D0759253

CHRISTIANITY & WESTERN THOUGHT

A History of Philosophers,
Ideas & Movements

Steve Wilkens &
Alan G. Padgett

VOLUME 2

FAITH & REASON IN THE 19TH CENTURY

InterVarsity Press
Downers Grove, Illinois

InterVarsity Press
P.O. Box 1400, Downers Grove, IL 60515
World Wide Web: www.ivpress.com
E-mail: mail@ivpress.com

InterVarsity Press® is the book-publishing division of InterVarsity Christian Fellowship/USA®, a student movement active on campus at hundreds of universities, colleges and schools of nursing in the United States of America, and a member movement of the International Fellowship of Evangelical Students. For information about local and regional activities, write Public Relations Dept., InterVarsity Christian Fellowship/USA, 6400 Schroeder Rd., P.O. Box 7895, Madison, WI 53707-7895.

Cover illustration: S. Buonsignori, Pianta detta "della Catena". Florence, Mus. di Firenze com'era. Used by permission of Scala/Art Resource, N.Y.

ISBN 0-8308-1753-0

Printed in the United States of America ∞

Library of Congress Cataloging-in-Publication Data

The Library of Congress has cataloged the first volume of this series as follows:
Brown, Colin, 1932-
    Christianity and western thought Vol. 1/Colin Brown.
     p. cm.
    Includes bibliographical references.
    ISBN 0-8308-1752-2
    1. Christianity—Philosophy. 2. Faith and reason—History of
doctrines.   3. Philosophy—History. I. Title.
    BR100.B6483   1990   *89-48564*
                                                                                CIP

19 18 17 16 15 14 13 12 11 10 9 8 7 6 5 4 3 2 1

15 14 13 12 11 10 09 08 07 06 05 04 03 02 01 00

To our parents,
with gratitude and love.

Preface

This book is the continuation of a project that began with Colin Brown's publication of *Christianity and Western Thought,* volume 1, in 1990. When Colin decided not to finish this project, he graciously gave us his blessing to complete the task. We both felt that a survey of Western philosophy (and some theology) from a Christian perspective was a useful and important task, especially for students. The work that lies before you is the product of our labors over the last three years toward this end. The nineteenth century proved so complex and interesting that we found it took up the whole of volume two. A projected final volume will cover the twentieth century.

As an overview for students, our book is primarily a survey. Our purpose is to introduce the major figures in Western thought, primarily philosophers, from a Christian perspective. This is not a book in apologetics, and it does not have as its primary function the criticism of ideas and systems that are contrary to the Christian faith. Rather, we seek to fairly explain the philosophical arguments and conclusions of great thinkers that have influenced our culture. Of course, from time to time, some criticisms are advanced—but they are preliminary, meant to stimulate further reflection. A purely objective, neutral perspective is impossible. We have striven to be "objective" in another sense, that is, to focus on the objects of our study and present their philosophies in as unbiased a manner as we can. To write this from a Christian perspective means that we are Christianly interested in the work of these thinkers, their view of God and religion, and their impact upon theology as well as philosophy and culture. We do not pretend to be without presuppositions, but we firmly believe that our Christian faith has not distorted our exposition but rather stimulated and guided it.

We thank God for the opportunity to work in a Christian academic environment with so many wonderful resources and fellow workers, viz. Azusa Pacific University. This work was supported financially by the faculty research council at APU and several Accomplished Scholar's Awards from the office of the provost. The library staff, especially the ILL staff headed by Jane Thorndike, has been very helpful and understanding. Our research assistants deserve a special thanks, including Jeremy Schipper, Dillon Enderby, Finney Premkumar and especially Sally Bruyneel for extensive bibliographical research, Melissa Hester for a careful reading of the entire work, and Lisa Welch for working on the index. Our colleagues and friends have helped with criticisms and comments from time to time, and we are grateful to Tim Fenderson, Gayle Beebe, Cahleen Shrier, Les Eddington, Brian Eck, Richard Christopherson and Don Thorsen. We also thank our editors and friends at IVP, Rodney Clapp and Jim Hoover, for their long-suffering support of this project. While we have been very careful, there are, no doubt, some errors that remain, but don't blame our friends who worked very hard to show us the error of our ways. (Each of us thinks, instead, you should blame the other author.)

Not only has this project provided opportunities for us to grow in friendship, but our long-suffering families have become close as well. We dedicate this book to our parents. Without their support and love, our education (and hence this book) would not have been possible. I, Alan, wish to thank with all my heart my mother, Mary Cavalier; my father, Hank Padgett; my stepmother, Yrsa Padgett; my stepfather, Jack Kent; and my father-in-law, Roy Bruyneel. I am particularly mindful of my late mother-in-law, Bonnie Bruyneel. Her tragic death in a freeway accident last November was a real loss to my family and me, and I dedicate this book to her memory; also, under the mercy, I commend her soul to the risen One.

I, Steve, want to express my deep appreciation to my late parents, Kenneth and Louise Wilkens, who continue to teach and shape me, and my father-in-law and mother-in-law, Monroe and LaNorma Kreutziger, extraordinary people who have entrusted me with their wonderful daughter and filled a very special place in my life.

This labor has been completed with students in mind. If some of them find it useful and learn from it, our labor will not have been in vain. But no labor for the Lord (as this book has been) is entirely without its blessings.

Steve Wilkens and Alan Padgett
Azusa Pacific University

1. A CENTURY OF TRANSITION

T he nineteenth century in the West was characterized by great movement and excitement. Change was not limited to any one sphere but covered the entire spectrum of life in such a way that it is often difficult to distinguish between cause and effect. Instead, we find symbiotic relationships in which one engine, driving change, both feeds and is fed by others. This interrelationship of causes makes analysis of the various movements, schools and ideas in this century difficult. We do not get a clear and clean chronological schema in which one belief system rises, dominates, wanes and is followed by the next. In the vitality of the nineteenth century temporal sequence is collapsed and even the logical order of ideas is difficult to untangle because of multiple influences.[1]

As a backdrop to the philosophical and theological dynamics we will examine, there are corresponding political and social revolutions. Many of the democratic ideals of the Enlightenment found their way from theory to practice in the political systems of Europe. The nobility's power was dispersed, sometimes by force, and was increasingly invested in a broader base of society. Centuries-old traditions of social stratification began giving way in the face of democratizing impulses. These changes were accompanied and facilitated by an increasing level of literacy, with basic educational skills becoming available even to those on the lowest rungs of the social ladder. When people have direct access to information, the power of authoritarian structures that would control interpretations is blunted.

Economic change, while often resulting in the exploitation of labor and resources, also provided a foundation for a higher standard of living. We find an increasing freedom in the economic sphere from the control of government, and the ideals of capitalism become firmly rooted in much of the West. The nineteenth century is marked by the birth of the machine. "The Machine Age" separates us from earlier human societies more than any other factor of modern life. In addition to greatly increasing capacity for production, it leads to massive population displacement from farm and field to city and factory. All of this was facilitated, in large part, by a relative absence of military conflict between the major powers of the West—for the time being.

This sense of progress and growth also was evident in the popular Christianity of the day.[2] Many of the earlier renewal movements such as the Wesleyan revival and the Great Awakenings continued to grow and mature. As gains were consolidated, they manifested themselves in the founding of colleges, missionary organizations, Bible societies and other institutional expressions. The rapid proliferation of denominations, especially evident in the United States, mirrored the new sense of confidence in individual judgment and freedom from traditional centers of authority and power. However, much of the energy behind the splintering of denominations was internal. In correspondence to innovation in theological approaches a number of groups came into existence that were identified by their acceptance of or opposition to these new ideas. Also somewhat unique to this century was the extent to which people felt freedom *from* Christianity. While previous centuries had their critics of the church, many of them retained their association with it. It is only in the nineteenth century that we find growing confidence that there was little danger in forsaking Christianity altogether.[3]

This same sense of freedom and innovation spilled into the intellectual sphere. The literary arts were revitalized by individuals such as Goethe and movements such as Romanticism. The natural sciences were coming into their own, and scientific method displaced revelation as epistemologically authoritative for many. The middle and later parts of the century witnessed the birth of the social science disciplines. The desire to understand human social nature, drives, cultural practices and past followed from the democratizing impulses of the early part of the century. Thus, anthropology, history, psychology and sociology began staking out their own territory independent of philosophy and theology—and sometimes in opposition to their intellectual parents.

One of the most remarkable features of the nineteenth century was its almost unrestrained belief that the next step in history would lead us to the goal for which we had been destined. From Kant's belief that he had initiated a "Copernican revolution," to Hegel's dialectical schema of God's writing his autobiography in history and nature, to Comte and Spencer's evolutionary interpretations of human social structures, to Marx's dream of a socialist utopia, the intellectual world was in almost unanimous agreement in its rosy view of the future. All it would take, of course, was adoption of the solution suggested by a particular philosopher surveying the human situation. There were exceptions to belief in inevitable progress, notably Kierkegaard, Nietzsche and Schopenhauer, who are all the more remarkable because of the tremendous energy necessary to resist this overwhelming tide of optimism. In general, however, the belief that history was at the penultimate stage of salvation continued unabated until brought to a grinding halt by two world wars in the next century.[4]

Kant as Agenda Setter

The opening of the nineteenth century marks an end of the movements that had dominated the previous two centuries and the emergence of new beginning points that would establish the direction of philosophy and theology in the twentieth century. Without too much exaggeration, the philosophy of Immanuel Kant (1724-1804) can be identified as the transition point. While the rationalistic foundations of the Enlightenment had already suffered severe damage at the hands of Hume's skeptical philosophy, Kant's *Critique of Pure Reason* (1781) decisively slammed the door on its confident pronouncements. Very few post-Kantians indicate any inclination to return to the methods and systems of the past after his criticism of Enlightenment metaphysics.

At the same time, Kant's writings open new avenues for future development, which were immediately seized upon by his successors. In spite of his massive influence it would be a mistake to think the philosophers who follow are only fleshing out a Kantian program. While there is a great deal of dependence on his thought, the innovation and impatience

of the age can be seen in the fact that few nineteenth century philosophers can be called "Kantian" in the strictest sense.[5] Instead their
responses to his philosophy pick and choose from the numerous points
of departure suggested in his works and usually take them to conclusions
Kant himself would not endorse. Since Kant's thought was handled quite
competently by Colin Brown in volume one of this series,[6] it is not our
concern to provide a full exposition of his philosophy. However, it is necessary to revisit some of his conclusions to gain perspective on where
Western thought will go during the nineteenth century.

First, the impact of Kant's *Critique of Pure Reason* on metaphysics is profound. In sum, he argues that the mind does not passively receive and
reflect data from the world outside. Instead, the mind has a priori categories through which this data is interpreted, and these categories shape
what we can know. Kant's position might be illustrated with the example
of a rock breaking a window. We can easily acknowledge that the actual
event of a rock crashing through a pane of glass occurs in a different
manner and location from our perception of it. The rock and the window
are "out there." They are part of what Kant calls the noumenal world, the
"thing-in-itself." However, our perception and memory of this event
occur "in here," in the mind. This perception of the external world is
called "phenomena." The Enlightenment tended simply to assume that
the perceptions of the mind (phenomena) matched the events in the
noumenal world. However, Kant destroys this assumption by arguing that
even the most fundamental structures of human knowledge, such as
time, space and causation are not supplied by the external thing-in-itself
but by our mind. Therefore, the temporal sequence of the event witnessed, the frame of reference within which it occurs (space), and the
concept of a rock "causing" a window to break all have their origin within
our mental world, not in the external world of rocks and windows. Since
we cannot step outside the mind's interpretive filters to experience this
external world directly, it should never be assumed to be the same as our
experience of it in the mental realm.

With Kant's conclusion that human reason cannot gain access to the
external world but only knows the world as it is processed by our categories of understanding, metaphysical speculation seems to be trapped in a
cul-de-sac. Such a position appears to limit our investigations to inner

experience since the built-in categories by which our mind organizes the data of the noumenal world are insurmountable barriers. And in fact this conclusion was adopted by a number of the antimetaphysical philosophers and theologians, such as Nietzsche, Kierkegaard and Schleiermacher. If, they argue, the finitude of human experience blocks access to reality, this effectively eliminates metaphysics as a valid field of study. This position was also assumed by many prominent figures in the natural and social sciences in the latter half of the century. While they were quite interested in the idea that human experience was the realm open to investigation, they frequently ignored or openly disputed the idea that there was some discoverable reality behind natural and social phenomena. This point of view was evident in their approach to religion. Social scientists wanted to know what influence religious beliefs had in the lives of people. However, the question of whether these motivations correspond to any divine reality was often deemed to be unanswerable or answerable with a firm no.

The destructive nature of Kant's first *Critique* for metaphysics is paralleled in its effect on current theological approaches. By the same means, he transforms metaphysical discussion; he also undermines the traditional arguments for God's existence. Since these arguments rely on ideas supplied by the mind (space, time and causation), they cannot give us access to God's existence. In addition, Kant's critique is devastating for natural theology and deism. These movements were constructed on the belief that conclusions about divine reality could be grounded in empiricism.[7] However, if it is true that the senses tell us nothing about the thing-in-itself, our perceptions are useless as a basis for theological claims.

The destructive facet of Kant's first *Critique* should not overshadow the fact that his division between the noumenal world (the world as it is) and the mind's activity in shaping it (the world as it appears to us) provides new opportunities for metaphysical speculation. Metaphysics simply moves to a new plane as later thinkers search Kant for new ways to get at reality. In fact, post-Kantians found a fresh approach in the very element Kant saw as the blockage between the noumenal world and our experience of it: the mind and its categories. If the mind is not simply a passive receptor of data but rather is active in the shaping of that data, it is possible to reconstruct metaphysics from the activity of the mind. It is a

short step to extend the role of the mind from the means by which the
material presented by the world of objects is processed to the means by
which the world is, in some sense, *created*. This is precisely the direction
taken by Idealism and, to a lesser extent, Romanticism. In other words,
they believed that the solution had been discovered by Kant himself, and
he just did not see it clearly. The mind does not simply process data presented by some thing-in-itself external to it but is the source of that
world. The issue that divides Idealists and Romanticists is the means by
which this creative mental activity takes place.

The divisions between the post-Kantians about how the mind shapes
the world depend on their response to Kant's two later *Critiques*. Kant's
own resolution to the problem of metaphysics is found in his *Critique of
Practical Reason* (1788). Here he argues that we gain partial entrance to
the noumenal world via moral freedom. Freedom, which is not itself subject to proof, is the necessary assumption of moral behavior. One who
does not have liberty to act cannot be held morally responsible. However, by asserting moral freedom we have gone beyond the spatiotempo-
ral realm. Further, in order to make sense of our moral impulses we must
assume that there is a self that acts. Moreover, this moral impulse is
rational only if there is some final accounting of our moral activity that
rewards good and punishes evil. Since it is clear that this moral reckoning does not occur in our lifetime, Kant argues that there is a postmortem
judgment of our actions by a perfectly just and all-knowing God. In short,
although we cannot approach metaphysical concepts such as freedom,
ethics, God or the self through the senses, they are necessary postulates
of moral reasoning. This understanding of the ethical basis of religion
has an advocate during the latter part of the century in Ritschl. However,
the more immediate proponent of such a position is Fichte, who combines it with his understanding of the world as a product of mind. For
Fichte, the purpose of the mind's creative activity is to provide the context
in which moral activity is possible.

While we should not understate the influence of Kant's view of practical reason on the intellectual world, the more common mistake has been
the tendency to overlook the significance of Kant's *Critique of Judgment*
(1790). This text inspires the basic direction of Romanticism as well as
the Idealism of Schelling and Hegel. Kant's first *Critique* leaves the status

of the thing-in-itself in limbo. We may be able to suspend judgment and deal with the uncertainty of what is really "out there" on the intellectual level. However, we cannot suspend our actions or our expectation that those actions will be efficacious. To refer to human action as rational requires that it is also purposeful. Purposefulness, in turn, requires that our teleological activity corresponds to some sort of aim in the unconscious world: the world of rocks, windows and aardvarks. However, we do not have access to their perspective of the world. Thus, we have no way of proving the directionality of nature. Nor do we have any foundation for thinking of the world as a unified entity since, according to Kant's *Critique of Pure Reason*, unity is an attribute of the mind's activity rather than of the noumenal world. Therefore, any concept of teleology and unity in the universe must be taken as a necessary metaphor that can be described only by analogy with our own conscious intentionality and unity. As we will discover in short order, this view of the world as an organic, unified, teleological entity is crucial to much of post-Kantian thought.

Beyond Kant

While Kant's philosophy was strongly influential for nineteenth century thought, there were two places in particular that represent important departures from a Kantian perspective. As mentioned immediately above, Kant did allow for an organic model for understanding the world in his *Critique of Judgment*. However, the more mechanistic view of his first *Critique* tended to dominate, and Kant did not provide a satisfactory way to bring the two views together. As a result the majority of the seminal thinkers of the nineteenth century rejected Kant's ahistorical approach in favor of the more dynamic concept of an organism that grows toward a goal. The world was no longer viewed as a static target on which we score a direct hit if the proper methodology is used. Instead, history and its movements toward a higher end had to be factored into the philosophical and theological equation, and this paradigm is closely linked to the optimism of the era.[8]

In addition to the influence of this dynamic view in Romanticism and Idealism (to which we will turn shortly), the concept of organism is prevalent in the evolutionary thought of the nineteenth century. Of course, the name Charles Darwin will come to mind. However, it is important to recognize that biological evolution was already assumed by many in the natural sciences by the time Darwin wrote *Origin of Species*. Furthermore, the concept of evolution entered these disciplines only after it had enjoyed widespread popularity in philosophical and religious thought. Thus, in thinkers such as Schelling, Hegel, Baur, Marx, Comte and others, history can be analyzed in terms of well-defined periods in which we grow toward increasingly better understandings of the world and its workings. In addition to the numerous attempts to explain the meaning and telos of history and its progression, there is a new interest in historiographical methods that seek to establish criteria by which we can best determine what "really happened." In part, the intuition behind this is that the accuracy of our interpretation of history is dependent on accurate knowledge of the events being interpreted.

While many of the notable historical interpretations derived from this organic paradigm focused on the future, this new model of the world also brought about a new appreciation for the past. For Kant and the Enlightenment philosophers, the ideas of previous ages were something to be "gotten over." Their goal was to purge science, religion and culture of its superstition and ignorance. In contrast, most of the post-Kantians view earlier institutions, practices and rituals as necessary stages in the movement from simpler to more complete and complex expressions. This organic model, rooted in Romanticism, is developed by Idealism in terms of an ever-increasing consciousness of self. Later, natural and social scientists found that it fit easily with biological and social evolutionary theories, which were applied to every facet of life by individuals such as Mill, Marx, Comte and Spencer.

A second departure from Kant by his successors is greater allowance for the full range of human experience as a matter of philosophical and theological interest and even authority. Although he maintains in his own thought a strict requirement of rationality as the ultimate authority, it is Kant who provides the impetus for development of this broader range of investigation. Early Romanticism had certainly emphasized the validity of the creative, intuitive and affective domains, but it tended only to assert their value. By arguing that our mental processes are themselves creative, shaping experience by internal structures that are independent of the external world, Kant opens the door to a new examination of human existence and gives intellectual credibility to Romanicism's position. Thus, Romanticism's interest in the aesthetic side of life is readily blended into Idealism's attempt to provide an all-inclusive analysis of the full spectrum of human experience. This broadened perspective also allows Nietzsche and Schopenhauer to weigh in with their philosophy of the irrational will, a human force distinct from the Enlightenment ideal of the rational mind. In addition, the new respectability in the study of human impulses beyond the rational gives credence to the social sciences. History, culture, religious sensibility and the different facets of the psyche are not impediments to understanding human nature, but the means by which it must be approached.

Christianity in the Nineteenth Century

This brief prospective on the general philosophical directions of the nineteenth century sets the stage for the opportunities and problems that confront Christian thought through the century under consideration and up to the present.[9] First, while the role of reason in relation to faith had been a matter of debate for centuries, the new perspective of reason and its limitations reopens the issue with new vigor. The affective side of human experience that had been such a prominent feature in revival movements in the previous century had been contemptuously dismissed as "enthusiasm" by the intellectuals of the Enlightenment. Displays of emotion and talk of the "heart" violated the canon of rationality they had established for religious truth. However, as a result of Hume's radical skepticism and Kant's division of the noumenal from the phenomenal, the Enlightenment's faith in reason is undercut, and their empirically based theologies are in full retreat for a time. In their place, new approaches to the grounding of theological truth are tested. Do we separate reason and theology into independent realms of authority (Hamann, Coleridge)? Can theology be viewed as an outgrowth and handmaiden of ethics (Kant, Fichte)? Do we look to the aesthetic and intuitive for religious guidance (Schleiermacher)? Are we forced by the finitude of discursive reason into subjectivity (Coleridge and Kierkegaard), or do we put forward a new concept of reason as the essence of Reality (Hegel)?

While all the options above, and others, were entertained, Christianity also faced new threats to its claims. A significant challenge came from the social sciences. Efforts to analyze religious life from a sociological or psychological perspective seemed to many to fill a gap previously occupied by claims of divine authority. Thus whether religion is explicable in terms of a weapon wielded by wealthy oppressors (Marx), weaklings bent on controlling the strong (Nietzsche), alienation from our own native goodness (Feuerbach), a necessary but adolescent stage of cultures growing toward social adulthood (Comte) or a cry for Daddy from within arrested development (Freud), its claims are put in doubt.

A related challenge to Christianity is rooted in the growing awareness of other religions. While Christianity maintained its dominance in the West, growing literacy and mobility made it clear that Christian belief and practice was far from monolithic. Moreover, anthropological research made it impossible to assume that Christianity was the only living form of religious expression. This new awareness created the need to revisit the claims of Christianity vis-à-vis other religions. The insights of historical research intensify this question. Not only did Christianity vary in its contemporary manifestations, it also appeared to develop over time. Thus, theology must address the question of whether its claims to ultimate authority can be supported. Some attempted to do this by seeking to strip away cultural appendages and return to a pristine form of Christianity. Of course, among advocates of this approach there are serious disagreements about what constitutes the unedited teaching of Jesus and what picture of the church represents a purified Christianity. Others, rather than looking to the past for the essence of Christianity, embraced a forward-looking view in which Christianity grows toward, not away from, its highest expression. Thus while acknowledging a certain validity in the religious consciousness of all religions, most proponents see Christianity as the apex.

On the other hand, there were those in this century who took Christianity to be only one among many religions. Sometimes this leveling process occurred as a result of methodologies that approached religion as one mode of social behavior that can be expressed in descriptive, not normative, categories. In other cases, Christianity's claims are questioned by new knowledge of religions alive at its birth. Some concluded that elements that parallel Christian rituals and doctrines indicate that Christianity is not to be understood as the sole means of salvation. It is, instead, a sociological product of the age. Its only real claim to fame, in this view, is that it managed to adapt in ways that allowed it to survive changing times while the religions that birthed it faded into the background or disappeared completely.

The recognition of change within Christianity is closely connected with paradigms that understand reality as organic. This shift in worldviews has important implications in two areas of central importance to theology. First, in the all-encompassing systems of the Idealists, change occurs not only in human social structures and in nature but involves God himself in the dynamic process. The definition of God's perfection that grows out of Classical philosophy seemed necessarily to require a static God. However, because Kant's immediate heirs sought to unify the divine with the mental and the natural, God could no longer be understood apart from history. This also has ramifications for our concept of revelation. It is impossible, in the view of many, to rely on unchanging sources of revelation. Instead, our consciousness of God develops and grows with history. Therefore, questions are raised about the role and interpretation of Scripture in relation to the dynamics of history.

2. EXPANDING RATIONALITY

T he European intellectual world immediately following Kant's death is dominated by two main schools: Romanticism and Absolute Idealism. There are a number of connections between these movements. Both flourished during the same period, and there was frequent interaction between the major figures. The main center of activity was Jena, where the tenures of Schelling and Fichte overlapped with Romantic figures such as brothers Friedrich (1743-1819) and August Wilhelm Schlegel (1767-1845), the poet Friedrich Hölderlin (1770-1843), and the most famous figure of this movement, Johann Wolfgang von Goethe (1749-1832). In addition to chronological proximity there are so many points of interest common to both movements that the line between them is often blurred. Despite the intersecting lines, we will identify important distinctions between them as well, which lead to different perspectives in significant areas.

Romanticism

While Romanticism reached its zenith about the same time as Absolute Idealism, it had been a force in Germany since the 1770s. Tracing its roots back to Rousseau in France and Herder in Germany, the early expressions of Romanticism in the *Sturm und Drang* (Storm and Stress) movement were something of a counterculture rebellion against the Enlightenment.[1] Spurred on by Johann Georg Hamann's (1730-1788) attacks on the cold rationalism of the latter,[2] Romanticism refused to allow reason to act as a gatekeeper that determines what aspects of human experience should be seen as valid pointers toward reality. In fact, rather than viewing reason as a filter that removed the pollution of irrationality and subjectivity, the Romantics saw it itself as a limitation. In their view, reason allows access only to exterior realities. As Frederick Copleston puts it, "Romanticism was characterized by a feeling for and longing for the infinite."[3] The desire for the infinite requires that we give attention to the realms of human existence that provide the most direct access to human feeling and longing: the affective, the intuitive, the mystical and the artistic. Inclusion of these elements presents a challenge in outlining this school. Given its starting point, Romanticism is not simply a designation of a type of philosophy but has corollaries in art, music and literature as well as religious thought.

In its early stages Romanticism did not argue its position as much as it asserted it. It built on the inner sense that the world is a connected and meaningful place, that we are in some way continuous with nature and that our purpose is bound up in it. These assertions received additional credibility with the appearance of Kant's *Critique of Pure Reason*, which removed the empirical, rationalistic foundations of Enlightenment thought. However, Kant's second *Critique* only supports the Romantic's claim *against* reason. The positive claims of the Romantics found an ally elsewhere in Kant's writings. As Paul Tillich puts it, "Romanticism . . . used Kant's *Critique of Judgment* more than anything else because there Kant offered the possibility of accepting the fundamental restrictions of his previous *Critiques* and at the same time of going beyond them."[4] The opportunity for "going beyond" is found in Kant's portrayal of nature as organic and teleological in his third *Critique*.

The aesthetic and organic orientation of Romanticism leads to a new concept of epistemology. With the help of Kant's *Critique of Pure Reason*, Romanticism argues that empirical methods only allow us to get at the external. Novalis (1772-1801) summarizes the problem, stating, "The members (of the Enlightenment) were tirelessly cleaning the poetry off Nature, the earth, the human soul, and the branches of learning—obliterating every trace of the holy, discrediting by sarcasm the memory of all ennobling events and persons, and stripping the world of all colorful ornament."[5] In short, rather than directing us toward the real, rationalistic philosophy obscures it by removing the mystery and poetry. When we see only the exterior of nature, we inevitably end up with naturalism.

To get beyond the phenomenal we need to rely on subjectivity. This accounts for Romanticism's dependence on the aesthetic, the mystical and the imaginative. Freidrich Schlegel argues that a philosophy of life must be more than a "philosophy of reason." Instead, "Philosophical thought and knowledge, with that diversity of illustration and variety in method which follows from its universality, is in this respect somewhat in the same case with poetry. Of all the imitative arts poetry alone embraces and by its nature is intended to embrace the whole man."[6] Both poetry and philosophy attempt to speak of that which is beyond human description: the Infinite. Both the philosopher and the poet, then, merely suggest that which is grasped intuitively, not rationally. This difference in the attitude toward intuition marks a division between Romanticism and Idealism. While the former does not, in general, dispute the use of reason as a means of structuring and expressing our experience of the infinite, Romanticism is critical of Idealism for its reliance on reason as the *source*. Friedrich Heinrich Jacobi (1743-1819) states that "it is only *with* the understanding and *with* reason that we can experience, and become aware; and never *through* the understanding or *through* reason, as if these were *particular powers*."[7]

The belief that the aesthetic and intuitive allow access to the infinite presupposes another important difference between Romanticism and the Enlightenment.

Nature is not simply the environment in which we live but is rather the expression of the divine mind. By this means Romanticism replaces the Enlightenment's static view of the thing-in-itself with nature as the progressive revelation or unfolding of the Infinite in history. This sense of divine immanence goes beyond a view in which a transcendent God only periodically, if ever, intervenes in the temporal. Instead Romanticism emphasizes immanence to such an extent that it becomes in some cases pantheism or something close to it. As Novalis puts it, "If God could become man, then He can also become stone, plant animal, and element, and perhaps in this way there is a continuous redemption in Nature."[8] This view of divine immanence is also responsible for the teleological tone of Romanticism. Neither nature nor humankind can be viewed apart from God. God's purposes mirror those of the world.

An understanding of nature as a realm infused with the divine sheds additional light on Romanticism's rejection of rationalism. The tendency in the Enlightenment was to divide our lives into separate spheres, which were understood in a hierarchical schema that put the affective aspects at the bottom and the rational at the top. However, if God is present in all facets of life, reason is not the sole and true indicator of human nature. Romanticism also gives epistemological standing to other human impulses such as language, the arts, religion and cultural factors.[9] Moreover, the Romantics inverted the Enlightenment hierarchy and put the creative above the rational.

Romanticism and Religion

While subjectivity was viewed negatively by Kant and a majority of the theologians of the Enlightenment, for Romanticism subjectivity was positive. It allows for the interiority that is characteristic of religious life and allows us to escape determinism, skepticism or a subjugation of religion to purely ethical ends. Nature considered from only an external perspective causes us to see the world as a machine. Nature viewed through intuitive means is revealed as a dynamic, vital and unified entity. For Romantics such as Hamann, this reopens the door to faith, which the Enlightenment tended to oppose to reason. Faith as our subjective, experiential response to our awareness of the infinite is given centrality. Moreover, Romanticism's emphasis on the intuitive is seen to inoculate faith from challenges posed by rationality. "Faith is not the work of reason, and therefore cannot succumb to its attack, because faith arises just as little from reason as tasting and seeing do."[10] To others within the Romantic movement such as Novalis, Jacobi or the Schlegel brothers, the creative imagination supplies the content of religious belief.

Second, the view of God as immanent in history brings about a new understanding of revelation. Earlier approaches tended to rely on that which was thought to be static and objective. When this objective source was reason, as in the Enlightenment, the "ideal religion" was that which conformed to rational standards. This criterion requires that we strip away extraneous elements that have been superimposed upon this ideal religion, such as changeable rituals and practices. Since reason itself does not change, true religion was thought to be static and unchange-able. For Romanticism, however, interest was centered on religion as it exists and evolves, as it is manifested historically. Thus Romanticism finds in religious practices, myth, magic and ritual evidence of the human intuition of the Infinite. These are aesthetic presentations of reli-gious consciousness that can act as a spur to our awareness of God. Uni-formity is no longer viewed as desirable. Instead individuality, change and variation allow us to see different parts of the Whole.

This new concept of revelation has important ramifications for the understanding of Scripture as well. For Romanticism, the Bible does not contain the final, immutable revelation of God. It does offer insights into the religious consciousness of past generations, but its status is often viewed as no different from that of other sources. Novalis sums up this belief in two of his aphorisms:

☐ "If the spirit sanctifies, every real book is a Bible."

☐ "Who has declared the Bible completed? Should the Bible not be still in a process of growth?"[11]

Rather than being fixed and final the Romantics saw revelation as ongo-ing through the imperfect expressions of our experiences of the infinite. For many in the movement it would not be too much to say that imagina-tion and experience supplant Scripture's traditional role.

Finally, Romanticism causes a reexamination of the nature of God. Romanticism can be seen as a highbrow sibling to the popular reli-gious movements of the day. Both have in common their rebellion against the lifelessness imposed on religion by rationalism. One of the main distinctions however is that while the renewal movements within Christianity saw God as personal, Romanticism, with its monis-tic tendencies, often has difficulties maintaining the personality of the divine and its distinction from created reality. The movements within Christianity that gave attention to the affective also maintain a strong dualism between nature and divine, whereas this distinction disap-pears with Romanticism's emphasis on immanence.

Transcendentalism and Romanticism

A movement closely aligned with Romanticism was New England Tran-scendentalism. Transcendentalism was not "transcendental" in the Kant-

ian sense. It eschewed the technicalities of European transcendental philosophy and only adopted the label because outsiders refused to let them
shed it. One of its early proponents, Orestes A. Brownson (1803-1876),
defines Transcendentalism simply as "a doctrine founded on that which
transcends or surpasses sense and understanding."[12] Other than this
emphasis on transcendence, few overarching principles define the
school: intuitive epistemology, an organic view of the universe, individualism and rejection of doctrinal rigidity. Because of the last two, about the
only other common characteristic of Transcendentalism is fervent disagreement in almost every other matter.

This list of attributes reveals similarities with Romanticism, and the
close relationship between them is undeniable. However, it would be a
mistake is to see them as identical schools with different names; important differences push Romanticism's American cousin toward unique trajectories. One such difference grows out of the background of the
American Revolution. The reality of national independence was still
being digested, and Transcendentalism wanted to explore the ramifications of democracy and equality. The vision of America's potential is
clear in Emerson's question, "If there is any period one would desire to
be born in, is it not the age of Revolution; when the old and the new
stand side by side and admit of being compared; when the energies of all
men are searched by fear and by hope; when the historic glories of the
old can be compensated by the rich possibilities of the new era?"[13] This
awareness of standing between two ages with almost complete freedom
to define the future forms the horizon for Transcendentalism in a way
not possible in Europe, with its long-established cultural and social structures. This sense of transition is especially evident in the recurring theme
of individuality.

A second difference is the intellectual background from which the two
movements originate. The literary, artistic and philosophical community
provided the original impetus for European Romanticism. While its proponents had a keen interest in the implications of romantic notions for
religion, the situation in Transcendentalism is reversed. Its founders
were primarily pastors with interests in literature, art and philosophy.
Therefore while the interests overlap significantly, the shape of Transcendentalism is determined in large measure by the religious back-

ground against which they are reacting as religious figures. Transcendentalism is, from start to finish, a religious movement.

A third contrast between Romanticism and Transcendentalism is the time frame. The latter did not come into being until well after European Romanticism was beyond its peak. This time lag is not surprising since, by accident of its geography and its still young intellectual culture, America only absorbed intellectual movements a generation after they had run their course in Europe. Transcendentalism drew on and reacted to not just the materials of the German Romantics but also the writings of the Idealists and works in biblical criticism unavailable at the height of German Romanticism. Therefore, while the European resources confirmed and expressed ideas characteristic of Transcendentalism, we need not look to the other side of the Atlantic to find its origins. The context and raw materials from which it sprang were already present in early nineteenth-century New England.

New England Transcendentalism
The immediate context of Transcendentalism's birth was Boston Unitarianism. Many of the original Transcendentalists, including Ralph Waldo Emerson (1803-1882), Orestes A. Brownson, Theodore Parker (1810-1860) and George Ripley (1803-1880), were Unitarian ministers, all of whom, with the exception of Parker, eventually resigned their positions. An early crisis for Unitarianism arose because it relied on Jesus' miracles to establish his message and unique status. As time went on, Unitarianism found itself increasingly unable to reconcile miracles with the empiricism behind natural theology since miracles seemed to resist both empirical testing and conformity with natural law. This tension was intensified as biblical criticism made its way to America and cast doubts on the historicity of the biblical miracle stories.

While the question of miracles was the initial sticking point, the situation was somewhat parallel to the Protestant Reformation in that the initial tensions were only symptomatic of deeper issues that gradually took center stage. Transcendentalism eventually separated from Unitarianism for several additional reasons. Like Romanticism, it rejected the Lockian empiricism on which natural theology depended. Because, as Kant demonstrated, empiricism could not provide access to divine realities, Transcendentalists substituted an intuitive approach. Closely related to their reliance on intuition is the question of religious experience. Unitarianism was a highly intellectual movement and viewed religious experience and enthusiasm with suspicion. In contrast, Transcendentalism considered the emotive and intuitive the core of spirituality. Finally, while Transcendentalists agreed with Unitarianism's rejection of doctrinal rigidity, they saw this as a partial measure. They sought also to do away with what they viewed as rigidity in Unitarian church practice.

It was the question of praxis that led to Emerson's departure from Unitarianism. Generally acknowledged as the chief spokesperson for Transcendentalism, Ralph Waldo Emerson's pedigree included eight generations of Puritan pastors.[14] His father, who died when Emerson was eight years old, was a Unitarian minister. Although the family was poor, both he and his brother were able to attend Harvard. Emerson moved on to its Divinity School and after graduation took a position at Second Unitarian Church in Boston in 1829. At Harvard he had been immersed in the natural theology and Scottish Common Sense philosophy of the day but did not find their solutions to Humean skepticism satisfying. This inconclusiveness on so central a matter festered throughout his years at Second Church.

Emerson's discontent came to a head over the question of administering the Lord's Supper. He saw this rite as a form of institutional coercion that interfered with individual freedom. Even within a Unitarian system, in which the sacrament had become detached from its usual doctrinal accompaniments and its significance was seen primarily as commemorative, elimination of a sacrament ordained by Jesus went too far. There was a parting of the ways, and Emerson resigned his ministerial orders in 1832. Following his resignation, he read widely in mystical, neoplatonic, Eastern, idealist and romantic works and traveled to Europe to meet with William Wordsworth and Samuel Coleridge. This formative period in his thought was followed by publication of *Nature* (1836), which led to lecture opportunities on the lyceum circuit.[15] These lectures were collected into two volumes that received a great deal of attention, *Essays—First Series* (1841) and *Essays—Second Series* (1844).

The Divine Unity

A central theme in Emerson's philosophy and throughout the Transcendentalist writings is the continuity between the divine and the natural. Though not usually reckoned a Transcendentalist himself, William Ellery Channing (1780-1842) was an important source for this idea. Channing rejected the strict dualism between God and humanity common in traditional theology. Instead, divine attributes are identical to those in the human realm but in attenuated form. "The idea of God, sublime and awful as it is, is the idea of our own spiritual nature, purified and enlarged to infinity. In ourselves are the elements of the Divinity."[16] This idea was acceptable to most Unitarians, but the Transcendentalists went beyond Channing's idea of the potential perfectibility of human nature to state that both humanity and nature are divine. Nature is just "a remoter and inferior incarnation of God."[17]

The divinization of humanity and nature raises the question of whether Emerson is a pantheist. Statements such as, "This universal soul he calls Reason: it is not mine, or thine, or his, but we are its; we are its property and men,"[18] and "I become a transparent eyeball; I am nothing; I see all; the currents of the Universal Being circulate through me; I am part or parcel of God"[19] seem to support this conclusion. However, it should be kept in mind that Emerson intends to evoke intuitions, feelings or moods rather than offer logical analysis. After all, he is the source of the much misquoted line: "A foolish consistency is the hobgoblin of little minds, adored by little statesmen and philosophers and divines. With consistency a great soul has simply nothing to do."[20] Although he is loath to be pinned down to definite doctrines and believes systematization of ideas is a hindrance rather than a help to discerning truth, Emerson does present a level of unity between the divine and natural that could be identified as panentheistic if not pantheistic.

Whatever the label, a cornerstone of Emerson's philosophy is the doctrine of correspondence. Correspondence argues that nature and mind are two sides of the same coin. "He shall see that nature is the opposite of the soul, answering to it part for part. . . . Its laws are the laws of his own mind. . . . And, in fine, the ancient precept, 'Know thyself', and the modern precept, 'Study nature', become at last one maxim."[21] To know nature properly is to have self-knowledge as well as knowledge of the divine.

Knowledge is necessarily holistic because the World-Soul, or what Emerson variously refers to as Mind, God or the Over-Soul, permeates all things: "The world is not the product of manifold power, but of one will, of one mind; and that one mind is everywhere active, in each ray of the star, in each wavelet of the pool; and whatever opposes that will is everywhere balked and baffled, because things are made so, and not otherwise."[22]

The basis of Emerson's belief in the unity of all things is found in language. He observes that words drawn from natural entities are often employed to refer to spiritual realities. "We say the *heart* to express emotion, the *head* to denote thought; and *thought* and *emotion* are words borrowed from sensible things, and now appropriated to spiritual nature."[23] Such figurative language is universal because "every natural fact is a symbol of some spiritual fact. Every appearance in nature corresponds to some state of the mind, and that state of the mind can only be described by presenting that natural appearance as its picture."[24] What is true of the parts is possible because the same is true for the whole. "Parts of speech are metaphors, because the whole of nature is a metaphor of the human mind."[25]

The correspondence between nature and the spiritual realm allows Emerson to speak of nature as revelatory. And because nature encompasses all, no one has an inside track on knowing the mind of God. In the opening paragraph of *Nature* he asks, "The foregoing generations beheld God and nature face to face; we, through their eyes. Why should not we also enjoy an original relation to the universe? Why should not we have a poetry and philosophy of insight and not of tradition, and a religion by revelation to us, and not the history of theirs?"[26] Emerson's answer is that revelation cannot be limited to any one age, person or book. Failure to recognize this is the trap into which most religion has fallen. "The stationariness of religion; the assumption that the age of inspiration is past, that the Bible is closed; the fear of degrading the character of Jesus by representing him as a man;—indicate with sufficient clearness the falsehood of our theology. It is the office of a true teacher to show us that God is, not was; that He speaketh, not spake."[27] For Transcendentalism, not only is God's word ongoing, it is complete insofar as we are open to Nature. "We must trust the perfection of the creation so

far as to believe that whatever curiosity the order of things has awakened
in our minds, the order of things can satisfy."[28]

The prerequisite to a proper moral reading of nature is sympathetic
unity with its Author. "Every scripture is to be interpreted by the same
spirit which gave it forth,—is the fundamental law of criticism. A life in
harmony with Nature, the love of truth and of virtue, will purge the eyes
to understand her text."[29] Empiricism thus constitutes an improper
approach to interpreting nature because it sees nature as essentially different from God. It begins with the particular facts of what is assumed to
be a merely physical world and attempts to arrive at conclusions about a
divine being of a completely alien nature. Since empiricism constitutes a
false start, it will never lead to a proper understanding of the universe.
Instead, since the world is essentially soul, its spiritual essence can only
be known by our soul. Like knows like. All knowledge begins from the
divine and general, not the physical and particular.[30] Thus, when nature
is approached as a symbol of the spiritual, the divine becomes manifest
through it.

> We lie in the lap of immense intelligence, which makes us receivers of
> its truth and organs of its activity. When we discern justice, when we
> discern truth, we do nothing of ourselves, but allow a passage to its
> beams. If we ask whence this comes, if we seek to pry into the soul that
> causes, all philosophy is at fault. Its presence or its absence is all we
> can affirm. Every man discriminates between the voluntary acts of his
> mind, and his involuntary perceptions, and knows that to his involun-
> tary perceptions a perfect faith is due. He may err in the expression of
> them, but he knows that these things are so, like day and night, not to
> be disputed.[31]

As we see at the end of this quote, Emerson believes that the introspec-
tive approach avoids the uncertainties that attach to empiricism. Our soul
already possesses truth through its participation in the World-Soul; it only
needs illumination. Once illuminated, these innate truths are self-evident.

When nature's inspiration is properly interpreted, it reveals a religion
defined primarily by morality. "The moral law lies at the centre of nature
and radiates to the circumference."[32] When we adopt an intuitional
approach to revelation, nature becomes a means to knowing morality

rather than an obstacle to be overcome. "Therefore is nature ever the ally of Religion: lends all her pomp and riches to the religious senti- ment."[33] Morality now becomes a matter of inner experience, not discur- sive knowledge, and moral purity is the means by which one finds unity with oneself and God. "If a man is at heart just, then in so far is he God; the safety of God, the immortality of God, the majesty of God do enter into that man with justice. If a man dissemble, deceive, he deceives him- self, and goes out of acquaintance with his own being."[34] This shifts the ethical center of gravity away from actions and ideas to the sentiments. Moral goodness (or spiritual attunement) is the resonance of our spirit with the spirit that permeates the entire universe.

Although this concept of religion seems to take us far afield from Christianity, most Transcendentalists see it not as a departure but as a return to the pure message of Christ before it became encrusted with stagnant doctrines and practices. As Theodore Parker puts it, "Christian- ity is a simple thing, very simple. It is absolute, pure morality; absolute, pure religion; the love of man; the love of God acting without let or hin- drance. The only creed it lays down is the great truth which springs up spontaneous in the holy heart—there is a God. Its watchword is, Be per- fect as your Father in heaven. The only form it demands is a divine life; doing the best thing in the best way, from the highest motives; perfect obedience to the great law of God."[35]

This redefinition of Christianity requires a corresponding redefinition of the role of Jesus. The mistake of what Transcendentalism calls "histor- ical Christianity" is that it, "has dwelt, it dwells, with noxious exaggera- tions about the *person* of Jesus. The soul knows no persons. It invites every man to expand to the full circle of the universe, and will have no preferences but those of spontaneous love."[36] To put the accent on Jesus' *person* does not guarantee the truth of Christianity, as historical Chris- tianity believed, but leaves it vulnerable to doubt. Instead, the *principles* Jesus taught and modeled constitute the truth of Christianity, and these derive their authority through intuition. "If Christianity were true, we should still think it was so, not because its record was written by infallible pens, nor because it was lived out by an infallible teacher; but that it is true, like the axioms of geometry, because it is true, and is to be tried by the oracle God places in the breast."[37]

Historical Christianity distorted the original message by limiting incarnation to a single individual. In contrast, Transcendentalism argues that the heart of Jesus' message is that God is incarnate in each person. "One man [Jesus] was true to what is in you and me. He saw that God incarnates himself in man, and evermore goes forth anew to take possession of his World."[38] A related position was taken on the question of miracles. For the Transcendentalists, miracles are not occasional events imposed from above. Instead, the line dividing the divine from the natural is removed, and all is considered supernatural. This rejection of dualism is a direct attack at the foundation of Unitarianism, which relied on miracles as divine testimony of Jesus' authority. About this method Emerson says, "To aim to convert a man by miracles, is a profanation of the soul. A true conversion, a true Christ, is now, as always, to be made by the reception of beautiful sentiments."[39]

Transcendentalism seeks to replace doctrine with sentiment because doctrine is impersonal and static. Since life is experienced as a process, revelation can only be understood in dynamic and experiential terms. Emerson warns us, "Do not require a description of the countries towards which you sail. The description does not describe them to you, and to-morrow you arrive there and know them by inhabiting them."[40] In place of doctrine Emerson suggests poetry, music and symbol as better vehicles for religious ideas. These evoke our affections and have a fluidity that reminds us that truth is always becoming. Moreover, while doctrine seeks to create a uniform understanding, symbols awaken different ideas in individuals and invite their ongoing participation. It is this personal engagement with the World-Soul that constitutes an individual's true being. "In the right state he is *Man Thinking*. In the degenerate state, when the victim of society, he tends to become a mere thinker, or still worse, the parrot of other men's thinking."[41]

The belief that revelation was accessible to each person and only available to them experientially, led to a high degree of individualism in Transcendentalism. Henry David Thoreau (1817-1862) argues for a form of individualism that takes us beyond even democracy. "Is a democracy, such as we know it, the last improvement possible in government? Is it not possible to take a step further towards recognizing and organizing the rights of man? There will never be a really free and enlightened

State, until the State comes to recognize the individual as the higher and independent power, from which all its own power and authority are derived, and treats him accordingly."[42] This sense of individual rights and equality finds a different basis in Transcendentalism than is given in the founding documents of the United States. The latter relies on Lockian empiricism for its foundation, while the Transcendentalists ground human rights in our participation in the divine and the innate capacity of each individual to attain illumination.

Even though illumination is possible for every person, most do not experience the degree of self-realization available to them. As Thoreau put it, "The mass of men lead lives of quiet desperation."[43] One cause of this desperation is social structures and ideas that hinder self-realization. Thus many Transcendentalists became active in abolitionist and women's rights movements. Their emphasis on the personal character of nature led to a strong protest against industrialization, which views the physical world as an object of exploitation. They disliked the economic inequities created by capitalism and believed that its dependence on machinery removed us from nature. Transcendentalism took a great interest in democratizing educational opportunities and reforming the process to develop the intuitive powers of children.

However, the Transcendentalists believed that the greater hindrance to self-realization is internal. When we are not conscious of our divinity, our attention becomes fixed on externals. The result is that "at present, man applies to nature but half his force. He works on the world with his understanding alone. He lives in it and masters it by a penny-wisdom; and he that works most in it is but a half-man, and whilst his arms are strong and his digestion good, his mind is imbruted, and he is a selfish savage."[44] Ultimately, however, the Transcendentalists possess an unrestrained optimism about human possibility if we are attuned to divine realities. "Whilst we behold unveiled the nature of Justice and Truth, we learn the difference between the absolute and the conditional or relative. We apprehend the absolute. As it were, for the first time *we exist*. We become immortal, for we learn that time and space are relations of matter; that with a perception of truth or a virtuous will they have no affinity."[45]

Transcendentalism's Significance

There are always differences in evaluations of a movement's influence, and that is probably more true with Transcendentalism than with other philosophies. Some see it as America's defining school, noting not just its literary impact but also its continuing legacy of individualism and social criticism. Others respond that its influence was a mile wide and an inch deep. The inner circle of the Transcendentalists never numbered more than fifty, and its reach was largely confined to Boston and its immediate environs. And even though many college students go through their "Emerson" or "Thoreau" stage, this is more indicative of youthful idealism than Transcendentalism's intellectual significance.

As is usually the case the truth is probably somewhere in between. Perhaps the significance of Transcendentalism is not that its ideas are particularly innovative. The general concepts were supplied by movements in Europe and the social realities of early America. Instead, its genius seems to be in how it combined and communicated these ideas. The power of Thoreau's descriptions of the New England countryside in *Walden* or the towering strength and irrepressible optimism of Emerson's lectures still inspire today. Moreover, Transcendentalist writings resonate with the tradition of self-reliance and independence of the American mindset. Therefore, when situations arise in which our freedom and equality are threatened or when spiritual values are submerged in a mechanistic, consumer-oriented culture, Thoreau's "Civil Disobedience" and Emerson's *Nature* are discovered by a new generation of readers.

While the intuitive aspect of both Transcendentalism and Romanticism had great appeal to many, the vagueness with which these positions were stated was a nagging obstacle to others. Differences within both camps reveal that one of the few commonalities was general agreement in methodology, but this method produced divergent beliefs. What do we do when individual intuitions lead to vastly different conclusions? Replacing the Enlightenment's autonomous reason with an autonomous intuition seems to guarantee as many belief systems as there are individuals with intuition. Given this reality the Idealists, as we will see in chapter four, attempted to expand the definition of reason to include the intuitive, without making it autonomous, in order to free truth from subjectivity.

A second problem many have found within Transcendentalism and Romanticism is the relationship between religion in general and Christianity. Most within these schools did not want to forsake Christianity and considered their views a return to the original message. Outsiders, however, were often suspicious that rather than reading the ideas of Romanticism *from* Scripture, they were read *into* Christianity illegitimately. Therefore we find a new generation of theologians who appropriate Romantic and Transcendentalist ideas for religious expression but want to integrate these concepts in a manner that is more faithful to Christianity. The most prominent spokespersons for this trend are Coleridge and Friedrich Schleiermacher, the subjects of our next chapter.

3. ROMANTICISM CHRISTIANIZED/ CHRISTIANITY ROMANTICIZED

The question of how we balance the doctrines of Christianity and the philosophical constructs we inevitably bring to our expressions of religious ideas is one that every scholar must grapple with. In the previous chapter we surveyed a number of figures who developed their ideas on religion from the perspective of a Romantic/Transcendentalist philosophy. While they did this within cultural horizons strongly influenced by Christianity and generally viewed their work as a rediscovery of a true Christian message, one easily gets the impression that their philosophical concepts are the tail that wags the dog and the religion they ultimately embrace is watered down to the point that it can no longer be recognized as Christianity.

The two individuals we will consider in this chapter maintain a keen interest in Romanticism, but want to shift the balance of authority back toward Christian doctrine. Therefore, when Friedrich Schleiermacher, who we will meet later in this chapter, writes to the "cultured despisers of religion" of the Berlin salon, he does not approach his readers from an alien philosophical perspective. Like these "despisers," he also highly values the ideas of Romanticism. Where he and his audience part ways is that Schleiermacher is convinced that Christian dogma and Romanticism do not confront us with an either/or choice. The central tenets of the Christian faith can be maintained along with the interpretive grid provided by Romanticism. Indeed both Schleiermacher and Coleridge, to whom we will turn immediately, argue that the only means of protecting the foundational doctrines of Christianity against critical methods is to reinterpret them along the experiential directions offered by Romantic philosophy.

Samuel Taylor Coleridge

Samuel Taylor Coleridge (1772-1834) is known to most as a literary figure, penning works such as "The Nightingale," "The Eolian Harp," "The Rime of the Ancient Mariner," "Christabel" and "Kubla Khan."[1] However, he was also an influential force in English philosophy and theology and a major inspiration for the American Transcendental movement.[2] Coleridge was the youngest of ten children and seems to have been something of a favorite of both parents. His father, a pastor, was a man of impressive intellectual skill and, though he died before Samuel's tenth birthday, exerted a major influence in his son's early love of literature, poetry and philosophy.

Coleridge's first philosophical hero was Voltaire, whose work led him to declare himself an infidel. While infatuation with Voltaire was short-lived, he was attracted to other ideas considered rather liberal in his time. These forays were reinforced by his education at Jesus College at Cambridge, which he entered at the age of nineteen. While there, he abandoned his devout Anglican upbringing for Unitarianism, returning to trinitarianism only after a ten year absence. He became close friends with Robert Southey, the future poet-laureate, who shared his fascination with radical social theories. The two made plans to establish a utopian socialist commune, which they referred to as a Pantisocracy, in America. However, disagreements between the members of this future community, problems in financing the project and Coleridge's shifting political views doomed the plan.

Coleridge showed great academic promise, but a lack of discipline, a curse throughout his life, interrupted his Cambridge studies. A considerable debt accumulated through carelessness, while a love affair gone bad led him to despair. To escape, he enlisted under a false name with the Light Dragoons, an English cavalry unit. Soon realizing his complete lack of fitness for military life, he begged his older brother to save him. His commitment to the Dragoons was bought out by family members and friends, and he returned to Cambridge, only to leave a year later without completing his studies. Shortly after, he became engaged to Sarah Fricker, for whom he had no love, mostly out of obligation to Southey, who was engaged to Sarah's sister. The two couples married on the same day and moved to Nether Stowey. In the years after Cambridge, Coleridge was a frequent preacher at Unitarian churches and reluctantly became a candidate for a full-time pastoral job to relieve financial pressure. Financial salvation came the day after his candidacy sermon, when he received an annual patronage of 150 pounds from the Wedgwood brothers. This income allowed him to withdraw from candidacy and devote his energies to literary pursuits.

An important alliance was formed in 1795, when he met William Wordsworth. Though each benefited from the ideas of the other, Coleridge always felt himself the inferior, and Wordsworth did nothing to discourage his friend's deference.[3] In 1798 the two spent a year in Germany, where Coleridge became acquainted with the currents of German philosophy and literature. During this time Coleridge was extremely productive and penned his best poetry. However, the years following his return from Germany reveal a story of personal decline. He was permanently separated from his wife in 1806. In 1810 he became estranged from Wordsworth, and though there was some reconciliation later, the relationship was never the same. His annuity was cut because of lack of productivity, leaving him in financial straits. Finally, to find relief from nagging illness (and perhaps also from personal problems), Coleridge began taking opium and fought addiction to the drug for the remainder of his life. In 1816 he enlisted the help of Dr. James Gillman to bring his opium use under control, an effort that was moderately successful. Although this relationship was intended to be temporary, Coleridge lived with Gillman and his wife at Highgate until his death in 1834. During the final twenty years of his life, his writing of poetry slowed considerably, and most of his work focused on philosophy and theology. In view of his tremendous early literary output, one can only marvel at what could have been if Coleridge had managed his personal life more judiciously.

Understanding and Reason

On one level Coleridge's story is one of religious pilgrimage from early Anglican piety, through dalliance with Voltaire's philosophy, to Unitarianism and the materialistic philosophy of David Hartley (1705-1757), and back to Anglican orthodoxy. A decisive benchmark in this process was the trip to Germany in 1798. During this time he became acquainted the biblical criticism (with special interest in Hermann Reimarus and Gotthold Lessing) that was yet to make an impact on England. Coleridge had the foresight to realize how damaging these ideas would be to the natural theology that buttressed much of English theology. At the same time he also discovered in German Romanticism what would become the foundation for his experiential theology. However, while Romanticism generally rejected Christianity's claim to exclusivity, Coleridge used romantic ideas in a distinctively Christian manner.

During this time natural theology was reacting to David Hume, whose skeptical treatment of miracles led to a flood of works on the objective evidence for Christianity. The principal figure in this counterattack was William Paley (1743-1805), who Coleridge came to view as a grave danger to true Christianity. "I believe myself bound in conscience to throw the whole force of my intellect in the way of this [Paley's] triumphal Car, on which the tutelary Genius of modern Idolatry is borne, even at the risk of being crushed under the wheels!"[4] The problem, as Coleridge sees it, is Paley's assertion that we can move from disbelief to faith through objective evidences. These evidences originate in what Coleridge calls "understanding." Because they begin from empirical data, "the Judgments of the Understanding are binding only in relation to the objects of our Senses, which we *reflect* under the forms of the Understanding."[5] When confined to the sensible order, understanding is of value. However, when theological or philosophical method begins from physical senses, it limits its reach to physical objects, and *meta*physical truths become inaccessible. As a result natural theology turns the natural realm into a lifeless machine and inevitably degenerates into materialism. Thus on the practical level, Coleridge considers reliance on objective criteria nothing more than a variation on atheism.

Coleridge contrasts the understanding upon which natural theology relies to "reason," which he describes as "the Power of Universal and necessary Convictions, the Source and Substance of truths above Sense, and having their evidence in themselves."[6] Reason thus goes beyond understanding. The latter is reliant on fallible senses that can know only provisional entities. It possesses the power to reconfigure the givens of the physical world as a means to achieve an end. However, only reason admits us to the realm of ultimate reality in which we know ends and not just means. The key that unlocks the metaphysical realm is moral will. Speculative thought alone cannot reveal truth in its fullness. "But if not the abstract or speculative Reason—and yet a Reason there must be in order to a Rational Belief—then it must be the Practical Reason of Man, comprehending the Will, the Conscience, the Moral Being with its inseparable Interests and affection—that Reason, namely, which is the Organ of Wisdom, and (as far as Man is concerned) the Source of living and Actual Truths."[7]

It is not difficult to hear Kant's voice behind Coleridge's appeal to practical reason. Discursive reason, what Coleridge calls *understanding*, cannot pierce the veil of the noumenal world. However, through practical reason, or what Coleridge simply calls *reason*, we gain access to moral and religious truth. Through our moral sense and will, we express our freedom and responsibility and thus enter a domain that transcends the senses.[8] However, with his addition of "interest and affections" to the definition of reason, Coleridge adds an experiential spin absent in Kant. Kant was suspicious of anything that smacked of interest, emotion or desire. Coleridge, on the other hand, fully embraces them and pulls them within the purview of reason, which moves us beyond a world that we "know about" into one in which commitments are required. Therefore, for a belief to be rational, "I must have an *interest* in this belief. It must *concern* me, as a moral and responsible Being."[9]

Coleridge illustrates the limitations of understanding in his contrast between fancy and imagination.[10] Fancy is that power by which memories of phenomena are reconfigured to generate new ideas about sense objects. However, "It has no other counters to play with but fixities and definites. The fancy is indeed no other than a mode of memory emancipated from the order of time and space; and blended with, and modified by that empirical phenomenon of the will which we express by the word *choice*. But equally with the ordinary memory it must receive all its materials ready made from the law of association."[11] The problem is that fancy derives from passive faculty; understanding fabricates from ideas presented by the senses but cannot create. However, "If the mind is not *pas-*

sive, if it be indeed made in God's Image, and that, too, in the sublimest sense, the Image of the Creator, there is ground for suspicion that any system built on the passiveness of the mind must be false, as a system."[12]

In order to unleash the creative powers of our mind, we must employ imagination, the vital capacity of reason. "The primary imagination I hold to be the living power and prime agent of all human perception, and as a repetition in the finite mind of the eternal act of creation in the infinite I AM. The secondary I consider as an echo of the former, co-existing with the conscious will, yet still as identical with the primary in the kind of its agency, and differing only in degree, and in the mode of its operation. It dissolves, diffuses, dissipates, in order to re-create; or where this process is rendered impossible, yet still, at all events, it struggles to idealize and to unify. It is essentially *vital,* even as all objects (as objects) are essentially fixed and dead."[13] Through imagination we transcend the givens of nature and ascend to divine reality. Therefore, when natural theology builds on understanding, its power of fancy binds us to the sensible realm. Reason, with its imaginative faculty, elevates us above nature and unifies us with God.[14]

This search for unity with the divine brings with it awareness of disunity both within ourselves and between ourselves and God. Thus rationality cannot be separated from the question of salvation, and Coleridge is convinced that Christianity is the apex of rationality because it resolves our estrangement. "The truth revealed through Christ has its evidence in itself, and the proof of its divine authority in its fitness to our nature and needs;—the clearness and cogency of this proof being proportionate to the degree of self-knowledge in each individual hearer."[15] When self-knowledge creates openness, the truth of Christianity "finds me" and makes itself evident. "In short whatever *finds* me, bears witness for itself that it has proceeded from a Holy Spirit, even from the same Spirit, *which remaining in itself, yet regenerateth all other powers, and in all ages entering into holy souls maketh them friends of God, and prophets* (Wisd. vii.)."[16] This intuitive certainty is of such strength that speculative arguments are powerless against it. "The Law of Conscience, and not the Canons of discursive Reasoning, must decide in such cases. At least, the latter have no validity, which the single veto of the former is not sufficient to nullify."[17] The ability of our moral veto to override speculative reasoning demonstrates the priority of our subjective nature and the folly of attempting to evangelize or resolve religious issues by discursive thought alone.

In sum, Coleridge argues that reason is bipolar. "Revealed Religion (and I know of no religion not revealed) is in its highest contemplation the unity, that is, the identity or coinherence, of Subjective and Objective. It is in itself, and irrelatively, at once inward Life and Truth, and outward Fact and Luminary. But as all Power manifests itself in the harmony of correspondent Opposites, each supposing and supporting the other,—so has Religion its objective, or historic and ecclesiastical pole, and its subjective, or spiritual and individual pole."[18] Natural theology gives such prominence to the objective pole that the subjective is overshadowed or rejected.[19] In contrast, while Coleridge urges balance, he also gives the subjective at least a temporal priority over the objective. Objective truth cannot be apprehended until a subjective commitment to that truth exists. "In order to an efficient belief in Christianity a man must have been a Christian, and this is the seeming *argumentum in circulo* incident to all spiritual truths, to every subject not presentable under the forms of time and space, as long as we attempt to master by the reflex acts of the understanding what we can only know by the act of becoming."[20] Without commitment we substitute "a barren acquiescence in the letter for the lively *faith that cometh by hearing;* even as the hearing is productive of this faith, because it is the word of God that is heard and preached."[21]

The priority of commitment requires further clarification. Coleridge does not equate faith with reason, although they are closely related. Reason refers to our awareness of need, while faith speaks of our commitment in response to that self-knowledge. Therefore the position of both reason and understanding in relation to faith is somewhat analogous to the relationship between reason and understanding. "Faith elevates the soul not only above Sense and sensible things, but above reason itself. As Reason corrects the errors which Sense might occasion, so supernatural Faith corrects the errors of natural Reason judging according to Sense."[22] Therefore Christianity, "though not discoverable by human reason, is yet in accordance with it; that link follows link by necessary consequence; that religion passes out of the ken of reason only where the eye of reason has reached its own horizon; and that faith is then but its continuation."[23]

By defining reason and faith in intuitive terms, Coleridge believes that he has put Christianity out of reach of both Humean skepticism and biblical criticism. Coleridge states confidently that the believer should "never be alarmed by Objections wholly speculative, however plausible on speculative grounds such objections may appear, if he can but satisfy himself, that the Result is repugnant to the dictates of Conscience, and irreconcilable with the interests of Morality. For to baffle the Objector we have only to demand of him, by what right and under what authority he converts a Thought into a Substance, or asserts the existence of a real somewhat corresponding to a Notion not derived from the experience of his Senses."[24] Since biblical criticism and skeptical arguments ignore the existential and moral facet of life, they are trumped by intuitive moral knowledge and experience.

Moreover, Coleridge's definition of reason allows him to discard natural theology's intellectual proofs for Christianity in favor of an experiential one.[25] "I more than fear the prevailing taste for Books of Natural Theology, Physico-Theology, Demonstrations of God from Nature, Evidences of Christianity, &c., &c. Evidences of Christianity! I am weary of the word. Make a man feel the want of it; rouse him, if you can, to the self-knowledge of his need of it; and you may safely trust it to its own Evidence—remembering only the express declaration of Christ himself: No man cometh to me, unless the Father leadeth him."[26] The Christian message has no authority apart from our sense of sin and need but is self-authenticating to all who approach with awareness of moral deficiency.[27] Thus Coleridge's challenge to those who would know whether Christianity is true is, "Try it!"

Scripture and Experience

Coleridge applies this experiential criterion to Scripture as well. He accepted biblical criticism's basic tenet that Scripture should be studied like any other literary work since "they [the writers of Scripture] refer to other documents, and in all points express themselves as sober minded and veracious writers under ordinary circumstances are known to do."[28] However, this does not mean that the Bible is only one more ancient writing. Instead we should come with a willingness to be transformed and then read its [Scripture's] contents with only the same piety which you freely accord on other occasions to the writings of men, considered the best and wisest of their several ages! What you find therein coincident with your pre-established convictions, you will of course recognise as the revealed Word, while, as you read the recorded workings of the Word and the Spirit in the minds, lives, and hearts of spiritual men, the influence of the same Spirit on your own being, and the conflicts of grace and infirmity in your own soul, will enable you to discern and to know in and by what spirit they spake and acted,—as far at least as shall be needful for you, and in the times of your need.[29]

Instead of relying on external props for its authority, the Bible has an internal authority of which we become conscious when we find our needs addressed in the concrete experiences of the writers. "In the Bible there is more that *finds* me than I have experienced in all other books put together; that the words of the Bible find me at greater depths of my being; and that whatever finds me brings with it an irresistible evidence of its having proceeded from the Holy Spirit."[30] It is the fitness of Scripture to the believer's "nature and needs" that provides all the authority necessary for viewing the Scripture as the divine Word. In short, Coleridge states that "the Bible and Christianity are their own sufficient evidence."[31]

This approach to biblical authority and inspiration is in opposition to the view that the Bible's words were "dictated by an Infallible Intelligence; that the writers, each and all, were divinely informed as well as inspired."[32] While this position maintains that "whatever is contained in the Bible is religion, and was revealed by God," Coleridge argues instead, "The Bible contains the religion revealed by God."[33] Though Scripture "contains the religion revealed by God," not everything contained therein is of divine origin. There are factual errors, contradictions and other human impurities. But while his opponents sought to bolster Scripture's authority by reducing any human role to a minimum, Coleridge asserts that the Bible's power depends on the humanity of its writings. We can know who God is for us only when God's Word comes in full humanity, even though the necessary implication of this humanity is error. However, error in incidental matters does not negate the efficacy and authority of Scripture. "The Bible, considered in reference to its declared ends and purposes, is true and holy, and for all who seek truth with humble spirits an unquestionable guide, and therefore it is the Word of God."[34]

Coleridge cites several reasons for rejecting the inerrantist approach. First, it becomes "bibliolatry"; it makes the Bible an object of worship rather than the means. Thus he argues that the dictation view kills the spirit by dedication to the letter. When humanity is squeezed from Scripture's words, its relevance for our life is lost as well. "This breathing organism [Scripture], this glorious *panharmonicon*, which I had seen stand on its feet as a man, and with a man's voice given to it, the Doctrine in question turns at once into a colossal Memnon's head, a hollow passage for a voice, a voice that mocks the voices of many men, and speaks in their names, and yet is but one voice and the same;—and no man uttered it, and never in a human heart was it conceived."[35] Second, Coleridge argues that, ultimately, the dictation doctrine's attempt to avoid human fallibility is "nugatory" because we cannot bypass all human activity. "Every sentence found in a canonical Book, rightly interpreted, contains the *dictum* of an infallible Mind;—what the right interpretation is,—or whether the very words now extant are corrupt or genuine—must be determined by the industry and understanding of fallible, and alas!, more or less prejudiced theologians."[36] Finally, Coleridge believes that this doctrine requires its advocates to dishonestly interpret Scripture, avoiding obvious meanings that do not accord with their conclusions.[37] Rather than attempt to explain away critical problems through intellectual tricks and contortions, Coleridge argues that the erroneous chaff is simply overcome by the practical value of Christianity.

Significance

While Coleridge's ideas did not gain great notice immediately, as the impact of biblical criticism grew and the arguments of natural theology failed to satisfy, his ideas began to take hold. For many, he offered an alternative that did not strain the tenets of Christian orthodoxy the way Romanticism and Idealism did but still found a way to speak of the unity that appealed to these two schools. It sought a middle ground between the arid rationalism so characteristic of English deism and Unitarianism without sacrificing reason itself, while maintaining the objective pole so frequently missing in the Romantic figures with whom Coleridge otherwise has much in common. Moreover, Coleridge's theology was able to address the findings of biblical criticism instead of ignoring them, as many orthodox thinkers did. By shifting the theological basis to experience, he was able to absorb the impact of biblical criticism by accepting its method without acquiescing to the often radical conclusions drawn by its advocates.

This experiential aspect of religion constitutes the most powerful draw for Coleridge's ideas. The tendency of theological and philosophical systems is to move toward the objective pole, and occasionally figures such as Coleridge reintroduce the personal and subjective aspect of faith. When religious and philosophical systems become overly rationalistic, the idea that truth is what "finds me" gains a renewed hearing. Thus in his argument that experience creates the basis for our faith, Coleridge represents an important link that reaches back to Blaise Pascal, anticipates Søren Kierkegaard and finds strong representation in one of England's most prominent nineteenth century theologians, F. D. Maurice (1805-1872). This approach also surfaces later in the thought of William James, Karl Barth and the existential authors of the twentieth century.

The danger of taking up a position in the middle of the field is that you take shots from all sides. This was the case for Coleridge. However, since the loudest voice of the age came from rationalism in its various forms, Coleridge's reliance on the intuitive left him most vulnerable to charges of irrationality. His response to this is twofold: "To be *called* irrational is a trifle: to *be* so, and in matters of religion, is far otherwise; and whether the irrationality consists in men's believing *against* reason, or *without* reason, I have been early instructed to consider it as a sad and serious evil, pregnant with mischiefs, political and moral."[38] Coleridge is adamant that Christianity is rational but that current definitions of rationality are so severely restrictive that they neglect the most important aspects of our life. Thus he seeks to bring the subjective element under the domain of rationality. The weakness in his broadened definition is that he has the romanticist's tendency to avoid systematization and is not always clear how the objective and subjective fit together. This more than anything else may explain why his thought was overshadowed by Friedrich Schleiermacher's theology, which also explores the experiential element of religion.

Friedrich Schleiermacher

At a party celebrating Schleiermacher's twenty-ninth birthday, a reluctant promise was extracted from him by his friend Friedrich Schlegel that he would try his hand at writing. The product of these proddings, *On Religion: Speeches to Its Cultured Despisers* (1799), would appear two years later. This book created a great stir and moved Schleiermacher (1768-1834) into the center of an ongoing debate about the viability and nature of religion.[39] The situation Schleiermacher addressed in this inaugural text sounds surprisingly contemporary. While there were pockets of great vitality in popular Christianity, in the intellectual circles (such as the Berlin Romantics he addresses in his *Speeches*) it was often seen as outmoded, fit only for the uncultured and even a positive danger to the intellect and humanity. While Schleiermacher agrees with many of the concerns that lead to the "cultured despisers'" hostility toward religion, his main argument is that their criticisms do not address religion per se. Instead what they despise is something peripheral to the heart of religion.

Schleiermacher's main contribution to the debate concerning the validity of religious belief was to shift authority to what he terms *Gefühl*, or feeling. He came by his interest in the inner aspect of religion honestly. His father was an army chaplain with strong pietistic tendencies, who guided his son toward education in Moravian schools at Niesky and Barby. While Schleiermacher eventually rejected many of their doctrinal formulations and their tendency to hold culture at arm's length, evidence of a strong Moravian piety is apparent throughout his writings. Schleiermacher later made his way to Halle, which had been founded as a pietist school but had, like Schleiermacher, abandoned much of its original theology. There he was able to immerse himself in philosophy, especially that of Kant.

Unlike many other intellectuals of the time, his theological education culminated with ordination. While chaplain at Charity Hospital he became active in the intellectual circle of Berlin as a frequent participant in discussions held in the home of Henriette Herz (1764-1847). In these *salons* he met the leading figures of the Romantic movement and developed a strong friendship with Friedrich Schlegel. The Romantic influence is greatest during these early years, and Schleiermacher's first writings were contributions to the *Athenaeum* (1798-1800), a critical journal that was the primary vehicle of Romantic thought.

In 1804 he was invited to join the faculty at Halle, and there he discovered his passion for the academic world. However, his enjoyment of the teaching profession was interrupted in 1806 when Napoleon's armies invaded Prussia and shut down the university. In 1810 he went to Berlin as one of the charter faculty members of the new university (with Johann Gottlieb Fichte) and remained there until his death in 1834. Upon his arrival he wrote his *Brief Outline on the Study of Theology* (1811) in preparation for his lectures in theology. This gradually expanded to culminate in his greatest work, *The Christian Faith* (1821-22, revised 1831-1832). Over his career he lectured on a wide range of subjects: ethics, dialectics, education, church history, philosophy of religion, theology, hermeneutics, political thought, psychology, aesthetics and New Testament. Schleiermacher was also the first to translate most of Plato's dialogues into German, a project he continued for over thirty years but was unable to complete before his death. Many still consider them the authoritative German translations. In addition to his brilliant academic reputation Schleiermacher continued his preaching even while at the university (his collected sermons number ten volumes).

Although often introduced in modern texts as the "father of modern theology," Schleiermacher's impact was not fully recognized during his life. Even the liberal theologians of the nineteenth century most indebted to him are quick to criticize him without fully acknowledging his influence. Toward the end of the century this oversight was partially corrected with Dilthey's biography of Schleiermacher's life.[40] In a rather ironic twist his importance was finally recognized by his opponents with the rise of neo-orthodoxy early in this century. Both Barth and Emil Brunner traced the roots of liberal Christianity back to Schleiermacher. In spite of his rejection of Schleiermacher's theology, Barth states, "The first place in a history of the theology of the most recent times belongs and will always belong to Schleiermacher, and he has no rival."[41] We will consider Schleiermacher's defense of religion in general, primarily through *On Religion: Speeches to Its Cultured Despisers* (hereafter *Speeches*). We will then see how he built on this basis as a means of reframing Christian theology in *The Christian Faith*.

At the opening of the nineteenth century, pessimism about the future of Christianity was common in academic circles. Traditional orthodoxy was widely dismissed as untenable because it built on sources of authority such as the church or Scripture that were themselves open to question. At the same time, the rationalistic theology of the earlier century faced the same problem as orthodoxy since its own foundations were under assault in the philosophies of Hume and Kant. Both approaches appeared to lack proper grounding. Schleiermacher's *Speeches* acknowledges these concerns. "You are doubtless acquainted with the histories of human follies, and have reviewed the various structures of religious doctrine from the senseless fables of wanton peoples to the most refined Deism, from the rude superstition of human sacrifice to the ill-put together fragments of metaphysics and ethics now called purified Christianity, and you have found them all without rhyme or reason."[42] Surprisingly, Schleiermacher follows this description of their feelings with the statement, "I am far from wishing to contradict you."[43]

The concept of religion Schleiermacher defends is not religion as the cultured despisers defined it. Instead he offers a radically new conception, or at least new to them, of what is central in religion. He asks them to "turn from everything usually reckoned religion, and fix your regard on the inward emotions and dispositions."[44] For Schleiermacher, religion is intuited; it is a *feeling*. The term he uses, *Gefühl*, is only imperfectly translated as "feeling." This, along with Schleiermacher's own ambiguity, has led to an ongoing debate as to what he means by the term. However, he clearly intends something more than simple momentary emotion. Instead, it is intuition of the supernatural. It is an immediate consciousness of the divine that is deeper than and prior to reflection or discursive knowledge.

Most of the critics addressed in *Speeches* equated religion with metaphysics or ethics, or as Schleiermacher phrases it, with knowing or doing. Schleiermacher wants to establish *Gefühl* alongside knowing and doing as a valid and distinct realm of human experience. Rather than relying on some form of argument to establish this, however, he turns to experience itself. "Why do you not regard the religious life itself, and first those pious exaltations of the mind in which all other known activities are set aside or almost suppressed, and the whole soul is dissolved in the immediate feeling of the Infinite and Eternal?"[45]

Schleiermacher's point is that our most profound encounters with God have little to do with doctrine, metaphysics and ethics. Our awareness of God, what Schleiermacher calls *piety*, is immediate. The immediacy of piety is the reason he is comfortable with a direct appeal to experience. Since it is prior to argument, evidence or doctrine, true religious experience cannot be confirmed by or built upon them. It is self-authenticating. "All is immediately true in religion, for except immediately how could anything arise?"[46] This reliance on immediacy does not mean that doctrine, metaphysics and ethics have no theological use. They are instead the tools by which we communicate the significance of our experiences of piety and act on them. However, because they belong to spheres other than religion, philosophical or ethical claims require different avenues of verification than does *Gefühl*.

We should notice the impact of this move in the context of the cultured despisers' criticisms of religion. They had assumed that religion was dependent on metaphysics or ethics. However, if Schleiermacher's position is correct that religious sensitivities are something different from knowledge and activity, or metaphysics or ethics, he has deftly sidestepped their criticisms. Invoking arguments against metaphysical systems or ethical schemas does not touch religion because it is a third thing. Religion can only be criticized on religious criteria.

At this point we have only part of Schleiermacher's definition of religion. Our sense of the divine is not just any feeling. Instead, authentic religious experience is the *feeling of absolute dependence*. "The self-identical essence of piety, is this: the consciousness of being absolutely dependent, or, which is the same thing, of being in relation with God."[47] For Schleiermacher, our sense of absolute dependence is the recognition of our finitude before the Infinite and Eternal. This feeling is not to be confused with the wonder inspired by things in this world. As C. W. Christian aptly phrases it, "Religion is not awe for 'big finitude'; it is awareness of the mystery on which the world itself depends."[48]

The crux of Schleiermacher's message to the cultured despisers is that, try as they might to escape it, they are by nature religious creatures. "This feeling of absolute dependence, in which our self-consciousness in general represents the finitude of our being is therefore not an accidental element, or a thing which varies from person to person, but is a universal element of life."[49] Since it is universal, "Piety cannot be an instinct craving for a mess of metaphysical and ethical crumbs. If it were, you would scarcely oppose it."[50] We cannot simply ignore the feeling of absolute dependence as we might an ethical or metaphysical theory. To reject it is to deny something constitutive of our humanity. Thus while metaphysics and ethics have their place, "Only when piety takes its place alongside of science and practice [metaphysics and ethics], as a necessary, an indispensable third, as their natural counterpart, not less in worth and splendour than either, will the common field be altogether occupied and human nature on this side complete."[51]

Having reestablished the foundations of religion on an experiential basis, Schleiermacher turns to criticisms of religion in its concrete manifestations. One frequent target of the cultured despisers was religious dogma, which was frequently attacked as baseless or irrational. Schleiermacher's appeal to feeling blocks this route of attack. He is, like the despisers, highly critical of Protestant Scholasticism's tendencies to equate doctrine and piety by reducing theology to finely interwoven propositions and then contentiously battling over each doctrine. The problem with this, in Schleiermacher's view, is that doctrine is not religion. Instead, "Those things [doctrines] are only the shadows of our religious emotions."[52] Doctrine is external and capable of being learned from another. Neither is true for piety. "From within, in their original, characteristic form, the emotions of piety must issue. They must be indubitably your own feelings, and not mere stale descriptions of the feelings of others, which could at best issue in a wretched imitation."[53]

While erasing the confusion between doctrine and piety, Schleiermacher also argues that piety cannot dispense with doctrine. First, it is the means by which we communicate to others the significance of our experiences of piety. Second, in this process of communication, creeds and doctrinal statements "stimulate what should properly precede them,"[54] namely, piety. In other words, doctrine can direct us back toward its source and generate feelings of piety. Therefore, while religion and doctrine are related, their relationship must be rightly understood. For Schleiermacher, creeds and confessions are not the foundation of piety but its byproduct.

For this reason, Schleiermacher is no less charitable to those who seek a solution in natural theology. Natural theology appealed to many of the cultured despisers who "have always borne more easily with what for distinction is called natural religion."[55] Proponents of the natural religion sought to make religion a private affair built on a few inoffensive doctrines to which, presumably, any rational person could consent. The assumption was that natural theology would lead to a universal form of religion. However, Schleiermacher will have nothing to do with natural theology's abstract and uniform religion. Behind religious practices that "may long ago have degenerated into a long series of empty customs, into a system of abstract ideas and theories, will you not, when you examine the original elements at the source, find that this dead dross was once the molten outpourings of the inner fire?"[56] For Schleiermacher, religious customs and rituals are not themselves problematic. They are an inevitable means by which we give voice to our feeling of absolute dependence. The danger is that these can lose connection with the universal God-consciousness that birthed them. Nor should we seek to overcome diversity in religious practice and doctrine, as natural theology sought to do. Since expression of universal God-consciousness is determined by cultural and historical circumstances, we should expect and welcome diversity in religious practice and belief. This only becomes negative when one religion claims finality for itself.

Schleiermacher's affirmation of a single source of spiritual experience does not force him to view all religions as equally valid, however. For example, polytheism is seen as inferior to monotheism because it fails to recognize the unity of the divine. Among the monotheistic religions Schleiermacher finds Christianity to be the highest form. His main argument is that it possesses a capacity for self-criticism not found in other monotheisms. "Christianity then demands as first and essential that piety be a constant state. It scorns to be satisfied, even with the strongest displays of it, as long as it only rules certain portions of the life."[57] In other words, Christianity, above all other religions, makes the religious consciousness primary.

The means by which this heightened religious consciousness is possible in Christianity, according to Schleiermacher, is Christ. While his Christology in *Speeches* is extremely brief, he gives us a hint of how this will be developed later in *The Christian Faith*. "But the truly divine element [in Christ] is the glorious clearness to which the great idea He came to exhibit attained in His soul. This idea was, that all that is finite requires a higher mediation to be in accord with the Deity, and that for man under the power of the finite and particular, and too ready to imagine the divine itself in this form, salvation is only to be found in redemption."[58] While Schleiermacher sees Christ's mediation of redemption as key to Christianity's superiority, in *Speeches* he refuses to attach ultimacy to the work of Christ or the Christian faith. "Yet He never maintained He was the only mediator, the only one in whom His idea actualized itself. And He never made His school equivalent to His religion, as if his ideas were to be accepted on account of His person, and not His person on account of His idea."[59]

The Christian Faith

While the core idea of religion as the feeling of absolute dependence remains the same from Schleiermacher's *Speeches* to his later work *The Christian Faith*, the tone of the two works is distinctly different. Whereas *Speeches* represents Schleiermacher's early writing, *Christian Faith* gives us a view of the mature Schleiermacher at the height of his intellectual abilities. Second, the tone of *Speeches* is highly rhetorical, at times excessively so. In contrast, *Christian Faith* is tightly reasoned and logically integrated. Finally, like any good author, Schleiermacher understood his audience. In *Christian Faith* he no longer writes as a philosopher of religion to skeptical intellectuals but as a theologian to the believing community. It is therefore much more explicit in its Christian orientation and deals with specifically Christian doctrines more extensively than *Speeches*.

While very conscious of his role as a Christian theologian, Schleiermacher is also aware that, as a post-Kantian theologian, he cannot rely on prior approaches to theology for his model. As a result of Kant's first *Critique* Schleiermacher agrees that we cannot construct theology on supernaturalist or metaphysical bases. The reality (God) behind experience of the divine is inaccessible by direct means. Therefore, we must take a phenomenological approach to Christianity: we begin with the *experience* of the divine itself. Theology is to be understood as "descriptions of human states."[60] Or, as he describes it elsewhere, "Christian doctrines are accounts of the Christian religious affections set forth in speech."[61] When we "do theology," we systematize our encounters with God and thus refer only indirectly to God himself.

Although the subject of theology—God—remains the same, our relationship with God, which provides the data of theology, varies. Thus Schleiermacher structures *Christian Faith* to reflect the three potential states of our relationship to God. He begins with an explication of the general consciousness of the divine—the feeling of absolute dependence—that all have in common. The second section considers our experience in the context of consciousness of sin. Finally, doctrine is considered from the perspective of our relationship with God under grace.[62]

This structural difference leads to a unique treatment of the topics of Christian theology. For example, Schleiermacher argues, "All attributes which we ascribe to God are to be taken as denoting not something special in God, but only something special in the manner in which the feeling of absolute dependence is to be related to Him."[63] Thus discussion of the divine attributes is distributed among the three potential relationships to God. Schleiermacher considers in part one (religious consciousness in general) God's eternality, omnipresence, omnipotence and omniscience. When we experience finitude and absolute dependence in the face of God's infinity, these attributes are present to our awareness. In part two (religious self-consciousness as determined by sin) the mercy and justice of God is examined. In the final section (consciousness of grace) the wisdom and love of God are explicated.

Whereas Schleiermacher's Christology in *Speeches* is brief, *Christian Faith* makes it the centerpiece. His experiential approach to doctrine provides a third way between the older orthodoxy and the Enlightenment. Methodologically, this requires that he abandon the traditional approach to Christology, in which an examination of Christ's person precedes his work. Instead Schleiermacher argues that we must move in the opposite direction. We begin from our experience of redemption through Christ and draw from this our conclusions about his person. This experiential approach requires also a new understanding of Scripture. Scripture's witness to Jesus does not provide objective statements about his life and work. Instead it contains the theological reflection of the earliest Christians on the significance of their experience with him. They are interest-

ing from the perspective of historical theology but are not legitimate
bases from which we can begin our own theological endeavors.[64] Thus
while he argues, for example, that the concept of a supernatural birth is
required to safeguard Jesus' preeminence, "the more precise definition
of this supernatural conception as one in which there was no male activity has no connexion of any kind with the essential elements in the peculiar dignity of the Redeemer."[65] Similarly, the "facts of the Resurrection
and the Ascension of Christ, and the prediction of His Return to Judgment, cannot be laid down as properly constituent parts of the doctrine
of His Person."[66] Even if historically grounded (which he clearly doubts
in most cases), these events would be mere objective matters of fact and
not our subjective experience of the divine.

While rejecting traditional approaches to Christology, Schleiermacher
also avoids the attenuated Christology of the Enlightenment that reduces
Jesus to the role of moral instructor and exemplar. He agrees that Jesus
represents the perfection of human nature and in this way can lay claim
to the role of exemplar *(Vorbild)*. However, Schleiermacher wants to
define Jesus' perfection in terms other than morality. Instead Christ's
uniqueness is the primacy of his God-consciousness. Indeed the perfection of Jesus' sense of absolute dependence seems to function as a divine
element in him. "The Redeemer, then, is like all men in virtue of the
identity of human nature, but distinguished from them all by the constant potency of his God-consciousness, which was the veritable existence of God in Him."[67] Thus Christ is not simply the *Vorbild*, or exemplar
of moral perfection, but the *Urbild*, or ideal, of the sense of absolute
dependence required of all humanity. We should note that Schleiermacher dismisses most versions of atonement theory that focus on a single
event in Jesus' life. Instead the significance of Jesus is the constancy of
his God-consciousness throughout his life.

The significance of Jesus is not merely that the ideal of absolute
dependence became historical in his life. The benefits of his perfect
God-consciousness are also communicated to the church. For Schleiermacher, this sets Christianity apart. The church is the community of
redemption created through Christ's sense of dependence on God. "In
this corporate life which goes back to the influence of Jesus, redemption
is effected by Him through the communication of His sinless perfec-

tion."[68] Or, as he phrases it elsewhere, Jesus "assumes believers into the power of his God-consciousness."[69] This signals a significant departure from his position in *Speeches*. Whereas Schleiermacher appears to affirm in the earlier book the possibility that Christianity may be superseded by a new religious expression, the tone shifts dramatically in *Christian Faith*. In other religions, Schleiermacher says, God-consciousness is "dominated by the sensuous self-consciousness." In contrast, Christ "alone mediates all existence of God in the world and all revelation of God through the world, in so far as He bears within Himself the whole new creation which contains and develops the potency of the God-consciousness."[70]

Just as Schleiermacher's use of religious experience as the point of departure for theology influences his Christology, it has a profound effect on how other doctrines are formulated as well. For example, the concept of creation ex nihilo tells us nothing about how creation occurs. There is "neither motive nor guidance for a treatment of origination taken by itself" since the question of *how* the universe originated is distinct from the question of religious self-consciousness. We are best served by "handing over this subject to natural science."[71] Instead, creation ex nihilo is the vehicle by which the complete dependence of all creation on God is affirmed. "The expression 'out of nothing' excludes the idea that before the origin of the world anything existed outside God, which as 'matter' could enter into the formation of the world. And undoubtedly the admission of 'matter' as existing independently of the divine activity would destroy the feeling of absolute dependence, and the actual world would be represented as a mixture of that which existed through God and that which existed independently of God."[72]

As we might expect, if piety is the feeling of absolute dependence, sin is defined as the denial of absolute dependence, a distortion of our consciousness of the Infinite. This definition of sin is combined with Romanticism's concept of the universe as an interconnected organism in his exposition of original sin. Since all humanity is organically linked, the sin of one is the sin of all, and each sinful act is kept in play through its effect on society. "The sinfulness of every individual has its root in the previous generation."[73] Original sin cannot be traced back in history to an event involving the original pair.[74] In fact, he states that sinfulness must have been in existence prior to the actual sin of the first pair.[75] Although Schleiermacher states that the question of sin's origin is a natural one, it is "not a question arising directly out of the interests of Christian piety."[76] Instead the essence of sin is our refusal to recognize our finitude before the Infinite.

Schleiermacher's Significance

Due to the amorphous nature of Romanticism it is difficult to affix this label to any thinker. This is doubly true of Schleiermacher. He has moved some distance from Romanticism by the end of his career and is more interested in giving new expression to Reformed theology than in working out the implications of a philosophical system. However, if we must engage in the necessary evil of associating Schleiermacher's theology with a philosophical school, he is clearly linked to Romanticism by a number of things. The view that feeling provides the raw data of theology and is independent of philosophical or ethical verification is perhaps the clearest example of Schleiermacher's fusion of Romanticism and theology. That which is most basic to our lives is not discursive or rationally acquired. Instead, it is subjective and experiential. Like Romanticism, Schleiermacher firmly believes that philosophy is useful in the ordering of religious expression. However, philosophy cannot judge the validity of our experiences or provide the source material from which theology begins. Therefore, we should not see the affective and mystical side of human life as inferior to other capacities. Instead feeling is set alongside philosophy and ethics as an independent realm with a unique mode of verification.

Related to the above, Schleiermacher lines up with Romanticism's belief that our access to the deepest realities is always indirect. This is behind his phenomenological approach to doctrine. Since theology cannot begin with God, experience is the starting point. This anthropological point of departure becomes the norm for much of the theology that follows in this century. Similarly, his concept of Scripture is a natural outgrowth of his methodology. Rather than providing a reservoir of material for theology, Scripture contains the early church's theological expression of its experience of redemption.

Finally, Schleiermacher mirrors Romanticism in his analysis of history. Movements and transitions are understood under the paradigm of continuous growth and development rather than as a discontinuous series in which the old holds only dangers to be avoided. This is most apparent in Schleiermacher's understanding of different religions. While all find their origin in a universal impulse, he is certain that the movement of religious development is inevitably in the direction of Christianity. Moreover, Christianity itself progressively discovers more adequate expressions of the underlying experience of God-consciousness.

Schleiermacher's understanding of Christianity is decisive for much of the direction of later nineteenth century theology. The sharp either/or dualisms of traditional theology disappear and are replaced by a model that sees distinctions as a matter of degree. Revelation is no longer handed down from a wholly supernatural sphere but springs from within the God-consciousness of all. The doctrine of sin is interpreted as a lack of development progressively being overcome. Non-Christian religions are not adequately subsumed under a single heading but are seen as more or less capable of expressing our sense of absolute dependence.

4. IDEALISM AND THE END OF DICHOTOMY

A s philosophical movements go, Romanticism and Transcendentalism were relatively accessible to nonphilosophers. This is something of a double-edged sword. On the one hand, the ability of these schools to present themselves through media outside philosophy proper by many who were not philosophers by trade allowed Romanticism and Transcendentalism to find a broad audience. On the other hand, these two schools were often intellectually suspect within philosophical circles. Part of the reason for wariness might be attributed to academic hubris. Philosophers are often suspicious of movements originating outside the fold. However, another cause for reluctance was the considerable element of subjectivism inherent in Transcendentalist and Romantic thought. To many, it seemed more than ironic that these schools would strive for a comprehensive view of reality by employing a highly individualistic methodology. Concern about the subjectivist tendencies led to the ascent of Idealism. Idealism represents an attempt to retain the comprehensiveness of vision in Romanticism and Transcendentalism while avoiding their subjectivism. As a result, this school appealed to many who were dissatisfied with the dualisms between nature and supernature or human and nonhuman that had long dominated philosophy and theology. At the same time, it retained an allure for philosophy by attempting to build on rationality rather than intuition.

Idealism

Idealism has always been something of a "philosopher's philosophy." Because of its highly abstract and comprehensive nature, this school has never been able to sink roots directly into popular culture. However, Idealism's relative obscurity to the layperson can lead to the dangerous illusion that it has been less influential than other movements that have more immediate appeal and can thus be ignored. The fact is that Idealism's influence has been deep and long-lived, even if not always recognized. Because of its desire to explain everything at once, one of its characteristics is the ability to spin off its influence through other disciplines and derivative movements. Thus while Marxism, existentialism and personalism may be more readily recognized than Idealism, they owe their existence in large part to the Idealism that preceded them.

In G. W. F. Hegel's early work contrasting the philosophies of Fichte and Friedrich Schelling, he states, "Dichotomy is the source of *the need for philosophy.*"[1] This provides insight into the impetus behind Idealism.[2] The fundamental dichotomy with which Idealism was concerned was the Kantian distinction between the thing-in-itself and our experience of it. This distinction leaves Kant with a difficult problem because he appears to contradict his view of causation as a category of the mind when he argues also that objects provide the data of experience. The latter makes the thing-in-itself causal; it brings about our experience of it in some way. However, the point of Kant's *Critique of Pure Reason* is that causation, precisely because it is a category in our mind, tells us nothing about objects but works solely on the phenomenal level.

The task of the Idealists, as they saw it, was to resolve this dichotomy. This aim is accomplished by viewing all reality as a product of mental or spiritual agency. It is not just ideas, perceptions and memories that are created by the mind. What appears to us to be a world external to us, the realm of objects, is also actualized by the self. The internal and external universes are ultimately one. The reason Idealism feels justified in uniting the intellectual and natural realms is summed up by Schelling. Rather than attempting to find a connection between "what comes from without and what comes from within," he argues that

> in the process of explaining it [the connection between external and internal] I posit a region of consciousness where this separation *does*

not yet exist, and where inner and outer worlds are conceived as inter-
fused. So certain is it that a philosophy, which does not make it an
absolute rule to leave nothing unproved and without derivation, will
arrive, almost without willing it and through its own mere consistency,
at idealism.[3]
Thus the function of the thing-in-itself in Kant is taken over by the mind
in Idealism. The knower is also the source of that which is known at
some primordial level of consciousness. The world of objects is not ultimately separate from our knowledge but is dependent on a conscious
agent.

For the German Idealists, the argument that the world is a product of
thought should not be confused with solipsism, the belief that each individual creates his or her own world. In order to avoid the accusation of
solipsism, which was frequently leveled at them, the Idealists speak of a
supraindividual mind, an Absolute (hence the label Absolute Idealism).
The primary attribute of the Absolute is creative thought. It is the concept
of the Absolute Mind, by whatever name it goes in Idealistic philosophy,
that allows Idealism to reestablish metaphysics. Rather than fighting a
war on two different fronts in which we must hold together both the
objective world of the thing-in-itself and the mental world, we now are
able to gain access to the objective world *through* the mental. By this
means, the dichotomy of which Hegel speaks is overcome.

This new approach to metaphysics is accompanied by a different view
of epistemology. If the world is dependent on the mind, we are not
engaged in a process of the mind seeking to know what is external to it.
Rather, the mind explores its own activity. Since thought is a process of
internal discovery, as the Romantics argued, a subjective approach is necessary. It is through the self that the Absolute is revealed. While Romanticism stresses the aesthetic, Idealism's redefinition of the intellect absorbs
the rational within the subjective. Both movements broaden the scope of
what is epistemologically valid to encompass more than what the Enlightenment allowed into the category of reason.

This subjective approach also reveals other similarities between the
two schools. Both tended toward monism, refusing to sharply distinguish
between the natural and the divine, and so faced the same problem of
clearly expressing how God is distinguished from the world. They were

of a common mind in viewing the universe as organic and purposeful. Despite these similarities in emphasis, the older Romantics like Novalis, Hölderlin and the Schlegel brothers did not attempt an all-encompassing philosophy. While some within the Romantic school saw the systematization of intuition as its death, the concern of Idealism is to provide a consistent presentation of the subjective. It is one thing to speak of the creative and intuitive. It is another to explain how it works. Thus as Welch puts it, "If the Enlightenment had to be spiritualized, romanticism had also to be intellectualized."[4] When ideas common to Romanticism are systematized, the movement is in the direction of Idealism. Hegel's magisterial system is the height of this systematization. However, his ideas should be seen against the background of Fichte and Schelling, two fellow Idealists with whom his life and ideas are closely intertwined.[5]

Johann Gottlieb Fichte

A key figure in the transitional period between Kant and Hegel is Johann Gottlieb Fichte (1762-1814).[6] Born in Saxony to a poor family, his intellectual abilities were recognized early and a local landowner financed his education. At age eighteen, Fichte enrolled at Jena as a theological student and later studied at Wittenberg and Leipzig. His first major philosophical influence was Baruch Spinoza, whose comprehensive scope and disciplined logic impressed him deeply. However, he was later repelled by Spinoza's determinism and spent the rest of his life combating it.

Fichte's second philosophical hero was Kant, whose writings he became acquainted with while working as a tutor in Zurich. It was through the idea of moral freedom that formed the core of Kant's *Critique of Practical Reason* that Fichte was able to find his way free of Spinozan determinism and set the direction for his own philosophical contribution. The second *Critique* was also the inspiration behind a manuscript Fichte sent to Kant, hoping to gain a meeting with the master. Although it is not clear that Kant initially read the entire work, his response to the work was positive, and he helped Fichte find a publisher. When the book *Toward a Critique of All Revelation* (1793) was published, Fichte's name was not on it. Whether intentional on the part of the publisher or not, this oversight worked nicely to Fichte's advantage. Due to the strongly Kantian tone of the work, it was wrongly assumed that it was the much-anticipated fourth *Critique* from Kant. The book received quite favorable responses, including positive comments from Kant himself, who felt it necessary to clarify the misunderstanding and boosted Fichte from obscurity.

This recognition led to an invitation to join the philosophy faculty at Jena in 1794 as the second occupant of a chair created to propagate the philosophy of Kant. However, things did not go smoothly during his stay at Jena. Fichte's political views put him at odds with many colleagues, and his attempts to impose rigorous moral constraints at the university brought such a strong response from students that he was forced to flee for his life in 1799. His return a few months later was short-lived. He became embroiled in a controversy in which he was accused of atheism. At the center of the debate was an essay entitled, "On the Ground of Our Belief in a Divine World-Order," (1798) in which Fichte identifies God with the moral structure of the universe.[7] As a result he was forced to leave the university toward the end of 1799.[8] Fichte's academic career was revived when he received a faculty chair at Erlangen in 1804. Six years later he was installed as dean of the philosophy faculty at the newly created University of Berlin, where he remained until his death in 1814.

Idealism is a difficult philosophy to explain, and Fichte's writings do little to make it easier. To further complicate matters, he tends to dismiss those who disagree with him as either too incompetent to understand or too stubborn to be persuaded. His *First Introduction* (1797) and *Second Introduction* (1797) to his most significant work, *The Science of Knowledge* (1794), however, are written with the layperson in view. Also intended for the nontechnical reader is his *Vocation of Man* (1800). While our brief survey will focus on his philosophical ideas, Fichte was an important figure in political thought as well. His *Addresses to the German Nation* (1808) is a useful means to understanding the emerging natural consciousness of Germany during this period.

Knowing as Creative Act

In his *First Introduction to the Science of Knowledge* Fichte writes, "I have long asserted, and repeat once more, that my system is nothing other than the *Kantian;* this means that it contains the same view of things, but is in method quite independent of the *Kantian* presentation."[9] While

Fichte does use Kant as a starting point, what he sees as the logical synthesis of Kant's ideas takes him in a very different direction from the master. The reason behind the move from Kantianism to Absolute Idealism is found in Fichte's analysis of types of philosophy, which he reduces to two categories. On the one hand, we can argue that objects exist independently of our perception of them. This is essentially the position of Kant's *Critique of Pure Reason*. The problem with such an approach if not modified in some manner is that it necessarily leads to materialism and eliminates the possibility of freedom. If actions and perceptions are shaped by that which is external to us, choice is lost. This philosophical approach is labeled "dogmatism" by Fichte.

On the other hand the second type of philosophy, Idealism, argues that perceptions within the mind are not dependent on objects. Instead, these objects *result from* our consciousness. As Fichte puts it,

> The object of this system, therefore, actually occurs as something real in the consciousness, not as a *thing-in-itself,* whereby idealism would cease to be what it is and would transform itself into dogmatism, but as a *self-in-itself;* not as an object of experience, for it is not determined but will be determined by me, and without this determination is nothing, and does not even exist; but as something that is raised above all experience.[10]

In other words either the intellect is independent of the world of objects (idealism), or the thing-in-itself is independent of and determinative of the mind (dogmatism). We cannot have it both ways.

At the heart of Fichte's *Science of Knowledge (Wissenschaftslehre)* is the belief that philosophy is a science, a systematic body of knowledge. Such a system demands that all knowledge proceeds from one basic, self-evident principle. Once this principle is in place, everything else follows from it. For Fichte, that principle is "the *self posits itself.* "[11] No possibility for activity exists apart from a self that is capable of engaging in activity. In the process of consciousness, then, we posit the self or the ego. Thus for Idealism, the process of knowing is not just epistemologically significant but is metaphysically important as well. Since there is no difference between subjective and objective, thinking and knowing is a creative act. As Fichte puts it, "Seeing and being are inseparably united."[12] Consciousness of something's existence is simultaneously the cause of its existence.

Thus the self-positing of which Fichte speaks is the process of our coming into being.

The act of self-positing accounts for our existence, but Fichte has not yet explained why we also encounter a world of objects. This is where the theme of moral freedom in Kant's second *Critique* exerts significant influence. Freedom requires choice, and there must be a realm in which opposition occurs in order for choice to be possible. Struggle and opposition are inherent in the idea of freedom. This struggle leads to a second principle that derives from the first: the "I posits the non-I." We posit that which is other than and opposes us. In other words, we posit the objective world. This world, which holds the barriers we must overcome, is not simply a phantom. Instead it is the external reflection of opposing powers that are internally presented to the self. Fichte says:

> And the objective, that which is contemplated and of which I am conscious, is also myself—the same self which contemplates, but which now floats as an objective presentation before the subjective. In this respect, consciousness is an active retrospect of my own intuitions; an observation of myself from my own position; a projection of myself out of myself by means of the only mode of action which is properly mine—intuitive consciousness.[13]

The purpose for the opposition of the nonego is moral.[14] For Fichte, there is no distinction between the objective structure of the universe and its moral structure. They are identical and fulfill the same purpose. "My world is the object and sphere of my duties, and absolutely nothing more."[15] By free activity in which we seek to fulfill our moral duty, we transcend the sensual and mechanical. Our knowledge is not determined by the world around us. Instead this world comes to be through consciousness. This allows Fichte to bring together two more strands of Kant's philosophy: the cognitive and the moral. The world that we experience is not just naked fact but is the sphere of moral struggle.

Fichte's Idealism erases the distinction between objects and our consciousness of them as well as the line between cognition and ethics. However, there are two additional domains that Fichte wants to unite. As Josiah Royce states the problem, "The two expressions of self-consciousness, 'I know,' and 'I do,' stand, in Kant's account, in a profoundly baffling relation."[16] For Kant, the self is a thing. Fichte on the other hand views the self as activity. "The intellect, for idealism, is an *act*, and absolutely nothing more; we should not even call it an *active* something, for this expression refers to something subsistent in which activity inheres."[17] We never see consciousness per se. Instead we become aware of it in the very process of consciousness: through activity. Consciousness is indemonstrable in the abstract; each must discover it through their own reflective processes because consciousness *is* an activity. In other words it is known practically, not theoretically. It is in our freedom that we are aware of our self-positing. All knowledge of ourselves and nature is shrouded in doubt if it is established on a theoretical basis, as Kant demonstrated in his first *Critique*. However, we can avoid doubt if we move to practical reason, which focuses on the activity of free agents. We cannot ignore or refute our acting.[18]

When the self is represented as a creative agent, the constant danger is solipsism, which Fichte avoids by introducing the Absolute, or Pure Ego. Pure Ego transcends individual consciousness. It is that from which we originate and in which we participate. In other words it plays the role generally assigned to God in traditional theism. Like the individual intellect, Pure Ego is not a "something" that acts but the activity of intuition itself. It cannot be objectified. Pure Ego is the consciousness in which the world and individual minds are grounded.

The combination of the two previous ideas, the concept of the Pure Ego and Fichte's ethical concerns, provides the essence of his philosophy of religion. As in Kant the moral life is the goal of religion. Also as in Kant, God's existence finds its proof in moral freedom.[19] Where Fichte and Kant diverge is in their understanding of the nature of God. While Kant concludes that a personal God is a moral necessity, for Fichte God cannot be reduced to a something or someone, even a divine someone.[20] If the Absolute is infinite, we cannot think in terms of substance or personality. The problem, as he expresses it, "In the Idea of *person* there are imperfections, limitations—how can I clothe Thee with it without these?"[21] Further, when he speaks of the Pure Ego as a divine consciousness that contains the world, he eliminates any means of clearly speaking of the transcendence of God. Similarly, the idea of God as Creator becomes problematic. If the Absolute is infinite, all things are eternally found in it.

Fichte's Idealism attempts to fuse many areas that had previously been seen as discreet. He removes the barriers between subjective and objective, between being and doing, between cognition and ethics, and between God and the world. We might say that Fichte synthesizes the conclusions of Kant's first *Critique* with the organic orientation of the third *Critique* by means of the second *Critique*. In the resulting fusion the world does not exist apart from our perception but is presented to us by the self as an obstacle in order that we might exercise moral freedom. However, disagreement with this narrow view of nature as simply the realm of moral activity accounts for the divergence between Fichte and his erstwhile disciple, Schelling.

Friedrich Wilhelm Joseph Schelling

In contrast to the humble background of Fichte, Friedrich Wilhelm Joseph Schelling (1775-1854)[22] was born into a highly regarded family. His father was a Lutheran pastor and a noted expert in Semitic languages. Schelling was enrolled at Tübingen at the age of fifteen, where he developed strong friendships with two roommates who were to make their own mark on intellectual history: Hegel and Hölderlin. His extraordinary talent allowed him to receive a philosophy lectureship at Jena at the age of twenty-three, and he was an extremely prolific writer during his early years.

Early in his career he was an ally of Fichte and for a brief time a colleague at Jena. However, relations between the two men cooled as Schelling's philosophy moved in the direction of Romanticism, partly under the influence of the Schlegel brothers and Novalis, also at Jena during this time. His next alliance was with Hegel who, though five years his senior, was strongly influenced by the younger Schelling. As Hegel's fame eclipsed that of Schelling, however, relations between the two men became strained. Schelling became rather obsessed with the idea that Hegel had stolen his concepts of identity and the Absolute. Partly out of bitterness toward this experience, Schelling wrote almost nothing the last forty years of his life. Most of the books from this period are compilations of his lectures. Schelling did to some degree get the last word in the debate with Hegel. In 1841 he was invited to occupy Hegel's philosophy chair in Berlin, which had remained vacant for the ten years following

Hegel's death. The purpose of the appointment made by Friedrich Wilhelm IV, who had strong romantic sympathies, was to refute the Hegelian philosophy sweeping German intellectual circles.

While Schelling was forced into the shadow of Hegel, there is some truth to his claim that Hegel had borrowed much from him. Hegel was not alone in this. Schelling's thought was influential in Roman Catholic thought during his time,[23] and it shaped the existentialism of Kierkegaard, who attended Schelling's lectures in Berlin. Many of the Romantics also found in Schelling's writing the intellectual foundation for their own views. In more recent times his ideas have been channeled through the philosophical theologies of Paul Tillich and Martin Heidegger.[24] Schelling had a restless brilliance that never allowed him to settle on a particular approach and develop it to the full. As a result, a favorite game of Schelling scholars is arguing about the number of "periods" represented in his philosophy. Indeed his thought is more suggestive and evocative than systematic and consistent. In our survey we will focus on Schelling's philosophy of identity, his understanding of aesthetics and his philosophy of religion.

Reality as Creative Organism

Schelling wants to expand the role that nature plays in Fichte's thought, and his modifications move him into a closer relationship with Romanticism than what we find in Fichte. He believes that nature is more than simply a field posited by the ego within which moral activity occurs. This concept, in Schelling's evaluation, is subjective, making nature dependent on individual egos, which renders it inert and lifeless. By contrast he views nature as objective and vital, existing apart from our consciousness of it and teleological in itself. A second divergence is that Fichte sees the conscious self as eternally divided. The tension between ego and nonego is, for Fichte, the necessary precondition for moral striving. Schelling, however, argues that reality is always unified. Behind the appearance of conflict and division is an essential unity.

Behind Schelling's departure from Fichte's concept of nature as nonego is his principle of identity (or indifference). As he puts it, "We can all agree on this fundamental notion: the idea [of the Absolute], wherein all opposites are not just united, but are simply identical, wherein all opposites are not just canceled, but are entirely undivided from one another."[25] This means that both the thinking subject and the unconscious object are not ultimately different but are manifestations of the same thing. They are two poles of a dialectical process in which nature moves toward consciousness and conscious existence seeks concrete expression. Through the principle of identity we not only rid ourselves of old dualisms such as soul and body, but Schelling believes that he has also removed Fichte's residual dualism of ego and nonego, or nature and consciousness. Instead, all things move toward a harmony of objective and subjective.

An additional dichotomy eliminated by Schelling is that between God and world. The world does not exist apart from God but is rather a manifestation of the Absolute. However, Schelling's view is not so much pantheistic as it is pan*en*theistic. God is unified with his creation but is also its Creator. Creation occurs in God's act of going outside himself. The world comes to be as God's self-expression. In creation the same characteristics possessed by God are manifest in the individual self and in nature, which as we will see, allows him to incorporate the concept of creativity into his philosophy.

It is important to recognize in Schelling's understanding of creation, however, that God is not an entity that can be known in the normal sense of the word. We do not have consciousness of God but *are* the consciousness of God. To state otherwise assumes that God is an object external to and apart from us. If God is to be described as "living," which Schelling certainly believes is necessary, then God contains within himself the same tensions and oppositions that humanity and nature possess. The consciousness of the Absolute evolves, just as ours does. Or to put it more accurately, our consciousness evolves as a result of the evolving consciousness of God. Thus traditional views of the divine simplicity are replaced in Schelling by the dynamic complexity that is characteristic of the whole of human and natural existence.

While the harmony of opposites is perfected in God, it is never final in ourselves and nature. Instead history and the movements of nature are a story of salvation in progress. Salvation, however, is not achieved individually. The principle of identity requires that it be a salvation of the whole, and Schelling's vitalistic view requires that it be progressive. Schelling speaks of this unity in search of salvation as a "world-soul." Contained within this world-soul are both nature and spirit, each of which moves in the direction of its opposite in order to find a unity of the whole. Humans, who possess consciousness (spirit), seek to become objective, to represent themselves concretely by creating. Our life is a journey of finding unity between the opposing forces of spirit and nature within. From the other end, concrete but unconscious nature moves toward consciousness in its attempt to find balance. While it does not stretch us to grasp the desire of humans to give external expression to their thoughts and ideas, it is more difficult to comprehend the idea of objective reality moving toward subjectivity. However, if we recall that spirit and nature are not ultimately distinct, it is no more difficult for Schelling to argue that nature evolves toward mind than it is to argue that intellect seeks concrete representation.

At the heart of Schelling's system is a concept of divine freedom that grows out of his principle of identity.

But absolute freedom is identical with absolute necessity. If we could imagine an action in God, for example, it would have to be absolutely free, but this absolute freedom would simultaneously be absolute necessity, since in God we can think of no law or action that does not spring from the inner necessity of His nature. Such an act is the original act of self-consciousness; absolutely free, since it is determined by nothing outside the self; absolutely necessary, since it proceeds from the inner necessity of the nature of the self.[26]

With this view of freedom as a beginning point we can understand why Schelling believes the Enlightenment had lost its way. The latter saw nature as the realm ruled by law. This perspective separates nature from the realm of the mind, in which freedom resides. When Idealism tears down the wall between the objective and subjective, however, we can no longer see what was labeled natural law as operating independently of mind. Therefore, since God's chief characteristic is freedom, and the world is the mind of God, no set of laws can act as arbiter concerning the activities of the Infinite within history. We cannot limit what is possible for and within the world. When the line separating mind and nature is abolished, the boundary between natural law and miracle disappears, and all things are subsumed under God's freedom.

God's freedom is reflected through humanity in our desire to understand and produce art. It is here that Schelling's dependence on Kant's
third *Critique* is most evident and his Idealism forges its closest links with
Romanticism. When we engage in creative activities such as poetry, art or
religion, we seek to express the infinite within us in objective form. As
Schelling writes, "Art is paramount to the philosopher, precisely because
it opens to him, as it were, the holy of holies, where burns in eternal and
original unity, as if in a single flame, that which in nature and history is
rent asunder, and in life and action, no less than in thought, must forever
fly apart."[27] Philosophy and art are endeavors in which we objectify the
absolute and bring together mind and nature, albeit in provisional and
partial ways.

One way of viewing Schelling's thought, and idealism as a whole, is as
an assault on typically Western approaches to philosophy. The tendency
in the West is to understand by separating, defining and categorizing in
search of the timeless and universal. Schelling believed that Christian
thought had been distorted by this approach, particularly in its view of
Scripture. If Scripture is seen as the final and complete revelation of God,
we lose the idea of a living God.[28] Schelling's view is that Scripture should
be seen as myth. By this he understands Scripture to contain the expressions of an awareness of the divine within history. As long as we recognize that myths are provisional and partial, they offer insight into the
Absolute. However, Christianity has allowed these myths to become ossi-
fied, leading to the belief that God also is a fixed and unchanging entity.

Against this, Schelling calls for the return to that which had been
anathema during the Enlightenment. Instead of seeking a rational objectivity and finality, he argues that philosophy should be speculative. Speculative philosophy, which allows us to maintain the open-endedness of
revelation, is "the true organ of theology as science, wherein the highest
ideas of the Divine Being, of nature as its instrument, and of history as
the revelation of God become objective."[29] In order to retain the historical character of revelation Schelling suggests that we think of it in terms
of two ideas common to Christianity but in radically redefined ways. First,
he speaks of revelation as *incarnation*. For him, incarnation is not a once-
for-all event in which "God took on human nature at a given moment of
time." Instead, "The process of God's becoming man has been going on

from all eternity."[30] That this sounds more Eastern than Western is indirectly acknowledged by Schelling. In speaking of the experiences of mis-
sionaries proclaiming the incarnation to the Hindus, he says, "But the
Hindues were not surprised; they did not in the least contest the incarnation of God in Christ, and only thought it strange that an event that
occurs frequently among them should have occurred only once among
the Christians."[31] For Schelling, incarnation reminds us that the divine is
present in all things because all things are divine.

A second term used by Schelling to speak of revelation is *providence*.
He understands history to be divided into periods delineated by how the
divine presence in the world is interpreted. With typical nineteenth century optimism he intends to show the way to the third and highest stage.
"The third period of history will be that wherein the force which
appeared in the earlier stages as destiny or nature has evolved itself as
providence, and wherein it will become apparent that even what seemed
to be simply the work of destiny or nature was already from the beginning of a providence imperfectly revealing itself."[32] Thus God's presence
has always been evident. It has simply been misinterpreted in the past as
fate or the movement of nature's laws. With a new awareness of the world
as God's consciousness we now understand the same events under the
rubric of providence. However, we should recognize that for Schelling
providence is not simply God's ongoing activity through which he maintains the world. The world *is* God's activity.

Georg Wilhelm Friedrich Hegel

The greatest philosopher of his century in the West,[33] Georg Wilhelm
Friedrich Hegel (1770-1831) was a philosophical genius whose speculative
system influenced the rest of Western cultural history. Karl Marx is the
best-known example of Hegel's influence (as we shall see), but psychology,
social and political theory, aesthetics, theology and of course philosophy
have all felt his impact. Others have built philosophical systems but not as
influential as Hegel's, while the other influential philosophers have not
built original speculative systems. In some ways Western philosophy since
his time has been fragmented, even anti-systematic. This is partly in reaction to Hegel (and his student, Marx). In fact, much of Western philosophy
and intellectual culture from his death to the present could be understood

as a series of skirmishes with Hegel's great system.

Some intellectuals, especially those trained in analytic philosophy, find Hegel's thought to be nonsense, illogical gibberish or just plain silly. This prejudice will not withstand sustained reflection. That Hegel's language and thought prove difficult, even tortuous, will be admitted by all students of his work. That his philosophy is based upon a few simple logical blunders or that it can safely be ignored by contemporary thinkers, flies in the face of his enormous impact and the importance that many of his key ideas continue to have. Even though some of his views were false or exaggerated, this does not detract from the impressive character of his philosophical achievement. Hegel continues to deserve the serious, growing attention he receives from scholars throughout the world.[34]

Hegel's Development

Born and reared in Stuttgart, in the Duchy of Württemberg, during that age when Germany was divided into many local principalities,[35] Hegel did well in the local school (or Gymnasium) and earned a ducal scholarship to the seminary at Tübingen. Like most established middle-class families in Stuttgart, the religious atmosphere at the Hegels consisted of Lutheran piety. Many sons of such families entered civil service, law or the ministry. Indeed Hegel's father, Georg Ludwig, was a civil servant in the duke's revenue office.

Thus Hegel came to the Tübinger-Stift (theological school or institute) with the intention of becoming a clergyman, but such was not his destiny. At seminary he became fast friends with the likes of important German Romantics and "radicals," especially Schelling and the poet Hölderlin, his roommates at school. From an early age Hegel was influenced by the love of Greek culture typical of the Romantics. He read Rousseau with great interest at seminary, as did his friends. With them he shared an enthusiasm for the ideals of the French Revolution. His early theological writings (never published) show the deep influence of Kant as well as Romanticism upon the budding philosopher.[36] Hegel rejected the theology of his day but nevertheless continued to speculate on the meaning and importance of religion for life and society.

After working as a tutor, Hegel's first job in philosophy came through his

friendship with Schelling at the University of Jena. He worked as an unpaid
lecturer at the University and began developing his own philosophical system. This period of his life culminated in the publication of his greatest
work, *The Phenomenology of Spirit*.[37] But history interrupted the peaceful philosopher's life. Napoleon crushed the once-proud armies of Prussia at the
battle of Jena in 1806. While Hegel admired Napoleon, the war greatly disturbed the city, and Hegel's job at Jena came to an end. Indeed Hegel had to
flee the city with the manuscript of the *Phenomenology* still in his pockets.
Despite his fears the book arrived safely at the publisher.

Hegel was forced to take whatever job came his way, including newspaper editor. He eventually settled in as the headmaster of a Gymnasium in Nuremberg, where he finally married in 1811 at the age of
forty-one. During this time of relative security he published the most
extensive exposition of his philosophical system, *The Encyclopaedia of
Philosophical Sciences in Outline* (1817). This work is divided into three
parts: Logic, Philosophy of Nature and Philosophy of Mind. It was used
by Hegel as a textbook for his lectures and was later published with his
comments and some student notes (3rd ed., 1830).[38] He also published
during this period his massive *Science of Logic* (1812-1816).[39] In part as a
result of his publications, Hegel's fame began to grow, and he was
eventually offered the chair of philosophy at Berlin left vacant after
Fichte's death.

Berlin was the capital of Prussia and a center of commerce, culture
and influence. There Hegel grew in stature and influence, and his lectures attracted many students, men of influence and culture, from
throughout the German-speaking world. He published his philosophy of
Recht (justice or Right) in 1821, the last book he saw through the press by
his own hand.[40] Hegel's thought eventually eclipsed all other professors
of philosophy (including Schelling, whose friendship grew cold over the
years). His fame and followers spread to all German universities. At the
apex of this influence he was elected rector (president) of the University
of Berlin but died one year later in 1831 of a swift illness. His death was
felt as a great loss by the intellectuals of Germany. His students eventually published his lectures on the history of philosophy and on the philosophies of art, of history and of religion in an edition of his collected
works spanning eighteen volumes.[41]

Hegel's System

While Hegel's works cannot be ignored by students of Western philosophy, English-speaking students are at a disadvantage in approaching his thought. The style and vocabulary of Hegel are strange to us, and his prose is notoriously difficult to follow. Philosophers writing in English today typically create clear and precise arguments, set forth in logical form, leading from generally accepted premises to a conclusion. Hegel's style is quite different. He appeals to our common experience but always from his own systematic perspective. While Hegel can create ordinary arguments when need requires it, for the most part he appeals to our own sympathetic understanding of his point. He presents an interpretation of our experience, or of our common knowledge: an insight into reality rather than a tight logical argument. This style is typical of phenomenological and existential philosophies, too, and Hegel is—for better or worse—their model.

Hegel was, more than any other great philosopher of the West, a holistic thinker. This emphasis on the unification of reality, especially of human being and nature, shows the impact of Romantic ideals on Hegel. As an example of such influence consider this: "Pagan religion contains from the start a more serene state of reconciliation, . . . [whereas Christianity lost] the natural unity of spirit (i.e., the unity of humanity with nature)."[42] This sentiment smacks of Rousseau and indeed of Romantic thought in general with its longing for unity with nature. For Hegel, philosophy can provide such a unity but only as a complete system of knowledge. Truth must be seen from all sides, or it is incomplete. "The true shape in which truth exists can only be the scientific system of such truth. . . . The True is the whole."[43] Hegel's term *Wissenschaft,* translated as "science," means any rigorous, disciplined inquiry into knowledge. It is not limited to the natural sciences, as the English term tends to be. For Hegel, as for Aristotle, philosophy is the supreme science.

Hegel was a dialectical thinker, the greatest since Plato. Thus for Hegel, each particular truth is only partial. It needs to be placed into the larger whole of reality in order to be fully understood. And when it is placed within the larger system, its character as only partial truth is revealed. It needs to be supplemented with another, different, even contradictory truth. This is why Hegel was a dialectical thinker. He believed that the truth of reality, and indeed the history of reality, only unfolded in the context of a dialectical movement between a thesis, its opposite (antithesis) and a larger conception that synthesized both. The final synthesis keeps the best of both thesis and antithesis, rejecting what was fallible and false in prior, tentative expressions of reality. Hegel's term for this simultaneous acceptance-and-rejection was *Aufhebung*, a term that can mean both "canceling" and "preserving" and is usually translated as "sublation." This concept of the dialectic can be traced historically from Hegel through Fichte to Kant and all the way back to Plato. But Hegel gave it a new meaning and power in his own system.

We can illustrate Hegel's holistic view of reality with a quotation from a classic Chinese text, the *Tao Te Ching*. In the second chapter we read:

Being and non-being create each other.

Difficult and easy support each other.

Long and short define each other.

High and low depend upon each other.

Before and after follow each other.[44]

Every aspect of reality may seem to be independent, but fundamentally all things are related and depend upon the Other for their being. In Hegel's own words:

If the many determinate properties [of a Thing] were strictly indifferent to one another, if they were simply and solely self-related, they would not be determinate; for they are only determinate in so far as they *differentiate* themselves from one another, and *relate* themselves *to others* as to their opposites. . . . In other words the Thing has its essential being in another Thing.[45]

We begin life thinking that each thing is separate, unique, isolated. Hegel's point is this: in order for a thing to be what it is, it must be related to other things different from it, which define it and distinguish it. "Long and short define each other."

Let us take as an example the opposites of light and dark. A dark room is dark because it is not light: darkness is the absence of light. So "dark" has a relationship with "light" and vice versa: each is the negation of the other. Each can only be what it is in this relationship of opposition to the other. Hegel sometimes called this relationship "contradiction." We must bear in mind that he did not always mean logical contradiction but rather any kind of opposition (for example, one person oppressing another, or two states at war).[46]

But Hegel's dialectic does not stop at the point of contradiction, negation or difference. Hegel argued that one idea already contains within it both its own negation and the development of its opposite concept. This provides thought with movement toward a greater synthesis. To stick with our example, the very idea and reality of "darkness" already includes something of "light." Imagine waking up in the middle of the night and noticing that it is dark outside. Dark, we said, was the opposite of light. But there must be some light outside in order to notice that it is dark. If we cannot see at all, then we see nothing. We do not think, "It is dark outside," but rather, "I can't see!" Imagine being in a sensory depravation tank with blinders on so that you see nothing at all: that is not what we perceive when we know it is dark outside. So "It is dark outside" already includes some (very small amount) of light. To see that it is dark, some light must be present. A similar fact reveals itself if we imagine being before pure light: we would be blinded. Some darkness (a lessening or lowering of pure light) must occur so we can know that it is light outside.

Light and dark are not just contradictions. They already contain something of their opposite in order to be known. In fact, "light" and "dark" are two moments on a great spectrum; it is the fuller spectrum that is the Hegelian synthesis. Light and dark are "sublated" (to use Hegel's word) in the Concept of a spectrum from pure light to pure darkness. The word "Notion" or "Concept" (*Begriff*) is an important one for Hegel. It stands for the fullest scientific and therefore dialectical conception of an object in philosophy (such as light, in our example). Hegel believed that the whole of reality obeyed this dialectic.

He called the whole of reality the "Absolute," borrowing a term from Schelling. Reality is dialectical: not just philosophy or ideas but the world as it is. The Absolute is not static. Instead, the Absolute is always moving toward a greater synthesis, a great embodiment of the truth. "The Truth is the whole. But the whole is nothing other than the essence consummating itself through development. Of the Absolute it must be said that it is essentially a *result*, that only in the *end* is it what it truly is."[47] The whole of reality is moving toward an end or goal, and that end or goal is the Absolute. The course of this movement, for Hegel, is described by the dialectic. History moved to the threefold pattern of status quo (thesis), conflict (antithesis) and resolution (synthesis). Hegel thus understood reality to be dynamic, historical and goal-oriented. If he is any kind of idealist at all, therefore, he must be considered *a historical idealist.*

Hegel was indeed an idealist. His writings are full of the idea of *Geist,* a word that can mean "mind" or "spirit." He held that "History is Mind clothing itself with the form of events or the immediate actuality of nature."[48] Hegel was not a subjective idealist like Bishop George Berkeley who held that material objects collapsed into mental sensations.[49] For Hegel, the particular events of history or the particular things of nature are real and important facts. But nevertheless they are part of a whole, the Absolute, which is at bottom Absolute *Geist,* Infinite Mind. Hegel argued that when we consider the whole of reality, the subjective or mental aspect is the most fundamental. "Substance is essentially Subject."[50] That is why for Hegel all things—historical events, finite minds such as you and I, social institutions and natural objects—are all expressions of Absolute Spirit. Reality is in the end rational, and rationality (Absolute Mind) is the basis of all reality. "The rational is the real, and the real is the rational. . . . To comprehend what is, that is the task of philosophy, because what is, is reason."[51]

Hegel's Philosophy of History and Society

As a historical idealist Hegel understood the historical process (which obeyed the dialectic) to be the outworking of Infinite Mind in the development of nature and society. "Science sets forth this formative process in all its detail and necessity, exposing the mature configuration of everything which has already been reduced to a moment and property of Spirit."[52] If history is the outworking of Spirit (Infinite Mind), then it is important to understand culture in each of its independent epochs. We think this way "naturally" today, seeking to understand the past in the wholeness of each period. Hegel called the social and cultural institutions of each epoch "objective Mind" and sought to expound the basic ideas and institutions of each culture, in each historical period, and connect them to the whole of history. This was a fascinating exercise to the intellectuals of Hegel's day. The importance of history was rediscovered in the Renaissance and was a central idea of the German Romantic movement (e.g., J. G. von Herder). Hegel took this emphasis into the heart of his system of thought. Western culture has been historical in its orientation ever since. We study a new culture by looking at its history. At some point in our study of a new discipline (e.g., psychology), we will look at the history of its development. We owe this historical emphasis to Hegel as much as to anyone else.

Hegel's work on the history of philosophy was the first publication on this subject by a major philosopher since Aristotle. Prior to Hegel Western philosophers such as Kant thought in ahistorical terms about abstract logical truths or essential properties of things. Hegel shattered this myth of "pure, timeless" abstract philosophy. Rather he exposed philosophy as the expression of the Spirit in a particular historical epoch. Nevertheless Hegel did not fall into historicism (or cultural relativism). Because he believed in history as the expression of Absolute Spirit, he held to long-term and transcultural truths. But such transcultural truths find their expressions only in the particular developments of the historical process. Hegel's lectures on the history of philosophy thus provide an excellent example of Hegel's historical method and a fine introduction to his work.

In Hegel's works on the philosophy of religion and of history, he followed this same historical method. Only in his *Science of Logic* and the *Encyclopaedia* did he summarize his system in a nonhistorical manner. In these books he pursues "pure" conceptual knowledge, "The exposition of God (i.e., pure Reason) as he is in his eternal essence before the creation of nature and a finite mind."[53] Hegel considered logic to be the highest science. "In the Logic we have to do with pure thought or with pure thought-determinations. . . . The other philosophical sciences—the Philosophy of Nature, and the Philosophy of Mind—appear, in contrast, as applied logic, so to speak."[54] But Hegel's logic is not what we usually learn in college as logic. While it includes things like formal arguments, it is really an abstract metaphysical system. It covers such topics as being, being-for-itself, infinite Being, the Concept and the Absolute Idea. In fact Hegel explicitly said, "Thus *logic* coincides with *metaphysics,* with the science of *things* grasped in *thoughts.*"[55] In the rest of his *Encyclopaedia* as well as his lectures on the philosophy of art and of Right, he applies his logic in a topical rather than historical manner (but nevertheless Hegel presupposed a historical development for art and politics).

The Philosophy of Right represents Hegel's mature reflection on ethics, politics and society. In keeping with his historical idealism, Hegel understood the State in each culture and epoch to be "the actuality of the ethical Idea. . . . The state is the actuality of concrete freedom."[56] True to his holistic bent, Hegel saw the life of the family, ethics and law, civil society, and religious practice all united in the ethical State. The individual's freedom must be recognized by the state, and yet (dialectically) individuals "not only achieve their complete development and gain explicit recognition for their right . . . they also pass over of their own accord into the interest of the universal."[57] Noble citizens find their fulfillment only in the state. This is a very "idealistic" political philosophy (pun intended). Hegel has been severely criticized for his overly optimistic understanding of government and of the need for individuals to be obedient to the State. These objections are particularly poignant in the light of Kaiser Wilhelm and Adolf Hitler. The book later philosophy has admired most, however, is his *Phenomenology of Spirit*.

The *Phenomenology of Spirit* is developmental too but in a different way. In this seminal work Hegel traces the development of consciousness rather than historical epochs. He traces the dialectical pathways of consciousness from basic sensations to the highest reaches of the realms of Spirit in art, religion and philosophy. The book was published as the introduction to a "System of Science," which never saw the light of day. Nevertheless it does function as a good introduction to Hegel's mature system and was his first important publication. It continues to be his most influential work. Of this book Hegel himself wrote:

> In the *Phenomenology of Spirit* I have exhibited consciousness in its movement onwards from the first immediate opposition of itself and the object to absolute knowing. The path of this movement goes through every form of *the relation of consciousness to the object* and has the Notion of science for its result.[58]

Just as each thing has its existence only in another thing, so Hegel argued that each person can only develop in the context of other people and society: only over against the Other. While Hegel starts with the individual consciousness, his goal is to bring us to understand our finite minds as expressions of Infinite Mind seeking to understand itself in self-conscious freedom. Needless to say, most of us are unaware of our roles in this great drama. But the brilliance of Hegel is demonstrated in a careful reading of his argument. All of us are, in the end, caught up in the history of God coming to understand himself through our finite minds, that is, in society and history.

Hegel's Philosophy of Religion

Such an understanding of history and society raises the question of Hegel's theology. What exactly did Hegel understand God to be? This question has been debated for over a century because Hegel's works can be understood in several ways.[59] Clearly Hegel was not a traditional *monotheist*. In his mature thought Hegel did return to Lutheran orthodoxy and considered himself to be a Christian philosopher. He certainly adopted many Christian ideas and terms into his philosophy and argued that Christianity is the one true religion. Yet his identification of God with Absolute Spirit can hardly be considered the same theology as, say, that of Thomas Aquinas. God is dynamic for Hegel, integrated with the historical process, the totality of finite minds and with social institutions.

On the other hand, Hegel was hardly an *atheist*.[60] Absolute Spirit does not reduce to the many finite expressions of spirit. Hegel really did believe in God. Perhaps, then, Hegel was a *pantheist*. He was accused of this in his own day. Such an interpretation takes seriously Hegel's identification of God with the Absolute. But a careful reading of Hegel's work yields a more balanced view. Hegel argued that God both transcends the world and yet is immanent within the world. He was, after all, a dialectical philosopher. Pantheism, as a view of Hegel, ignores the transcendent moment of his dialectic.

The most likely interpretation of Hegel's theology is that of *panentheism*.[61] This is a modern term, used to designate a philosophy in which God is distinct from but dependent upon the world. God is different from all finite things but is intimately connected to all things. A good metaphor for panentheism is one of a mind with its body. The universe is not God but is God's "body." For Hegel, therefore, creation and incarnation become the same thing.

We have noted that in his mature thought, Hegel returned to an orthodox Christian theism. He affirmed the incarnation, the Trinity, human sinfulness and the need for redemption. But for Hegel, theology is not the highest or absolute knowledge. Only philosophy, in particular Hegel's own philosophy, attains a scientific knowledge of God. The Christian religion is true but remains at the level of "representation" or picture-thinking. It must be sublated by a scientific philosophy of religion.

This form of picture-thinking (i.e., religion) constitutes the specific mode in which Spirit, in this community, becomes aware of itself. This form is not yet Spirit's self-consciousness that has advanced to its Notion qua Notion: the mediation is still incomplete.[62]

Religion is incomplete and unscientific because it has not finished the dialectal movement toward the Concept of God. Only Hegel's own philosophy can supply that! And thus Hegelian philosophy replaces theology in the long run.

Hegel's Influence

Hegel's view of human consciousness, art and the State has had tremendous impact upon culture, philosophy and the social sciences. It's hard to imagine what political theory, sociology or psychology would be like if we took away the seminal insights of the *Phenomenology*. Both existentialism and phenomenology drank deep from Hegelian streams as well. These currents will be more fully explored in volume three of this series. Ironically, the Hegelian synthesis of transcendent and immanent soon broke apart. In our next chapter we shall focus on Hegel's impact upon religion, especially Christianity.

5. HUMANITY AS DIVINE INCARNATION

From the layperson's vantage point it may be difficult to understand the appeal of Hegel's philosophy of religion, which can seem obscure and far removed from traditional theology. However, it quickly became an important factor in the mid-nineteenth century, a fact explained in part by the theological void that existed at this time. Conservative orthodox theology required assumptions that no longer seemed tenable in the face of scientific advances and the growing awareness of historical development in Christianity. At the same time, the rationalist approach to Christianity had been badly damaged by Kant's philosophy. Hegel's metaphysics offered a third path, and a number of theologians quickly seized upon this new alternative.

The Hegelian Legacy in Christianity

Because Hegel was more concerned with providing an overarching metaphysical program and suggesting applications than with actually working out the implications of his philosophy in relation to specific disciplines, his religious thought is open to varying interpretations. In the face of this ambiguity it was hard for theology and philosophy to maintain the dialectical balance of Hegel's thought. David Friedrich Strauss (1808-1874), one of Hegel's more important students, noted that the followers of Hegel divided into two camps: the "left" and the "right" Hegelians. The right-wing Hegelians held on to the transcendent aspect of Hegel's system but also to a somewhat conservative defense of Prussia and Lutheranism.

Advocates of this position such as Philip Conrad Marheineke (1780-1864) and K. F. Göschel (1784-1861) remained closer to orthodoxy while using Hegelian thought to give new expression to Christology. While the right-wing Hegelians were prominent in many of the universities of Germany through the middle of the nineteenth century, they contributed little either to Hegelian thought or to theology and soon faded into history.

It was the left-wing, or young, Hegelians like Strauss that won the day and created exciting, new philosophies that took Western thought by storm, while at the same time often coming into conflict with governmental, ecclesiastical and academic authorities.[1] These thinkers went beyond the views of Hegel but adopted his methods and logic. They emphasized the immanent character of the Absolute and reduced Hegel's God to the totality of human being or the historical process. Among the luminaries of this group are David Friedrich Strauss, Ferdinand Christian Baur (1792-1860), Ludwig Feuerbach (1804-1872) and Karl Marx. Strauss and Baur, the subjects of this chapter, were highly critical of traditional Christian thought but sought to rebuild from within Christianity. In contrast, Feuerbach and Marx argued that Christianity was beyond salvage and was instead a problem to be overcome. All four rejected theism, and all but Baur eventually embraced atheism. While Hegel and his right-wing followers remained politically conservative, the Young Hegelians tended toward political radicalism.[2]

David Friedrich Strauss

Little is known of the early life of David Friedrich Strauss (1808-1874).[3] In his early teens he entered the lower seminary at Blaubueren in preparation for a career in the pastorate. There he came into contact with a young professor named F. C. Baur, whose career would eventually become intertwined with that of his student. From there Strauss went to Tübingen, where the curriculum consisted of philosophy and language studies the first two years and theology in the final three years. Unsatisfied with the quality of philosophical education during these early years, Strauss and several friends, including the gifted Christian Märklin (1807-1849) and Friedrich Vischer (1807-1887), began studying the Romantics on their own and were especially drawn to Schelling. These works sparked his initial interest in the idea of God as immanent. Another turning point occurred the year Strauss began his theological studies. His professor from Blaubueren, Baur, had been granted a position at Tübingen, and through his influence Strauss became interested in the theology of Schleiermacher. While Strauss was never really a devotee of Schleiermacher's theology, he found in his implicit panentheism the possibility of carving out an alternative between supernaturalism and rationalism. In 1827 Strauss and his friends began their private study of Hegel's *Phenomenology*. It was Hegel's speculative philosophical approach that had the most profound influence on Strauss's theology.

Following graduation from Tübingen, Strauss served short stints as a pastor and teacher at a preparatory school, after which he went to study at Berlin. The university was at its height during this time. August Neander (1789-1850), the most respected church historian of the time, Ernst Wilhelm Hengstenberg (1802-1869) in Old Testament and Philipp Marheineke (1780-1846), the right-wing synthesizer of Hegel and theology, were at the university. However, the two main draws were Schleiermacher and Hegel, although by now the latter was the greater attraction to him. While at Berlin Strauss met briefly with Hegel and attended two of his lectures. Less than a month after his arrival, however, Hegel died, one of the last victims of a cholera epidemic that had ravaged the city. During Strauss's first meeting with Schleiermacher, he was told of Hegel's death. Reportedly Strauss's response to the news was, "But it was for him that I came." Whether true or not, relations between Strauss and Schleiermacher following this were cordial but cool. Although disappointed that he would not have the chance to hear the master, he remained to study with other Hegelian thinkers at Berlin.

Strauss left Berlin in 1832 to become a tutor at the Tübingen *Stift*, where his lectures were extremely well-attended. His popularity with the students as well as his espousal of Hegelian philosophy earned him the enmity of the philosophy faculty. Partly because of his desire to avoid further contention over his lectures and partly to rapidly complete his study of the Gospels, Strauss discontinued his lectures after the year. The first volume of *Life of Jesus* was published in 1835 when Strauss was twenty-seven, and it would not be an overstatement to see it as the turning point of nineteenth century theological studies. He had hoped the book would be a vehicle for reinterpreting the Christian faith and expected considerable disagreement within academic circles. Instead he found himself embroiled in a fierce controversy that extended far beyond the academy.[4]

While we will examine the reasons for the furor below, the fallout was devastating to Strauss's career. Though not dismissed outright from his position, Strauss received a "call" to a secondary school in Ludwigsburg, a position everyone knew he would find unacceptable. The next opportunity for an academic appointment did not come until 1839, when he received the offer of the dogmatics chair in Zürich. However, popular uproar over the appointment of an arch-heretic forced the Great Council to pension him off. Shortly thereafter he turned to literary and political pursuits, and he did not write on theology for the next twenty years. Toward the end of his life he abandoned even his Hegelian version of Christianity for materialism.[5]

The Life of Jesus Controversy

Although Strauss's writings span four decades, his first published work, *Life of Jesus,* was by far his most significant. It quickly became the most controversial book of the century in biblical studies and laid the foundation for the historical-critical study of Scripture. Its significance was so profound that one contemporary New Testament scholar states that "this book was the most revolutionary religious document written since Luther's Ninety-Five Theses."[6] The text itself consists of three sections. The first is a brief history of myth that includes an overview of the supernaturalist and rationalist approaches to the Gospels. Strauss was unable to accept the uncritical acceptance of the miraculous by the supernaturalists, nor did he find convincing the attempts of the rationalists to reinterpret miracles as misunderstood natural events. By showing the supposed difficulties in the two most common approaches to the Gospels, Strauss positions his own mythological approach as the only satisfactory alternative.

The second part of *Life of Jesus,* and by far the most extensive, is a detailed story-by-story analysis of the Gospel accounts of Jesus' life. Throughout this section the pattern remains consistent: Strauss reviews the interpretations of the supernaturalists and the rationalists, pointing out the absurdities of both views, and then gives his own mythological rendering. He almost invariably concludes that, while there is a historical core to some stories, little in the accounts themselves is historical.

Strauss shows scant concern about the absence of historical fact in the Gospels, and the final part of *Life of Jesus* reveals the reason for this. In this brief "concluding dissertation" he reconstructs Christology apart from reliance on the historical Jesus. The root problem of both supernaturalism and rationalism is a dualism that maintains a strong distinction between the divine and human. Hegel's monism, as modified by Strauss, supplies an alternative that unveils the true significance of the incarnation: the *idea* of the union of the divine and human rather than its historical manifestation. Thus Christology does not depend on a historical reconstruction of Jesus' life and teachings but on a concept.

It is rare that a book stirs up controversy in so many quarters, and it is difficult to see, even in hindsight, why a text intended for the scholarly community would excite such contention as did *Life of Jesus*. None of the elements taken separately were particularly novel. Strauss had been introduced to the mythological approach by Baur as a student. The historicity of the biblical accounts of the life of Jesus had been challenged by the *Wolfenbüttel Fragments* of Lessing more than a century earlier and by several other works written in the interim. Moreover, the monistic idealism that governs Strauss's conclusions was at the cutting edge of German academics. Thus rather than isolating any single element as the source of the controversy, a more satisfactory explanation is found in a combination of factors.

Style, skill and specificity are certainly involved in the strong response elicited by the book. Strauss is frequently sarcastic in the evaluation of supernaturalist or rationalist interpretations. Second, *Life of Jesus* possessed a quality rarely found in academic texts—it was well-written. Albert Schweitzer says of it, "Considered as a literary work, Strauss' first *Life of Jesus* is one of the most perfect things in the whole range of learned literature."[7] Finally, Hegelian thought was tolerable to many as long as it remained theoretical. But when Strauss systematically applied Hegelian theory to the Gospels, non-Hegelians had a concrete example to support their opposition to his philosophy. Strauss himself states, "I was not surprised that when my book appeared the many opponents of the Hegelian philosophy used its conclusions to demonstrate the destructive consequences of the Hegelian method of philosophizing."[8]

Predictably the supernaturalists were concerned about Strauss's attacks on their approach to the Gospels. While they assumed the historicity of biblical material and linked it with the authority of Scripture, Strauss questioned both. He presupposed that the miraculous is excluded by a scientific worldview and logical consistency. "The proposition that God works sometimes mediately, sometimes immediately, upon the world, introduces a changeableness, and therefore a temporal element, into the nature of his action."[9] Most troubling to the supernaturalist faction was that the biblical materials most central to Christology, such as the resurrection and ascension accounts, were determined by Strauss to be laden with myth. If these are historically unreliable, the biblical foundation of the supernaturalists' Christology is undermined. In other words, the supernaturalists equated the Jesus of history with the Christ of faith. If Strauss effectively demonstrated that the two are dissimilar, the supernaturalist view of Christ falls apart.

While the rationalists applauded Strauss's interrogation of the supernatural elements of the Gospel stories, their position is also sharply criticized. Strauss treats their explanations of miracles as scornfully as he does the supernaturalist position, skillfully demonstrating how the rationalists stretched stories to discover natural causes behind the miracle stories. Strauss also erodes the historical core the rationalists relied on for their understanding of Jesus. Furthermore, Strauss disagrees with their conclusions about the actual Jesus. He argues that Jesus saw himself as an apocalyptic messianic figure rather than an ethics professor, as the rationalists tended to picture him.

There was also a political angle behind the fierce response to Strauss's book. Whereas older scholars had sought, or at least accommodated, a truce between theology and other disciplines, this respite melts away with the advent of Strauss's *Life of Jesus.* His conclusions reopened the often bitter attacks on religion dating back to the Enlightenment. This was seen as a threat to the fragile peace between church, university and government, no small consideration when these institutions were as closely interlinked as they were in mid-nineteenth century Germany. In addition, *Life of Jesus* brought to a head the debate between those who used Hegel's philosophy as an apology for the Prussian monarchy and Hegel's opponents. Because these views threatened the alliance between orthodox theologians and the Prussian government, right-wing Hegelians were sent scrambling either to disavow this philosophy or to show that Strauss had incorrectly applied Hegel's thought to Christianity.[10]

Finally, Strauss's belief that it was necessary to destroy in order to make room for a Hegelian reformulation of theology contributed to the firestorm generated by *Life of Jesus*. His attempts to undermine the historicity of the Gospel accounts, as well as his rejection of God's transcendence and personality, guaranteed strong opposition. Moreover, if one does not find Hegelianism convincing, the Christology Strauss constructs upon it will also be rejected, and all that remains are his negative conclusions. Thus as Hegelian philosophy faded from prominence, the destructive aspect of Strauss's work became his legacy. In summary then, *Life of Jesus* managed to alienate almost every interest group in Germany, and Strauss was forced to defend his views on several fronts.

The Gospels As Myth

Life of Jesus is an attempt to face head-on the tensions within the Gospel accounts and reformulate theology accordingly. Strauss argues that these tensions cannot be resolved by harmonization or appeal to God's intervention in history since the latter is "irreconcilable with the known and universal laws which govern the course of events."[11] Moreover, we should not resort to fanciful chronologies and rationalistic explanations that stretch biblical accounts beyond believability. Instead the problem of the Gospel accounts is an artificial one that arises because both the supernaturalist and rationalist positions have a theological stake in preserving the historicity of these stories. However, if we read these stories as myth, historical veracity becomes unimportant and "the innumerable, and never otherwise to be harmonized, discrepancies and chronological contradictions in the gospel histories disappear, as it were, at one stroke."[12]

Strauss provides some elementary guidelines for identifying mythological elements in Scripture. Events that violate laws of nature, that are internally inconsistent or contradict other accounts should be viewed as myth. Second, "If the form be poetical, if the actors converse in hymns, and in a more diffuse and elevated strain than might be expected from their training and situations, such discourses, at all events, are not to be regarded as historical."[13] Similarly, "If the contents of a narrative strik-

ingly accords with certain ideas existing and prevailing within the circle
from which the narrative proceeded . . . it is more or less probable,
according to circumstances, that such a narrative is of mythical origin.[14]

Strauss's basic definition of *myth* is "a narrative relating directly or
indirectly to Jesus, which may be considered not as the expression of a
fact, but . . . the product of an idea of his [Jesus'] earliest followers."[15]
Myth can be further reduced to two subcategories. *Pure myth* results from
the messianic expectations of the culture or from the "impression which
was left by the personal character, actions, and fate of Jesus."[16] In other
words, they are stories created to illustrate the significance attributed to
Jesus by the church. The story of the Transfiguration, which portrays
Jesus as glorified Messiah, is an example of this category. *Historical myth*
"has for its groundwork a definite individual fact which has been seized
upon by religious enthusiasm, and tinged around with mythical conceptions culled from the idea of the Christ."[17] Thus while an actual event or
saying of Jesus may supply the background, the present setting is so far
removed from the historical foundation that it can no longer be located
within the story.

If much of the material in the Gospels is to be considered mythological, we must ask how it came to be presented in this fashion. First, Strauss
says that it would be a mistake to consider the first believers capable of a
philosophical or historical report of their experience of Jesus. Instead
they would express their ideas by means current in their world. Since the
literature of this age is highly mythological, we should not be surprised to
find similar means of expression in the Gospels. Not only would the Jewish disciples use the literary forms of the day, but they would also draw
from the Old Testament stock of ideas to speak of Jesus' significance.
Chief among these is the messianic concept. "So that for the period
between the formation of the first Christian community and the writing
of the Gospels, there remains to be effected only the transference of the
Messianic legends, almost all ready formed, to Jesus, with some alter-
ations to adapt them to Christian opinions, and to the individual character and circumstances of Jesus: only a very small proportion of myths
having to be formed entirely new."[18] Given the cultural horizon of Jesus'
followers and their beliefs about Jesus, Strauss exonerates them of intentional deception. "Whatever view may be taken of the heathen mythol-

ogy, it is easy to show with regard to the New Testament, that there was the greatest antecedent probability of this very kind of fiction having arisen respecting Jesus without any fraudulent intention."[19]

Strauss argues that the reason Jesus became linked with messianic expectations is relatively simple: Jesus claimed to be the Messiah. If social and religious context shapes the form and content of one's communication, it also influences one's self-understanding. Jesus as a product of first-century Judaism might be expected to view himself as the anticipated Messiah. This messianic consciousness, as reconstructed by Strauss, was birthed by his contact with John the Baptist.[20] The model of a prophet of repentance that he saw in John the Baptist gradually evolved into a belief that he was the Messiah. The most influential strand of Jesus' messianic conception was not the restoration of David's throne over an earthly realm but that of the Son of Man returning to earth after his death.[21] This picture is combined by Jesus with the Old Testament picture of the Suffering Servant. The result is Jesus, by means of the Suffering Servant motif, believes that he may be killed but will return as the Son of Man.[22]

Other than this rather elaborate reconstruction of Jesus' messianic consciousness, Strauss professes to know little more about the historical Jesus than that he was baptized by John, had a band of disciples, taught, considered himself to be the expected Messiah, predicted his death and was crucified. Beyond this the image is cloudy. The birth narratives, the temptations, transfiguration, triumphal entry, the cleansing of the temple, resurrection and ascension are largely or completely fictional. It is impossible to reconstruct a chronology of Jesus' life. "Throughout the interval between the baptism of Jesus and the history of the Passion, their [the Synoptics] narratives resemble a collection of anecdotes, strung together mostly on a thread of mere analogy and association of ideas."[23] John's Gospel, described as "mainly free compositions of the Evangelist,"[24] is of even less historical value. He allows that the Gospels have preserved some of Jesus' teachings, which, "like fragments of granite, could not be dissolved by the flood of oral tradition." But he immediately adds, "They were not seldom torn from their natural connexion, floated away from their original situation, and deposited in places to which they did not properly belong."[25]

Strauss's Hegelian Reconstruction

At the end of his survey of the Gospels, Strauss anticipates the reaction to his conclusions thus far. "The results of the inquiry which we have now brought to a close, have apparently annihilated the greatest and most valuable part of that which the Christian has been wont to believe concerning his Saviour Jesus, have uprooted all the animating motives which he has gathered from his faith, and withered all his consolations."[26] However, even with little historical footing remaining Strauss believes that there is a happy Hegelian ending for Christology. By means of philosophical speculation, we can "re-establish dogmatically that which has been destroyed critically"[27] and bring forward conclusions acceptable to the modern mind.

Against orthodoxy and rational theology, which stressed the distance between God and humanity, Strauss followed Hegel's monistic view. The core of religion is that the natural and divine are not ultimately distinct but polarities of the same reality. Thus Strauss says of Hegel's metaphysics, "In my years at the university, my friends and I thought that the point of Hegel's system most relevant for theology was his distinction in religion between representation and concept, which, although different in form, could still have the same content. In this distinction we found respect for the biblical documents and church dogmas reconciled as nowhere else with the freedom to reflect on them."[28]

The ultimate unity of representation *(Vorstellung)* and concept *(Begriff)* is what makes the incarnation central to both Hegel and Strauss. For Hegel, the incarnation is the highest form of religious representation, the concrete unification of the human and divine on the historical plane that synthesizes the contradiction between the human and divine. Unfortunately Hegel leaves the details of the relationship between historical incarnation and the concept of the unity of divine and human vague. Strauss sees it as his mission to clear up this ambiguity and correct Hegel's Christology. "In an individual, a God-man, the properties and functions which the church ascribes to Christ contradict themselves; in the idea of a race, they perfectly agree. Humanity is the union of the two natures--God become man, the infinite manifesting itself in the finite, and the finite spirit remembering its infinitude."[29] Thus Strauss cannot embrace the incarnation of God in the historical. The idea *(Begriff)* captured by Christianity is that finite and infinite are unified in the whole of humanity.

> If reality is ascribed to the idea of the unity of the divine and human natures, is this equivalent to the admission that this unity must actually have been once manifested, as it never had been, and never more will be, in one individual? This is indeed not the mode in which Idea realizes itself; it is not wont to lavish all its fulness on one exemplar, and be niggardly towards all others—to express itself perfectly in that one individual, and imperfectly in all the rest: it rather loves to distribute its riches among a multiplicity of exemplars which reciprocally complete each other—in the alternate appearance and suppression of a series of individuals. And is this no true realization of the idea? is not the idea of the unity of the divine and human natures a real one in a far higher sense, when I regard the whole race of mankind as its realization, than when I single out one man as such a realization? is not an incarnation of God from eternity, a truer one than an incarnation limited to a particular point of time?[30]

For Strauss then the person of Christ is not central to Christianity. Jesus holds a unique place because of his recognition of the oneness of the divine and human but is not himself the sole embodiment of this unity.[31] Once again Strauss employs Hegelian dialectics to defend this conclusion. While the idea of Jesus as the incarnate Son of God was necessary for people during an age incapable of abstract thought, it is only a representation *(Vorstellung)* of a deeper truth. For those able to grasp the speculative idea *(Begriff)* of the unity of the human and divine, the historical incarnation can be discarded.[32]

But mind, having once taken occasion by this external fact to bring under its consciousness the idea of humanity as one with God, sees in the history only the presentation of that idea; the object of faith is completely changed. Instead of a sensible, empirical fact, it has become a spiritual and divine idea that has its confirmation no longer in history but in philosophy. When the mind has thus gone beyond the sensible history and entered into the domain of the absolute, the former ceases to be essential; it takes a subordinate place, above which the spiritual truths suggested by the history stand self-supported. History becomes as the faint image of a dream which belongs only to the past, and does not, like the idea, share the permanence of the spirit which is absolutely present to itself.[33]

Summary

In *The Christ of Faith and the Jesus of History*, Strauss provides what might be considered his primary agenda for theology. "Nowadays we view all things in heaven and on earth differently from the New Testament authors and the founders of Christian doctrine. What the Evangelists tell us we can no longer take to be true in the way they tell it; what the apostles believed and the way they believed it we can no longer hold necessary for salvation. Our God is another, our world is another; also Christ can no longer be for us who he was for them. To admit this is the duty of truthfulness; to want to deny or cover it up leads to nothing other than lies, distortion of the Scriptures, and hypocrisy with regard to faith."[34] If we are to remain both Christian and scientific, Strauss argues, supernaturalism or rationalism, as currently formulated, are untenable in view of modern knowledge. The anger he aroused in these schools indicates that his evaluation was not without some merit.

Strauss's *Life of Jesus* establishes an important benchmark in biblical interpretation. Its application of the historical-critical method is the best early attempt to consider biblical materials through the tools applied to other documents of history. By this Strauss lays the foundation from the work of Baur and the Tübingen School and redirects the focus of theology from doctrine alone to the community that gave it birth. In view of his methodology he also brings the discussion of our knowledge of the historical Jesus to a new level. Without the impetus provided by *Life of Jesus*, the "quest of the historical Jesus" would have started much later and would have taken a different direction. Strauss sets the agenda for the discussion of the relationship between the Jesus of history and the Christ of faith, a discussion that is ongoing still. Finally, he adds a new dimension to the discussion of the relationship between theology and philosophy with his speculative refashioning of Christian doctrine.

While Strauss raises a number of significant questions concerning the historicity of the Gospel accounts, he is not as successful in answering the question of why the accounts arose in such forms as they did. His definition of myth is a rather blunt interpretive instrument and a variety of differing features of the Gospels are simply tossed into this broad category.

A second problem is that although Strauss addresses the question of how certain messianic conceptions were applied to Jesus, he is surprisingly silent about *why* his followers were ready to speak of Jesus in these terms.[35] Moreover, Strauss's own conclusions also reflect a blind spot common to many of his time. While his argument assumes the relativity of knowledge of ages past, for some reason this relativity does not apply to his own conclusions. Thus he does not seem to recognize that, like the mythological worldview he wanted to put behind him, his own Hegelian understanding of the world soon would be considered antiquated. Finally, even as many of his opponents came to reject a total identification of the Jesus of history and the Christ of faith, to argue as Strauss did that the former is almost wholly unrelated to the essence of Christianity appears to stretch the definition of Christianity to an extreme. Stated otherwise, if Straussian Christianity would be unrecognizable as Christianity to the first church as it was to many of his contemporaries, can we honestly call it Christianity anymore?

Ferdinand Christian Baur

Ferdinand Christian Baur (1792-1860), though Strauss's teacher and sixteen years his senior, did not achieve any real measure of recognition until after the ascent of his precocious student. His most influential writings came later in life, and many were published posthumously.[36] However, Baur set the tone for theological discussion in the latter part of the nineteenth century by his establishment and leadership of the Tübingen School, giving his views the institutional voice Strauss never had.[37] Baur was educated at home by his father, a pastor, until he went to lower seminary at Blaubeuren at thirteen. Like his father he later attended the theological school at Tübingen. The old Tübingen School was at its height during Baur's student days, and the rational supernaturalism embraced at the school provided a transition between the orthodox supernaturalism of his youth and his subsequent speculative monism. Following graduation from Tübingen he pastored for two years, followed by two years as a tutor at Tübingen and then nine years as professor of philosophy and classics at Blaubeuren.

After completing his formal education Baur's reading of Fichte, Schelling and Schleiermacher brought a new perspective to his theology. In particular he appreciated their expansion of the divine from a purely transcendent reality to one that encompassed the natural sphere as well. His later reading of Hegel reinforced this perspective and helped complete his conversion to speculative monism.[38] Because of his Hegelian inclinations he was opposed by some of the old guard at Tübingen when he was nominated to a chair in 1826. However, Baur was able to garner enough support, bolstered by a petition signed by 124 seminary students (including Strauss), to receive an appointment. He remained there until his death in 1860. While at Tübingen his focus shifted to New Testament, patristics, history of dogma and church history. His writing production was as prolific as his interests were broad. Bauer rose every day to begin work at 4:00 a.m., and his publications amounted to 16,000 pages.

Over time Baur was able to assemble around himself a number of like-minded scholars and establish what has come to be known as the Tübingen School, built on the foundation of historical criticism pioneered by Strauss.[39] Some clarification is necessary to differentiate the various uses of the name "Tübingen School." The old Tübingen School attended by Baur as a student was dominated by theologians who attempted to apply critical methodology while maintaining orthodoxy. However, the new Tübingen School under Baur's leadership rejected the supernaturalism of the old and desired to examine Scripture and church history from a critical perspective. While the conclusions of these scholars often drew hostile fire, even their staunchest opponents were forced to incorporate much of the historical-critical method they championed. Tübingen also had a separate Roman Catholic faculty of repute.

When Strauss's *Life of Jesus* was published in 1835, Baur, as a respected scholar in a visible position and Strauss's former teacher, was required to respond in some way. However, many of the conservative scholars who had attempted to block his appointment to Tübingen still held considerable sway nine years later, and Baur's approval would have brought renewed attacks on him. It was a no-win situation since there was little to gain by falling into line with Strauss's views, and Baur's support at the time was tepid. It is clear, however, that he was in accord with Strauss on several fundamental issues. First, both assume that critical methods are necessary to prevent theological presuppositions from determining conclusions or limiting progress. "Dogma in general cannot be expected to remain always the same throughout its development. Its sphere of development may not be limited merely to ecclesiastical dogma. No specific limits may be set for it; the content of its development is not to be prescribed in advance; it must be permitted a free, self-generating movement."[40] In addition, both Strauss and Baur seek to replace supernaturalist and rationalist interpretations of Christianity with a scientific approach built around an Idealist core.

However, Baur argues that Strauss leaves the theological task half-finished. "For all the work's [Life of Jesus] imposing and masterful exposition of the view that the history of dogma is also its criticism, it is nevertheless also to be seen that in this linking of the history of dogma with dogmatics, history itself always comes off badly. Not history as such, but rather criticism, is the major concern. Since criticism is negatively rather than positively directed, dogma allows itself to be constructed only to have its structure destroyed, and to show how it contains nothing that can endure. As a result, dogma seems to exist merely for the sake of criticizing itself."[41] In Baur's judgment then, Strauss's historical criticism only tells us what theology cannot believe because it severs theology from history. What Baur seeks is a more positive theological synthesis achieved by holding theology and history together.

The difficulty for the theologian or Christian historian is combining the historical and the theological in a way that does not steal from one to give to the other. On the one hand, even a cursory overview of the church's history reveals movement, conflict and development in both doctrine and praxis. On the other hand, Christianity also lays claim to a truth that transcends time and place. What then is the eternal truth of Christianity and how can it be reconciled with changes in what the church believes and does? The answer, according to Baur, is to bring together the divine and human—theology and history—through dialectical monism. Building on the Idealism of Schelling and Hegel, he argues that nature and supernature are not separate but two facets of the same reality. Spirit seeks actualization in the concrete, and the natural strives for Spirit. The dynamic activity of the Spirit means then that the movements and controversies of church history are not simply changes: they are growth toward an ideal. Without development Baur says, "The Christian faith would have become the faith of a mere Jewish sect, in whose keeping the whole future of Christianity would have been imperiled."[42] What binds this activity together throughout is the Idea of the oneness of the divine and natural.

Baur believes that we are forced to reconsider several aspects of historiography if we apply this monistic paradigm to the study of the church. First, the events of history cannot be viewed as distinct from the inner logic of the universe. Events are intimately linked with and grow out of ideas. This metaphysical paradigm shapes Baur's methodology. History requires more than simply the observation of empirical events. It must be supplemented with the theoretical input of speculative thought in order to gain an understanding of what events mean and where they are taking us. Finally, Baur addresses the practical and ethical aspect of his view. "The word *history* has both an objective and a subjective meaning.... History is both what has happened objectively and the subjective knowledge of what has happened."[43] The task of the historian is to align our subjective knowledge with the Spirit's work within history, the objective aspect, so it becomes part of individual self-consciousness. Although Baur's approach does not allow for easy abstraction of one aspect from another, we will attempt to examine each of these items separately and show why Baur finds them a useful corrective to supernaturalist and rationalist historiography.

Monistic Historiography

To know whether historical understanding is possible, we must ask "whether history, despite all the variety of its spiritual tendencies, is something other than a mere aggregate, a variegated play of powers in which there is no unity and therefore no single moving principle determining the course of development."[44] For Baur, there is a "single moving principle behind the multiplicity of events." Church history is not a random sequence of policies, structures and power brokers but the story of the Idea become historical. Event and Idea are facets of a whole. Therefore, "Only when he [the historian] knows the essence of the subject matter [the Idea] and what is included within it, does he also know what he is to look for in history so as to include everything that belongs to the subject matter itself, and not to overlook anything that represents a moment of its development."[45] If history is a whole, then a constant—the Idea—is required to unify it. Once the Idea is understood, the stream of historical activities becomes comprehensible.

If this is true, rationalist dualism fails because it radically separates events from the Idea. It places God outside the historical process, not within as its impetus and foundation. As a result, rationalism's strict separation of the divine from the historical realm leaves no room for providence and opens the door to subjectivism. "But generally once church history is viewed according to the utility of its substantial content, its value and utility will always be identified with very subjective interests and particular purposes."[46] In other words, without a unifying principle working within history, church history becomes a tool by which each rationalist gains free rein to interpret history in a manner that advances a private agenda.

Ontological monism requires that we bring history and speculation together. History, as Baur uses the term, includes church history, the history of dogma and the history of philosophy since they all deal with occurrences and doctrines that are public in nature. And because the Absolute manifests itself in the particulars of history, our understanding of the Absolute requires that our beliefs about history be justified. "Since Christianity belongs to the succession of historical phenomena, what it is in its essence can be determined only in a historical fashion."[47] Only in an accurate reconstruction of the past stretching back to the beginning is the whole clear. On the other hand, history by itself is insufficient without speculation, which includes both theology (or dogmatics) and philosophy. While the two differ in method, Baur virtually identifies their conclusions.[48] "If one perceives in history only contingent, subjective beliefs and views, only an endless multiplicity and change, . . . then no Absolute Truth exists. Everything crumbles into an indeterminable multiplicity; there is no unity, no unity of movement, of moving principle. That an Absolute Truth exists, however, and therefore also a consciousness of the Absolute, is the fundamental presupposition of speculative thinking."[49] The Absolute both makes possible and is the subject of speculative thought. Thus speculation has as its focus the Idea, which holds together the particulars of history.

For Baur the term *speculative* did not carry the same connotation of subjectivity that it holds today. On the contrary, because the Idea is objective, speculation is the means by which subjectivity is overcome. "The historian can be equal to his task only in so far as he transposes himself into the objective reality of the subject matter itself, free from the bias of subjective views and interests, whatever they may be, so that instead of making history a reflection of his own subjectivity, he may be simply a mirror for the perception of historical phenomena in their true and real form."[50] Thus Baur brings history and philosophical theology together. History without philosophy is meaningless. It is the task of speculation to illuminate the shape and structure of events. By understanding the divine logic within the development of the world, we can discern the pattern of external events that mirror it. At the same time, history provides the data with which speculation must work. Baur sums up by stating, "The task of historiography is completed only in the union of these two mutually complementary methods, which make up the two aspects of the same process—moving from the particular to the universal and from the universal to the particular."[51]

The symbiosis of universal and particular illustrates the problem in supernaturalist historiography. By relying on the miraculous to explain the occurrence of events, the supernaturalist historian moves from the divine (universal) to the natural (particular). Therefore, natural causes reveal little about history's meaning. Indeed they are no longer actually causes but merely the results, the epiphenomena, of divine activity. Moreover, miracle, which Baur defines as "an interruption of the natural continuity, established by an immanent law, between cause and effect, which natural causes can do nothing to explain, and which must be produced by the impact of some external power,"[52] makes historical investigation impossible. History requires continuity within a sequence of events, and since miracle is the intervention of a factor without antecedents, it reduces history to a series of unrelated new beginnings rather than an interconnected fabric.

The final dialectic Baur considers is that of historical reality and our awareness of this reality. The Spirit's activity in history is the object of theology. Since development occurs with the unfolding of the Spirit, this growth is reflected in our attempt to describe the significance of events and ideas. Developments in doctrine and praxis within the church follow from the consciousness of the various ages. Like the overall activity of the Spirit, which through a process of dialectic moves toward more complete expression in history, so also does our understanding of dogma experience growth and development. This involves a shift in the traditional view, which conceives of dogma as a final statement of theological truth. In contrast to this, Baur states that, "What dogmatics would regard as permanent is already, for the history of dogma, the first member of a new progression."[53] Since dogma has as its object the work of the Spirit, its continuing activity in different ages is self-correcting. "Every successive form in this forward-moving process thus becomes the negation of what has preceded it, and dogma in its own development always labors to remove everything negative and inadequate, the history of dogma is also its criticism; and thus quite naturally the critical consciousness itself appears as an element in history."[54]

The goal of the dialectical approach is to bring our subjective awareness into line with the objective reality of the Spirit's work. So that the Spirit might be known inwardly and not just as a concept, we must know history, the sphere within which revelation occurs, in order to recognize the Spirit in its various concrete manifestations. "Revelation is the act of Spirit in which an objective reality confronts subjective consciousness as an immediate given, and becomes for the subject the object of a faith whose content is the absolute Idea."[55] The reason history can provide subjective certainty of the Idea is once again tied in with Baur's monism. The Spirit we seek to know through history and speculation is not distinct from the Spirit *by which* we know. "Religion itself, however, is essentially a relation of Spirit to Spirit, in which Spirit mediates itself with itself through the activity of thinking. All thinking is the mediation of Spirit with itself, in order to be for consciousness what it is in itself, and thus to become thinking, self-conscious Spirit through the mediation of thinking."[56] The divine permeates all nature, thus human nature has a point of contact with the divine mind and can through thought recognize the work of the Spirit.

The dynamic nature of the Spirit's activity in history betrays another gap in supernaturalist and rationalist historiography. If all theological truth is embedded in Scripture, then all theological truth is available from the beginning, and there can be no development in doctrine. Any divergence from Scripture must be viewed as heresy. Baur charges that no history of dogma is possible under these assumptions. Instead this model allows only a history of heresy. However, a dialectical approach overcomes this problem. Since there is an evolution of the Spirit, our theology must reflect this progression or become obsolete. "The whole history of dogma is a forward-moving process of development; indeed, it is the developing process of Spirit itself."[57] Change within theology is therefore not a departure from truth but the means by which we keep up with growth in our consciousness of truth.

Baur sums up his judgment on supernaturalism and rationalism in true Hegelian fashion. The earlier supernaturalist approach fixed our attention on the divine reality within the movements of history but did so at the expense of the natural. Later, rationalism provided the antithesis by stressing the nexus of cause and effect but held the divine at such arm's length that the Spirit had no place in history. Thus "as the respective theological systems of rationalism and supernaturalism have outlived their usefulness, having each evolved to a degree that oversteps the antithesis between the two, so is it impossible for the most recent historiography of the Christian church, if it is not to remain attached to an obsolete standpoint, to be either rationalistic or supernaturalistic in the older, absolute sense."[58] The only viable option, in his view, is his monistic historiography, which perceives the divine and natural as two sides of the same coin.

Baur's Application of Dialectical Historiography

If the views of each generation mirror a stage in our awareness of the Idea, we understand the development of the Spirit only to the degree that we understand each generation's theological perspective, or what Baur calls its *Tendenz*. Thus he introduces *Tendenz*, or tendency, criticism as a vital tool of historical criticism.[59] Every writer has a theological bias created by his or her history and interest, and Baur argues that church history's task is to discover this *Tendenz* in order to understand the situation in which dogma came into being. Baur's employment of tendency criticism is then coupled with another innovation. Since Scripture is not a repository of changeless truths but a reflection of the earliest church's awareness of the unfolding Spirit, the New Testament writers are theologians with aims of their own, shaped by their cultural and religious horizon. Thus church history begins with the New Testament, not at the close of the apostolic age.

The traditional view of the New Testament church was one of relatively smooth and quick transition from Jewish particularism to an inclusive Christianity that embraced Gentile converts. Baur argues that a very different picture of the New Testament church is disclosed when we apply tendency criticism. Since the earliest documents of the church are the Pauline epistles, church history begins its investigations there. These materials, especially Galatians and the Corinthian correspondence, reveal an intense struggle between Jewish and Gentile factions and are at odds with the more conciliatory view we find in Acts (e.g., chap. 15). In this Pauline correspondence we find references to a faction of the original Jerusalem Christians who wanted to maintain their Jewish identity. Therefore, when Paul teaches that the Law had been superseded by justification by faith, Galatians and the Corinthian letters provide evidence that a group of Judaizers hound him and seek to impose Judaism on Gentile converts. However, Paul saves Christianity from Jewish particularism and makes the Idea truly universal.

It is the death of Jesus that transforms Paul from a narrow Jewish legalist into the apostle to the Gentiles preaching salvation by faith for all. "A death which ran so directly counter to all the facts and presuppositions of the Jewish national consciousness, could not be confined in its significance to the Jewish nation, it must have a scope far transcending the particularism of Judaism. There can be no doubt that this was the thought in which the apostle first discerned the truth of Christianity."[60] This "truth of Christianity" is of course a Hegelian monism read back into Paul. "In his [Paul's] Christian consciousness as an essentially spiritual one, the Christian knows himself to be identical with the spirit of God; for only the spirit, the spirit of God, the absolute spirit, can know the divine contents of the Christian consciousness."[61] This interpretation of Paul's view of reconciliation as the unity of the divine and human found its fullest expression in the person of Christ. However, Baur, like Strauss, implies that once the idea of the Spirit's unity has been grasped, we can dispense with the historical Jesus. That Paul says so little of the sayings and events of Jesus' life "only shows us how large and how spiritual his conception of Christianity was. The special and particular vanish for him in the contemplation of the whole."[62]

Baur uses the conflict between Jewish and Gentile Christianity as a tool to establish the date and setting of the individual New Testament books. Jewish Christianity, which wanted to maintain the role of Old Testament law, is reflected in the Petrine epistles, Revelation and Matthew. Thus he argues that Matthew is the earliest of the Gospels, originally written in Hebrew, because Jesus is presented as the expected Messiah. The Hellenistic perspective of Paul, which is antithetical to Jewish Christianity, is evident in 1 and 2 Corinthians, Galatians and Romans. Beyond this the other letters attributed to Paul are dubious. Luke's Gospel, written after A.D. 70 since it contains an allusion to the fall of Jerusalem, also represents Hellenistic Christianity.

Gradually the thesis and antithesis of Jewish and Hellenistic Christianity resolves into the synthesis of early Catholicism, and evidence of the previous tensions disappear. This synthesis is necessitated by Gnosticism, which posed a threat for both previous forms of Christianity. The early Catholicism reflected in the Pastorals, Acts, Hebrews and the two remaining Gospels requires a late dating of these materials. Mark was written in the last part of the second century. John's Gospel is placed somewhat earlier and is pivotal to Baur since he sees John's presentation of Jesus as a primitive version of his own attempt to express the idea of Christ in speculative terms.

Although the strains between Jewish particularism and Pauline theology dissolve in early Catholic theology, the dialectic through which the Spirit's manifestations grow assumes new forms in the post-apostolic church. In this period, which Baur separates into three distinct epochs, we find an ongoing dialectic between the inner consciousness and appropriation of the object of faith and the church's doctrine and external structure. "The two major forms in which the Idea of the church realizes itself are dogma and polity. In both the development of the church proceeded to realize the Idea of that unity in such fashion that Christian consciousness could find in it the adequate expression of its Idea."[63] Each stage represents a partial realization of the Idea, and subsequent stages preserve the truth of the past while correcting imbalances between the internal consciousness and external expression of Christianity.

The first period, which Baur calls the "substantiality of dogma," extends through the first six centuries of the church. The theological foundation established during this period was powerful and creative.

However, these doctrinal formulations confronted the believer as a series of abstract propositions to be accepted on the basis of church authority. Thus the Idea becomes identified with the empirical church. As a result ecclesiastical structure, which provides an external unity for the church, stands as a hindrance to the freedom of individual consciousness. "Since everything that the church had once sanctioned through public proceedings and decision was regarded as irrevocable dogma, the individual was no longer free to form his own opinions about the doctrine of Christian faith; he had to submit in unconditional belief to the authority of the church."[64]

During the second epoch of church history (seventh century to the Reformation), an attempt was made to infuse dogma with piety. The external structure of the church and its dogma had overwhelmed individual self-consciousness, and there was need to incorporate the Idea internally. "The major point of view in which scholasticism must be placed is precisely the endeavor, which lies at the basis of all its major manifestations, to remove dogma from the externality and immediacy it possessed as an absolute given, resting on the bare authority of ecclesiastical faith, and to place it in subjective consciousness, to mediate it with consciousness."[65]

Baur is unclear about why the liberation of self-consciousness, which was the goal of the medieval scholasticism, was not attained. However, the freedom of the individual over against the external structures of the church comes to fruition in the Reformation's emphasis on the priesthood of all believers. There is now a unity of subjective consciousness and objective dogma within the believer rather than a truth imposed by external authority and simply accepted on faith. "Dogma no longer confronted him [the Christian] in its externality and with the externally imposed authority of ecclesiastical doctrine; rather, it derived its significance only from the subject's knowing himself to be internally at one with divine truth, which he recognized as the essential content of dogma."[66]

While the emergence of Protestantism allowed for a greater internalization of "the essential content of dogma," the unification of the object of dogma and the external structure of the church was still unrealized. As Baur puts it, "The Idea still hovers indefinitely and at a great distance over the manifestations to which it must be related."[67] Both Catholicism and Protestantism present only a partial view of Christianity. The former appropriates the unity of the church but does not give complete account of the subjective element of the faith. Protestantism, on the other hand, provides for the freedom of individual consciousness but gives up external unity in the bargain. Baur believes that both the unity and diversity of Christianity can be achieved in his speculative approach.

Summary

While Hegel attached a certain finality to his philosophy, viewing it as the goal of Christian thought, Baur disputed the idea that dogma had reached its conclusion. The future of dogma remains eternally open to the unfolding of the Spirit. On the other hand it does seem clear that Baur claims finality for his historical *method*. In his view the Idea, which is objectively given in history, is only accessible through the speculative approach he advocates. Only this method links theology and philosophy and results in a more comprehensive understanding of dogma than was previously available.

Even if the equilibrium between openness to the future and the finality of the dialectic method is sustainable, heavy reliance on Hegelianism creates severe weaknesses in Baur's entire program. When the Hegelian foundation underlying this method crumbles, so does much of Baur's method. For example, although he professes confidence that the dialectical model by which history is truly understood is not imposed on the concepts and events of history by the interpreter but is rather discovered from it, it is not clear how this is possible. He argues that, because the theologian is not radically distinct from the thinking Spirit, we can get beyond a mere subjectivity and know the subject matter in its reality, not simply its present historical manifestation. However, it is difficult to see why Baur's interpretation should be any less determined in his interpretation than any other historian. If historical context determines one's perspective and goals, it becomes the double-edged sword that calls into question, not only the methods and conclusions of our predecessors, but our own as well.

At the same time, when stripped of its Hegelian appendages, Baur's work marks a stride forward in a number of areas. The recognition of various theological tendencies and aims in the New Testament materials is an important insight, and while the specific conclusions he draws from his application of tendency criticism found few adherents, the use of *Tendenz* criticism to determine the setting of New Testament writings is a common fixture in New Testament scholarship. Similarly the general outline of the conflicts in the early church and the fundamentals of the different faction's positions are widely accepted. Finally, Baur's acknowledgment of the influence culture and background wield over theological views and ecclesiastical practices set the course for the discussion of church historiography that continues. His critiques of supernaturalist and rationalist historical approaches required that advocates of these positions reformulate support for their claims. And though Baur's own dynamic monism failed to win a significant number of followers, his work suggests new directions and thus lays the groundwork for what is possibly the most innovative period in historiography and social theory. His demand that we confront the questions of the individual in relation to social context, the relationship of objective reality and our interpretations, and the interplay of the human and divine in history, assures that theology and philosophy cannot proceed until it defends its assumptions in these areas. His discussion of the continuity of history and the forces that move it set the table for the historical and social criticism of Ludwig Feuerbach, Karl Marx and Max Weber.

6. HEGEL INVERTED

When a movement dominates the scene to the extent that Hegel's Idealism captured the middle of the nineteenth century, it often takes some time for possible trajectories of the system to bubble to the surface. However, as a second generation of intellectuals attempted to flesh out Idealism, unforeseen interpretations of an Idealist system begin to emerge. The beginning of an important transition in Hegelianism may be seen in Strauss's conclusion later in life that the only difference between Idealism and materialism is linguistic (see endnote 5 in the previous chapter). If all reality is essentially a single whole, why would terms such as idea and matter designate different realities? Once this question has been posed, it is not difficult to see (at least in hindsight) that rather than providing a philosophical system that places the universe under the sway of the divine, Idealism may provide a foundation for materialism. This is precisely the direction that Idealism takes in the thought of Ludwig Feuerbach and Karl Marx, who turn Hegel's dialectic on its head.

From Theology to Anthropology

Feuerbach and Marx view their philosophies as the next logical step (as well as the final step) for Hegelian thought. Like Strauss and Baur, they rejected the idea of God as transcendent of the historical. However, Feuerbach and Marx go one step farther and regard God as a *product* of historical development rather than its author. Once they removed God as the force behind historical movements, they then sought to explain the past and prescribe for the future from an entirely secular perspective. Thus in contrast to Strauss and Baur, who argue that we know God through human history, Feuerbach and Marx assert that we know humanity by understanding the history of religion.

Feuerbach and Marx, like Strauss and Baur, follow Hegel in his rejection of metaphysical dualism but resolve the dualisms of traditional philosophy differently. Instead of dissolving all into a rational monism, Feuerbach has something of a practical monism. We do not function as a body distinct from a soul. Reason and affection do not exist as separate compartments of human existence. Instead our division of the world into dual realms is a product of alienation from our true nature. Marx draws on the theme of alienation but stresses its social dimensions. We are estranged from our true humanity by oppressive economic structures. Second, while retaining Hegel's dialectical process, Feuerbach and Marx turn it on its head. Whereas Hegel uses dialectical philosophy to demonstrate the real meaning of Christianity in order to save it, they use it to explicate the real meaning of Christianity in order to destroy it for the purpose of saving humanity. Christianity contains truth, but for that truth to be of service to us it must be uncoupled from Christianity and transformed into anthropology.

Ludwig Feuerbach

Ludwig Feuerbach (1804-1872)[1] was the son of a distinguished lawyer and one of five brothers who each made their mark in different fields. Like so many of the philosophers of this age his initial academic pursuit was theology. In 1823 Feuerbach entered the university at Heidelberg, where he studied under the most prominent rationalist theologian of the day, H. E. G. Paulus (1761-1851). However, he found the rationalist explanations of biblical and theological tensions contrived. The Hegelian-influenced approach advocated by right-winged Hegelian Karl Daub seemed to be the only viable theological method. Daub had been influenced by Schleiermacher and Hegel, and since both these scholars were at Berlin, continuing his studies there was the natural next step for Feuerbach.

In spite of a promise to his father not to become a disciple of Hegel, Feuerbach became so close to the older scholar while at Berlin that he referred to him as his "second father." However, he disagreed with Hegel about the compatibility of philosophy and Christianity and came to find theology so unbearable that he eventually dropped his classes with Neander and Schleiermacher and moved to the philosophy faculty. When King Max Joseph of Bavaria died, the stipend he received as the son of a government employee was discontinued, and Feuerbach was forced to move to the university at Erlangen, where costs were lower, to complete his studies.

Feuerbach was granted his doctorate in 1828 with a dissertation that hinted at differences with Hegelian orthodoxy.[2] He became docent at Erlangen and lectured on philosophy from 1829 to 1835. However, publication of *Thoughts on Death and Immortality* (1830), a scathing attack on Christianity that was confiscated by government authorities as subversive, doomed his chances of a university appointment.[3] He did not consider exclusion from the academy a big loss and desired instead the solitude of writing. This wish was fulfilled by his marriage to Berta Löw, whose family owned a porcelain factory. Her wealth allowed Feuerbach to spend most of his midlife writing in rural isolation.[4] The publication of *The Essence of Christianity* (1841) brought widespread attention and made him something of a spokesperson for the Young Hegelians, which included the young Karl Marx and Friedrich Engels, through the 1840s.[5]

The comfortable existence Feuerbach enjoyed for almost thirty years came to a rather abrupt end when his wife's porcelain factory went bankrupt in 1860, and the remainder of his life was spent in relative poverty. For a short time he considered going to America, but his financial situation made immigration impossible. Simultaneously, Feuerbach's stature had diminished for the philosophical and political left after the midpoint of the nineteenth century. Hegelian philosophy ceased to be the force it had been earlier, and Feuerbach's use and criticism of Hegel's thought did not capture the attention of the new generation. Second, his admirers were disappointed that he stayed on the sidelines during the revolution of 1848. Even though his own thought was received with stronger criticism from Marx as time went on, Feuerbach was greatly impressed with Marx's *Capital* when it was published in 1867, and he became a member of the German Social Democratic Party two years before his death in 1872.

The Origin of Religion

Although some see Feuerbach as one of the seminal thinkers of his time, even his strongest advocates must allow, as Feuerbach himself did, that the scope of his work is limited to the question of religion and its abolition. At the same time, it is incorrect to view him, as some have, as just another atheist with an ax to grind. Feuerbach goes beyond the eighteenth century Enlightenment thinkers who argue that religion should be discarded as an outmoded remnant of an irrational worldview. While Feuerbach agrees that these earlier philosophers successfully demonstrated that God did not exist, they left unanswered the question of why religion came to exist.

Feuerbach's attempt to explain the genesis of religion combines the Hegelian dialectic with a criticism of Christianity from an anthropological perspective. Like Hegel he argues that there is an inseparable connection between the structure of religion and the prevailing ideas of the age. However, Feuerbach reverses Hegel's order, arguing that religion, rather than creating human self-consciousness, instead *reflects* our awareness of ourselves in various ages. Religious belief and praxis is the key to rightly analyzing all human endeavors in history and is the starting point for scientific anthropology when demythologized. However, while Feuerbach relies on Hegel's dialectical model to outline the development of our awareness, he distances himself from Hegel's emphasis on reason. Religion is not a rational endeavor but a reflection of human need. We project our fears and goals in such a way that we produce from our needs the concept of a divine being. Thus Feuerbach argues that the Genesis account has inverted the story. "For God did not, as the Bible says, make man in His image; on the contrary man . . . made God in his image."[6] As a result, religion and philosophy, generally viewed by their proponents as the antidote for privation and want, are actually the *product* of human desires and fears. Because this has not been recognized, theology and philosophy became part of our self-deception. Their otherworldly orientation obscures legitimate human needs by fixing our attention on an invisible realm. Therefore, while Feuerbach denies the objective claims of religion, he also sees them as expressions of truths about the valid needs of humanity, albeit veiled truths as long as they remain entrapped within religion.[7]

Feuerbach's aim is to decode the way we speak of our needs and goals and restate them anthropologically, without the haze produced by philosophy and religion. "The task of the modern era was the realization and humanization of God—the transformation and dissolution of theology into anthropology."[8] For Feuerbach, the beginning point is a proper understanding of human self-consciousness. While human beings are differentiated from animals in that only the former have religion, there is something yet more basic. Only humans have consciousness, which Feuerbach defines as "present only in a being to whom his species, his essential nature, is an object of thought."[9] This is the core of our humanity. While animals are trapped within their individuality and particularity, human beings know themselves as a species—as humanity. "Man is himself at once I and thou; he can put himself in the place of another, for this reason, that to him his species, his essential nature, and not merely his individuality, is an object of thought."[10]

This view of human consciousness is grounded in Hegelian dialectical assumptions. In the absence of another, we would have no means of knowing the essence of human being. Consciousness is always consciousness of something—an object of thought is required. To know ourselves as human, we must objectify ourselves. Only by this means do we know what and who we are. And the object against which we come to know ourselves is humanity itself, represented in another. "My fellow-man is *per se* the mediator between me and the sacred idea of the species."[11] We are what Feuerbach calls a "species-being." Our awareness is molded by our consciousness of being like the other.

In the other, then, we discover our true nature. "What, then, *is* the nature of man, of which he is conscious, or what constitutes the specific distinction, the proper humanity of man? Reason, Will, Affection. . . . Man exists to think, to love, to will."[12] As individuals, we possess these qualities only in a limited way. However, Feuerbach believes that reason, will and affection reach perfection in humanity as a whole because they force us out of ourselves into reciprocal relations with others. These capacities are infinite because they allow us to transcend individuality and know ourselves as a species. "Solitude is finiteness and limitation; community is freedom and infinity. Man for himself is man (in the ordinary sense); man with man—the unity of I and thou—is God."[13] Our awareness of an object over against ourselves, humanity, is therefore the genesis of our concept of infinity.

The combination of humanity's infinity and the awareness of individual finitude is the source of religion. As finite individuals we experience need and desire. "But the sense of limitation is painful, and hence the individual frees himself from it by the contemplation of the perfect Being; in this contemplation he possesses what otherwise is wanting to him."[14] To overcome our boundaries we look to an infinite source. Our proper complement, the Absolute that fulfills our lack, is humanity. However, we mistakenly understand the source and object of our awareness of the infinite. The absolute, which we know in humanity, is objectified, projected into another sphere and given the name of God. In short, the idea of God is simply human consciousness externalized. "Every God is a *creature* of the imagination, an image, and specifically *an image of man,* but He is an image which man places outside himself and conceives of as an independent being."[15] The creation of God does not arise from our consciousness of ourselves as purely individual but rather is the result of our awareness of ourselves as species-beings. We do not find the origin of God in our individual capacity to think, create and feel. Instead as social creatures we universalize what we find in ourselves as a species. Our mistake is in predicating these capacities of the wrong subject. It is not God but humanity as a whole that perfectly thinks, creates and feels.

Religion as Egoism

To view limitation and need as the origin of religion marks a departure from the Enlightenment, Kant and Hegel, who considered religion from the perspective of rationality. Feuerbach says instead that religion's primary purpose was never satisfaction of intellectual needs but the resolution of the practical and concrete questions of human existence. We have wants, and religion promises to meet them. This introduces a major theme: religion as egoism. "In short, religion has essentially a practical aim and foundation; the drive that gives rise to religion, its ultimate foundation, is the striving for happiness, and if this is an egoistic drive, it follows that the ultimate foundation of religion is egoism."[16]

It is in this light that Feuerbach understands the incarnation. While on the one hand the incarnation expresses the concept that the human and divine are the same, on the other hand it betrays our egoism. "God did not become man for his own sake; the need, the want of man—a want which still exists in the religious sentiment—was the cause of the Incarnation."[17] Feuerbach interprets the concept of eternal life similarly. Our mortality is the ultimate limitation: all who share this life will die. "Therefore, there must exist a second life, a life that is not determined and restricted by the conflict and dissimilarity of any qualities, a life that is lived out in an element as bright and transparent as the purest crystal water, in order that the pure light of personhood may penetrate and shine through this element without limitation, without coloration, without resistance."[18]

One might protest that the doctrine of universal sinfulness presents a counterexample to Feuerbach's charge that religion is egoistic. After all, why would those driven by self-interest describe themselves as sinful? Feuerbach says in response: "Is he who always inspects his faults and defects in the mirror less vain and self-satisfied than he who only thinks of his virtue and handsomeness? . . . Religion should be a matter of God, of the will of God, of God in and for himself. Yet does not everything seem to turn only on *their* deliverance and reconciliation, on *their* salvation and immortality? God is only on the periphery of their religion; individuals themselves are its focal point."[19] Thus Feuerbach argues that the concept of sin, which reveals our sense of limitation, is only a minor point. The real concern is our desire for ultimate salvation.

In order to create God we magnify and purify what is already present in human nature, objectify the result, then project it onto God. Therefore, all the characteristics attributed to God by Christianity are actually human attributes. "In the divine omniscience man merely fulfills his own desire to know everything. . . . In divine ubiquity, he fulfills his desire not to be tied to any place, or objectifies the faculty of the human mind to be everywhere at once. In divine eternity, he merely fulfills the desire not to be restricted to any time. . . . In divine omnipotence, man merely fulfills his desire to be able to do everything, a desire that is related to, or a consequence of, the desire to know everything . . . in divine omnipotence man merely objectifies and deifies his own universal powers, his unlimited capacity to do all things."[20]

While these metaphysical qualities attributed to God grant him the power to meet our needs, they are insufficient by themselves because they exclude personal qualities and therefore do not encompass the whole of human nature. "Only a being who comprises in himself the whole man can satisfy the whole man."[21] Therefore, Christian theology amends metaphysical attributes with personal qualities as well. Of particular interest to Feuerbach is the doctrine of God as love. A loving God is a projection of our social nature, and this provides the motive of salvation—God desires fellowship. However, the doctrine of the Trinity lets the truth slip about the human origins of this concept. The impossibility that a solitary being could be perfect in love requires that God also has a social nature within himself. "The Trinity was the highest mystery and the focal point of absolute philosophy and religion. But . . . the secret of the Trinity is the secret of communal and social life; it is the secret of the necessity of the 'thou' for an 'I'; it is the truth that no being—be it man, God, mind, or ego—is for itself alone a true, perfect, and absolute being, that truth and perfection are only the connection and unity of beings equal in their essence."[22]

Christianity's combination of metaphysical attributes with personal characteristics is ultimately unavoidable, according to Feuerbach, because if religion is a reflection of our needs, only a God with the first type attributes would have the capacity to meet such needs, and only a personal God would have the motive. However, Feuerbach says that the attempt to assign both metaphysical and personal attributes to God leads to contradictions. In an argument that anticipates process theology, Feuerbach states that metaphysical perfections, which require a static state of being, are mutually exclusive of personal attributes, which presuppose change. However, unlike process theology, he states that theism cannot be modified to make it comprehensible. We must instead dispense of it. If we attempt to divorce from the divine any hint of the human, we end up with an indescribable entity. Instead we should acknowledge "the divine being is nothing else than the human being, or, rather, the human nature purified, freed from the limits of the individual man, made objective—i.e., contemplated and revered as another, a distinct being. All the attributes of the divine nature are, therefore, attributes of the human nature."[23]

The Evolution of Human Consciousness

Feuerbach's second line of argumentation against religion relies on Hegel's dialectical view of human consciousness. Following the tendency of this century to view history as a series of segments, he proclaims the religious worldview to be "man's earliest and also indirect form of self-knowledge."[24] Religion, humanity's first and most primitive stage of getting to know itself, is later superseded by speculative philosophy, then by atheism, which Feuerbach sees as the final destination of human consciousness. Based on this evolutionary model, he states that, "The identity of the subject and predicate is clearly evidenced by the progressive development of religion, which is identical with the progressive development of human culture."[25] Religious practices assume the shape of our understanding of the world; therefore, religion must be the result of historical consciousness. "The difference between the pagan god and the Christian God is solely a difference between pagan and Christian man, taken both collectively and individually. The pagan is a patriot, the Christian a cosmopolitan; consequently the pagan's god is a patriotic god, while that of the Christian is a cosmopolitan."[26]

As humanity advances from a religious worldview to the age of speculative philosophy, one might anticipate that Feuerbach's criticism would differ. However, he sees religion and philosophy as variations of the same problem. "Modern philosophy proceeded from theology; it is indeed nothing other than theology dissolved and transformed into philosophy."[27] Previously human striving was transposed by theology into otherworldly concerns and offered otherworldly solutions as a remedy. Philosophy simply takes its subject matter from Christianity and adds yet another layer of mysticism. While in Christianity we can find a remnant of the human in the idea of a personal God, philosophy turns religion's otherworldly realities into abstractions such as ideas, being, nature or substance. Thus while Feuerbach attacks both philosophy and religion, he gets at the former by his critique of the latter. Both do the same thing: they take what is human and project it into the transcendent realm.

When Feuerbach attacks philosophy, he has in mind primarily the speculative philosophy of Hegel. He credits Hegel for the dialectical approach and his recognition of the unity of the human and divine, and he sees Hegel's philosophy as the apex of the evolution of human consciousness to that time. However, it fails to recognize the truth of human nature. Hegel's mistake is that he begins with the universal and moves to the particular. The problem is that universals such as Spirit or Idea speak only of our awareness of the external world but not of the world itself. In other words, Idealism addresses actual human functions and capacities, but it leaves us without any world to which these functions might be applied or any subject who engages in these activities. There is in Idealism no world about which to think and no thinker to exercise the function of thought. World and self are mere abstractions.

Alienation and Its Resolution

Feuerbach thus argues that Hegel contributes to human alienation by reversing the order of things. God does not posit humanity as a means of writing his story. Instead humanity (wrongly) posits God and thus wrongly understands human consciousness. By emphasizing the transcendent nature of rationality, speculative philosophy loses sight of the material. "The essence of theology is the *transcendent;* i.e., the essence of man posited outside man. The essence of Hegel's *Logic* is *transcendent* thought; i.e., the thought of man *posited outside man.*"[28] For Hegel, the Absolute reaches concrete expression as the material strives toward Spirit. The implication of this, according to Feuerbach, it that God exists only by negating the physical. Therefore, we must in turn deny any aspect of our existence that is not rational. Because we are not solely rational but are also feeling and volitional beings, Idealism alienates us from ourselves.

Feuerbach argues that this alienation is paralleled in Protestantism. With its strong individualism, Protestant thought accents the distinction between soul and body in order to make room for immortality, a life free of the conditions of nature. However, this creates desires that are not grounded in reality. If our aims are unharnessed from physical existence, we desire the goods of a nonexistent world and ignore the legitimate needs of this one. "Christianity set itself the goal of fulfilling man's unattainable desires, but for that very reason ignored his attainable desires. By promising man eternal life, it deprived him of temporal life, by teaching him to trust in God's help it took away his trust in his own powers. . . . Christianity gave man what his imagination desires, but for that very reason failed to give him what he really and truly desires."[29]

The result of alienation is not only a neglect of real needs but a diminution of our nature. While we can deceive ourselves about our real needs, we cannot ignore the fact that we participate in nature and must live within the confines it establishes. Since God is in reality a construction of attributes of the human subject, when we project these predicates outside ourselves and onto God, we bring about our own destruction. God now possesses the perfections of humanity; therefore we are forced to define ourselves in distinction from God. "To enrich God, man must become poor; that God may be all, man must be nothing."[30]

Feuerbach's solution to our self-imposed impoverishment is atheistic humanism. We must reclaim what rightly belongs to us: the love now directed toward God must be redirected toward humanity. This puts Feuerbach's atheism in the proper context. Rejection of God's existence is not an end in itself. Instead Feuerbach considers his atheism an affirmation of humanity: "If atheism were a mere negation, a denial without content, it would be unfit for the people, that is, for man or for public life; but only because such atheism is worthless. True atheism, the atheism that does not shun the light, is also an affirmation; it negates the being abstracted from man, who is and bears the name of God, but only in order to replace him by man's true being."[31]

Anthropology as Religion

That which displaces religion is anthropology. Feuerbach sometimes speaks of anthropology as a new philosophy that begins, as human consciousness does, from the concrete. "The task of philosophy and of science in general consists, therefore, not in leading away from sensuous, that is, real, objects, but rather in leading toward them, not in transforming objects into ideas and conceptions, but rather in making visible, that is, in objectifying, objects that are invisible to ordinary eyes."[32] This new philosophy surpasses the old because it does not reduce us to disembodied, rational soul but considers instead the whole person. "Man must therefore replace the religious ideal with another ideal. Let our ideal not be castrated, disembodied, abstract being but the whole, real, many-sided, fully developed man."[33] In other places Feuerbach speaks of anthropology as a new religion. Although the language of religion is somewhat surprising in view of his atheism, his humanism should not be confused with materialism. While he denied the objective existence of God apart from human existence, he does argue that humanity is in some way divine and infinite, and the vocabulary of religion is appropriate. Similarly, to act for the betterment of humanity is a spiritual activity. Therefore, "Should philosophy be able to replace religion, it must, qua philosophy, become religion. This means that it must, in a way suited to its own nature, incorporate the essence of religion or the advantage that religion possesses over philosophy."[34]

When we approach human problems and goals anthropologically, we see them as they are and can successfully change the conditions of life. Because the highest expression of humanity is collective and not individual, answers to the human situation are political in nature. However, true political reform is not a viable possibility until atheism has displaced Christianity. "There can be an instinctive transformation of politics into religion, but what we need is a distinctively ultimate ground for such a transformation, and official principle. This principle, negatively expressed, is nothing other than atheism, or in other words, the renunciation of a God who is other than man."[35]

Feuerbach's hope is essentially spiritual in nature: we must become God to ourselves. *"Homo homini Deus est:*—this is the great practical principle:—this is the axis on which revolves the history of the world."[36] He sums up his vision in his concluding words in *Lectures on the Essence of Religion.*

> If we no longer *believe* in a better life but decide to *achieve* one, not each man by himself but with our united powers, we will *create* a better life, we will at least do away with the most glaring, outrageous, heartbreaking injustices and evils from which man has hitherto suffered. But in order to make such a decision and carry it through, we must replace the love of God by the love of man as the only true religion, the belief in God by the belief in man and his powers—by the belief that the fate of mankind depends not on a being outside it and above it, but on mankind itself, that man's only Devil is man, the barbarous, superstitious, self-seeking, evil man, but that man's only God is also man himself.[37]

We cannot hope human conditions will change but must instead actively transform our world. However, the only way this can occur is by reclaiming our humanity in its fullness.

Feuerbach's Significance

With the exception of a few dissenters, most consider Feuerbach an important transitional figure rather than a profound, original thinker. He turns a significant historical corner in the "movement away from a theological interpretation of the world to an interpretation in which man himself, considered as a social being, occupies the centre of the stage."[38] It is not enough to attack God's existence exclusively, as many of Feuerbach's predecessors had, because it still leaves religion and other traces of transcendence unexplained. What he provides then is an approach that attempts to account for the origins of metaphysical belief. This contribution is recognized by Friedrich Engels, who says of Feuerbach's *Essence of Christianity,* "The spell was broken. The 'system' [Hegelian Idealism] was exploded and cast aside. And the contradiction, shown to exist only in our imagination, was dissolved. One must himself have experienced the liberating effect of this book to get an idea of it. Enthusiasm was general; we all became at once Feuerbachians."[39] Shortly thereafter, however, this self-proclaimed Feuerbachian and his closest associate, Karl Marx, became sharply critical of many aspects of his thought, and they saw him only as a passage to a new phase.

Of particular importance to Marx is what appears to be a critical gap in Feuerbach's materialism. It is clear that Feuerbach is not a materialist in the traditional sense. He does not attempt to reduce will, affection and reason to material categories, but he is also adamant that these in no way point to the existence of God. Instead reason, affection and will are infinite and perfect in humanity and are thus transcendent of nature. However, with this view he appears to fall back into the type of abstraction he seeks to overcome. As Marx points out, Feuerbach simply replaces metaphysical categories like God, Spirit or Reason with a new one: Humanity. But if the earlier metaphysical constructs are subject to Feuerbach's criticism of wish-fulfillment, why should his own view of humanity be exempt from the same attacks?

A second criticism goes right to the heart of Feuerbach's argument concerning the human origin of God. Feuerbach assumes that because religious doctrines fulfill human desires, they are the result of human desires. It is one thing to argue that there is a correspondence between human need and religion's various pictures of God. However, this does not necessarily mean that religious ideas are therefore *nothing but* human needs and that language about God is *nothing but* language about ourselves since it expresses human need. Related to this is the fact that arguing against Feuerbach's view of religion is something like attempting to dispute Freud's interpretation of dreams. Since Feuerbach is engaged in decoding actions and ideas whose significance is unknown to the actor, he is open to the charge that he finds in them what he expects or wants to find. For example, he argues that the idea of the virgin birth fulfills the desire that the purity of virginity be combined with the positive aspects of sexuality and motherhood.[40] Feuerbach is stating that humans have cloaked their language in such religious terms without any realization of what truths about human nature such words really refer to. It is a rather audacious claim that only he now knows their true meaning.

Karl Marx

Both of Karl Marx's (1818-1883) parents were Jewish, and ancestors on both sides of the family included several generations of rabbis.[41] However, his father felt compelled to submit to Christian baptism when his work as a lawyer was jeopardized by limitations placed on Jews after Napoleon's defeat. Early on it seemed that Marx would follow in his father's footsteps when he enrolled as a law student at Bonn. In his first year at the university the young Marx gained a reputation as a spendthrift and spent time in jail for creating excess noise while drunk. At his father's behest he made a new start the next year by moving to the university at Berlin, where the academic atmosphere was more serious. Once there Marx went to the other extreme and withdrew from social life, spending long hours in the library, and became something of an academic recluse.

While at Berlin Marx encountered new and radical political ideas and became enamored with them. Convinced that the university would be a better forum than law for disseminating his newfound political ideas, the nineteen-year-old Marx wrote to his father to gain his blessing for a move to philosophy.[42] In it he gives evidence of being influenced by

Hegelian thought. What attracted him, as it did others we have considered previously, was Hegel's ability to overcome the dualism of idea and nature, and the social and political implications of this paradigm. After completing his doctorate in philosophy at Berlin, Marx anticipated receiving a position at Bonn through Bruno Bauer's assistance. These hopes evaporated when Bauer was relieved of his teaching post because of his political radicalism. After this Marx took up journalism and became a regular contributor to the *Rheinische Zeitung.* In 1838 he became the editor, but the paper was suppressed a few months later because of its political positions. He went to Paris and joined with Arnold Ruge (1802-1880) to become the editor of the *Deutsch-Französishe Jahrbücher.* Only one volume was published before the journal folded because of disagreements between the two over Marx's growing communist sympathies.[43]

Shortly thereafter an important alliance was formed. Marx met with Friedrich Engels (1820-1895), the son of a wealthy textile manufacturer from Manchester, England, to discuss political and social views. Engels had been something of a playboy in his youth. His father, a strong Calvinist, decided his son should learn the virtues of hard work and consigned him to labor on the docks at Bremen. While there he became sympathetic with the plight of the working class and was influenced by the ideas of Moses Hess (1812-1875), the individual who helped shape Marx's communism. These new convictions led him to Karl Marx. In the discussions between Marx and Engels, which spanned several days, they discovered a great deal of agreement in their ideas. This led to a collaboration that lasted until Marx's death and actually continued beyond as Engels edited and prepared Marx's notes for posthumous publication. In their collaborative efforts Marx provided the theoretical foundations, and Engels was instrumental in supplying empirical data and rendering Marx's sometimes-torturous writing style more palatable.

Soon after these discussions Marx was expelled from France and went to Brussels for three years. Engels joined him there, and they began work on *The German Ideology* (1845-1846) and deepened links with political and union groups. One such group was the Communist League, which held its first congress in 1846. Marx was prevented by finances from traveling to this meeting but did attend the second one in 1847. Out of this congress emerged one of the benchmark documents of world history. It was determined that a position paper should be prepared to clarify the mission and beliefs of the Communists, and the job fell to Marx and Engels. The result was the *Communist Manifesto* (1848).

After the congress it appeared that France was on the verge of a worker's revolt. Marx quickly went to Paris then to Germany where revolution was in process. However, the Revolution of 1848 failed, and he was prevented by the French government, under pressure from Prussian authorities, from returning to Paris. He moved to London, where he lived the remainder of his life. The first several years in London were difficult. The Marxes, now a growing family, occupied a two-room apartment in Soho during most of their first six years in London due to their poverty. Their fourth and fifth children, born in London, died very young. A few years later an eight-year-old son died, and the wolf was continually at the door. For some time Marx's only regular income came from weekly articles written for the *New York Daily Tribune*.

Marx was constantly torn between everyday financial concerns, political activities and his true love: writing. His research on economics was constantly interrupted by his obligations to the *Tribune* as well as the need to defend members of the Communist League in Germany who had been arrested and put on trial. This required that most of his work and research on the massive *Capital* took place deep into the night. Financial salvation finally came from inheritances and an annuity from Engels that allowed the Marx family to significantly improve their standard of living.

The first volume of *Capital* (the English translation of the well-known German title *Das Kapital*) was finally completed in 1867. Marx was unable to finish the remainder of the work before his death and the last two volumes were compiled from his notes, edited and released for publication by Engels in 1885 and 1894. *Capital* is a unique combination of social commentary, political theory, history, economics, statistical studies and philosophy, and quickly became the communist bible. After *Capital* most of Marx's work and writing was political in nature. The International Workingmen's Association was formed in 1864, and for several years Marx headed it, demanding unbending adherence to his own version of communist orthodoxy. Constant ill health limited his activity for the final ten years of his life. He never fully recovered from the death of his wife, Jenny, in 1881; Marx died two years later.

Dialectical Materialism

It is important that Marx's philosophical, social and political ideas be put in context. The industrial revolution created great social upheaval throughout Europe. Small guildsmen were increasingly unable to compete with larger factories. The sense of identity that came with family, guild and region eroded as great segments of the population moved from rural areas to the cities in search of jobs. This demographic shift resulted in a glut of labor that allowed factory owners to keep wages low. The machinery produced in the factories replaced manual labor, there was no minimum wage, the workday was long, and child labor was commonly used to keep manufacturing costs low. Conditions were often deplorable, and industrialization made it difficult for workers to feel a connection with mass-produced goods.

Marx argues that such an economic structure is dehumanizing. He bases this position on his concept of human nature. We are not primarily *homo sapiens* (thinkers) as Hegel and a host of previous philosophers argued. We are instead *homo faber* (makers). "As individuals express their life, so they are. What they are, therefore, coincides with their production, both with *what* they produce and with *how* they produce. The nature of individuals thus depends on the material conditions determining their production."[44] We find meaning in life through creating. Work is an end, not simply a means. This is what distinguishes us from animals. "Of course, animals also produce. . . . But they . . . produce only under the compulsion of direct physical needs, while man produces when he is free from physical need and only truly produces in freedom from such need. Animals produce only themselves, while man reproduces the whole of nature."[45] Through our productivity we find identity in objectifying ourselves and in doing so say something about how we see ourselves. Therefore, when our creative efforts are constricted or controlled by someone else, we become alienated.

This understanding of human nature reveals why Marx saw capitalism as so destructive. The laborer does not own or control what he or she makes. When the direction of their energies is controlled by others, a part of them is taken away, and they become alienated from themselves. The result is that the creative effort that is meant to be expressive of ourselves becomes instead a matter of survival. "For labour, *life activity, productive life,* now appear to man only as *means* for the satisfaction of a need, the need to maintain his physical existence."[46] When work is reduced to a means of keeping ourselves alive, we are reduced to the level of animals.

If we are indeed *homo faber,* history is a story of the systems within which we work. More precisely, human history is created by the economic structures within which we live. Thus Marx understands himself as a social scientist whose mission is a scientific redefinition of history. There is an ultimate order to world events, determined by a clash of thesis and antithesis that inevitably moves history forward. Our role is to anticipate the direction based on scientific laws. "The theoretical conclusions of the Communists are in no way based on ideas or principles that have been invented, or discovered, by this or that would-be universal reformer. They merely express, in general terms, actual relations springing from an existing class struggle, from a historical movement going on under our very eyes."[47] However, this disclaimer of scientific neutrality often stands in uneasy tension with the activist side of Marx, who also states that, "The philosophers have only *interpreted* the world, in various ways; the point, however, is to change it."[48]

In outlining the philosophical underpinnings of his social thought, Marx draws from a number of sources, most notably Hegel and Feuerbach. He takes up Hegel's ideas that opposition and struggle are necessary components of progress. Upward movement occurs in the clash of opposing forces that leads to new and higher syntheses. Also, like Hegel, Marx argues that the ultimate goal is not individual but corporate salvation. The disagreement between Hegel and Marx concerns the engine of history. For Hegel, history is moved by ideas. It is thought becoming concrete; competing ideas direct the religious, political and economic structures of life to higher planes. Marx agrees with this dialectical model but states that, with Hegel, it "is standing on its head. It must be turned right side up again, if you would discover the rational kernel within the mystical shell."[49] This "rational kernel" is that ideas do not have causal power. They are instead the *products* of social and economic realities. Our way of life and the social structures that facilitate it *create* ideas, not the other way round. "With me, . . . the ideal is nothing else than the material world reflected by the human mind, and translated into forms of thought."[50]

Marx's materialism finds its support in Feuerbach's philosophy. Feuerbach had demonstrated that Hegel's dialectic could be abstracted from his Idealism and applied to this-worldly concerns. Moreover, Marx appreciates the way Feuerbach presented human consciousness as the result of our social nature. Thus ideas that were formerly understood as finding their source in God or some other transcendent source were now grounded in the here and now. However, he faults Feuerbach for two related problems. First, Marx says that Feuerbach had done an incomplete job of grounding human existence in the material. Feuerbach believed that the salvation of humanity would come at the level of ideas. In contrast, Marx argues that there will be no salvation until social conditions are reshaped. This is the same error Hegel had committed in his failure to recognize that ideas result from material conditions, not vice versa. This problem is related to a second deficiency. "Feuerbach resolves the religious essence into the *human* essence. But the human essence is no abstraction inherent in each single individual. In its reality it is the ensemble of the social relations."[51] Feuerbach conceives of humanity as the source of our concept of God, but Marx argues that Feuerbach's "humanity" is itself an abstraction created by social structures. There is no transcendent from which to work, even if it is pulled down from the sky and vested in humanity as a whole. Instead all realities and relationships are material.

Once purified of Hegel's and Feuerbach's mistakes, the resulting system is often called dialectical materialism.[52] The gist of this position can be summarized in a few sentences. First, we are really and only material beings and lead meaningful lives only when we are in accord with the laws governing the natural world. Since this is the case, material goods are necessary for our existence. At the same time we are social beings whose self-understanding is molded by social institutions. Third, the way we acquire material goods is determined by economic structures. Therefore, our identity results from the type of economic system in place. However, economic systems do not remain stable and new ones do not arise in a vacuum but are the logical outcome of social forces present before-

hand. Finally, these forces are opposing economic classes whose interests are in direct conflict with each other.

Marx feels no compulsion to provide an extended argument for his
materialism. Instead, based on his empirical point of departure he simply
points to our reliance on the material world. "Men must be in a position
to live in order to be able to 'make history.' But life involves before everything else eating and drinking, a habitation, clothing and many other
things. The first historical act is thus the production of the means to satisfy these needs; the production of material life itself."[53] What Marx
would have us keep in mind, however, is that these productive processes
involve more than simply our interaction with inanimate nature. We
engage in transactions with another aspect of nature as well: our fellow
human beings. "Man is the direct object of natural science, because
directly *perceptible nature* is for man directly human sense experience (an
identical expression) in the form of the *other person* who is directly presented to him in a sensuous way. His own sense experience only exists as
human sense experience for himself through the *other person*."[54] In other
words, our awareness of ourselves is social.

While we can hear strong echoes of Feuerbach in the quote above,
Marx differs in his conception of how self-consciousness arises through
interpersonal relations. Feuerbach argues that in the other we gain the
picture of the perfection of humanity, which we project into the heavens
to create the concept of God. In contrast, Marx says that in the other person, we find opposition. Humanity is divided into two camps separated
from each other by economic status. Therefore, Marx and Engels write in
the opening lines of the *Communist Manifesto:* "The history of all hitherto
existing society is the history of class struggles. Freeman and slave, patri-
cian and plebeian, lord and serf, guild-master and journeyman, in a
word, oppressor and oppressed, stood in constant opposition to one
another, carried on an uninterrupted, now hidden, now open fight, a
fight that each time ended, either in a revolutionary re-constitution of
society at large, or in the common ruin of the contending classes."[55]

What Marx argues, then, is that history is an account of human beings
in conflict with each other. However, the opposing classes do not meet
on a level playing field. The rich have the advantage, not simply because
they control the economy but also because through their wealth they

determine the thought world of the age. "The ruling ideas of each age have ever been the ideas of its ruling class."[56] To preserve their status those in dominance create ideas that support their position. This is then incorporated into an economic system in which the poor have no voice but upon which they rely in order to meet their physical needs. As Marx and Engels argue:

> In the social production which men carry on they enter into definite relations that are indispensable and independent of their will; these relations of production correspond to a definite stage of development of their material powers of production. The sum total of these relations of production constitutes the economic structure of society—the real foundation, on which rise legal and political superstructures and to which correspond definite forms of social consciousness. The mode of production in material life determines the general character of the social, political and spiritual processes of life. It is not the consciousness of men that determines their existence, but, on the contrary, their social existence determines their consciousness.[57]

The products we make determine how we live. In turn, the way we live produces ideas about who we are. Our religions, philosophies, laws, our political systems are, therefore, under the control of those who control the production of goods.

Marx frequently points to religion as an example of how ideas are shaped by economics.[58] "The basis of irreligious criticism is this: *man makes religion;* religion does not make man. Religion is indeed man's self-consciousness and self-awareness so long as he has not found himself or has lost himself again."[59] This helps explain his opposition to the church. Religion is a tool of the wealthy to make the oppressed satisfied with their lot. It can do this by appeal to predestination or original sin, by encouragement that suffering prepares us for the rewards of the next life, or by some other doctrine. The tragedy of this, in Marx's eyes, is that people believe that these ideas are eternal truths about a beneficent God when they are, in reality, the means by which their oppressors hold them in submission.

The reason people look to the sky for salvation is that they are alienated from this life and have lost hope in salvation on earth. Because the economic deck is stacked against them, they cannot achieve fulfillment in the here and now. Thus he agrees with Feuerbach by saying that religion, though not the answer to our alienation, reveals a genuine recognition of our estrangement. *"Religious* suffering is at the same time an *expression* of real suffering and a *protest* against real suffering. Religion is the sigh of the oppressed creature, the sentiment of a heartless world, and the soul of soulless conditions. It is the *opium* of the people."[60]

Marx believes that the fates of class conflict and religion are intertwined. When one disappears, so does the other. This will happen when we reorder our lives according to the laws by which the material world operates. "The religious reflex of the real world can, in any case, only then finally vanish, when the practical relations of everyday life offer to man none but perfectly intelligible and reasonable relations with regard to his fellowmen and to nature."[61] However, he is unclear about the "chicken and egg" question. At points the activist Marx shows up and states that the abolition of religion precedes the abolition of class. "The abolition of religion as the *illusory* happiness of men, is a demand for their *real* happiness. The call to abandon their illusions about their condition is a *call to abandon a condition which requires illusions.*"[62] In other places Marx the social scientist states that once the conflict between the classes is resolved, religion will simply melt away because it no longer serves any purpose. "Religious alienation as such occurs only in the sphere of *consciousness,* in the inner life of man, but economic alienation is that of *real life* and its supersession, therefore, affects both aspects."[63]

The Stages of History

Like so many others of his day Marx argues that history should be analyzed in terms of epochs. However, his stages are not defined primarily by ideas but by the economic structures that hold sway. The earliest of these five historical stages was the communal (or Asiatic) epoch. This was an agrarian stage suited for a simple, rural life, but its productive potential was limited by a lack of technology and specialization. What follows is a slave economy, which provides for specialized labor by dividing society into classes: slave and master. A higher level of productivity that arises from increased specialization among workers makes possible the emergence of towns and small cities. Once we arrive at this concentration of skilled workers, craft guilds, which relied upon the proximity of skilled workers to one another and provided an even greater level of specialization and productivity than the slave economy, became an important economic force.

Out of this comes a third stage, a feudal economy in which apprentices were essentially slave labor to guild masters and the serfs who produced the food were virtually slaves of the feudal lord. Therefore, while the nature of both the haves and have-nots changed, the division of society into classes that began in the slave economy continued in the feudal stage. As the goods manufactured by the guilds increased productivity, fewer workers were needed in the agricultural economy, which resulted in an outflow of labor to the cities. Moreover, the increasing specialization of labor in the guilds brought about the need for money. When people produce only one product but need a number of material things to maintain life, they must trade for that which they themselves do not make. Money, because it is a more efficient means of economic exchange, gradually replaces the barter system of feudalism. This sets the stage for the fourth economic system: capitalism.

Money results in a greater level of productivity because it is a portable form of wealth. Since it can be transformed into and out of different forms of wealth—real estate, machinery, stocks or any one of many other vehicles—it creates a new way of working. Most importantly, it allows individuals to invest and acquire greater wealth while not producing anything directly. This newly created wealth is not necessarily consumed but can be reinvested to generate even greater amounts of capital. This accumulation of wealth allows its possessors to hire others to manufacture the goods for them, which results in the large-scale manufacturing and concentration of labor near natural resources and transportation centers. Because of the scale of their production, possessors of capital eventually displace the guild masters and small merchants.

Marx argues that the historical movement through these various stages could be predicted, given the proper paradigm, because the conditions of the existing system make necessary the movement to a new structure. For example, the merchant class, like the serfs, had been oppressed by the nobility in the feudal system. However, the feudal system lacked mechanistic production and required new sources of goods. The dialectical process thus dictates that a merchant class arise to facilitate the creation and procurement of these goods. Eventually, because of the machine age and the discovery of the new world, fueled by the demands of the nobility, the merchants gained such influence that they were able to wrest power from the nobility and become the new oppressor. "The modern bourgeois society that has sprouted from the ruins of feudal society has not done away with class antagonisms. It has but established new classes, new conditions of oppression, new forms of struggle in place of the old ones."[64] For Marx then each successive economic system represents a different and more efficient way of producing wealth. What they all have in common is an oppressing class and those who are oppressed by them.

With the merchant class, or bourgeoisie, now in charge, capitalism comes into being. However, Marx would remind us that capitalism is not just an economic program but brings with it an entire ideological infrastructure. For example, competition is not an idea that leads to capitalism. Instead, it is viewed as a public virtue *because of* capitalism. Capitalism creates the idea that competition is virtuous, and then creates laws, institutions and systems around this idea designed to keep the classes in their places. It is built into our education systems in the form of grades. It appears in the "Protestant work ethic." The capitalists provide their own definition of success and the good life and then sell us what they produce so we can attain these goals.

Similarly, while noble birth determined one's place in the feudal world, control of capital now confers the power to define reality. "My own power is as great as the power of money. The properties of money are my own (the possessor's) properties and faculties. What I *am* and *can do* is, therefore, not at all determined by my individuality. I *am* ugly, but I can buy the most beautiful woman for myself. Consequently, I am not *ugly,* for the effect of ugliness, its power to repel, is annulled by money."[65] Thus Marx argues that control of wealth grants the power to remake reality. To put it differently, money alienates by defining ourselves and our world in ways contrary to their true nature. "The power to confuse and invert all human and natural qualities, to bring about fraternization of incompatibles, the *divine* power of money, resides in its *characteristic* as the alienated and self-alienating species-life of man. It is the alienated *power of humanity.*"[66]

Money represents the "alienated power of humanity" because its source is the labor of another person. Under capitalism all surplus value—the difference between the cost to produce an item and price it brings—goes to the owner. The surplus value of goods, however, is created by the worker, who does not benefit proportionally from his or her work. Thus the fruits of their creative labor are alienated from them and enjoyed by someone else. "The worker puts his life into the object, and his life then belongs no longer to himself but to the object. The greater his activity, therefore, the less he possesses."[67]

Marx argues that the dehumanization of the worker under capitalism is inescapable. Because of competitive pressures the worker becomes a cost of doing business: another commodity. "The whole system of capitalist production is based on the fact that the workman sells his labourpower as a commodity."[68] For the working class, which Marx calls the proletariat, the need to sell their labor becomes an increasingly self-defeating cycle. Since they are a commodity that, like all other commodities, decreases in value as the supply increases, they unwittingly become their own enemy. "The worker becomes an ever cheaper commodity the more goods he creates. The *devaluation* of the human world increases in direct relation with the *increase in value* of the world of things. Labour does not only create goods; it also produces itself and the worker as a *commodity*, and indeed in the same proportion as it produces goods."[69] One example of how this occurs is found in the production and use of machinery. "The instrument of labour, when it takes the form of a machine, immediately becomes a competitor of the workman himself. The self-expansion of capital by means of machinery is thenceforward directly proportional to the number of the workpeople, whose means of livelihood have been destroyed by that machinery."[70]

Marx would point out that the alienating nature of capitalism is not exclusively economic. Its most devastating effect is the various forms of psychological and social alienation that issue from it. First, human beings, who as *homo faber* should find their identity in what they create, become alienated from what they produce. They do not participate in deciding what to make or how it is done, nor do they reap the benefit from their efforts. Moreover, for the owner, the product becomes the matter of first importance rather than the worker. The product is the source of their wealth while the worker is simply a cost of production.

Therefore, "the object produced by labour, its product, now stands opposed to it as an *alien being,* as a *power independent* of the producer."[71]

Second, capitalism alienates us from the material world. We depend upon the natural world for our life. However, capitalism requires the exploitation of anything in nature that has the potential to yield profit. In doing so, workers deplete that which they rely on for their existence. "But just as nature affords the *means of existence* of labour, in the sense that labour cannot *live* without objects upon which it can be exercised, so also it provides the *means of existence* in a narrower sense; namely the means of physical existence for the *worker* himself. Thus, the more the worker *appropriates* the external world of sensuous nature by his labour the more he deprives himself of *means of existence.*"[72]

A third facet of capitalism's alienating character is self-estrangement. Capitalistic economies are problematic because under them our work does not reflect our creative impulse but is rather a route to supplying physical needs. The only remaining outlet for the creativity that should characterize the workplace is our leisure time. "The worker, therefore, feels himself at home only during his leisure time, whereas at work he feels homeless. . . . We arrive at the result that man (the worker) feels himself to be freely active only in his animal functions—eating, drinking and procreating, or at most also in his dwelling and his personal adornment—while in his human functions he is reduced to an animal."[73] Marx acknowledges that our physical functions are genuinely human. They have become animal functions, however, because they are transformed into ends rather than means. Furthermore, because of the demands of capitalism, the worker becomes his or her occupation. What individuals do is who they are, but under capitalism our doing is controlled by others. We are therefore stripped of our humanity and become identified with a particular task.

This identification of ourselves with our occupation highlights a fourth form of alienation. "A direct consequence of the alienation of man from the product of his labour, from his life activity and from his species-life, is that *man* is *alienated* from other *men.*"[74] Not only do we come to view ourselves in the light of our occupation, capitalism causes others to see us in the same way. The worker is a painter, farmer or weaver rather than a human who paints, farms, or weaves. Owners see employees as commodities that have value only because of what they can produce, the proletariat considers the bourgeoisie the enemy, and the workers are divided among themselves as they compete for wages. There is even competition within the bourgeoisie as they vie with other owners for profits.

While Marx is almost totally focused on the plight of the proletariat, he also believes that capitalism ultimately dehumanizes the bourgeoisie. "There is a kind of wealth which is inactive, prodigal and devoted to pleasure, the beneficiary of which *behaves* as an *ephemeral*, aimlessly active individual who regards the slave labour of others, human *blood and sweat*, as the prey of his cupidity, and who sees mankind and himself as a sacrificial and superfluous being."[75] Such individuals cannot become whole because, when their wealth is created by others, they do not fulfill their calling as *homo faber* nor do they allow their employees to do so. Instead they direct their energies toward consumption. Consumption is not evil in itself, but when it displaces our need to engage in creative work, it turns us into one-dimensional individuals who satisfy only our animal needs.

The End of History
For Marx then history is the account of the ongoing alienation of human beings from what they do, from themselves and from others. However, the fact of the workers' alienation is not necessarily matched by their awareness of it. Thus Marx views his task as consciousness raising. People need to be made aware of the nature and source of their alienation. This consciousness raising is difficult because it pits us against the ideology created by the bourgeoisie. This ideology tells the proletariat that their low station has honor. They are promised reward (either here or in the hereafter) if they cheerfully accept their status. Bourgeoisie ideology "explains" why those at the top deserve their spoils. Thus Marx argues that the process begins in helping people recognize that the current situation and the belief-systems that support it are creations of economic forces, not part of the ontological structure of the universe.

Despite the difficulties of changing economic and political structures, Marx is an optimist about the future and argues that capitalism creates the conditions that will spell its demise. "But with the development of industry the proletariat not only increases in number; it becomes concentrated in greater masses, its strength grows, and it feels that strength more. The various interests and conditions of life within the ranks of the proletariat are more and more equalized, in proportion as machinery obliterates all distinctions of labour, and nearly everywhere reduces wages to the same low level."[76] The proletariat, as they become concentrated in factories, will come to recognize their kinship in oppression. Eventually, capitalism will collapse of its own weight because, as more and more people are replaced by machines, it will not be able to sustain even the bare minimum of wages it now gives to workers, and they will become wards of the state. "What the bourgeoisie, therefore, produces, above all, is its own grave-diggers. Its fall and the victory of the proletariat are equally inevitable."[77] However, this descriptive analysis of capitalism's collapse is in conflict with his more activist side, which we see in the final words of the *Communist Manifesto:*

> The Communists disdain to conceal their views and aims. They openly declare that their ends can be attained only by the forcible overthrow of all existing social conditions. Let the ruling classes tremble at a Communistic revolution. The Proletarians have nothing to lose but their chains. They have a world to win.
>
> WORKING MEN OF ALL COUNTRIES, UNITE![78]

Regardless of whether capitalism simply falls or must be pushed, since the bourgeoisie are not as firmly entrenched in some countries as others, eventually the laborer will recognize, "The proletarian is without property; his relation to his wife and children has no longer anything in common with the bourgeois family-relations; modern industrial labour, modern subjection to capital . . . has stripped him of every trace of national character. Law, morality, religion, are to him so many bourgeois prejudices, behind which lurk in ambush just as many bourgeois interests."[79] When the worker discovers that the social structures are merely tools by which they are oppressed and not metaphysical realities imprinted on the universe, communism will replace capitalism.

The goal of communism is to free workers of capitalism and its alienating nature and to make them people rather than tools of labor. In order to do this the entire system of private property must be destroyed: "The theory of the Communists may be summed up in the single sentence: Abolition of private property."[80] Because private property is the source of class antagonism, when it ends, so does history. By this Marx means that historical movement is created by alienation and lack within previous systems. In the past the oppressor relied on its opposite for its own existence. There can be no bourgeoisie without the proletariat. When private property is abolished, so is a class-based society. The dialectical process of history will cease because the proletariat needs no opposite, and history will reach its culmination.

Once alienation ends, there is no further development to new economic systems and the ideologies that prop them up. We will have achieved earthly salvation in which work becomes a fulfilling activity, and we no longer need to look to the hereafter for comfort and hope. There will be social peace and well-being because that which created division—private property—no longer exists. Marx describes this idyllic situation:

> For as soon as the distribution of labour comes into being, each man has a particular, exclusive sphere of activity, which is forced upon him and from which he cannot escape. He is a hunter, a fisherman, a shepherd, or a critical critic, and must remain so if he does not want to lose his means of livelihood; while in communist society, where nobody has one exclusive sphere of activity but each can become accomplished in any branch he wishes, society regulates the general production and thus makes it possible for me to do one thing today and another tomorrow, to hunt in the morning, to fish in the afternoon, rear cattle in the evening, criticise after dinner, just as I have a mind, without ever becoming hunter, fisherman, shepherd, or critic.[81]

Significance and Problems

It is difficult to overstate the influence of Marx's ideas in the last century. His thought reshaped maps as communism became the form of government under which about one half of the world's population lived at one time. This is not to say that these governments have been models of Marxist orthodoxy; it would be just as erroneous to judge the truth of his ideas on the actions of those who call themselves Marxist as it would be to judge Christianity by the actions of those identifying themselves as Christian. Nonetheless, it is truly questionable whether communism would have had such political and social impact without the ideological foundation Marx offers.

A less visible but still formidable influence is found in his understanding of how ideology comes into being. Marx is a forerunner of many groups, including the Frankfort School, some liberation theologians and many postmodern thinkers, in his view that ideas are not so much the cause of our self-understanding as the social constructs devised by various power groups to further their agendas. Most of these thinkers have broadened Marx's reduction of ideas to exclusively economic causes to include other forms of power, but the essential core of Marx's relativism of ideology remains.

Finally, Marx's philosophy strikes a nerve when he discusses the importance of work in the context of human nature. To this extent he is one more nail in the coffin for philosophies that approach human nature only from the perspective of rationality. More specifically, he represents one of the last in a long line of Hegelian-inspired thinkers who uses Hegel's own thought to destroy itself. In Marx's case he borrows Hegel's ideas of the dialectic and alienation only to use them as tools to dispute Hegel's Idealism. Seen from the other side Marx represents an early phase of a growing tendency to rely on (or at least claim to) empirical methods. In this way he stands as a precursor of social and philosophical positivism.

One result of Marx's view of the determinative impact of economics on our ideas, as we have seen above, is a relativization of knowledge. The ideas of any age are the necessary result of the economics of that age. At the same time he believes that his theories are true and not constructions of some power group. It is difficult to avoid the question of whether this is consistent. Why is his view true rather than being a byproduct of and relative to prevailing economic systems? A related problem arises with his view of historical movement. Despite his statements about his status as social scientist who is only describing the inevitable, it is clear that he finds communism to be morally superior to any other social structure. However, this would be difficult to sustain given his pronouncements about the relativity of truth.

A final criticism of Marx's ideas is that it is difficult to avoid the conclusion that his view of communist society (the achievement of which receives scant attention) is overly confident. As Bertrand Russell put it, "Marx professed himself an atheist, but retained a cosmic optimism which only theism could justify."[82] After documenting centuries of human oppression and inequality, it is difficult to believe that class disparity will cease and people will find a higher motivation in cooperative communities than in competitive individualism because of a change in economic structures, no matter how radical the change. Put otherwise, it seems doubtful that the alienation of which Marx speaks can be eradicated by economic, social and political means alone. And because this theory of human nature stands at the heart of Marx's philosophy, it throws many of his prescriptions and conclusions into question.

7. REBELLION AGAINST RATIONALITY

While it may not be accurate to call *Romanticism* and *Idealism* inherently optimistic philosophies, it is difficult to avoid the conclusion that they have tendencies in this direction. These tendencies, coupled with the positive social developments in the middle nineteenth century, resulted in philosophies that were unrelentingly sunny in their outlook for the future. The strength of this confidence can be felt when we observe that even when materialists such as Feuerbach and Marx removed the divine as the director and guarantor of a grand future and replaced God with natural forces, hopefulness remained. The prospect of universal salvation was simply relocated from heaven to earth.

Three Dissenters

Amid the tide of optimism found in Romanticism and Idealism as well as in most later nineteenth century thought, we find three notable dissenters: Arthur Schopenhauer, Søren Kierkegaard and Friedrich Nietzsche. At the heart of their protest against a positive evaluation of human existence is a rejection of reason. Whereas Idealism and Romanticism did not fully adopt the Enlightenment's definition of reason, their expanded formulation of rationality still promised them entry into the metaphysical realm. In contrast, all three of the philosophers surveyed in this chapter thoroughly rejected rationality, regardless of its definition, as a means of knowing the noumenal world. While they disagree strongly among themselves in just about every other conclusion, they are united in the belief that the world is inexplicable by means of reason and that the future of this world offers nothing positive for the whole of human society. Because of the unique approach of these philosophers it is difficult to know where to place them. Chronologically they belong to the mid-nineteenth century. They are also properly placed here in the sense that they all represent a reaction against Hegelian thought. In another very important way, however, these three philosophers are temporally misplaced. They received relatively little attention while they were alive. In the present century, on the other hand, they have become immensely popular and influential.

Arthur Schopenhauer

The earliest of the antirationalists, Arthur Schopenhauer (1788-1860), proudly took on, even insisted on, the title: "the philosopher of pessimism."[1] His family was of Dutch heritage and had moved to the German city of Danzig to pursue economic opportunities. His father was a well-to-do merchant, his mother a novelist of some fame. The elder Schopenhauer had in view for his son a career in business and, in return for an extended period of travel in Britain and France, received assurance that those wishes would be fulfilled. Much to the displeasure of his father, however, Schopenhauer developed an interest in philosophy during his travels. Before he could guide his son in a more sensible direction, Schopenhauer's father died.

After his father's death the younger Schopenhauer found it impossible to remain with his mother, who was cursed with a sunny personality and love of life, contrasting sharply with his own pessimistic disposition. He eagerly welcomed the opportunity when it arose to escape to the university at Göttingen in 1809, where he enrolled as a medical student. Once there he quickly switched to philosophy and immersed himself in the writings of Plato and Kant. He later attended lectures in Berlin under Fichte and Schleiermacher, both of whom he held in great contempt in his writings. Schopenhauer received his doctorate from Jena with a dissertation entitled *On the Fourfold Root of the Principle of Sufficient Reason* (1813). The book greatly impressed Goethe, an approval usually guaranteed to bring success in this age but not in Schopenhauer's case.

Fourfold Root was the first in a long string of failed endeavors. An essay submitted for the contest at the Royal Danish Academy of the Sciences,

On the Basis of Morality, was not awarded the prize, although it was the only submission. Most copies of Schopenhauer's magnum opus, *The World as Will and Idea* (1819), had to be sold at scrap paper prices. Undaunted, he managed to get a second edition published in 1844.

In 1820 he began lecturing at the University of Berlin, even though he had been awarded no chair. This was hugely unsuccessful because he intentionally scheduled his lectures during the same time as Hegel's. This was done out of spite for the master, whose philosophy Schopenhauer described as "sheer nonsense . . . senseless and maddening webs of words, such as had previously been heard only in madhouses . . . the instrument of the most ponderous and general mystification that has ever existed, with a result that will seem incredible to posterity, and be a lasting monument of German stupidity."[2] Schopenhauer's stay at the university lasted less than a year, although he remained in Berlin until 1831, when he fled the cholera epidemic that claimed Hegel's life. Recognition finally came in 1851 with the publication of *Parega and Paralipomena,* a collection of essays on a wide-ranging array of topics. The final forty years of Schopenhauer's life were spent in study and writing, which he was able to pursue as a result of the inheritance left by his father. Following the example of one of his few heroes, Kant, he took a two hour walk at precisely the same time each afternoon, rain or shine. Schopenhauer's routine differed from Kant's, however, in that he was always accompanied by his dog and a loaded revolver, the latter the result of his view of human nature.

The World As Idea

The foundation of Schopenhauer's philosophy is summarized in the opening line of *World as Will and Idea:* "The world is my idea."[3] When Schopenhauer speaks of the world as "idea," he does not use the word in the usual sense. The world is not something we contemplate or imagine. Instead *idea* means something closer to "representation"; the world is "re-presented" to the consciousness. Schopenhauer argues that the world we know is not something "out there." It is, rather, an idea, an object in relation to a subject. To one who understands this it "becomes clear and certain to him that he does not know a sun and an earth, but only an eye that sees a sun, a hand that feels an earth; that the world around him is there only as presentation, in other words, only in reference to another thing, namely that which represents, and this is himself."[4]

It is not difficult to find here the influence of Plato and Kant, the two philosophers whose writings so enamored Schopenhauer at Göttengen. Both believed the world of perception to be illusory and easily confused with reality. Thus any metaphysics built on it would be fatally flawed. Schopenhauer agrees but goes even farther. He concludes that reason, which had been the way out of perception for the older philosophers, is also relevant only on the phenomenal level. It is a practical tool for use in dealing with the world of perception, but it cannot get beyond it.

Essentially Schopenhauer claims that all previous Western philosophy was built on an error, which he now seeks to correct. "All philosophers have made the mistake of placing that which is metaphysical, indestructible, and eternal in man in the *intellect*. It lies exclusively in the *will*, which is entirely different from the intellect, and alone is original."[5] For Schopenhauer, "the *will* is *thing-in-itself*," the Kantian noumenon.[6] All that is perceived is an expression of the will; nature is will become concrete. Thus we have in Schopenhauer Idealism with a twist.[7] The external world has no independent existence but neither does it arise from an underlying rationality, as Fichte and Hegel believed. It is created by will.

Will should not be misunderstood as a capacity by which individuals make conscious choices from among a number of options. Individuality and plurality are illusion. Schopenhauer argues, "We know that *plurality* in general is necessarily conditioned by time and space, and only in these is conceivable."[8] In short, we cannot distinguish between things without time and space. However, these categories belong to the phenomenal world and thus tell us nothing about what really is. "But time has no absolute existence; it is not the mode and manner of the being-in-itself of things, but merely the form of our *knowledge* of the existence and the inner being of ourselves and of all things."[9] When we erase the categories of time and space from external reality, we also remove the distinction between ourselves and others. All is will, and will is unified. It is not something we possess. We as individuals are an expression of will.

Schopenhauer defines will more precisely as the *will to live*. We see the drive to sustain life throughout the universe, even in "the force by with the crystal is formed, the force that turns the magnet to the North Pole . . .

and finally even gravitation."[10] This will to live is even more apparent in the animate world, especially in each species' quest to sustain itself through procreation. This desire is replicated in all living things, although it manifests itself differently in humans from the animal and plant world because of our rational capacities. "In the animal we see the will-to-live more naked, as it were, than in man, where it is clothed in so much knowledge, and, moreover, is so veiled by the capacity for dissimulation that its true nature only comes to light almost by chance and in isolated cases."[11] The fact that reason "veils" the will to live reveals that reason is not the source of our drive for survival but the *means*. It is at the service of the will to live and is thus secondary. Stated otherwise, rational activities geared toward survival are simply an objectification of the will.

It is the overwhelming drive of the will to live that accounts for Schopenhauer's famous pessimism. In a nutshell this will to live is always frustrated. Everything and everyone eventually dies. More significantly, for one entity to live, others must die. "This world is the battle-ground of tormented and agonized beings who continue to exist only by each devouring the other."[12] This cycle of life, created and sustained through the taking of other life, is not just characteristic of the animal world. It is duplicated in the human world, although in a more subtle way. In the end, however, all human activity is "the utmost exertion of its strength for something that has no value."[13]

It would be a mistake to conceive of the will to live as rational or purposeful. Rationality is a category relevant to the phenomenal level only, not to any noumenal reality. "The will, considered purely in itself, is devoid of knowledge, and is only a blind irresistible urge."[14] Therefore, the will to live is not a will to live *for* something or some purpose. It is a naked will to live. While the cycle of life may be longer or shorter, depending on the species, it is a cycle in the truest sense. We do things for the purpose of perpetuating our life, and because we have perpetuated our lives, we do them again to perpetuate our life. The will to live is a vicious circle with no goal other than itself.

Schopenhauer's bleak outlook on life is rooted in his analysis of will. Willing is a form of pain because desire reveals a state of deprivation. "The basis of all willing, however, is need, lack, and hence pain, and by its very nature and origin it is therefore destined to pain."[15] The tragedy of the human situation is that fulfillment of desire brings only temporary relief. "Now absolutely every human life continues to flow on between willing and attainment. Of its nature the wish is pain; attainment quickly begets satiety. The goal was only apparent; possession takes away its charm. The wish, the need, appears again on the scene under a new form; if it does not, then dreariness, emptiness, and boredom follow, the struggle against which is just as painful as is that against want."[16]

This concept of will represents a radical reversal of the typical view of happiness. Traditionally philosophy considered happiness to be the goal of or reality behind human endeavors, while pain and unhappiness are the lack thereof. Schopenhauer disagrees: "All satisfaction, or what is commonly called happiness, is really and essentially always *negative* only, and never positive. It is not a gratification which comes to us originally and of itself, but it must always be the satisfaction of a wish."[17] To wish for or will something is to experience deprivation. Thus the wish (pain) is primary, and happiness is accidental. To view happiness as essential, as is often the case in Christian theodicies, is to deny experience. Thus he turns Leibniz on his head. "But against the palpably sophistical proofs of Leibniz that this is the best of all possible worlds, we may even oppose seriously and honestly the proof that it is the *worst* of all possible worlds."[18]

Schopenhauer does not conceive of any final salvation of the type generally found in Western religion. Whatever salvation he envisioned was fashioned more along Buddhist lines.[19] If misery is the result of the impulse of will, then relief comes by circumventing or suppressing it. One temporary respite from pain is found in art. Through art we rise above the individual and egoistic—the unreal. This is because a particular object or impulse becomes in aesthetics "a representative of the whole, and equivalent of the infinitely many in space and time."[20] When we speak of love in a poem, for example, we do not speak only of *our* love but of love in general. Therefore, artistic endeavors allow us to get beyond the individual or to see the whole through the individual object.

The other means of provisional relief from will is sympathy, or disinterested love. Sympathy requires that we discover a sense of unity with another; we "feel with" another. Sympathy allows a glimpse through what Schopenhauer calls the "veil of Maya," the belief that we exist as separate and discrete individuals. "If that veil of Maya . . . is lifted from the eyes of a man to such an extent that he no longer makes the egoistical distinction between himself and the person of others . . . it follows automatically that such a man . . . must also regard the endless sufferings of all that lives as his own, and thus take upon himself the pain of the world. No suffering is any longer strange or foreign to him."[21] However, sympathy can never be more than a temporary refuge. "As soon as any relation to our will, to our person, even of those objects of pure contemplation, again enters consciousness, the magic is at an end. We fall back into knowledge governed by the principle of sufficient reason; we now no longer know the Idea, but the individual thing."[22]

Schopenhauer's final word on this life is that "a genuine, lasting happiness is not possible."[23] This leads to his evaluation that "the shortness of life, so often lamented, may perhaps be the very best thing about it."[24] The end of life is to be welcomed because it is really the death of an illusion since individual existence occurs only on a phenomenal level.[25] Death forces metaphysical clarity upon us. "Egoism really consists in man's restricting all reality to his own person, in that he imagines he lives in this alone, and not in others. Death teaches him something better, since it abolishes this person, so that man's true nature, that is his will, will henceforth live only in other individuals."[26]

Therefore, we find that Schopenhauer does have a doctrine of immortality.[27] However, he admits that it is not much comfort to those attached to the illusion of individual existence. The blind, impersonal, unified will to live is eternal; this is all that is. All that is real about us is immortal. However, Schopenhauer, ever fearful of being mistaken for an optimist, hastens to remind us that this doctrine of immortality is ultimately nihilistic. "Before us there is certainly left only nothing; but that which struggles against this flowing away into nothing, namely our nature, is indeed just the will-to-live which we ourselves are, just as it is our world. That we abhor nothingness so much is simply another way of saying that we will life so much, and that we are nothing but this will and know nothing but it alone."[28] Schopenhauer's final words in *World as Will and Idea*, "This very world of ours with all its suns and galaxies, is—nothing,"[29] thus logically follow from his opening sentence, "The world is my idea."

Philosophy of Religion

After his graduation from Jena, Schopenhauer came in contact with the
Hindu *Upanishads*, which had only been translated into Latin at the
beginning of the century. While he would admit to no influence of Eastern philosophy upon his own, he was delighted by the West's growing
awareness of Eastern thought. Its appeal to Schopenhauer derived from
the belief that what we take for individual realities is actually only the
appearance of one unified reality. Moreover, the concept of salvation
embraced by Schopenhauer was very similar to that prevalent in Eastern
thought, especially in Buddhism. Both said that since striving fails to satisfy desire, the only path to salvation is to empty ourselves of desire.
Schopenhauer finds a similar concept in Christian forms of asceticism
and renunciation. "We cannot sufficiently wonder at the harmony we
find, when we read the life of a Christian penitent or saint and that of an
Indian. In spite of such fundamentally different dogmas, customs, and
circumstances, the endeavour and the inner life of both are absolutely
the same; and it is also the same with the precepts for both."[30]

Schopenhauer's positive evaluation of Christian asceticism does not
carry over to his opinion of popular Christianity, toward which he is
especially critical. His primary criticism is that it is an inaccurate metaphysical perspective. All humans, as a result of misery in the world, are
metaphysicians. "If our life were without end and free from pain, it
would possibly not occur to anyone to ask why the world exists, and why
it does so in precisely this way, but everything would be taken purely as a
matter of course."[31] While pain provides the need for metaphysics, rationality offers the opportunity. Our awareness of mortality is accompanied
by rationality, which allows us to contemplate death. "The same reflection that introduced the knowledge of death also assists us in obtaining
metaphysical points of view. . . . All religions and philosophical systems are
directed principally to this end, and are thus primarily the antidote to the
certainty of death which reflecting reason produces from its own
resources."[32]

The problem is that most people, in Schopenhauer's view, are "unable
to devote themselves to thinking, [therefore] religions fill very well the
place of metaphysics in general, the need of which man feels to be
imperative."[33] In short, religion is counterfeit metaphysics. True meta-

physics requires reasoned argument, while religion is based on authority and, when imparted to people in childhood, its "dogmas grow into a kind of second inborn intellect."[34] The greatest fault of popular Christianity is that it perpetuates the ultimate mistake. "There is only one inborn error, and that is the notion that we exist in order to be happy."[35] For Schopenhauer, optimism is not just false "but also a pernicious doctrine, for it presents life as a desirable state and man's happiness as its aim and object."[36] Christianity's view that this life has meaning, according to Schopenhauer, is a delusion rooted in the inability to come to grips with our mortality and misery. In other words, it is a rejection of true (i.e., pessimistic) metaphysics.

For Schopenhauer, the most accurate means of classifying religions is not under categories such as monotheism, polytheism or pantheism, but with regard to the question of "whether they are optimistic or pessimistic."[37] He argues that the correct interpretation of Christianity is a pessimistic one. "Christianity is the doctrine of the deep guilt of the human race by reason of its very existence, and of the heart's intense longing for salvation therefrom."[38] This requires that we reject a literal interpretation of Scripture for the allegorical. By this means, then, Schopenhauer equates original sin with existence itself and favorably quotes the poet Calderon's words, "man's greatest offense is that he has been born."[39] Similarly, "We should interpret Jesus Christ always in the universal, as the symbol or personification of the denial of the will-to-live, but not in the individual, whether according to his mythical history in the Gospels, or according to the probably true history lying at the root thereof."[40]

While Romanticism nibbles around the edges of rationality, Schopenhauer represents a frontal assault on reason. While he is in accord with the Idealists in the denial of the independent existence of the world of objects, the terms of this denial have shifted in a decisive way. At the heart of his monism is not a rational power providing the meaning and *telos* of the world. Instead we find a blind irrationality, the nature of which creates an absurd and torturous situation. The will to live seeks nothing other than life, and this will to live destroys life in its impulse for survival and ultimately ends in our own death.

Schopenhauer's Impact
Although nineteenth century Germany was not ready to fully appreciate

a philosophy of pessimism, Schopenhauer did have an impact. He is one of the first to seriously question the roots of Western philosophy and introduce Eastern concepts into the discussion. The question of what is primary in human nature is also given new direction by his analysis of will. Reason can no longer be taken as a given. Moreover, his concept of change without teleology is absorbed by many who consider the philosophical implications of biological evolution. As is the case with Kierkegaard and Nietzsche, however, Schopenhauer's full impact was not felt until this century, when pessimism seemed to many to be a logical outcome of experience. Only then did his nihilistic perspective receive widespread attention.

Søren Kierkegaard

The biographical sketches of most philosophers focus heavily on the influence of teachers and the universities attended. However, educational background offers little insight into the life and thought of Søren Kierkegaard (1813-1855).[41] He argues that knowledge and education have little to do with human existence (which may account for his attractiveness to some). Instead to comprehend human life, we need to consider the individual within the crucible of life and its decisions and relationships. It should not surprise us then that the most significant formative experiences of Kierkegaard's life come from his relationships. These and not his academic pedigree provide a glimpse into the thought and psychology of "the melancholy Dane."

The first key to understanding Kierkegaard is his father. Michael Pedersen Kierkegaard was a pious community leader of some wealth. However, his station at the end of his life is deceiving because things did not begin that way. He was born to an impoverished family in Jutland and sent to live with relatives in Copenhagen as a teenager because his family was unable to feed and clothe him. He eventually took over his uncle's successful businesses and was able to retire comfortably at forty. However, Michael Kierkegaard had dark secrets, one of which his son mentions in his journal. "How terrible about the man who once as a little boy, while herding sheep on the heaths of Jutland, suffering greatly, in hunger and in want, stood upon a hill and cursed God—and the man was unable to forget it even when he was eighty-two years old."[42] The memory of cursing God as a twelve-year-old haunted Kierkegaard's father throughout his life. Second, Kierkegaard's mother had become pregnant while a servant in the home, and Michael Kierkegaard felt obligated to marry her. These two events, especially the first, led the elder Kierkegaard to believe that he lived under God's curse, an idea confirmed in his mind by the deaths of his second wife and five of his seven children prior to his own death. It created such an atmosphere that Kierkegaard states in retrospect, "Humanly speaking, it was a crazy upbringing."[43]

In reaction to his father's burden Søren tried his best to live the life of a carefree student. Outwardly he played the part well. He maintained an active social calendar, was involved in political matters at the university of Copenhagen and took his time (almost ten years) completing his degree. However, his own words reveal that he did not escape his father's melancholy. "From a child I was under the sway of a prodigious melancholy, the depth of which finds its only adequate measure in the equally prodigious dexterity I possessed of hiding it under an apparent gaiety and *joie de vivre*. So far back as I can barely remember, my one joy was that nobody could discover how unhappy I felt."[44] This unhappiness was so intense that he writes elsewhere, "I have just returned from a party of which I was the life and soul; wit poured from my lips, everyone laughed and admired me—but I went away—and the dash should be as long as the earth's orbit ——————————————————————————————— and wanted to shoot myself."[45]

A second relationship of importance is Kierkegaard's engagement to Regine Olsen. The two met shortly after her fourteenth birthday and became engaged three years later (1840). Immediately Kierkegaard came to believe that he had made a mistake, even though he had deep affection for her. A year later, despite Regine's pleas not to end the engagement, Kierkegaard broke the relationship. There is much debate about the reason. Kierkegaard had his own dark secret, which he refers to obliquely in his journal. One night after a drunken party, he woke up next to a prostitute with no memory of what had occurred. Perhaps he felt himself unworthy since he had not told Regine of this experience. In other places Kierkegaard says that he believed himself unable to love God with the requisite passion while also fulfilling his duty of love to a spouse. He felt himself forced into one of the "either/or" choices Christians must make.

Regine married another man shortly after the engagement ended, but Kierkegaard remained single throughout his life. He also did not accept a pastorate, although he passed his theological examinations and spoke occasionally of taking a parish. Instead he spent his life writing, made possible by an inheritance left by his father. In view of his short life he was extremely prolific, and there is evidence that the energy expended in his writing contributed to his early death at forty-two. However, he worked almost as hard at giving the impression that his writing came without effort. Kierkegaard was a constant fixture at concerts, plays and parties. Legend has it that he would arrive at a play, mingle beforehand, take his seat, leave as the lights went down to continue his writing and then return to the theater in time for the end to lead others to believe that he had been there throughout. At his death he was almost completely unknown outside the Scandinavian countries, and there was little evidence he would become the father of one of the most potent philosophical schools of the twentieth century: existentialism.

Kierkegaard's Mission

As complex as Kierkegaard's psyche was, his mission is simple. He wants to awaken Christendom to the difficulty of becoming a Christian. *Christendom,* as Kierkegaard uses the term, is institutional religion.[46] Christendom makes Christianity easy; it does not require a life-rending decision or passion. Instead one must only follow the crowd. As Kierkegaard describes it, "There are many people who reach their conclusions about life like schoolboys; they cheat their master by copying the answer out of a book without having worked out the sum for themselves."[47] This attitude toward Christianity was certainly possible in the Lutheran Denmark of Kierkegaard's day, where being a Christian was often considered the equivalent of being a good citizen.

In Kierkegaard's view the difference between Christianity and Christendom is radical: "The thought of Christianity was to want to change everything. The result of the Christianity of 'Christendom' is that everything, absolutely everything, has remained as it was, only everything has assumed the name of 'Christian'—and so (musicians, strike up the tune!) we live a life of paganism."[48] The goal of his writing is to awaken his readers to the danger of "copying the crowd's answers" and direct them toward the Christianity of passion and commitment. Following Christ means that Christians cannot "have their cake and eat it too." It is an either/or choice. "The inquiring subject must be in one or the other of two situations. Either he is in faith convinced of the truth of Christianity, and in faith assured of his own relationship to it; in which case he cannot be infinitely interested in all the rest. . . . Or the inquirer is, on the other hand, not in an attitude of faith, but objectively in an attitude of contemplation, and hence not infinitely interested in the determination of the question."[49] Kierkegaard argues that Christianity requires a decision of life-encompassing commitment.

The difficulty of Kierkegaard's mission is that "crowd-think" so permeated the minds of most people that they would not respond to a direct offensive against it. "No, an illusion can never be destroyed directly, and only by indirect means can it be radically removed. If it is an illusion that all are Christians—and if there is anything to be done about it, it must be done indirectly, not by one who vociferously proclaims himself an extraordinary Christian, but by one who, better instructed, is ready to declare that he is not a Christian at all."[50] This helps clear up some of the confusion created by Kierkegaard's style of writing. Several of his most important works are pseudonymous and reflect a view that is not fully his own in order to demonstrate the characteristics and shortcomings of different modes of life. By means of this indirect form of communication he hopes to awaken people to the folly of a life consumed with temporal concerns and move them toward a life of passionate commitment.[51]

Kierkegaard's message is a response to Hegel's philosophy, which was enjoying great popularity throughout the Continent at the time. As we have seen in chapter four, Hegel devised a philosophical system intended to address every aspect of life. However, Kierkegaard's response to Hegel is that despite its intentions his massive philosophical structure is far removed from everyday experience. We get an impressive system but are unable to locate ourselves within it because everything is reduced to the abstract. Kierkegaard, in contrast, argues that life demands decisions in concrete circumstances. Thus Kierkegaard says of the situation facing Hegel and all who rely on systematic thought, "A thinker erects an immense building, a system, a system which embraces the whole of existence and world-history etc.—and if we contemplate his personal life, we discover to our astonishment this terrible and ludicrous fact, that he himself personally does not live in this immense high-vaulted palace, but in a barn alongside of it, or in a dog kennel, or at the most in the porter's lodge."[52] Not even Hegel lives a system.

Philosophy has become separated from real life, Kierkegaard says, because it was lured away by math and science, which are reducible to abstract systems of objective knowledge. He acknowledges that science, or objective knowledge, has its place. As he writes in his journal, "I certainly do not deny that I still recognize an imperative of understanding and that through it one can work upon men." However, he follows this immediately with, "But it must be taken up into my life, and that is what I now recognize as the most important thing."[53] Objective information does little to address the human predicament because it views us only as knowing and not acting subjects. Once we know, we must decide. However, this second step—the decision—is one that most fail to take, and without it we fail to become truly human. Against the all-important demand that the individual commit his or her life by choice, objective knowledge becomes incidental.

Hegel's system allows that individuals might make choices, but these are ultimately irrelevant in relation to the gradual unfolding of the Spirit, which pulls all things toward some goal of its own making. For Kierkegaard, individual decision is the crux of life. It is only in the process of choosing that we exist. This indicates that the term "existence" assumes a unique meaning for Kierkegaard. It refers to much more than the fact of our being. A particular state of affairs, objective existence, is of little importance. As he puts it, "A fly, when it is, has as much being as God . . . for factual being is subject to the dialectic of Hamlet: to be or not to be."[54] Kierkegaard contends that true existence is not a factual matter but one of passionate commitment. Existence is determined by a person's decision to invest him- or herself. This is the result of two significant features of human life.

First, objects are what they are. Their identity is established from the beginning. Human beings are different; we are able to transcend the factual by means of choice. However, most never get beyond the factual. They follow the crowd and simply assume another's identity, thus becoming objects rather than true individuals. In contrast, the "existing individual" makes his or her identity a matter of conscious decision. This is not a once for all choice, however. "An existing individual is constantly in process of becoming."[55] The question of our identity is never settled as long as we are called to decide: in other words, as long as we live.

A second thing that distinguishes humans from objects is that we are not tied to the immediate. Human existence has also an eternal aspect. As Kierkegaard puts it, "Existence is the child that is born of the infinite and the finite, the eternal and the temporal, and is therefore a constant striving."[56] It is the eternal aspect of human existence that has the capacity to unify life into something meaningful, rather than simply a series of unrelated moments. Our sense of the eternal also tells us something of the nature of salvation. The longing that is characteristic of human life is not for the temporal but for the infinite. At the same time, this process of salvation is worked out within the temporal: in the process of existential decision. It is this tension between the temporal and eternal that accounts for the prevalence of terms like dread, melancholy, absurd and paradox in Kierkegaard. We strive for the infinite in the context of finitude.

The Three Stages

Kierkegaard's understanding of the problem of existence and identity is best illustrated by his analysis of what are often called the three stages. To refer to them as "stages" is proper insofar as they mark a movement from lower to higher. However, it is more precise to see them, not as stages, but as ways of living. While Kierkegaard believes we must move through the lower to get to the higher, the transition between the stages is not a seamless process of inevitable development. Neither is it simply a matter of changing paradigms or philosophies. A conscious decision, or leap, in which we dedicate ourselves to a particular posture toward life, is required to progress from one stage to another.

The first stage, the aesthetic, is one in which a person is consumed by the temporal and immediate. The needs, desires and impulses of the senses are the sole guide. This need not be a life of crass sensuality (although it can be). It may also manifest itself as a love of art, high culture, philosophy or religion. The common point is that the aesthetic individual does not choose in any real sense. Although the aesthete makes decisions, they are not *existential* decisions since the only question considered is whether this or that will fulfill a particular sensual desire. "The aesthetic choice is either entirely immediate and to that extent no choice, or it loses itself in the multifarious."[57] This mode of life, Kierkegaard believes, is unfortunately characteristic of most people. "The majority of men do never really manage in their whole life to be more than they were in childhood and youth, namely, immediacy with the addition of a little dose of self-reflection."[58]

Aesthetic individuals are condemned because they do not really live. He or she is only a spectator who fails to understand the importance or implications of decisions. There is no awareness that the either/or of choice represents real difference. Kierkegaard says of the aesthetic person, "You listen to their exposition of the case and then say, 'Yes, I perceive perfectly that there are two possibilities, one can either do this, or that. My sincere opinion and my friendly counsel is as follows: Do it/or don't do it—you will regret both.'"[59] This indifferent attitude toward choice can become cynicism, as we see in the quote above, or can manifest itself as a reckless and carefree attitude. In any event, the aesthetic individual refuses to make a choice and therefore cannot become an existing individual.

The result of the failure to choose is boredom and melancholy. The aesthetic life, which is "absolutely committed to relative ends,"[60] fails to give due attention to our need for the absolute. Because the resources of the immediate cannot bear the weight of our longing for the eternal, boredom is inevitable. The boredom of the aesthetic stage leads to despair and confronts us with a choice. *Either* we seek ever-new variations of the immediate in search of salvation, *or* we abandon the immediate and seek salvation elsewhere.

If the latter choice is made, we enter the ethical stage. In this mode of life we view others as valuable and acknowledge this by honoring their rights. Since the rights of one person assume the responsibilities of others, laws outlining these duties are necessary. "The ethical as such is the universal, and as the universal it applies to everyone, which can be put from another point of view by saying that it applies at every moment."[61] Recognition of law adds a feature not present in the earlier stage. On the aesthetic level, right and wrong are not yet relevant categories because decisions are accorded no significance. The possibility of the ethical life arises only when one sets aside sensual desire out of concern for universal standards. Choices, as Kierkegaard defines them, can now be made because a standard that transcends the immediate and transient is acknowledged.

Kierkegaard's description of this stage is a thinly veiled version of Kantian ethics. Kant pictures the human as autonomous moral agent. Everything depends on the individual. Each must formulate universal law and act in accordance with it. Moreover, Kant understood these duties as objective. They are obvious to any rational agent willing to put aside personal desires and wishes. Moral law's demands are absolute and binding on all people, and the moral agent's goodness or badness is tied to the degree of success attained in negotiating the duties imposed by these universal imperatives. For Kierkegaard, however, the ethical life is doomed to failure because it fails to recognize the totality of human sinfulness. The problem of seeking fulfillment in the ethical is threefold. First, the greater awareness we have of the demands of universal law, the more acutely we become aware of our failure to keep it. Moreover, our failures are not simply mistakes on the level of mathematical errors or incomplete information. Instead moral failure is what Christianity calls sin. Finally, because the law is abstract and impersonal, there is no hope of forgiveness. Forgiveness is a transaction that is possible only between persons.

With a recognition of the hopelessness of the ethical level comes despair. Just as the despair of the aesthetic level may prompt movement to the ethical, the despair of the ethical prepares us for the next stage. Movement to the third stage, the religious stage, requires a "leap of faith." Through faith we can know God, not as an object or component of an intellectual system but as subject and personal. While the hallmarks of the previous stage were objectivity and universality, the religious level is characterized by subjectivity and individuality. Stated otherwise, what distinguishes these two modes of life is not primarily what we do but the manner in which it is done. From Kant's perspective ethical activity requires detachment. This was the purpose of moral law. We rely on its dictates to direct our actions, and its objectivity takes our desires and whims out of play. In contrast, Kierkegaard states, "Now if Christianity is essentially something objective, it is necessary for the observer to be objective. But if Christianity is essentially subjectivity, it is a mistake for the observer to be objective."[62] The one who assumes an objective posture risks only the possibility of defending a wrong answer. However, the one who holds to Christianity with infinite passion risks everything: "Without risk there is no faith."[63] Thus the religious stage, unlike the ethical, requires subjective involvement.

A second distinction between the religious and the ethical stages is the goal toward which action is directed. Since the law has universal validity, the ethical stage is one in which talk of God as the source or guarantor of law is possible. However, while God can be a component of an ethical system, Kierkegaard disputes the notion that universal law is the means by which we enter into relationship with God. "The duty becomes duty to God by being referred to God, but I do not enter into relation with God in the duty itself. Thus it is a duty to love one's neighbour; it is a duty in so far as it is referred to God; yet it is not God that I come in relation to in the duty but the neighbour I love."[64] While our relationships with others are ordered by law, these relationships remain relative. The goal of the religious stage is, however, the realization of an eternal *telos*. Kierkegaard sees the ethical, which regulates our relationships with others, as valid, but its significance pales against our quest for the infinite, which is gained only through a leap of faith.

The Knight of Faith

Kierkegaard illustrates the individual and subjective character of faith by contrasting the knight of faith and the knight of infinite resignation. Kierkegaard uses King Agamemnon as an example of the knight of infinite resignation. On the way to battle the winds ceased, and Agamemnon's fleet is stranded at sea. He is informed that the gods have suffered offense and that the winds will resume only with the sacrifice of his daughter, Iphigenea. With provisions running low, Agamemnon is faced with a choice. *Either* he can heed his personal desire to spare his daughter's life *or* fulfill his ethical duty to act for the good of the greater number. In the face of this either/or situation Agamemnon chooses the latter and thus can be seen as a hero in the ethical sense. While his decision is tragic, his action is ethically comprehensible, even to the victim, because it conforms to the canons of rationality. "She [Iphigenea] is able to understand Agamemnon because his undertaking expresses the universal."[65]

In contrast to Agamemnon is the knight of faith, for whom Abraham is the model. Abraham, like Agamemnon, is called to sacrifice his offspring Isaac. What makes this case different, however, is that we cannot consider Abraham's willingness to sacrifice Isaac as laudable on moral grounds. Unlike Agamemnon's choice, this is not the tragic sacrifice of one for the good of the many. Isaac's death will not benefit others. In fact, Abraham fully intends to engage in an act that violates universal moral laws governing the sanctity of life and the obligation of parent to child with no greater good in view.

We see from this story, according to Kierkegaard, the subjective nature of faith. Abraham's actions are inexplicable in ethical terms. There is no objective standard to which appeal can be made. By any such standards Abraham must surely be seen as mad or murderous, not as a hero. "The difference between the tragic hero and Abraham is obvious enough. The tragic hero stays within the ethical. He lets an expression of the ethical have its telos in a higher expression of the ethical; he reduces the ethical relation between father and son, or daughter and father, to a sentiment that has its dialectic in its relation to the idea of the ethical life. . . . With Abraham it is different. In his action he overstepped the ethical altogether, and had a higher telos outside it, in relation to which he suspended it."[66]

Abraham's faith requires what Kierkegaard calls a teleological suspension of the ethical. While the ethical is God's demand on all, it can be suspended for that which is greater. The relative (Abraham's ethical obligation to Isaac) is superseded by the absolute (Abraham's relationship with God). The teleological suspension of the ethical involves our call as individuals to follow God. Since this call to faith has no universal validity but is always directed toward the individual, it cannot be explained in a manner that satisfies objective criteria. Therefore, against Kant's understanding of religion as universal, Kierkegaard elevates the individual above the universal. "Faith is precisely this paradox, that the individual as the particular is higher than the universal, is justified over against it, is not subordinated, but superior."[67]

Because faith is individual and subjective, Kierkegaard tells us, "He [Abraham] said nothing to Sarah, nothing to Eleazar. After all, who could have understood him? Hadn't the test by its very nature exacted an oath of silence from him?"[68] In short, the subjectivity of faith puts the believer in a dreadful situation. "The ethical expression for what Abraham did is that he was willing to murder Isaac; the religious expression is that he was willing to sacrifice Isaac; but in this contradiction lies the very anguish that can indeed make one sleepless; and yet without that anguish Abraham is not the one he is."[69] While on the one hand Abraham is certain of God's call, on the other hand he cannot explain himself on an ethical basis. This accounts for the "fear and trembling" of the person of faith. Abraham's silence is an important indicator that his willingness to sacrifice Isaac is born of faith. He accepts the anguish of faith and resists the temptation to explain himself. To explain is to retreat from faith because explanation is the attempt to ground our actions in objective knowledge.[70]

The question of whether life is grounded in the objective or the subjective is not simply a matter of intellectual interest. Instead Kierkegaard sees it as an either/or decision directly related to our salvation. "Let us take as an example the knowledge of God. Objectively, reflection is directed to the problem of whether this object is the true God; subjectively, reflection is directed to the question whether the individual is related to a something in such a manner that his relationship is in truth a God-relationship."[71] The existential issue confronting us is not that of a proper definition and knowledge of God but that of relationship with God. Thus Kierkegaard says that "subjectivity is truth."[72] He is not here advocating a facile "X is true for you, Y is true for me, and we are both right" type of subjectivism. Instead *subjectivity* as truth refers to the way we live. It is a life of conscious engagement and passion rather than one of detached objectivity. Since the central problem confronting Kierkegaard—how does one become a Christian—cannot be solved by objective knowledge, the question of whether we approach truth from an objective or subjective point of view is an either/or decision of highest significance. [73]

Kierkegaard's approach to truth represents an extreme juxtaposition to Hegel's. Rather than attempting to defend the rationality of Christianity, Kierkegaard revels in the irrationality of its doctrines. As Kierkegaard states it, "What now is the absurd? The absurd is—that the eternal truth has come into being in time, that God has come into being, has been born, has grown up, and so forth, precisely like any other individual human being, quite indistinguishable from other individuals."[74] The truth of Christianity, for Kierkegaard, is not found in its conformity to reason but in the very fact that it is a paradox. God's appearance in human form is an offense to our rationality.[75] Rather than attempting to synthesize this paradox into a coherent concept, as Hegel does, Kierkegaard argues that faith must embrace absurdity and paradox.

Against a background in current European thought that strives to make the divine comprehensible and rational, Kierkegaard presents God as the "Wholly Other." God confronts and confounds our finite resources for the purpose of giving us that which is infinite. Reliance upon our own powers, whether intellectual or ethical, is not the solution but the problem. Rationality and ethical activity become hindrances because they address only our relative concerns, not the object of our infinite passion. Thus Kierkegaard argues that "for the whole of Christianity it is one of the most decisive definitions that the opposite of sin is not virtue but faith."[76] Our guilt and sin are total because they are always measured against God. Therefore, the ethical and the intellectual are irrelevant as an answer to sin. Both are concerned with our relationship to this world and others, not our relationship to God.

Kierkegaard's Significance

Because the intellectual world of the day was propelled by the engine of Hegelianism, it is not difficult to understand why Kierkegaard was largely ignored. While Hegel's system understands salvation in a collective and social sense, for Kierkegaard salvation is radically individual. Against the great Idealist's concept of inevitable progress, Kierkegaard stresses that each generation begins in the same place with the same decisions confronting it.[77] While Hegel urges objectivity, Kierkegaard calls for subjectivity. In contrast to Hegel's presentation of Christianity as consonant with rationality, Kierkegaard understands it as paradoxical and absurd.

Kierkegaard's time was not to come until after World War I. With the changing circumstances of the beginning of the twentieth century, however, Kierkegaard's voice is finally heard. His philosophy reminds us that no analysis of human nature in generic and abstract terms is ultimately fulfilling. Without an awareness that our identity is defined by choices we make or fail to make, it is difficult to avoid the conclusion that the system deals with someone else and not us. Thus Kierkegaard brings into clear view the primary question of human existence: How are we related to God? Kierkegaard also reminds his readers of the danger that comes when Christianity and culture are identified, a warning that gained credence with both World Wars. Finally, although he couches it in a significantly different format and vocabulary, Kierkegaard represents a return to Luther's Reformation themes of New Testament Christianity (especially the Gospels), the totality of each individual's sin before God, the otherness of God, the centrality of faith, and the separation of Christianity and metaphysics. He is an important conduit through which these ideas reemerge in twentieth century theology, particularly neo-orthodoxy.

As is always the case, Kierkegaard's strengths also open him to criticism, even by those who agree with his fundamental position. First, the radical subjectivity underlying his call to commitment appears to leave us devoid of any aiming mechanism. What if one's infinite interest is directed toward some other type of God or no God at all? Might not someone's faith commitment to another form of deity provide the same subjective certainty Kierkegaard finds in Abraham? It is not clear how we can know whether the content of our faith is directed at the proper object, and Kierkegaard adamantly opposes any objective means by which we might avoid arbitrariness in the leap of faith. Similarly, his unrelenting subjectivity and individualism appears to leave little room for the doctrine of the church. Neither does it provide a sufficient foundation for understanding sin in its social dimensions. Finally, Kierkegaard is frequently criticized for the amount of distance he places between faith and reason. Although few theologians or philosophers would seek to identify one with the other, many will question whether faith and reason are at odds to the degree described by Kierkegaard.

Without seeking to downplay these criticisms, it is also important to put them in the context of Kierkegaard's mission. Because of his focus on that which is of infinite concern, Kierkegaard has no interest in the balance of a philosopher who seeks an objective, dispassionate picture of reality. The passion of faith requires him to play by a different set of rules than does the traditional philosopher. Thus that which is of relative concern, which the objective philosopher will include, is buried in Kierkegaard's quest for the infinite. Similarly, Kierkegaard's mission provides the necessary backdrop to his famous melancholy. While themes of uncertainty and suffering play a prominent role in his philosophy as well as his personal life, it should not obscure the fact that Kierkegaard is convinced that life does take on meaning within the sphere of faith. Behind the intensity of his description of the aesthetic and ethical stages is a recognition that these, when properly understood, are unfulfilling. Kierkegaard's melancholy then is not the pessimism of a Schopenhauer who tells us that darkness is the result of properly understanding the human predicament. The availability of salvation undergirds Kierkegaard's philosophy of faith. As he tells us, "No person who has learned that to exist as an individual is the most terrifying thing of all will be afraid of saying it is the greatest."[78] Kierkegaard's melancholy is perhaps more correctly understood as that of the prophet who sees the path of fulfillment, recognizes the cost involved and knows that few will heed the call.

Friedrich Nietzsche

Friedrich Nietzsche (1844-1900) was born into a family of strong Lutheran piety and in his youth seemed destined to follow his father and grandfather into the pastorate.[79] However, his early dedication to the Christian faith was not simply abandoned, but to a large extent his philosophy is defined by opposition to it. This reversal was preceded by an earlier tragedy and has led to much discussion concerning the connection between the two. In 1848 Nietzsche's father became insane and died the following year. The death of a younger brother in 1850 left Friedrich the sole male in a household that contained his mother, a sister, a grandmother and two unmarried aunts. His intelligence was apparent early in life, and he received a full scholarship to attend the renowned boarding school at Pforta beginning in 1858. From there he went to the university of Bonn, where he studied theology (briefly) and philosophy, later following his teacher, Friedrich Ritschl (1806-1876), to Leipzig. While at Leipzig, Nietzsche repudiated Christianity and discovered Schopenhauer's philosophy.

Ritschl proved to be an important ally. It was on the basis of the latter's glowing recommendation that Nietzsche received an appointment in philology at the University of Basel.[80] This was remarkable not only because Nietzsche was a mere twenty-four years old but also because he had not fulfilled the requirements for a doctorate. Even more exceptional was that upon his appointment Nietzsche was granted a doctorate without sitting for examinations. Ritschl's prediction that Nietzsche would soon move to the forefront of philological studies did not materialize, however. In a hint of what was to come, his first book, *The Birth of Tragedy*, was not the scholarly, technical tome expected of a philologist. Instead it was passionate and flashy in tone and presentation and earned him the scorn of his colleagues. After ten rather unsuccessful and unhappy years at Basel, Nietzsche was allowed to retire with pension because of poor health.

From 1868 to 1888 Nietzsche, moving frequently in search of some place where his fragile health might be restored, occupied his time with writing. Although he received little public recognition during most of this period, and a number of his books were financed on his small pension, he never questioned the importance of his ideas and wrote with the fervor of a missionary. In 1888 it appeared that his fortunes were changing. Nietzsche wrote five books, including the first part of what he hoped would be his magnum opus, and his thought had begun to gain notice. However, Nietzsche had a complete mental breakdown the following year. He was last seen in public in Turin, his arms draped around the neck of a draft horse, an event T. V. Morris describes as "perhaps the first time in history that both ends of a horse have gotten together."[81] The last eleven years of Nietzsche's life were spent in total insanity, probably caused by syphilis.[82]

Philosophizing with a Hammer

It is difficult for anyone to claim to have given the final word on Nietzsche's philosophy, and even those who have given years to studying his ideas admit the difficulty of wading through the enigmatic and frequently inconsistent works. The subtitle of Nietzsche's *Twilight of the Idols—or, How One Philosophizes with a Hammer*—provides a clue as to why this is true. His philosophy is iconoclastic. This in itself is not unusual for the nineteenth century, but the means by which he does it is. Nietzsche does not dismantle respected philosophies by use of logical methodology and argumentation. Instead he finds a vulnerable point and aims his aphorisms at them like projectiles. His short, stinging criticisms, often only a phrase, appeal to instinct or intuition. He creates suspicion. Moreover, he does not erect a new system of truth in its place. Truth and systematic thought, in all forms, are what he endeavors to replace. As he puts it, "I mistrust all systematizers and avoid them. The will to a system is a lack of integrity."[83]

Nietzsche intends to take his reader *beyond* truth. The traditional terminology of philosophy—reality, being, teleology or truth—is a symptom of the problem. These concepts obscure rather than clarify because they assume fixity and finality. For Nietzsche, whatever reality may exist is dynamic. This dynamism is paralleled in his method, which differs greatly from traditional philosophy. Nietzsche's ideas push the envelope in hopes of taking the reader beyond accepted methods and conclusions. It is a call to envision something not yet in existence. This helps us understand the diversity of judgments concerning his contribution. Depending on whom we read, Nietzsche is heralded as a precursor of existentialism, a proto-phenomenologist, the father of postmodernism, a genius of psychological theory, the intellectual engine of Nazism, a religious innovator or a mentally imbalanced pretender (even before his breakdown in 1889) whose outrageous statements are profound only to those who fear being accused of inability to recognize true genius.

The Will to Power

During his years at Leipzig, Schopenhauer's philosophy impressed Nietzsche on a number of different levels. He appreciated the older philosopher's concept of artistic genius, his rejection of rationality and found in Schopenhauer a kindred spirit in atheism. Although Nietzsche later became strongly critical of Schopenhauer, he can still say that he was "the last German of any consequence."[84] His major debt to Schopenhauer is the idea that will, not reason, is the key to human nature. Nietzsche wants to distinguish his own views on will at two critical junctures, however. First, while the older scholar considers the will to live the most powerful drive of human life, Nietzsche sees it as a byproduct of something more basic. The will to live occurs, "but as the exception; the general aspect of life is *not* hunger and distress, but rather wealth, luxury, even absurd prodigality—where there is a struggle it is a struggle for *power.*"[85] Thus in place of Schopenhauer's will to live Nietzsche substitutes the *will to power.* "Life itself is *essentially* appropriation, injury, overpowering of the strange and weaker, suppression, severity, imposition of one's own forms, incorporation and, at the least and mildest, exploitation."[86] The will to power is present in all of the movements of the universe. The impulse for conquest is expressed in the weed that forces its way up through the crack in the sidewalk, in the struggle of animals to establish their right as head of the pack, or in the attempts of individuals to modify other's lives by advocating a set of moral precepts.

This sets the stage for the second difference. Schopenhauer champions the view that pity is a virtue. We sympathize with all things in their quest for self-preservation, and by this we temporarily overcome the illusion of individuality. In contrast, Nietzsche sees nature as a bloody competition in which the powerful conquer in order to assert their individuality. Since we are but an aspect of nature, the same should be true of human society. "The scope of any 'progress' is measured by all that must be sacrificed for its sake. To sacrifice humanity as mass to the welfare of a single stronger human species would indeed constitute progress."[87] Thus Nietzsche concludes of Schopenhauer's view of sympathy, "Pity on the whole thwarts the law of evolution, which is the law of *selection.* It preserves what is ripe for destruction; it defends life's disinherited and condemned; through the abundance of the ill-constituted of all kinds which it *retains* in life it gives life itself a gloomy and questionable aspect."[88] Ultimately pity, because it seeks the survival of that which should be destroyed, is a vice; nature has no place for it. Nietzsche describes it as "hostile to life."[89]

Nietzsche's definition of power *(Machen)* is more complex than simple brute strength. In fact, on the human level the greatest form of power is the ability to impose your interpretation of reality on others. When we cause others to view life in a particular way, we have conquered. However, the categories through which we interpret the world—truth, reality, purpose or knowledge—are neither objective or neutral but the tools by which we, consciously or not, exercise power over others. Thus the problem of knowing the reality, truth and *telos* of the universe is not that these are obscured by sense experience. Instead they are not real categories. "'Reason' is the cause of our falsification of the evidence of the senses. In so far as the senses show becoming, passing away, change, they do not lie. . . . But Heraclitus will always be right in this, that being is an empty fiction. The 'apparent' world is the only one: the 'true' world has only been *lyingly added*."[90] Therefore, reason is not the tool by which we discover metaphysical truth; it clouds the issue by making us believe there is something to be known by it. "The 'real world'—an idea no longer of any use, not even a duty any longer—an idea grown useless, superfluous, *consequently* a refuted idea: let us abolish it!"[91] Therefore, the only truth Nietzsche accepts is negative: it is freedom from illusion.

Like other ideas Nietzsche seeks to refute, he argues that the concept of truth has a "genealogy." He considers ancient Greece prior to Plato to be the golden age. During this time early philosophers like Heraclitus understood statements about the world as the claims of individuals about their experience. Later philosophers such as Plato abstracted these statements from the changing physical world and presented them as universal truths. Once in place these truths, understood as resident in the "real world" to which we gain access by reason, are opposed to the sensible realm, the latter now seen as unreal or dependent. We then forget that metaphysics is merely an interpretation, and it becomes the means by which we judge our experience. Philosophy has with few exceptions been mired in this illusion of metaphysical truth ever since.

For Nietzsche, there is no underlying reality to the world to be investigated and classified. Instead what we call knowledge is simply the means by which we impose ourselves on the world. We exercise mastery over things through ordering and structuring. But not even logic, the most basic tool of ordering, has any eternal validity. Rather than viewing it as the test by which we know what is and is not the case, logic is only a grid of interpretation. "Our subjective compulsion to believe in logic only reveals that, long before logic itself entered our consciousness, we did nothing but introduce its postulates into events: now we discover them in events—we can no longer do otherwise—and imagine that this compulsion guarantees something connected with '—truth'. . . . The world seems logical to us because we have made it logical."[92] Therefore, it is not simply truth that is illusory. Any means by which we have sought to know unchanging realities are themselves provisional. This includes science: "Strictly speaking, there is no such thing as a science without assumptions; the very notion of such a science is unthinkable, absurd."[93] Rather than granting entrance into the "real" world, science instead allows us to see the relativity of knowledge. The attempts of science, philosophy or religion to understand the world are not a means by which we conform our ideas to an unchanging reality. Instead they are the tools by which we make nature conform to us. In more Nietzschean language, they are impositions of our will to power on that which is external to us.[94]

Because the thing-in-itself is a mirage, the same fate is shared by "meaning-in-itself." There are no bare, uninterpreted facts. What we call truth or teleology is actually a perspective we have imposed on our experience. More precisely, truth is *our* perspective. "Man really mirrors himself in things, that which give him back his own reflection he considers beautiful: the judgment 'beautiful' is his *conceit of his species*."[95] The view of truth as perspectival is evident as well in Nietzsche's understanding of history. It is illegitimate to compress the details of history into the mold of abstract metaphysical systems, as Hegel does. There is no history to be interpreted. Instead history itself is interpretation. Events are created by those who successfully win the right through strength to tell the story in a way that is advantageous to them. "Everything that exists, no matter what its origin, is periodically reinterpreted by those in power in terms of fresh intentions."[96]

God Is Dead

This relativistic approach might lead us to suppose that Nietzsche would see all views as equal. This is not the case, however. Some interpretations are dangerous, and Christianity is the most dangerous of the lot. Nietzsche recognizes that Christianity is attractive to people for a number of reasons. It claims to bring knowledge of the absolute and, by means of this knowledge, gives value to human existence. In addition it professes to make sense of evil and suffering and provides hope for perfection. In brief, it keeps nihilism at bay. As long as God lives, there is meaning. The problem for Nietzsche is that the desire to know ultimate reality and find value in suffering is a symptom of weakness, an inability to face the world on our own. Against this, Nietzsche issues his famous proclamation: "God is dead. God remains dead. And we have killed him."[97]

"God is dead" is intended to do more than just announce Nietzsche's atheism. It is a call to a certain stance toward life. Other atheists attempt to keep alive, without God, concepts such as truth or goodness. For Nietzsche, the death of God leads to nihilism: the undoing of all that gives order and meaning to life. This is what distinguishes him from most of his fellow atheists. "What sets *us* apart is not that we recognize no God, either in history or in nature or behind nature—but that we find that which has been reverenced as God not 'godlike' but pitiable, absurd, harmful, not merely an error but a *crime against life.*"[98] While other atheists jettison belief in God, they refuse to follow this to its logical implication. When God is dead, all attempts to discover meaning in or for life become futile.

It is in Nietzsche's conclusion that theism and all that flows from it is life denying that we find the core of his argument for atheism. In some of his earliest writings he suggests that God's role as guarantor of truth is displaced by the sciences. The problem with such an approach is that it implies a new metaphysical foundation, a position he wants to avoid. Therefore, in most of his writing, Nietzsche, who call himself an atheist "from instinct,"[99] focuses on what he considers to be the inevitable consequence of theism. It leads to decadence; theism is a denial of the will to power. "The Christian faith is from the beginning sacrifice: sacrifice of all freedom, all pride, all self-confidence of the spirit, at the same time enslavement and self-mockery, self-mutilation."[100] Moreover, God's existence means that the riddle of life and its sufferings have been solved. Christianity thus represents a protest against the intellect because it offers ultimate answers. Therefore, Nietzsche declares that "God is a gross answer, an indelicacy against us thinkers—at bottom merely a gross prohibition for us: you shall not think."[101]

This weakness is found also in any other system, theistic or not, that denies the implications of God's death. Thus Nietzsche's hostility toward Christianity does not arise because it goes farther afield than other metaphysical systems. Instead the problem is that theism has so permeated culture that the hope of truth, meaning, significance and goodness grounded in Christianity continues to live even after theism has been repudiated. Nietzsche argues that it is not the death of God alone but the death of the truth, meaning and purpose that spring from theism that is necessary for our "salvation." "The concept of 'God' has hitherto been the greatest *objection* to existence. . . . We deny God; in denying God, we deny accountability: only by doing *that* do we redeem the world."[102]

Master Morality/Slave Morality

Nietzsche's breakdown came before he was able to complete his *Revaluation of Values,* which was to be the capstone of his work. However, he had broached the topic of ethics frequently in other writings. He argues that there are two types of ethics—master morality and slave (or herd) morality. With the death of God—the current moral outlook of Europe—a form of slave morality grounded in theism would give way to the return of the older master morality, now in eclipse.

Master morality is the valuation of actions from the perspective of nobility. The noble class has its roots in the conquering warrior who is spontaneous and instinctual. These individuals do not act out of hatred or carefully weighed decision; the warrior mentality is simply the impulse of the strong to forge their own values. "The noble type of man feels *himself* to be the determiner of values, he does not need to be approved of, he judges 'what harms me is harmful in itself', he knows himself to be that which in general first accords honour to things, he *creates values.*"[103] The noble warriors are honest moralists because their behavior is not reactive. Their will to power is manifest as an open, sincere egoism that imposes itself on others, not by agreement of the weaker or a belief that everyone ought to conform to some standard of truth. Instead "it is the intrinsic *right of masters* to create values."[104] While acknowledging that such an individual would be seen as morally repulsive by contemporary standards, Nietzsche argues that they are the ideal: "Their superiority lay, not in their physical strength, but primarily in their psychical—they were *more complete* human beings."[105]

Since the original master morality has been replaced by slave morality, Nietzsche must explain the transition. The cause, he concludes, is the same as in all historical movements: it is the result of reinterpretation. Slave morality comes to ascendancy by redefining three ideas: the "good," the proper referent of goodness and the antithesis of good.

According to Nietzsche the original meaning of "good" was noble, strong and effective. It described that which was superior and powerful. Slave morality abandons this and substitutes an ethical understanding in which good is equated with altruism, mercy and humility. Second, as Nietzsche tells us, "It is immediately obvious that designations of moral value were everywhere first applied to *human beings,* and only later and derivatively to *actions.*"[106] Under master morality, "good" is properly predicated of individuals, not what they do. Finally, "It should be noted at once that in this first type of morality [master morality] the antithesis 'good' and 'bad' means the same thing a 'noble' and 'despicable'—the antithesis 'good' and *'evil'* originates elsewhere."[107] Nietzsche argues that the proper meaning of "bad" is base, common and weak. "The origin of the opposites *good* and *bad* is to be found in the pathos of nobility and distance, representing the dominant temper of a higher, ruling class in relation to a lower, dependent one."[108] It is only in slave morality that good is opposed to evil and given moral connotations.

The transition from the good-bad antithesis of master morality to the good/evil antithesis in slave morality involves a number of steps. In master morality the bad person was one unable to fulfill obligations to a creditor. Such failures are the source of punishment, which grows out of a creditor's rage at unpaid debt. This resulted in the infliction of pain on the debtor and served two purposes. First, pain is a powerful reminder of what one should not do and what should be taken seriously.[109] Second, the pain of the debtor is satisfaction to the creditor. In dominating another the creditor receives pleasure because it fulfills a will to power. Nietzsche says, "To behold suffering gives pleasure, but to cause another to suffer affords an even greater pleasure."[110]

That we will recoil from the idea that pleasure is received by inflicting cruelty comes as no surprise to Nietzsche. However, his response is twofold. First, we have been ethically conditioned by a slave morality interpretation of cruelty that is alien to our natural instincts. More importantly, however, we should not think that we have excised our instinct for gaining pleasure through cruelty; we have simply sublimated it. Morality begins in the domination of the weak by an external authority but later becomes internalized. This occurs when the weak try to make sense of suffering through philosophy or theology. No longer do we seek salvation by avoiding punishment at the hands of the strong but by escaping into transcendent truth. The endeavor to make sense of the senselessness of suffering is the purpose of salvation in all its forms.

When we seek salvation through transcendent truth, our instincts turn inward. No longer do we vent our will to inflict pain on others but use it against ourselves and call it conscience. This is a primary source of Nietzsche's opposition to Christianity. Christianity is destructive to our natural instincts because, through ideas such as sin, guilt, or the virtue of suffering, our cruelty is unleashed upon ourselves. "Man, with his need for self-torture, his sublimated cruelty resulting from the cooping up of his animal nature within a polity, invented bad conscience in order to hurt himself, after the blocking of the more natural outlet of his cruelty. Then this guilt-ridden man seized upon religion in order to exacerbate his self-torment to the utmost. The thought of being in God's debt became his new instrument of torture."[111]

This last element is a significant step. In our attempts to deny our desire for cruelty, we take all that Nietzsche considers positive in human nature—the instinct for power—and call it sinful. Human nature becomes that from which we must be rescued, thus, denial of the will to power results in our salvation. But it comes at the cost of what Nietzsche understands to be our true nature. We sacrifice our will to power to become debtors to a creditor God. "They called God that which contradicted and harmed them; and truly, there was much that was heroic in their worship! And they knew no other way of loving their God than by nailing men to the Cross!"[112]

With this, master morality is overcome by slave morality, which reverses all that is exalted in master morality and encourages instead sympathy, kindness, altruism and submission. As a result, "Lofty spiritual independence, the will to stand alone, great intelligence even, are felt to be dangerous; everything that raises the individual above the herd and makes his neighbour quail is henceforth called *evil;* the fair, modest, obedient, self-effacing disposition, the *mean and average* in desires, acquires moral names and honours."[113] From this point, it is not difficult to understand why Nietzsche sees Christianity as the antithesis of master morality. Any movement that calls its disciples to submit to each other, to take the role of a servant, to love the enemy and follow one who willingly goes to his death represents a decisive reversal of master morality.

Nietzsche finds resentment to be the motive behind this reversal of values. The strength of the masters grows out of their nature, not hostility toward those they exploit with their power. In contrast, weakness creates a hatred of the strong, which leads the slave to exact revenge against the strong by means of a morality that identifies force, egoism and strength as evils. Thus Nietzsche finds it predictable that Christianity originally had its strongest appeal to the slave class. "Christianity has taken the side of everything weak, base, ill-constituted, it has made an ideal out of *opposition* to the preservative instincts of strong life; it has depraved the reason even of the intellectually strongest natures by teaching men to feel the supreme values of intellectuality as sinful, as misleading, as *temptations*."[114]

Although slave morality is rooted in the slave's will to power, even if unrecognized or unconfessed, Nietzsche condemns it as dishonest. First, the weak person who refrains from what they call sin secretly resents those others who do what they want to do. Because they are too weak to live according to their instinct for power, they insincerely call their inability to do so a virtue. On the other hand, if the slave does sin, guilt—a resentment of self—follows. In either case the slave thrives on resentment. The only difference is whether it is directed at others or oneself. Second, in contrast to the master who knows true self-love, the revolt of the slave class is motivated by hate. The stated ideals of the weak—love, sacrifice, compassion—are really a disguise for envy. They are not happy simply to torture themselves but, claiming to act in love, turn their hate toward the strong as well. "Christianity has at its basis the *rancune* of the sick, the instinct directed *against* the healthy, *against* health."[115]

Those most culpable for resentment are the priests, who Nietzsche calls, "the greatest haters in history—but also the most intelligent haters."[116] They are, in Nietzsche's evaluation, parasites who control the herd by interpreting the forces of nature as evil. "The priest disvalues, *dissanctifies* nature: it is only at the price of this that he exists at all."[117] Moreover, by means of the cross, the Lord's Supper and other symbols glorifying suffering, the priest places blame on us. We are sick and sinful, and they have the cure. "From a psychological point of view, 'sins' are indispensable in any society organized by priests: they are the actual levers of power, the priest *lives* on sins, he needs 'the commission of sins.' "[118] In Nietzsche's view then, Christianity can survive only as long as people can be convinced of their sinfulness. "Christianity *needs* sickness almost as much as Hellenism needs a superfluity of health—*making* sick is the true hidden objective of the Church's whole system of salvation procedures."[119] Thus the priests verbally deny the will to power while at the same time using it to maintain their hold on people.

This illustrates a third objection to Christianity. Rather than exercise power via affirmation, it controls through prohibition. Nietzsche says that while master morality is motivated by self-affirmation, slave ethics "begins by saying *no* to an 'outside,' an 'other,' a non-self, and the *no* is its creative act."[120] This is the opposite of real creativity because it requires an enemy. "[Slave ethics] requires an outside stimulus in order to act at all; all its action is reaction."[121] Christianity's call for universality or uniformity is symptomatic of the fear of that which is alien. The master class recognizes that not all of nature is capable of strength and thus feels no compulsion to make the weak in their image. In contrast the weak seek to impose their values on all; they must resist all that is different because they cannot control it. Thus they demand patriotism, religious order and other types of uniformity. The result, according to Nietzsche, is mediocrity. Commonality is encouraged as the weak attempt to bring all to their level by stressing the virtues of weakness. A concrete example of the leveling-down process is the move toward democracy, which Nietzsche calls "an essential feature of decline."[122]

Nihilism

The good news, from Nietzsche's perspective, is that the day of herd morality is in its twilight. He has tapped the idols of moral, theological and metaphysical truth with his hammer, and they are unmasked as hollow shells. The stage is now set for a new ideal, one beyond good and evil, beyond God and beyond humankind. However, the transition will be painful and difficult. The death of God means that we have lost our moorings; there is no transcendent in which to ground our beliefs and actions. Without God some will seek refuge in secular systems such as socialism, evolutionism, utilitarianism or metaphysics. However, all attempts to forestall the inevitable will prove futile. The only honest option is nihilism.

Nietzsche believes that two responses to nihilism are possible. We can become embarrassed and disillusioned over the recognition that we had been deluded in the past. Now that we know that salvation in any of its forms is an illusion, many will drown in meaninglessness. All that has given us identity has been destroyed so we passively succumb to what Nietzsche calls "a new Buddhism," an acceptance of nonidentity. However, Nietzsche argues that at this point one is only a pessimist (his criticism of Schopenhauer), not a nihilist.

The true nihilist, which Nietzsche identifies by names such as Zarathustra, the Anti-Christ or the Superman (*Übermensch*) does not passively accept the loss of unity and identity that comes with the death of God. Instead the destruction of previous idols creates new opportunity. " 'Nothing is true; everything is permitted.' Here we have real freedom, for the notion of truth itself has been disposed of."[123] The Superman will actively embrace nihilism and create an identity, free of the strictures of the past. To live in such a manner is to forsake security; nature is not safe. "He possesses heart who knows fear but *masters* fear; who sees the abyss, but sees it with *pride*."[124] To create one's own meaning through strength, to *make* the world conform to one's own values in the face of danger, is the Superman's source of joy. "He who will one day teach men to fly will have moved all boundary stones; all boundary stones themselves fly into the air to him, he will baptize the earth anew—as 'the weightless.' "[125]

Nietzsche's vision of the Superman is individualistic and egoistic in nature. "The most cautious people ask today: 'How may man still be preserved?' Zarathustra, however, asks as the sole and first to do so: 'How shall man be *overcome?*' "[126] Greatness is never an attribute of the masses. Thus Nietzsche will have nothing to do with the dreams of the Idealists concerning the salvation of humankind as a whole. Instead his goal is to get beyond humanity. "What is the ape to man? A laughing-stock or a painful embarrassment. And just so shall man be to the Superman: a laughing-stock or a painful embarrassment."[127]

Summary

As popular as it is within Christianity to designate Nietzsche as the ultimate bad boy, it must be conceded that he proved to be prophetic in many ways. He predicted the onset of terrible war in the next century.[128] Against the prevailing mood of the age he warned that science and technology was not the long-awaited savior many hoped for. His expectation of a coming age in which many would feel cut adrift by the loss of divine moorings has also proved accurate. His position that the death of God, metaphysics and reality places all of our conceptions of government, education, religion and society in question has been absorbed by much of today's philosophy. Finally, he was one of the first to create the realization that our cultural horizon shapes our perspective of reality.

While Nietzsche's experimental approach has a great deal of visceral appeal to many readers, the fact that he uses suspicion rather than structured rational arguments to outline his position makes him difficult to critique. However, this method is often a point of departure for critics who argue that Nietzsche is more clever than profound. To direct an assertion against a philosophical or theological truth claim should not be mistaken for an argument that would legitimately shake such claims. To create suspicion is different from disproving. For example, Nietzsche is often brilliant in his insights concerning the misuse of Christianity, but it is difficult to locate in his writings a structured rebuttal of Christianity itself. Of course, Nietzsche will respond that rational argumentation is part of what needs to be destroyed. If this reply is accepted, however, Nietzsche seems to leave open the question of why we should accept his assertions rather than any other set of beliefs.

Related to this is the question whether his own philosophy can remain consistent with his assumptions. If morality is simply a battle of who gets to define good, are his views only a manifestation of his own will to power or are they intended as a paradigm for revaluing our own morality? Are his positions concerning the nature of the world, including his pronouncements about the will to power, simply subjective statements, or do they assume the very type of metaphysical categories he rejects? Is the *Übermensch* a personal ideal that should not be imposed on others? Does he intend for us to understand his views as objectively superior to those he so strongly opposes? In the end it may be that Nietzsche provides a rich source of thought-provoking observations and memorable aphorisms, but the problem of a system that is self-consciously experimental and iconoclastic is that it provides no intellectual infrastructure upon which we may build.

8. A RATIONAL SOCIETY

T he pivotal event for European social thought in the early nineteenth century was the French Revolution, and since France was the epicenter of the Revolution, the greatest impact was felt there. In the political confusion that reigned in the Revolution's wake, an abundance of new social and political theories emerged in France. Some, such as Joseph de Maistre (1753-1821), wanted to return to something approximating the pre-Revolutionary system. Others wanted to move forward with the democratic impulses, rooted in Jean Jacques Rousseau, that originally fueled the Revolution. Out of this grab bag of social philosophies Auguste Comte proposes a radically new social structure built on principles derived from a scientific philosophy.

While he is reluctant to admit it, Comte's ideas find much of their original impetus in the philosophy of another French thinker, Claude Henri de Saint-Simon (1760-1825), and it will prove helpful to briefly survey his ideas before moving forward. Saint-Simon was born to nobility but poor nobility.[1] He led a colorful life, participating in the American Revolution as an officer, proposing plans for a canal through Panama decades before the task was actually undertaken, making a fortune at an early age dealing real estate and squandering it by the time he was forty-five. While he possessed a keen mind, he was a visionary rather than a systematic thinker. Too impatient to work through the formal channels of education, he existed on the fringes of the Ecole Polytechnique, the premier scientific institution of France, and entertained the most prominent French thinkers of his day.

In the social ferment that followed the French Revolution, Saint-Simon, like so many other French intellectuals, pondered the question of what society needed. While he had long since abandoned Catholicism and royalism and was certain society could get along nicely without clergy and nobility, he did not think any modern society could survive without its scientists. Thus he undertook a restructuring of society under the governance of scientists that eliminated the inequalities of wealth and power that had invested so much power in the nobility and the church. The primary vehicle for promoting this new social message would be a new religion that celebrated the life and principles of Sir Isaac Newton and focused on a positive love of the world rather than an ethics of self-denial. Saint-Simon viewed religion not as the worship of a God who had objective existence but as a means of moving an industrial society forward for the betterment of society. Though many were impressed by Saint-Simon's intellect and ideas, he was highly unsystematic and prone to contradict himself or change his positions as he encountered new ideas. To his credit, he recognized the need to bring structure and consistency to his writings and hired a young secretary named Auguste Comte (1798-1857) to assist in this task.[2]

Comte, whose talents in mathematics were apparent early in life, had been allowed to enter the Ecole Polytechnique at sixteen, well before he had reached the customary age. During his short time there he distinguished himself as a top-level student. However, he took part in a student rebellion that closed down the school before he completed his studies. When it opened again, he did not reenter as a student but worked as a tutor and, like Saint-Simon, maintained loose connections with the Ecole for the rest of his life. Comte's attempts to earn a living as a mathematics tutor were largely unsuccessful, and he struggled financially until the opportunity arose in 1818 to become Saint-Simon's secretary. Though barely in his twenties he proved to be a valuable asset to the older scholar, providing a consistency that had been previously lacking in Saint-Simon's ideas and, more importantly, marrying his employer's concepts to a plan of application.

For all their differences in temperament the two men were surprisingly similar in a number of ways. Like Saint-Simon, who rejected his Catholic upbringing at the age of thirteen, Comte left Catholicism at the same age. Both were admirers of Marquis de Condorcet (1743-1794) and the French Enlightenment. Both thought that democracy inevitably led to anarchy. They rejected metaphysics and argued for a new society built on scientific principles. Although they were seen as leading intellectuals, neither completed formal education or held academic positions. The working relationship between Saint-Simon and Comte lasted for six years but became increasingly strained over the last few years. Part of the tension can be attributed to the fact that Comte never liked playing second fiddle, even to a person with the renown of Saint-Simon. And the older philosopher's insistence that only his name appear on publications written by both men became increasingly vexing to Comte. There were also ideological differences. A primary source of disagreement was Saint-Simon's growing tendency to invest the power of future society in the industrialists, contrary to his earlier belief that scientists would be the mainspring of the new order. While Saint-Simon had full confidence that laborers would assent to his ideas, Comte argued that the lower classes did not possess the intellectual capacity to recognize what society needed.

The parting of ways between Saint-Simon and Comte in 1824 had a profound effect on the younger man and was probably responsible for two rather unfortunate events in his life. First, discouraged and depressed when left without a source of income and accused of stealing Saint-Simon's ideas, Comte married Caroline Massin, a registered prostitute, the following year. The union was never a happy one, and they were chronically impoverished. She eventually left in 1842 on the same day he sent the last volume of *Positive Philosophy* to the publisher. Second, the year after his wedding Comte suffered a severe mental breakdown. He was hospitalized but left the institution a few months later even though he was declared incurable. During this illness he tried to kill himself by jumping into the Seine but was pulled out by onlookers. Comte's mother saw his weakened state as an opportunity to sanctify her son's marriage, conducted by civil authorities, in a religious ceremony. However, the ceremony had to be hurried along when Comte flew into a blasphemous outburst. It was almost two years before he recovered from his illness.

After his recovery he returned to tutoring mathematics and began writing his six volume *Positive Philosophy* (1830-1842). During this time his work caught the attention of many intellectuals of the age, most notably

John Stuart Mill, with whom he carried on a lively correspondence for six years.[3] Mill for a short time helped lighten Comte's financial difficulties by arranging support from wealthy friends. In what became the defining relationship for the last part of his life, Comte met and fell in love with Clotilde de Vaux. She was married, but her husband seems to have been serving a life sentence in prison. Clotilde declined Comte's request that she become his mistress. However, their close friendship continued until she died suddenly just a little more than a year after they met. If anything, Comte's devotion to her intensified after her death. He says of her, "Madame Clotilde de Vaux was the source from which I was at last initiated in the highest human emotions."[4]

It was this initiation into the affective aspect of life that became the focus of his second great work, *Positive Polity* (1851-1854), and the basis of his Religion of Humanity. While he maintains that a proper philosophical basis is a necessary beginning point for social reform, the masses will only be incorporated into a reorganized society through their emotions. To this end *Positive Polity* consists of an extremely detailed outline for the ordering of society. This polity revolved around the nucleus of a new scientific religion, which Comte created (with himself as high priest), that was designed to encourage altruistic attitudes among citizens. Many earlier admirers such as Mill and M. P. E. Littré distanced themselves when he attempted to transform his philosophy into religion, but several thousand disciples remained at his death. However, the movement melted away rather quickly in most places since he died without a designated successor.

Positive Philosophy

Comte's tone is similar to many other nineteenth century thinkers in that he saw all previous philosophies as preparation for his own program. And his program was, to say the least, ambitious. Comte's mission, like Marx's, was the total restructuring of society. Unlike Marx, he argued that this task must begin with new ideas. He wanted to correct philosophy by basing it on science and unify all disciplines under a new science—sociology—that he would create. Finally, he would bring this philosophy together with a new social polity and a religion he would found. The name Comte coins for his approach is positivism, or positive philosophy.

He considered the label "positive" appropriate because this new scientific philosophy would do nothing less than perfect human community. In the optimistic conclusion of *Positive Philosophy*, he asserts that "the positive philosophy will lead us on to a social condition the most conformable to human nature, in which our characteristic qualities will find their most perfect respective confirmation, the completest mutual harmony, and the freest expansion for each and all."[5]

Comte argues that previous philosophical theories had failed because they sought the origins, ultimate reality and purpose of the universe. However, the goal of discovering "first or final truths" had been attempted and failed so often that Comte believed the time was ripe to rid ourselves of metaphysical ventures for good. Instead we should "consider all phenomena as subject to invariable natural laws. The exact discovery of these laws and their reduction to the least possible number constitute the goal of all our efforts."[6] By discovering the "invariable natural laws" that exist between entities, we can predict and control events, a task not accomplished by other philosophical approaches.

Law of the Three Stages

While the natural sciences increasingly employed a phenomenological approach to their subject matter, Comte argued that empirical methods were necessary in the social sciences as well. At the heart of his scientific approach to social phenomena is a central observation. On the one hand there are certain enduring institutions in every society: religion, property, family, language and government. On the other hand the way these institutions are used and understood changes over time. Thus the study of human society, sociology (a word coined by Comte), is resolved "into two essential parts. The one, the statical, will treat of the structural nature of this, the chief of organisms; the other, the dynamical, will treat the laws of its actual development."[7] When sociology enables us to understand the dynamic of social change, we will be able to shape the enduring institutions in a way that allows for the greatest social happiness.

In tracing the evolution of social progress Comte isolates three distinct epochs that follow a logical progression. This he refers to as the "Law of the Three Stages."[8] Social development parallels our individual maturation, and awareness of this process allows us to anticipate the movement of social systems. "Now, does not each of us in contemplating his own history recollect that he has been successively—as regards the most important ideas—a theologian in childhood, a metaphysician in youth, and a natural philosopher in manhood? This verification of the law can easily be made by all who are on a level with their era."[9] Thus just as individuals eventually "grow out of" theological and metaphysical worldviews, Comte argues that human social institutions currently under the sway of a theological or metaphysical understanding of history will eventually adopt the perspective of natural philosophy (positivism).

The stages Comte identifies above—theological, metaphysical and positivist—are characterized by their different means of explaining events. In the first stage, the theological (or animistic) stage, the powers behind the universe are anthropomorphized. Thus when the crops fail or an epidemic ravages a city, it is explained by the will and activity of the gods. Because the will of God or the gods is arbitrary, we are left with little capacity to anticipate or modify occurrences. What little power to control circumstances we possess comes through currying the favor of the gods. This form of explanation leads logically to the social structure and virtues of the theological stage. If our meager control over the world depends on the good graces of divine forces, the people with social power are the priests and kings, who are appointed by the gods to explain the divine will and offer mediation. Correspondingly, the social virtues of the age are conformity and obedience to the divine powers, whose whims are communicated to us by the priests and kings.

The theological stage involves several intermediate steps. It begins with fetichism, moves to polytheism and culminates in monotheism. In fetischism almost every event is seen as magical, and divine involvement touches all facets of life. However, when monotheism matures, as in deism, God's intervention in the universe is viewed as infrequent or nonexistent. This sets the stage for the next period, the metaphysical stage, in which the mode of explanation changes. "In the metaphysical state, which is in reality only a simple general modification of the first state, the supernatural agents are replaced by abstract forces, real entities or personified abstractions, inherent in the different beings of the world. These entities are looked upon as capable of giving rise by themselves to all the phenomena observed, each phenomenon being explained by assigning it to its corresponding entity."[10] Thus the metaphysicians speak of "ideas," "nature," "Spirit," "mind" or similar abstract ideas as causal. This worldview leads to a political structure in which natural law is seen as the basis of "individual rights" and "popular sovereignty." The center of power shifts from the priesthood to the masses.

The root problem of the first two stages, in Comte's view, is that they ask the wrong question. Theologians and metaphysicians want to know "why"; they seek absolute truth. However, absolute truth is elusive. Therefore, Comte argues that in the final, or positive, stage, we should confine our questions to that which is observable. The positivist, as a scientist, only asks "how" things work. "Finally, in the positive state, the human mind, recognizing the impossibility of obtaining absolute truth, gives up the search after the origin and hidden causes of the universe and a knowledge of the final causes of phenomena. It endeavours now only to discover, by a well-combined use of reasoning and observation, the actual laws of phenomena—that is to say, their invariable relations of succession and likeness."[11]

While all true science relies on an empirical investigation of phenomena and their laws, the attempt to collapse all sciences into one, as in the theological and metaphysical stages, is impossible because it ignores the different types of relations that exist between phenomena. Thus Comte enumerates six disciplines that can be considered science—mathematics, astronomy, physics, chemistry, biology and sociology.[12] These sciences come into being in a logical sequence that represents a hierarchy. Mathematics, the lowest of the sciences, is the first to achieve scientific status because it is the most universal and abstract.[13] The intermediate sciences—astronomy, physics, chemistry and biology—are birthed in this order because each represents an ascending level of specificity. The earliest are almost completely grounded in scientific method, while the later still have some residue of theological or metaphysical perspectives.[14]

The crown jewel of the sciences is sociology: "All other sciences are but the prelude or the development of this."[15] Since sociology is the highest of the sciences, it is also the least developed. Stated otherwise, it is the last of the sciences to be emancipated from an unscientific perspective. "The theories of Social science are still, even in the minds of the best thinkers, completely implicated with the theologico-metaphysical philosophy; and are even supposed to be, by a fatal separation from all other science, condemned to remain so involved for ever."[16] Comte viewed his main task as purging theological and metaphysical remnants from social thought by submitting questions of social matters to phenomenological study. While it seems natural today to view the nonhuman world in terms of law, this had not been the case in the theological stage. Thus Comte argues that our social world—ethics, history, psychology, economy and social theory—though it does not appear to be under the control of laws analogous to those that control nature, is not to be given unique ontological standing. What differentiates the science of human behavior is not that humans are free of the power of law but that the laws that describe human activity are of greater complexity.[17]

Social Polity

From his perspective as a social scientist who sees the Law of the Three Stages as absolute, Comte has every confidence that all disciplines will eventually succumb to positivist methods. "It would evidently be absurd to suppose that the human mind, which is so disposed to unity of method, would yet preserve indefinitely, in the case of a single class of phenomena, its primitive mode of philosophizing, when it has once adopted for the other classes a new philosophic path of an entirely opposite character."[18] In his role as social engineer Comte's endeavor to bring all aspects of our experience under scientific scrutiny had a practical goal. "For it is only by knowing the laws of phenomena, and so foreseeing their occurrence, that we are able in active life to make these phenomena modify one another for our advantage."[19] The logic of his program is simple. When the sciences are properly constituted and organized, with sociology in the lead, history will experience a transformation that exceeds all previous reforms. "No preceding revolutions could modify human existence to anything like the degree that will be experienced under the full establishment of the positive philosophy."[20]

While Comte was in many ways a child of the Enlightenment, there are two notable departures. First, while the Enlightenment sought to disassociate the intellectual and emotional, Comte wants to unite them. Otherwise we deny an important facet of our existence. Second, although Comte shares with the Enlightenment the belief that rationality is the key to understanding the structure and order of the universe, he was not as confident that all people, given the right circumstances, would participate in the rationality and act in accordance with it. The intricacies of true science will be understood by only a few. Therefore, since those who wield social power shape the political structures, Comte believes democracy is unworkable, and he offers his alternative in his *System of Positive Polity*.

At the center of his finely detailed system of social existence under positivism is a new religion—the religion of humanity. He refers to it as a "proved religion," as opposed to "revealed religion," because it is constructed on principles provided by science. In view of Comte's atheism it is not immediately clear why he created a new religion, and the reasons he offers are not always consistent. At times it appears that its primary purpose was as a propaganda tool analogous to Plato's "Noble Lie." Convinced that "the real thinkers of the West" had accepted his philosophy, Comte's task was to reach those who would be controlled only by feeling.

> The next step was to prove that the *new philosophy*, which *directly organized modern thought*, could completely carry out its normal functions by becoming the foundation of the *only religion* capable of *reorganizing* also *our feelings*, the supreme motor power in human life. In a word, to the career of Aristotle that of St. Paul must succeed, or the incomparable mission I had at the outset ventured to assign myself would utterly fail.[21]

The "real thinkers" had succumbed to his philosophy, but Aristotle's appeal to the intellect would never play with the masses. Therefore, Comte must now assume the role of St. Paul and evangelize the populace through the emotions.

In most places, however, Comte argues that philosophy must unite head and heart—theory and practice—to bring about human perfection. "The natural result of making the emotional [religious] nature finally paramount will be to establish a complete agreement between theory and practice, as the impulse given by either concurs with that simultaneously derived from the other, both together aiding us in our systematic conception of the normal state and the last phase of the transition."[22] Christianity had failed in this integration of our existence because its appeal was directed solely toward the emotions. "It rejected Imagination, it shrank from Reason; and therefore its power was always contested, and could not last."[23] The salvation of religion is provided by sociology since it submits both the intellect and the affections to science. "The study of Humanity [sociology] therefore, directly or indirectly, is for the future the permanent aim of Science; and Science is now in a true sense consecrated, as the source from which the universal religion receives its principles."[24]

The proper object of worship is the "Great Being," the term Comte uses to refer to humanity. Worship of humanity is proper because it is not God but human beings who sustain and direct human existence. Moreover, Comte defines humanity more broadly than just those currently alive. "The Great Being is the whole constituted by the beings, past, future, and present, which co-operate willingly in perfecting the order of the world."[25] Our present life, what he calls our objective existence, is not our greatest contribution to humanity. Instead only after death do we enter what he calls subjective existence, in which the memory of our deeds and ideas inspire those who continue to progress toward the future. In subjective existence our influence is no longer spatially or temporally limited, thus our assistance in the furtherance of progress is enhanced, not diminished, by death.[26]

Worship in the Religion of Humanity has both a public and private aspect, corresponding to country and family, the two foundations of human social life. Public worship was designed to instill moral sympathies in the populace through commemoration, which "when regularly instituted, is a most valuable instrument in the hands of a spiritual power for continuing the work of moral education."[27] One aspect of the commemorative process was a celebration of human progress, which is brought to memory in a "yearly celebration of the three greatest of our predecessors, Caesar, S. Paul and Charlemagne, who are respectively the highest types of Greco-Roman civilization, of Mediaeval Feudalism, and of Catholicism, which forms the link between the two periods."[28] The core of commemoration was the Positivist Calendar, in which various positivist ideals and values are given special attention. The annual cycle is broken down into four week periods, each featuring a special focus of contemplation and its own list of saints. These periods are further subdivided so that "in every week of the year some new aspect of Order or of Progress will be held up to public veneration."[29] Similarly there is a cycle of nine sacraments that marks the individual's progress through the stages of life. These sacraments establish, among other things, the age of marriage, one's vocation and retirement.[30]

Those who lead in public worship are the priests. Their role differs in two ways from that traditionally assigned to the priests. First, since the Religion of Humanity is a scientific religion, the priests are the intelligentsia of the age, trained in all the sciences. Given this composition, "The chief function of the priest of Humanity is education, the encyclopaedic education which is needed to complete the training given in the family."[31] Second, because they have been trained in the sciences, including sociology, the priests are best able to understand what society needs. Thus they will be given a major role in governing. However, the rational foundation the scientist-priests offer society is insufficient in itself. "The direct influence of Reason over our imperfect nature is so feeble that the new priesthood could not of itself ensure such respect for its theories as would bring them to any practical result."[32] Thus Comte finds it necessary to combine the public worship under the priests with private worship and early childhood education in the family, where women are the primary force. In keeping with his strict delineation of social roles Comte argues, "Woman, if she is to attain her full intellectual, still more her full moral, value, must be concentrated on private life, whilst man's development is imperfect unless he look to public life as his true sphere."[33] While their service to society is restricted to home education, Comte believes that women possess a naturally sympathetic nature that is superbly adapted to foster altruism in children.

In further dividing social roles Comte separates the governing and religious powers of the priests from the administration of economic life. This will put men with industrial expertise in control of the material resources. "While the speculative class is thus superior in dignity the active class will be superior in express and immediate power, the division answering to the two opposite ways of classifying men, by capacity and by power."[34] Under these captains of industry is the fourth component of society—the workers who fuel the economy that any country needs for existence. They are completely excluded from leadership in religion, government or the economy. "It would be absurd however to extend this practice [national governance] to those still more numerous cases where the people is incompetent to express any opinion, and has merely to adopt the opinion of superior officers who have obtained its confidence."[35] While this might appear to be a condescending attitude, Comte assures us that the different role for the working class is favorable to them. "This difference is not only a guarantee of social harmony, but it is favorable to private happiness, which, when the primary wants are securely provided for, depends mainly on the small amount of habitual solicitude: and thus, the lowest classes really are privileged in that freedom from care, and that thoughtlessness, which would be a serious fault in the higher classes, but are natural to them."[36]

Thus in Comte's positive polity there are four avenues of human providence in which religion, science, government, family and economy are fully integrated. Women provide the moral and sympathetic fabric of society; industrialists direct production of material goods; the masses provide for the general providence, actually making the material goods; and the intellectuals control and rule the general direction of society as a whole. The moral core of this society is altruism (another term created by Comte), which binds the various social divisions into a whole. "The composite nature of Humanity involves its having as its principle, love, the sole source of voluntary cooperation. The constant supremacy of feeling over thought and action thus becomes the fundamental law of the human consensus."[37] While we also have innate egoistic impulses, these are contrary to our essential social nature. We do not find our deepest fulfillment and happiness on the individual plane. Thus "to love Humanity may be truly said to constitute the whole duty of Man."[38]

Influence and Problems
One of the reasons for Comte's popularity is that he not only tapped into the mood of the age but also found a way to combine so many of these elements into a system that encompasses both philosophy and social theory. First, the nineteenth century was an age very much taken with science and its methods. When Comte pronounced his agenda to reconstruct both philosophy and society on scientific principles, he found an interested audience, particularly in France and England. He

also held strong appeal for those attracted by the idea of human progress, and as previous chapters demonstrate, this represented a great number of the thinkers of the day. More specifically, Comte's idea of progress was more activist than that found in Idealism and captured the growing notion that the human race controls its own fate. Third, given the dissatisfaction in France with the traditional political structure and their impatience with what had replaced it, many were open to Comte's new vision of social polity. Moreover, in spite of great dissatisfaction in many quarters with traditional Christianity because of its complicity in old political systems and its reluctance to adjust to a more scientific outlook, religion itself was still attractive. Therefore, when Comte offered a philosophy that put science at the head of a new religion and system of governance (free of Christian clergy and the old nobility) as the means to a higher stage of social evolution, he received an eager hearing.

Perhaps Comte's most enduring influence has been as the founder of sociology. His attempt to examine human social institutions and their development, free of the encumbrances of metaphysics and theology, was readily picked up in an age that was developing an awareness of society's influence on its individual members. Similarly, with the rapid change occurring in Western Europe during this century, there was a growing interest in where they had come from and whether this might be able to provide direction for their future. Thus while Comte's assertion that our social development is as driven by laws as the inorganic world is not as confidently held by many who follow him in the study of human societies, his claim of the value of a phenomenalogical study of human institutions has found widespread acceptance.

Finally, Comte has made a lasting impression as the founder of positivism. Much of positivism's appeal is that it removes what has frustrated almost every student of philosophy 101. Philosophy confronts us with a succession of theories that lay claim to the final answer, with each theory displacing the old with a new "final answer." Comte says that instead of running into the brick wall of ultimate truth, backing up and running into it again, we simply go around the wall. Thus philosophy's traditional role is reduced from a search for final truths to that of a tool. It is now the means by which we compute and analyze sense data.

One of the problems with Comte's philosophy and positivism in general is that despite the initial attraction of putting the knotty problems of metaphysics at arm's length, it is not at all clear that he can leave metaphysics behind. For example, while he rejects the attempt to explicate the world in terms of natural law, he himself assumes a universe of interconnected laws behind all phenomena. The only real difference between his approach and some form of natural law theory, other than the fact that he rejects unification of these laws into one, is that he ignores the origin and purpose of these laws. Similarly, he builds his social science on a series of conclusions about human nature that assume both a direction for and certain abiding truths about human development. What seems to be missing, however, is some bridge between his *observation* that no foundations have been agreed upon concerning the teleology and essence of human nature and his *conclusion* that we can therefore dispense with questions of teleology and metaphysical truth.

A second problematic area for Comte concerns his method. During most of his life, he engaged in a practice he called cerebral hygiene. By this he referred to his refusal to read other philosophers or current news and journals in order to keep his own views unsullied. As a result there is little mention of competing ideas and even less active engagement of them than what we would expect in works such as his. It is this approach that leads W. M. Simon to pronounce that, "Comte's system is *ab initio* a feat of sleight of hand. It was programmatic in its own behalf, announced its own necessity, and prescribed its own tests for its own truth. It was, in other words, a tissue of begged questions, a wholly circular argument, a dogma entirely uncritical of itself."[39] While this evaluation is rather harsh, Simon cannot be faulted for calling Comte's rather infamous arrogance into account. Just as one cannot call for a rejection of metaphysical investigation simply on the basis that such questions are contentious and unlikely to yield universal agreement, those who desire credibility for their philosophical positions must make a case for their own views within the arena of philosophical discourse.

Finally, while Comte provides a good picture of the optimistism of the age and more specifically the sometimes cloudy humanitarianism that was so prevalent in nineteenth-century Europe, most such views can be passed off as naive and quaint. However, while he presents his social polity as an altruistic approach to society, it is not difficult to see how it degenerates into a rather totalitarian society under the control of the elite. While he celebrates the concept of the free interchange of ideas, he also calls for censorship of writings and speech that run contrary to positivism. He advocates the abolition of dogma and replaces it with a new dogma built on his own principles, all the while proclaiming that ultimate truth is inaccessible. Similarly, he is never clear why those in charge of the Religion of Humanity will have altruistic motives in encouraging the altruism of the masses, particularly when the masses are viewed as irrational.

Comte and Mill

It is not customary to link the ideas of Comte and John Stuart Mill, but despite attempts by each to distance himself from the other later in life, their thoughts and aims are strikingly similar. Their six year correspondence and Mill's book *Auguste Comte and Positivism* reveal a number of intersections. Mill states in his *Autobiography* with little apparent regret that he "had contributed more than any one else to make his [Comte's] speculations known in England."[40] His claim that "no great improvements in the lot of mankind are possible, until a great change takes place in the fundamental constitution of their modes of thought"[41] could have come straight from the lips of Comte. More importantly, the types of intellectual changes necessary and the goal of these changes are strikingly similar. Both considered metaphysics a hindrance to a scientific approach that would lead humanity forward. Both were ardent believers in the inevitable growth in human knowledge and that only by this means will true social reform occur. Similarly, Mill was in accord with Comte's elitism, stating that the masses must "accept most of their opinions on political and social matters . . . from the authority of those who have bestowed more study on those subjects than they generally have it in their power to do."[42] Mill, like Comte, "recognizes no religion except that of Humanity,"[43] and judges the validity of any religion by its ability to thrust us into the service of others. Finally, both believed that the affective side of human existence must be combined with the intellectual in order to satisfy the whole of our nature.[44]

This is not to suggest that Mill is simply the English echo of Comte's thought. There are differences in emphasis. Comte devotes a great deal

of attention to tracing the historical path by which society and its structures have come into present form, while Mill does not develop any such
detailed evolutionary pattern. Comte attempts to create new social structures *de novo* while Mill works from within existing institutions for
reform. While Comte intentionally avoided engaging other philosophers,
Mill read widely and commented on others' ideas in numerous essays.
There are also important differences in ideas. In contrast to Comte's condescending view of women's intellectual potential and social role, Mill is
an early advocate of gender equality. Mill also had no use for the French
philosopher's extensive religious program, which he describes as "a kind
of corporate hierarchy."[45] However, the difference that Mill most often
speaks of concerns the totalitarianism implicit in Comte's social polity,
stating that it "stands [as] a monumental warning to thinkers on society
and politics, of what happens when once men lose sight in their speculations, of the value of Liberty and of Individuality."[46]

John Stuart Mill

Every person's life involves a number of ironies, and John Stuart Mill's
(1806-1874) had its share.[47] He was ambivalent about his own educational
process, which deviated from the usual channels, but also believed education to be the key to human progress. He is the great advocate of individual liberty but constantly struggled to balance it with socialist
tendencies in his thought. Mill's fight for universal suffrage was ahead of
its time, but he mixed his democratic ideals with unapoligetic elitism. The
belief that the affective facet of human life must be developed in proportion to the intellectual went unrealized in his own life because of his
inability to break free of a sterile temperament. Time and again he
stressed the need for dialogue and contrary opinion as the condition for
discovering truth, but the basic truths he defended and died with were
those inculcated in him by his father.

Mill's story necessarily begins with his father. James Mill was educated
for the ministry but soon concluded that he could not follow the doctrines of any religious group. He left the pastorate and spent most of his
career as an officer with the East India Company. He was also a political
thinker and historian of some note[48] and the guiding force in his son's
education. He taught the younger Mill Greek, beginning at the age of

three, and John had read much of the prose material of the Greek classics by age seven. Instruction in Latin began at age eight, and within a few years he had read most of the classical Latin texts. The older Mill exposed his son to history, philosophy and logic, political and economic theory, often quizzing him during extended walks.

This education was enhanced by his father's friends, which included many of the most notable scholars in England.[49] For years the Mills lived next door to Jeremy Bentham (1748-1832), the greatest early proponent of utilitarianism. In addition to spending many evenings listening to and later engaging in discussions between Bentham and his father, John spent a year in France with Bentham's brother, also an accomplished scholar. Later he studied Roman law with John Austin (1790-1859). David Ricardo (1772-1823), the great political and economic theorist, was a frequent guest of the Mill family. Although John wanted to attend the university to round out his already exceptional education and the financial means were available, his father objected because of the religious orientation in the English schools. Instead he secured a position for his son at the East India Company, where the younger Mill remained from the time he was seventeen until the company was dissolved thirty-five years later. His work there was not overly arduous, and he had the leisure to complete much of his writing during business hours.

In spite of this careful attention to his son's education and career, the elder Mill was unable to provide affection and joy. Mill says of his father, "He thought human life a poor thing at best, after the freshness of youth and of unsatisfied curiosity had gone by."[50] His rather abnormal upbringing caught up with him in 1826, when he went through what he refers to in his *Autobiography* as "a crisis in my mental history." The nature of this crisis was a deep depression, during which, he says, "I seemed to have nothing left to live for."[51] Convinced that the reason for his breakdown was his underdeveloped emotions, he began to read Romantic philosophy and poetry. The poetry of Wordsworth, particularly his descriptions of the countryside, "proved to be the precise thing for my mental wants at that particular juncture."[52] Throughout his life he was appreciative of Wordsworth for helping him overcome this depression but remained strongly critical of his ideas.

As was the case for Comte, Mill's personal life was defined by a relationship with another person's wife. In 1830 Mill met Harriet Taylor, a married woman with two children, and there was an immediate mutual attraction between the two.[53] They took extended trips together, and Harriet entertained Mill in her home each week while her husband went to the club. This scandalized Mill's father and became a wedge between Mill and many of his friends. While Mill acknowledges that their frequent companionship raised suspicions, he writes that their relationship "was one of strong affection and confidential intimacy only. For though we did not consider the ordinances of society binding on a subject so entirely personal, we did feel bound that our conduct should be such as in no degree to bring discredit on her husband, nor therefore on herself."[54]

Mill and Harriet Taylor were married in 1851, two years after her first husband's death. While Mill had always discussed works with Harriet, her contribution became more pronounced after their marriage, and it is generally agreed that in *On Liberty* she was instrumental in moderating his tendencies toward government control. Harriet died in 1858, the same year the East India Company was dissolved. For the remainder of his life Mill spent about half of each year in a house overlooking her grave in Avignon. Toward the end of his life Mill spent three stormy years in Parliament (1865-1868), where he was a champion of women's suffrage. He died in 1873 and was buried next to his wife.

Mill's Logic
Mill is best known for his political and ethical thought, but his logic, an area of his philosophy often ignored, provides the epistemological horizon. Like Comte, Mill believed that scientific thought depends on proper logical method. Unlike Comte, he establishes this foundation by engaging competing approaches to logic. His basic argument, which pits him against Hegel and intuitionists such as Reid,[55] is that all knowledge relies on induction. Deduction alone cannot produce new knowledge. It only clarifies and tests what is already implicit in the propositions. Even axioms as basic as noncontradiction and fundamental mathematical principles are not a priori truths. "These original premises, from which the remaining truths of the sciences are deduced, are, notwithstanding all appearances to the contrary, results of observation and experience,

founded, in short, on the evidence of the senses."[56] Mill, using as an example the axiom that two straight lines can only converge once, states that "it receives confirmation in almost every instant of our lives, since we cannot look at any two straight lines which intersect one another without seeing that from that point they continue to diverge more and more."[57] What the intuitionists mistake as a priori truths are simply gained through experience and have become so habitual that their experiential origin is not recognized.

Mill's next step is to show that experience can be generalized into logical principles. Here he is at pains to distinguish himself from the "empiricists." Although his rejection of a priori knowledge would appear to put him in this camp, by "empiricist" he refers to philosophers such as Hume who reduced observation to isolated perceptions. When left at this, no foundation remains upon which to build science. Thus Mill endeavors to find an inductive approach that yields more than "a mere shorthand registration of facts known"[58] and instead arrives at an operation of the mind "by which we conclude that what is true of certain individuals of a class is true of the whole class, or that what is true at certain times will be true in similar circumstances at all times."[59] The linchpin is the uniformity of nature. Without this, causality (and science) collapses. "The uniformity of the course of nature, will appear as the ultimate major premise of all inductions, and will, therefore, stand to all induction in the relation in which . . . the major proposition of a syllogism always stands to the conclusion; not contributing at all to prove it, but being a necessary condition of its being proved; since no conclusion is proved for which there cannot be found a true major premise."[60] Nature's constancy need not be explained metaphysically but is instead a generalization constructed on earlier generalizations grounded in experience. Thus he, like Comte, argues that all that is necessary or possible is a description of the laws behind events. However, Mill appears to paint himself into something of a corner because he states earlier that "mere shorthand registrations of facts" is an insufficient means of establishing universality. It is difficult to see how he grounds the universality of nature except on an enumeration of occasions in which using it as a premise had led to truthful conclusions.

Mill assumes a similar approach and encounters a similar problem in his view of the external world. On the one hand he wants to avoid

Hume's skepticism, in which we cannot get beyond immediate perception to speak of a world external to ourselves. On the other hand he
wants to avoid metaphysical speculation about the nature and origin of
the external world and maintain perception as his sole epistemological
basis. In order to steer this middle course Mill states that the world is not
limited to that which is present to our senses during a particular time.
The world consists of a vast array of other sensations that might be accessible given different conditions—what Mill calls the "permanent possibility of sensation." This constitutes his definition of matter. Thus, "The
reliance of mankind of the real existence of visible and tangible objects,
means reliance on the reality and permanence of Possibilities of visual
and tactual sensation, when no such sensations are actually experienced."[61] However, Mill denies that this view of the external realm leads
to solipsism. "The world of Possible Sensations succeeding one another
according to laws, is as much in other beings as it is in me; it has therefore an existence outside me; it is an External World."[62]

A number of objections to this definition of matter are possible, but we
will confine ourselves to one that Mill himself raises. He recognizes that in
order to protect his phenomenalogical definition of matter he has no
recourse to the metaphysical category of mind. "We have no conception of
Mind itself, as distinguished from its conscious manifestations. We neither
know nor can imagine it, except as represented by the succession of manifold feelings which metaphysicians call by the name of States or Modifications of Mind."[63] However, if Mill argues that what has traditionally been
called Mind is simply a sequence of experiences, he must deal with the tricky
problem of how a sequence can have an awareness of itself as a sequence.
He seems to acknowledge the fix he is in when he states, "The wisest thing
we can do, is to accept the inexplicable fact, without any theory of how it
takes place; and when we are obliged to speak of it in terms which assume a
theory, to use them with a reservation as to their meaning."[64] This is clearly
inadequate since, in recognizing a problem that throws him back into the
Humean skepticism he seeks to avoid, he solves it simply by ignoring it.

Human Freedom
Mill is not content to apply inductive logic only in the natural sciences,
but he includes the social realm as well. Any phenomena, human activity

included, are subject to law and thus within the domain of science. Nor does Mill believe that imperfection in our ability to predict human actions is reason to exempt human nature from scientific investigation. He points out that we have no reservations about admitting that predictions about weather will always be imperfect, even though it is subject to the laws of nature, because of limited knowledge of the laws governing weather and what conditions are relevant to prediction. Similarly, "The actions of individuals could not be predicted with scientific accuracy, were it only because we cannot foresee the whole of the circumstances in which those individuals will be placed."[65] Moreover, these circumstances are so diverse that we will never encounter a situation in which conditions are identical. Thus while the study of human nature is a science, it will remain, Mill says, an "inexact science." However, given what is potentially knowable about human nature, it will be possible "to make predictions which will *almost* always be verified, and general propositions which are almost always true. . . . For the purposes of political and social science this *is* sufficient."[66]

Once one declares that human behavior is subject to law, there is need to address the matter of human freedom. Mill again must tread a delicate middle path between two extremes. On the one side he wants to avoid the conclusion that behaviors are arbitrary since this would undermine the possibility of sociology or psychology. On the other side he rejects fatalism, the view that all events are determined by a coercive and blind necessity. Mill's mediating view is that human activity is necessitated by antecedent causes, but these causes are partially subject to our control. In support of the necessity of our actions, Mill points to our everyday experience. The better we know a person—his character, background and drives—the more accurately we will be able to predict how he will act under certain circumstances. This does not contradict our sense that a person's actions are free, however, because character is one of the causal agents behind our actions and is to some extent under an individual's control. "Its [character] being, in the ultimate resort, formed for him, is not inconsistent with its being, in part, formed *by* him as one of the intermediate agents. His character is formed by his circumstances, . . . but his own desire to mould it in a particular way is one of those circumstances, and by the means one of the least influential."[67] Therefore, freedom means that one's actions would be different if one's character were different, and we have some ability to create our character. At the same time, "If we know the person thoroughly, and knew all the inducements which are acting upon him, we could foretell his conduct with as much certainty as we can predict any physical event."[68]

Mill's assertion that we play a role in shaping our character is a vulnerable point of his argument. If nothing is beyond the necessity created by antecedent causes, at what point are we free to shape our own character? Mill's response is that necessity is not a compelling force but an invariable sequence. However, while Mill believes that this definition of causation circumvents the problems normally associated with determinism, one can hardly avoid the impression that he only switches vocabulary. It is difficult to explain what makes a sequence invariable without compulsion.

Mill's Social and Political Thought

With Mill's phenomenalogical background in place, we are in a position to examine the areas for which Mill is most famous: political and ethical philosophy. At the heart of his social thought was advocacy of individual freedom, outlined primarily in *On Liberty*, which he considered his most important work. The evolutionary bent in Mill's thought is evident when he argues that in more barbaric times, dictatorship, with its distinction between governors and governed, was justified because of the infant state of intellectual development. However, "As soon as mankind have attained the capacity of being guided to their own improvement by conviction or persuasion (a period long since reached in all nations with whom we need here concern ourselves), compulsion, either in the direct form or in that of pains and penalties for non-compliance, is no longer admissible as a means to their own good, and justifiable only for the security of others."[69]

The quote above establishes Mill's benchmark for human freedom. As long as one's actions do not harm another, individuals should be given complete freedom to think, speak and do as they wish. "The sole end for which mankind are warranted, individually or collectively, in interfering with the liberty of action of any of their number, is self-protection. That the only purpose for which power can be rightfully exercised over any member of a civilized community, against his will, is to prevent harm to others. His own good, either physical or moral, is not a sufficient warrant."[70] Mill allows that an individual's choices may indeed cause that person harm, and, "These are good reasons for remonstrating with him, or reasoning with him, or persuading him, or entreating him, but not for compelling him, or visiting him with any evil in case he do otherwise."[71]

Consistent with his inductive method, Mill does not base his support for liberty on a metaphysical foundation of natural rights but on an argument in utility, or usefulness.[72] His argument focuses on two useful results of individual freedom. First, it is a corrective for our fallibility. A famous section in *On Liberty* begins with the sentence, "Mankind can hardly be too often reminded, that there was once a man named Socrates, between whom and the legal authorities and public opinion of his time, there took place a memorable collision."[73] Over the next few pages Mill chronicles the stories of individuals, including Jesus, whose teachings were suppressed because they went against accepted truths. Later these censored teachings were found to be useful. Mill's point is that "ages are no more infallible than individuals; every age having held many opinions which subsequent ages have deemed not only false but absurd; and it is certain that many opinions, now general, will be rejected by future ages, as it is that many, once general, are rejected by the present."[74] The best defense against human fallibility is free discussion of ideas. Therefore, "If all mankind minus one were of one opinion, and only one person were of the contrary opinion, mankind would be no more justified in silencing that one person, than he, if he had the power, would be justified in silencing mankind."[75] Unless society allows the voice of the eccentric, we constrict the possibility that new and better ideas will be heard.

In addition to the concern that we not squelch new ideas, Mill also champions liberty as a means to moral development. Freedom is a prerequisite for democracy because it requires the individual to consider his or her actions in a broader scope. We are moral beings only when we work for a goal that encompasses the whole of humanity. In Mill's view this altruistic vision of character development depends on liberty: "Wherever the sphere of action of human beings is artificially circumscribed, their sentiments are narrowed and dwarfed in the same proportion."[76]

While Mill is an ardent promoter of democracy, he is also concerned that it not degenerate into a "tyranny of the majority," in which individuals or minorities have their rights suppressed by the majority. To protect against this Mill argues for proportional representation. This is one place where his elitist ideals come through most clearly. Greater political voice should be given to those of greater education. "If with equal virtue, one is superior to the other in knowledge and intelligence—or if with equal intelligence, one excels the other in virtue—the opinion, the judgement, of the higher moral or intellectual being, is worth more than that of the inferior; . . . One of the two, as the wiser or better man, has a claim to superior weight."[77] While Mill, unlike Comte, makes no concrete suggestions as to how to proportion political power, he is confident that such a program can be devised, presumably by those of high moral and intellectual status.

Mill's Utilitarianism

Mill is the most famous proponent of utilitarian ethics but not its originator (although he claims credit for attaching the name to this system). In fact it has been said that Mill did not become a utilitarian but was raised one by his father (with assistance by Bentham).[78] In *Utilitarianism* (1863) he defines this ethical theory as "the creed which accepts as the foundation of morals Utility, or the Greatest-happiness Principle, holds that actions are right in proportion as they tend to promote happiness, wrong as they tend to produce the reverse of happiness. By happiness is intended pleasure and the absence of pain, by unhappiness, pain and the privation of pleasure."[79] In short, we determine the rightness or wrongness of an action not by reliance on rules or virtues that must be grounded in authority or metaphysics but by whether it results in pleasure or pain. This allows him to remain consistent with his reliance on sensation.

Mill is careful to qualify what is meant by happiness. First, it is not limited to immediate or physical happiness but is a state of being that includes all facets of human existence. Second, he distinguishes utilitarianism from egoism. Since we are naturally social beings, we cannot speak of our happiness apart from the happiness of the whole. "The social state is at once so natural, so necessary, and so habitual to man, that, except in some unusual circumstances, or by an effort of voluntary abstraction, he never conceives himself otherwise than as a member of a body; and this association is riveted more and more, as mankind are further removed from the state of savage independence."[80] Our social nature is the ground of our moral sympathies. We become moral beings when we consider individual happiness as secondary to the good of the whole. Moreover, Mill is convinced that individual happiness is not opposed to the greatest happiness for the greatest number but is dependent on it. Any sacrifice we make for the common good indirectly benefits us in greater measure.

Before Mill's period of depression he was wholly under the sway of Bentham's brand of utilitarianism. However, he later sees fit to modify these views. The most important adjustment was in the definition of "greatest happiness."[81] For Bentham, moral good results from the action that creates the greatest *quantity* of happiness for the greatest number of people. However, Mill argues that quantity is not the sole or even the most important means of measuring happiness. "It is quite compatible with the principle of utility to recognize the face that some *kinds* of pleasure are more desirable and more valuable than others. It would be absurd that while, in estimating all other things, quality is considered as well as quantity, the estimation of pleasures should be supposed to depend on quantity alone."[82]

The question that naturally follows this assertion is how we distinguish between higher and lower pleasures. Mill's answer, as expected, relies on experience. "Of two pleasures, if there be one to which all or almost all who have experience of both give a decided preference, irrespective of any feeling of moral obligation to prefer it, that is the more desirable pleasure."[83] Mill is certain that the pleasures deemed the more desirable are intellectual in nature. Once again his elitism is evident. Because of a lack of intellectual background most people are not in a position to make qualitative moral distinctions. As Mill puts it in his famous quote, "It is better to be a human being dissatisfied than a pig satisfied, better to be Socrates dissatisfied than a fool satisfied. And if the fool or the pig are of a different opinion, it is because they only know their own side of the question. The other party to the comparison knows both sides."[84] Since fools do not know both sides and will not choose the higher pleasures due to their ignorance, the elite must preserve them for the sake of society since, "Men lose their high aspirations as they lose their intellectual tastes."[85]

The centerpiece of utilitarianism is that happiness is the criterion of right and wrong. Mill views happiness as something of a moral first principle that cannot be argued *for*. It is instead the necessary assumption *from* which we argue. "No reason can be given why the general happiness is desirable, except that each person, so far as he believes it to be attainable, desires his own happiness. This, however, being a fact, we have not only all the proof which the case admits of, but all which it is possible to require, that happiness is a good, that each person's happiness is a good to that person, and the general happiness, therefore, a good to the aggregate of all persons."[86]

Two significant problems arise from such a position. First, while it is difficult to deny that each person desires happiness, Mill does not show how his view avoids the naturalistic fallacy, which states that "ought" cannot be derived from "is." In other words even if we agree that we *do* seek happiness, this does not answer the question of whether we *should* pursue it. Second, Mill does not answer the question of what makes one form of pleasure qualitatively better than another by appealing to pleasure itself. Thus it is difficult to avoid the conclusion that Mill assumes a standard other than happiness itself when he claims, "It is better to be a human being dissatisfied than a pig satisfied."[87]

Utilitarian Religion

Mill's utilitarianism also defines his approach to religion. Religion is beneficial when it fosters altruistic sentiments in people and is a means to the greatest happiness for all. Thus when he states, "If religion, or any particular form of it, is true, its usefulness follows without other proof,"[88] it is clear that he has no intent to ground ethics in divine authority. Although religion may have been the source and primary vehicle for some of the most profound moral principles, these principles no longer need religious props since their moral value is evident to reason. In fact Mill, following his father, argues that when divine authority is cited as the source moral teaching, "that origin consecrates the whole of them, and protects them from being discussed or criticized."[89] This exemption from criticism hinders progress in moral knowledge. Second, Mill notes that other aspects of religion, such as doctrine or ceremony, often become primary and obscure the central role of virtue.

While Mill does not rely on religion as the source of moral precept, he does accept the existence of a benevolent God. Even here, however, his views are less than orthodox. Although "the adaptations in Nature afford a large balance of probability in favour of creation by intelligence,"[90] the God revealed in his version of the teleological argument is not all-powerful. Instead the only view of God that can avoid intellectual contradiction "is that which, resigning irrevocably the idea of an omnipotent creator, regards Nature and Life not as the expression throughout of the moral character and purpose of the Deity, but as the product of a struggle between contriving goodness and an intractable material, as was believed by Plato, or a Principle of Evil, as was the doctrine of the Manicheans."[91] Although Mill sometimes refers to his own approach as natural theology, his adoption of a Manichean position requires him to reject a common feature of most versions of natural theology, which finds in nature the foundation upon which morality is constructed. If evil is bound up with the material, the moral duty of humanity is not discovered in the patterns of nature but in "perpetually striving to amend the course of nature— and bring that part of it over which we can exercise control, more nearly into conformity with a high standard of justice and goodness."[92]

Unlike his father, who was antagonistic toward organized religion, Mill has a more positive evaluation. In *Utilitarianism* he agrees with Comte's view that religion can provide "psychological power and the social efficacy" for moral sentiment.[93] The proper idea of God, even when removed as the origin of morality, can arm humanity with the ability "of carrying on the fight with vigour and with progressively increasing success."[94] The religion envisioned by Mill is similar to Comte's Religion of Humanity (a label Mill gladly adopts) but stripped of Comte's massive bureaucratic superstructure. This religion is a social tool designed to promote altruistic feelings. "The essence of religion is the strong and earnest direction of the emotions and desires towards an ideal object, recognised as of the highest excellence, and as rightfully paramount over all selfish objects of desire. This condition if fulfilled by the Religion of Humanity in as eminent a degree, and in as high a sense, as by the supernatural religions even in their best manifestations, and far more so than in any of their others."[95]

Mill's Significance

Mill is one of the few philosophers fortunate enough to rise to prominence during his lifetime, and this is perhaps as it should be, since his thought embraced the mood of the age. While it does not play as prominent a role in his writing as many of his contemporaries, Mill was highly optimistic about the future and certain that many of his programs would be adopted. He predicted that the future would bring the increasing popularity of democracies that were built on the principle of suffrage for all, facilitating greater protection of all people as well as growth in all areas of character and talent. "Yet no one whose opinion deserves a moment's consideration can doubt that most of the great positive evils of the world are in themselves removable, and will, if human affairs continue to improve, be in the end reduced within narrow limits. Poverty, in any sense implying suffering, may be completely extinguished by the wisdom of society, combined with the good sense and providence of individuals."[96] This social evolution will be paralleled by increased confidence in human knowledge. "As mankind improve, the number of doctrines which are no longer disputed or doubted will be constantly on the increase: and the well-being of mankind may almost be measured by the number and gravity of the truths which have reached the point of being uncontested."[97]

While Mill's political ideas anticipated movement in the West and his utilitarian ideas have informed much of the decision-making of budding democracies, he is not without critics. In addition to the challenges to his philosophical underpinnings mentioned above, which we will not revisit here, he is often criticized for his lack of detail in the implementation of his political and ethical ideas. For example, though he makes a case for maximal freedom in individual action as long as those actions do not harm others, he is extremely vague about what would count as harm to another. This is particularly discomforting since self-inflicted injuries, which Mill says we should not oppose, inevitably have a ripple effect that touches others. Similarly, he is not always forthcoming about how his high democratic ideals can be maintained in conjunction with his elitist views and who should be counted among the informed and privileged few. Finally, his modifications to Bentham's quantitative approach to utilitarianism seem naively optimistic concerning the possibility that all informed and properly educated individuals will find common ground in their evaluation of the higher goods necessary for the preservation of society.

Western Thought and the Struggle for Women's Rights

Mill's quest for political and ethical reform extended to a concern for the rights of women. The philosophical collaboration of Mill and Harriet Taylor was a significant event in the development of reflection on the role of women in society. Already in 1831 or so Mill and Taylor exchanged philosophical essays on the position of women in an enlightened marriage.[98] In addition to helping Mill think through the issues in his classic text *On Liberty,* Taylor was an important collaborator in Mill's volume *The Subjection of Women* (1869). In fact Taylor had published (with a forward by Mill) an article containing several of the key themes of *Subjection* already in 1851.[99] Elaine Storkey notes that this book "soon became the feminist centrepiece as educated women throughout the world read and discussed it. It had become available in twelve countries and eight languages by 1870."[100] The fact that Mill himself was an important political voice in the "suffragette" movement during his three years in Parliament is a natural outgrowth of his earlier philosophical collaboration with Taylor.

The struggle for women's right to vote, or suffrage, was not a new issue in the days of Taylor and Mill. In fact the political roots of women's suffrage are found earlier in books by women in both philosophy and religion. During the Reformation, women first began to write books advocating their equality in Christ.[101] The original concern was not equal rights in society but equal access to ministry and the right to speak in the church. A good example of this early Christian concern for women in ministry is Margaret Fell (1614-1702), a founder of the Society of Friends, or Quakers. Fell wrote the first book in English to advocate women's freedom in ministry.[102] *Women's Speaking Justified* (1667) is a good example of the Christian theological argument during the Reformation and post-Reformation period concerning women's equality in the work of the gospel.[103]

The nineteenth century saw these concerns within the church grow

more powerful, especially in Wesleyan, holiness and revivalist movements.[104] Concern for the equality of women grew in the same soil as
concern for the equality of all men, and the liberation of slaves in ante-
bellum America. Key evangelical leaders arose during the revivals of the
1820s and 1830s. This holiness and perfectionist message, grounded in
the theology of John Wesley, grew into a concern for immediate perfection and displays of the love of Christ. Prominent leaders of this movement like Theodore Weld (1803-1859) and Charles Finney (1792-1875)
demanded the abolition of slavery and were known as "abolitionists." But
the concern over equal rights for slaves and the rethinking of theology
and Scripture that lay behind it lead to similar revisions for the rights of
women. Abolitionism provided the space in which Christian women
began to preach and lead in the church and called for women to be
ordained alongside men. Antoinette Brown Blackwell (1825-1921), the
first woman to be regularly ordained in the United States, is just one
example of the path that the abolitionist movement provided for women
to step into church leadership. At her ordination Wesleyan minister
Luther Lee (1800-1889) preached "Woman's Right to Preach the Gospel"
(1853), a published sermon that was widely read.[105]

The concern for women's right to preach the gospel soon spilled over
into women's rights in society. Brown Blackwell was not only an early
abolitionist, but she also worked for the right for women to vote. In this
she was part of a larger movement of women in leadership from revival
to political reform. Perhaps the most politically important and influential
of these women was Francis E. Willard (1839-1898).[106] Willard was a Methodist Sunday school teacher, reformer, feminist and an important leader
in the temperance movement. A product of the holiness movement, the
Women's Christian Temperance Union provided the first international
political organization for women's power in church history. The WCTU
was for temperance but also provided a proving ground for women leadership and political power. Willard was educated, articulate and deeply
pious. She worked with D. L. Moody in evangelistic and educational ministry and in 1871 became the first woman college president in America to
confer degrees. While in the Chicago area Willard became involved in
preaching for the temperance movement. In 1879 she became president
of the National WCTU, a post she held until her death. Willard wished to

be ordained and published her *Woman in the Pulpit* (1889) to defend her claim. But the Methodist church denied her request.

Willard herself was influenced by a very popular Christian preacher and leader, Phoebe Palmer (1807-1874). Palmer taught Willard and thousands of women and men in the way of holiness and was one of the most influential religious women of her century. A laywoman in the Methodist church, her ministry of preaching, teaching and publishing—especially concerning holiness—was widely influential across denominations. She was "a woman to whom thousands of people looked for leadership, and by whom thousands were instructed, in a time when women were not generally accorded positions of leadership or authority in America."[107] Like Willard after her and Fell before her, Palmer found it necessary to defend her ministry. She published *The Promise of the Father, or a Neglected Specialty of the Last Days* in 1859. This volume is an extensive defense of women's right to preach. Palmer was part of a group of "transatlantic revivalists" that included Moody and Finney. Her travels and preaching in Britain brought such strong criticisms from clergy that Catherine Booth (1829-1890) published a small booklet defending her: *Female Ministry, or Women's Right to Preach the Gospel* (1891). General Booth herself was cofounder of the Salvation Army with her husband and another of Palmer's avid admirers.

The experience and popularity of women in the revival and temperance movements, which were deeply Christian, provided the platform for the struggle for women's suffrage. Two sisters, Sarah Moore Grimké (1792-1873) and Angelina Grimké Weld (1805-1879) provide good examples of this movement from abolition to women's rights.[108] Born and educated as aristocrats in the South, the Grimkés were part of the venerable Quaker tradition of antislavery reform and women's equality. Angelina's popular tract *An Appeal to the Christian Women of the South* (1836) was read avidly in the North but burned just as avidly in Charleston.[109] The Grimké sisters toured New England as speakers for the Anti-Slavery Society, and Angelina later married Theodore Weld. The conservative clergy of New England objected to their speaking in pulpits and public fora. In response Sarah published her biblical and theological defense, *Letters on the Equality of the Sexes, and the Condition of Women* (1838). The Grimké sisters, like some other gifted Christian women leaders, were convinced that rights for slaves were intimately connected to rights for women.

Evangelical religion, especially revivalist, abolitionist and temperance movements, was the seedbed for the growth of women's suffrage. Two American women in particular demonstrate this link, Susan B. Anthony (1820-1906) and Elizabeth Cady Stanton (1815-1902).[110] Anthony was a leader and speaker in the temperance and antislavery movements in New York state. She met Stanton in 1851, who was a leading figure in the struggle for women's rights. Their fifty-year friendship and collegial labors at reform changed the face of American society. In 1848 they helped to organize the first women's rights conference in North America, at Seneca Falls, New York. Stanton drafted its "Declaration of Sentiments," which called for women's suffrage. Together they published *The Revolution*, a weekly newspaper (1868-1870). They founded the National Wo-man Suffrage Association and became national leaders in the struggle for women's rights. Stanton was highly educated. She applied modern biblical criticism to the issue of women in the Bible in the landmark document *The Women's Bible* (2 vols., 1895, 1898). It is a testament to the conservative Christian character of the suffrage movement that many women leaders rejected this book because of its use of modern higher-critical methods. In 1896 her own Suffrage Association voted to reject the book and censure its author. Nevertheless, the volume was a bestseller and the first book in English to bring critical, feminist hermeneutics to the Scriptural texts.

When women were finally given the right to vote in the United States, and the House of Representatives voted in favor of the Nineteenth Amendment (1918), women in the gallery of the House of Representatives broke into the doxology "Praise God from Whom All Blessings Flow." Throughout the Western world, women were successful in their struggle to gain the right to vote during the early part of the twentieth century. While often overlooked by secular histories of feminism, the deeply Christian roots of women's suffrage associations is clear to those who care to examine the evidence. But religion alone did not provide the impetus for women's rights. Philosophers and political authors also contributed to the development of equality for women in the West.

Prior to the work of Mill and Taylor, radical French revolutionary women had already declared the rights of women. Based upon Enlightenment philosophy, several authors pressed for the equality of sexes.[111] Olympe de Gouges (ca. 1748-1793), for example, wrote "Declaration of the Rights of Woman" (1791) in reply to the "Declaration of the Rights of Man" (1789), which was a key political document in the French Revolution. De Gouges herself, along with many of the women radicals of the Revolution, was later to face the guillotine.[112]

In the period after the Revolution several women intellectuals continued to contend for the rights and equality of women based upon philosophical arguments. Before the work of Harriet Taylor and John Stuart Mill the most important of these women writers was Mary Wollstonecraft (1759-1797).[113] Her *A Vindication of the Rights of Woman* (1792) is arguably the first book of feminist political philosophy. Wollstonecraft was a journalist and lived in France to study the Revolution firsthand. She achieved lasting fame with her critique of Edmund Burke concerning the Revolution, which she published as *A Vindication of the Rights of Man* (1790).[114] Both of these books were widely read and discussed in her time.

Wollstonecraft argues that human beings are born in order to develop and perfect their rational and ethical powers. This obligation is laid equally at the feet of women and men. Wollstonecraft emphasizes the human capacity for self-development and socialization, which applies to both sexes. The function of society is to help with this process of human development, but corrupt societies too often thwart it instead. She particularly decries the oppression of women in European society during her day, but her point is a general one about people and society. It is corrupt societal environments that produce social injustice, including patriarchy. Thus Wollstonecraft called for social and family reform and the establishment of equal opportunities for women and men in human development.

Enlightenment philosophy carried to its logical conclusions led to an argument for equal rights for women. Romantic and Idealist philosophies that are characteristic of the nineteenth century were also sources for women philosophers to make a case for equality. A prominent and popular example of this trend is Sara Margaret Fuller (1810-1850), one of America's most important women intellectuals.[115] Margaret Fuller was born in Cambridge, Massachusetts, and educated fully by her father. She was conversant with Classical, Italian, French and German literature, and was a gifted student. The first woman member of the Symposium Club, a group of Transcendentalists in New England, Fuller was a philosopher and author in this American vein of intellectual idealism and romanticism. She was a devoted student of Ralph Waldo Emerson and served as the first editor of *The Dial* (a major organ of transcendental thought and literature). She began a series of annual philosophical "Conversations" with women in her home in Boston in order to develop their intellectual and moral virtues. A very popular article she wrote for *The Dial* (the only issue ever to sell out) advocated the liberty and equality of women on transcendentalist grounds. She later developed this essay into her book, *Woman in the Nineteenth Century* (1845).[116] Fuller's career continued in journalism, and she became a foreign correspondent for the *New York Daily Tribune* in 1844. She traveled extensively in Europe and met a number of leading intellectuals and artists. While there she met and was wooed by the Marchese d'Ossoli, an Italian nobleman and republican reformer. After the fall of Rome in 1850 to the enemies of the Republic, the new Marchesa d'Ossoli (Fuller) had to flee with her husband and son back to America. She died with her family when their ship went down off the East Coast during a storm at sea. Her body was never found, even after extensive searching by many friends, including Thoreau. Her death was felt as a loss to American culture itself.

Woman in the Nineteenth Century was widely read and well received by critics like Edgar Allen Poe. In it Fuller takes Emerson's philosophy of optimism, self-reliance and individualism and applies them to women's status. Arguing that the soul has no sex, Fuller insists that women as well as men can grow in mind and spirit, but they are hampered by ignorance and domination in society. Her book was very influential upon the suffrage movement, including upon both Anthony and Stanton. It provided a philosophical basis for the discussions at Seneca Falls. In some ways the book was America's first feminist manifesto.

Religion and philosophy thus combined to work for the equality and dignity of women in Western thought. Of course, theologians, clergy and philosophers like Rousseau could also argue for the continued exclusion of women from public power, while at the same time extolling their virtues as long as they remain in their "proper sphere," the home. Yet the nineteenth century certainly saw the most extensive movement in both Christian and philosophical circles toward equality for women that the Western world had yet developed. Harriet Taylor and John Stuart Mill were not lonely voices but part of a larger movement. Full-blown feminism, however, was only to flower in the 1960s. But that is a story of and for another time.

9. ACT AND IDEA: PRAGMATISM AND ANGLO-AMERICAN IDEALISM

The majority of Western European thinkers considered the United States something of an intellectual backwater. Even those Americans who achieved some level of philosophical recognition, such as the Transcendentalists, were seen as lightweight popularizers incapable of serious scholarship. While there is certainly an element of provincialism present in this evaluation, it is the case that American scholarship did not begin to catch up with European thought until the latter part of the nineteenth century. Moreover, although most of the residents of the United States at this time were immigrants or descendants of recent immigrants from Western Europe, the culture of America was very different. The circumstances, traditions, long-held loyalties and ideas that shaped the intellectual trajectories of Europe were less influential in the still-young, rootless and culturally diverse United States. When this new culture met philosophy, what emerged was what many consider America's first real contribution to the discipline: pragmatism.

Charles Sanders Peirce

Charles Sanders Peirce (1839-1914), the father of pragmatic philosophy, is seen by many as the greatest philosopher America has produced (an honor some find diminished by lack of competition).[1] The irony is that he did not publish a book on philosophy, never held a permanent teaching position[2] and received little recognition during his life, except from other philosophers who would later build on his ideas. Though often chided by fellow pragmatist William James to make his ideas accessible to a wider audience, Peirce's perfectionist tendencies made this almost impossible for him.[3] Instead he preferred to remain out of the spotlight and play the role of the pioneer whose work would guide the vanguard of the next generation.

In a number of ways Peirce's early biography parallels that of John Stuart Mill. His father was an eminent intellectual, a Harvard professor and America's premier mathematician, who played a major role in young Charles's education. The best minds in America were frequent guests of the Peirces and greatly enhanced his intellectual growth. Like Mill, Peirce's father was instrumental in obtaining for his son the only full-time job he held. After earning an undergraduate (1863) and two masters degrees from Harvard, Peirce worked for the United States Coast and Geodetic Survey in various capacities for thirty years.[4] In contrast to Mill's experience, however, Charles Peirce had a wonderful relationship with his father and always referred to him with great warmth.

After his retirement from the Geodetic Survey, he moved to a large, isolated farmhouse in Milford, Pennsylvania. He had hoped this would be a center to which followers would come to receive instruction from him. This dream did not transpire, and his small inheritance and pension were insufficient to maintain the large estate and pay the medical expenses from extended illnesses. Most of his meager income following retirement came from writing articles for magazines and philosophical dictionaries and from financial assistance from William James. It is reported that he would work in the garret of the house and pull a rope ladder up behind him so his creditors could not reach him. He died in dire poverty and his papers, numbering in the thousands of pages, were sold to Harvard by his widow for $500.

Pragmatism
Peirce's aim was the reform of science and philosophy. He considered the fundamental problem in each field to be methodological. On the one hand he rejected the unexamined philosophical presupposition, common among scientists, that science requires a nonteleological, naturalistic foundation. Many scientists (and philosophers enamored with scientific method) prematurely foreclosed on metaphysics and excluded a

great deal of the universe from their beliefs. Peirce argued that proper method accommodated both scientific discovery and metaphysics. On the other hand Peirce believed philosophy would benefit greatly from incorporating the empirical and experimental approach of science. Of foremost importance to Peirce is scientific method's reliance on results. Good beliefs, whether scientific or philosophical, lead to observable results that are open to testing by others.

It is around the idea of empirically verifiable consequences that Peirce builds his epistemology, which he calls pragmatism.[5] His pragmatic maxim states that, *"In order to ascertain the meaning of an intellectual conception one should consider what practical consequences might conceivably result by necessity from the truth of that conception; and the sum of these consequences will constitute the entire meaning of the conception."*[6] Pragmatism claims that truth is not a matter of knowing pure ideas but understanding the relationships between things. In other words the truth of a theory is found only in its actual or potential use and practical effects.[7] For example, if we claim that a diamond is hard, this statement can be judged only by considering whether our experience is consistent with what is claimed. If a diamond scratches the surface of many other substances but is itself unscratched by these, our statement that a diamond is hard is confirmed and can be similarly confirmed by others. There is nothing more to our conception of a diamond than this and other potential effects. "Our idea of anything *is* our idea of its sensible effects; and if we fancy that we have any other we deceive ourselves, and mistake a mere sensation accompanying the thought for a part of the thought itself. It is absurd to say that thought has any meaning unrelated to its only function."[8]

To illustrate the benefits of pragmatism as a means of establishing or, as he puts it, fixing belief, Peirce compares it to three competing methods—tenacity, authority and a priori philosophy. By tenacity Peirce refers to an arbitrary decision to hold to a belief by simply ignoring alternatives. This method has the admirable quality of developing steadfastness of character and is often satisfying to those who employ this approach. "When an ostrich buries its head in the sand as danger approaches, it very likely takes the happiest course. It hides the danger, and then calmly says there is no danger; and if it feels perfectly sure there is none, why should it raise its head to see?"[9] However, this ultimately fails because one's tenaciously held beliefs will clash with the ideas espoused by others and "it will be apt to occur to him in some saner moment that their opinions are quite as good as his own, and this will shake his confidence in his belief."[10] The only way to maintain beliefs in this manner is to avoid the testing of our ideas by others because, "Unless we make ourselves hermits, we shall necessarily influence each other's opinions; so that the problem becomes how to fix belief, not in the individual merely, but in the community."[11]

Authority, as a means of fixing beliefs, refers to ideas inculcated by culture, religion, family, tradition or other institutional sources. It is superior to tenacity because it includes the communal aspect and thus "has over and over again worked the most majestic results," especially in the development of a social consciousness.[12] The shortcoming of this approach is that institutions often seek to control ideas in every aspect of life and preserve beliefs beyond their usefulness by confusing culturally conditioned ideas with eternal truths. Authority's means of establishing beliefs is overcome when people recognize the influence of culture on their ideas and begin looking beyond the narrow community to seek a more stable foundation upon which to build.[13]

Because authority and tenacity are nonphilosophical means of fixing beliefs, Peirce is less interested in them than the a priori, or metaphysical approach.

Usually when he speaks of metaphysics, he has in view the deductive approach, of which Descartes is the paradigm. Although Peirce considers deduction an important tool for clarifying and testing the internal consistency of ideas, it is of no use as a source of knowledge: "Nothing new can ever be learned by analyzing definitions."[14] The problem is that when speculative thought attempts to spin new truths from the mind's inner workings it becomes vulnerable to subjectivity. Advocates select certain ideas to defend without recognizing that what seems reasonable is determined by what they want to believe.[15] For this reason the a priori method yields a measure of satisfaction because what we want to believe generally mirrors what is fashionable. But this satisfaction lasts only "until we are awakened from the pleasing dream by rough facts."[16] When "rough facts" disturb subjectively devised systems, as they have throughout the history of a priori metaphysics, doubt arises and the system collapses.

Therefore, while Peirce applauds the fact that the a priori approach has suggested many new and fruitful ideas, he believes it has done so blindly.

In summary, Peirce argues that pragmatism surpasses the other means by which beliefs are fixed for several reasons. First, it provides the best means for collectively pursuing truth. Tenacity and the a priori method do not provide avenues by which beliefs can be corporately tested. While authority is a community-based approach, its views are acceptable only within a specific culture or community with shared presuppositions and beliefs. In contrast, pragmatism requires confirmation by a community of philosophers, "where investigators, instead of contemning each the work of most of the others as misdirected from beginning to end, coöperate, stand upon one another's shoulder, and multiply incontestable results; where every observation is repeated, and isolated observations go for little; where every hypothesis that merits attention is subjected to severe but fair examination, and only after the predictions to which it leads have been remarkably borne out by experience is trusted at all, and even then only provisionally."[17]

A second difference concerns how the relationship between doubt and belief is understood. Tenacity, authority and a priori philosophy consider doubt a disturbance that must be banished to preserve existing beliefs. What Peirce proposes is a more constructive view of doubt in which "both doubt and belief have positive effects upon us, though very different ones. Belief does not make us act at once, but puts us into such a condition that we shall behave in a certain way, when the occasion arises. Doubt has not the least effect of this sort, but stimulates us to action until it is destroyed."[18] The action to which doubt gives rise is inquiry. The purpose of inquiry is to resolve doubt, "an uneasy and dissatisfied state from which we struggle to free ourselves," into belief, which "is a calm and satisfactory state."[19] In other words, doubt spurs us to move from less to more satisfactory beliefs. This gives pragmatism a capacity for self-correction lacking in the other methods. However, no particular belief should be considered a final resting point (which is the assumption in other means of fixing belief) but is instead an invitation for new doubt. "As it appeases the irritation of doubt, which is the motive for thinking, thought relaxes, and comes to rest for a moment when belief is reached. But, since belief is a rule for action, the application of which involves further doubt and further thought, at the same time that it is a stopping-place, it is also a new starting-place for thought."[20]

The quote above highlights two key concepts of pragmatism—beliefs as "a rule for action" and knowers as fallible. First, establishing the proper process of fixing beliefs is vital for Peirce because beliefs are not simply intellectual entities unrelated to practical concerns. Instead they govern how we act. What we should strive for, Peirce believes, is consistency in action, or what he calls habit. "The essence of belief is the establishment of a habit, and different beliefs are distinguished by the different modes of action to which they give rise."[21] However, because humans are fallible, beliefs must always be open to question and reform should experience require it. "The scientific spirit requires a man to be at all times ready to dump his whole cartload of belief, the moment experience is against them."[22] Thus through belief we can act, and through observation of actions we are led into further inquiry by doubt and eventually into revised beliefs that correct deficiencies in previous actions.

Peirce's Metaphysics

Many philosophers imbued with the scientific spirit saw fit to dispense with metaphysics, and Peirce himself describes it as "a subject much more curious than useful, the knowledge of which, like that of a sunken reef, serves chiefly to enable us to keep clear of it."[23] However, he does not reject metaphysics itself but its earlier manifestations constructed on flawed methods. Metaphysics becomes useful only when radically rebuilt on a pragmatic foundation. Peirce argues that experience, when processed pragmatically, requires a metaphysical realism. The world is "something upon which our thinking has no effect."[24] At the same time, the reality about which we think is not static. Not only is the process of knowing the world dynamic, but the world that is known also evolves. The openness required of the knower is necessitated in part by the openness of nature. Nature has an element of spontaneity, thus it cannot be interpreted in a mechanistic manner. However, this spontaneity is progressively giving way to law, or to state it differently, nature itself is developing and modifying its habits, just as human beings do.

To express this metaphysical schema Peirce finds it necessary to create a new vocabulary to refer to three modes of being. Firstness refers to what something is in itself, apart from its relation to anything else. Secondness refers to the reaction of something to another. Thirdness addresses the means by which a first and a second are related. While the idea of Thirdness bears similarities to Hegel's dialectic, Peirce broadens it to include, not just synthesis, but any kind of relationship, including symbolic representation. This final concept is of greatest interest to Peirce because this mode of being makes knowledge possible. Thirdness refers to the habituated processes of the universe. Given knowledge of a particular relationship we can anticipate future facts. These habitual relationships, generally referred to as laws, are the basis upon which scientific method depends. "Reality consists in regularity. Real regularity is active law. Active law is efficient reasonableness, or in other words is truly reasonable reasonableness. Reasonable reasonableness is Thirdness as Thirdness."[25]

The developing regularity, or reality, of the world requires introduction of three additional metaphysical terms—*tychaism, synechism,* and *agapasm.* Tychaism (from the Greek word for chance) refers to a spontaneous and nonteleological facet of the universe. These random elements exist outside the lawful behavior that generally characterizes the universe. "The tychastic development of thought, then, will consist in slight departures from habitual ideas in different directions indifferently, quite purposeless and quite unconstrained whether by outward circumstances or by force of logic."[26] The tychastic elements do not have the lawful regularity that allows them to be described as real or rational, but in their randomness they possess the potential for growth toward reality. Spontaneity gradually gives way to what Peirce calls synechism, which refers to the continuity demonstrated within the world. In explaining synechism Peirce notes that in order to understand an idea we must know something of its past, without which each idea would be spontaneous and inexplicable. However, our present concepts also have a future that will be connected with both the present and past. If certain conditions are present, specific future events can be anticipated. Synechism is the process that connects the past, present and future of an idea into a coherent whole. As synechism overcomes tychaism, ideas become more general and all-encompassing. Peirce's final concept, agapasm (from the Greek term for love), refers to the goal of the growing regularity and

scope of law. Love is the force behind the development of the universe
that seeks to bring all things under its domain. Thus evolution is not a
random process; agapasm pulls together the novelty of tychaism and the
continuity of synechism to create a moral universe.[27]

Religion and Ethics

Agapasm, the action of creative love, forms the basis of Peirce's religious
and moral views.[28] As the universe evolves toward greater unity, religion
will become a universal force through which we are bound together by
sympathetic love, which is the sum of all religious and moral thought.
Earlier religions and philosophies anticipate religion's climax in a message of love. However, the highest expression of religious life is found in
the teachings of Jesus. "Now what is this way of life? Again I appeal to the
universal Christian conscience to testify that it is simply love. As far as it is
contracted to a rule of ethics, it is: Love God, and love your neighbor; 'on
these two commandments hang all the law and the prophets.' . . . The
belief in the law of love is the Christian faith."[29] However, the evolutionary process does not culminate when all religion is brought under the
banner of sympathetic love. The even more generalized unity Peirce
envisions is the convergence of religion and society. "Man's highest
developments are social; and religion, though it begins in a seminal individual inspiration, only comes to full flower in a great church coextensive
with a civilization. . . . Its ideal is that the whole world shall be united in
the bond of a common love of God accomplished by each man's loving
his neighbor."[30]

An evolutionary process guided by love leaves room for the divine,
and Peirce argues that God's existence is evident from our experience of
this process. In what he calls the "neglected argument for God's existence," Peirce suggests that we enter into the "pure play of musement."
Musement requires that we put aside all external motives and allow
thought free rein to reflect on the whole of our experience because the
concept of God encompasses all things. Then, "in the Pure Play of Musement the idea of God's Reality will be sure sooner or later to be found an
attractive fancy, which the Muser will develop in various ways. The more
he ponders it, the more it will find response in every part of his mind, for
its beauty, for its supplying an ideal of life, and for its thoroughly satisfac-

tory explanation of his whole threefold environment."[31] In short, it is the interconnectedness, the synechism, of all things that leads the Muser to the conclusion of God's existence.

However, Peirce refuses to be pinned down to traditional metaphysical definitions of God. Since our hypotheses are subject to growth and revision, the hypothesis of God must be understood in a similar manner. The concept of God must be viewed as "vague yet as true so far as it is defined, and as continually tending to define itself more and more, and without limit."[32] For Peirce, then, the evolutionary nature of reality means that, "If a pragmatist is asked what he means by the word 'God', he can only say that just as a long acquaintance with a man of great character may deeply influence one's whole manner of conduct, so if contemplation and study of the psycho-physical universe can imbue a man with principles of conduct analogous to the influence of a great man's work or conversation, then that analogue of a mind—for it is impossible to say that *any* human attribute is *literally* applicable—is what he means by 'God'."[33]

Peirce's Significance

It may be noticed that Peirce's metaphysics is similar to absolute idealism in a number of ways. The view that reality is ultimately mind, the concept of reality evolving toward ever greater perfection, and the belief that evolution occurs in the tension between entities in relationship led Peirce to describe the goal of all things as a "Schelling-fashioned idealism which holds matter to be mere specialized and partially deadened mind."[34] However, there are significant differences. Unlike Hegel and Schelling he argues that we cannot gain final answers from the midpoint of historical processes but must always view our conclusions as provisional. More importantly Peirce does not arrive at his metaphysics through a deductive approach but believes his conclusions to be grounded in experience. Mind cannot be deduced from pure concepts but must be derived from observation of the external world.

This comparison helps us understand the role Peirce plays in philosophy. He seeks to bridge the worlds of science and metaphysics. He refuses to sacrifice metaphysics on the alter of science, as Comte and Mill had done, and draws many of the same metaphysical conclusions found in Idealism. On the other hand he believes that metaphysics can only be released from subjectivity inherent in Idealism by the empirical approach of science. As such, Peirce is at the forefront of a movement that attempts to combine empirical scientific method and metaphysics. This combination evolves into ideas such as those present in Whitehead's process philosophy[35] and the thought of Josiah Royce and F. H. Bradley.[36]

A second area of significance in Peirce's thought is that it gives philosophical expression to the characteristic bottom-line orientation, restlessness and optimism of the American mindset. Truth cannot be divorced from what is observable, and theory must correspond with results. However, in the process of investigation, struggle and inquiry, the underlying theme is that no problem is incorrigible. Though Peirce does not communicate his ideas in a manner that captures the imagination of the general public, he provides the platform from which later popularizers would work. Without Peirce the highly influential instrumentalism of John Dewey and the work of G. H. Mead would likely have taken a much different shape. However, Peirce's groundbreaking work finds its greatest outlet in the thought of fellow pragmatist William James, to whom we now turn.

William James

While Peirce sealed his obscurity by intentionally avoiding popularization of his philosophy, William James's (1842-1910) fate is much different.[37] His vivid presentation of pragmatism brought recognition and fame during his lifetime but at a cost. James was frequently lax in his use of language, and his popularization of philosophical concepts made him susceptible to caricature.[38] However, the often-repeated charge of intellectual shallowness does not stick. Unlike Peirce's metaphysical positions, which are tenuously linked with his pragmatic method, James masterfully brings pragmatism and metaphysics into close association. His analyses of religious experience and determinism offer major contributions to both difficult discussions. Moreover, he is a key figure in boosting the fledgling field of psychology to respectability, and his insights on how and why we believe add a new facet to the philosophy originated by Peirce. James's attempts to push pragmatism in new directions were not appreciated by Peirce, who attempted to distinguish his ideas from James's psychologizing approach by referring to them as pragmaticism, a label he described as "ugly enough to be safe from kidnappers."[39] In the end, however, the distinction Peirce sought to establish did not last, and the essential idea of linking truth and observable results remains a strong commonality between two philosophers who were radically different in interest and temperament.

James's grandfather emigrated from Ireland to America penniless but carefully and slowly built a considerable fortune. His strict Calvinism was passed on to his son, Henry, who attended Princeton with plans to enter the ministry but left school without completing his studies. However, he continued to study the Bible until, at age thirty-three, he had a mystical vision that radically altered his life. He rejected Calvinism, put away forever his extensive notes on the Bible and eventually became a devotee of Swedenborgianism. This event had a significant impact on William, the oldest of the five James children (which included younger brother Henry, the famous novelist, and the diarist Alice James), because Henry James vowed that his children's upbringing would be different from his own highly structured, doctrinaire background. Instead he encouraged their exposure to a wide variety of ideas and places. Leading intellectuals were often guests in the James home and household discussions were wide-ranging and often boisterous, with the expectation that everyone participate. Much of James's childhood was spent between America and Europe, never remaining in any one school for more than a year or two. As a result he acquired proficiency in several languages and a cosmopolitan perspective.

James developed a great love of art during his travels and aspired to become a painter. At eighteen he was given the opportunity to study with well-known portraitist William Hunt. However, he quickly realized that his interest in good art outstripped his capacity to produce it. He then entered Harvard and soon moved on to its medical school, graduating with a medical degree in 1869. James's health had been fragile all his life and worsened after he completed his medical studies. The result was a depression, brought on by fear that his fate was determined by powers beyond his control. This gloom was so deep that he contemplated suicide and was almost completely incapacitated for two years. His discovery of Renouvier's writing on free will provided a way out of his melancholy and greatly influenced his later views on the will to believe.

Shortly after this turning point James was invited to Harvard as a lecturer in physiology and anatomy. Recognizing the links between physical health and state of mind, he soon began lectures in psychology as well. His *Principles of Psychology* (1890) grew out of these lectures. It quickly became a standard and established James as the leading figure in the growing field. The writing of *Principles of Psychology* required James to address a number of philosophical issues, and in 1879 he began lecturing on philosophy. By 1900 philosophy had become his primary concern, and with Royce and George Santayana also in residence during this time, Harvard became a major philosophical center in America. James died from a chronic heart condition in 1910.

The Will to Believe

One of James's most important contributions is his view of the will's role in forming and maintaining our beliefs. While strongly empirical in his basic orientation, James disagreed with empiricists, most directly William Kingdom Clifford (1845-1879), who argued that we should accept only those beliefs grounded in adequate empirical evidence. This requirement unfairly circumscribes the whole of human experience. We are not simply rational beings but also have what James refers to as a "passional" nature controlled by the will. "Pretend what we may, the whole man within us is at work when we form our philosophical opinions. Intellect, will, taste, and passion co-operate just as they do in practical affairs."[40]

The impulse behind the radical empiricists' demand for irrefutable certainty, James believes, is a fear of falling into error. In other words, they were driven more by what they wanted to avoid than by what they might gain. However, James points out that we cannot suspend judgment on all that is intellectually uncertain; otherwise we would do little in our life. Instead we must and do act as if certain things are true, particularly in the ethical and religious realms of our lives. "To preach scepticism to us as a duty until 'sufficient evidence' for religion be found, is tantamount therefore to telling us, when in presence of the religious hypothesis, that to yield to our fear of its being error is wiser and better than to yield to our hope that it may be true."[41] But James argues that we ought to listen to "our hope that it may be true" in religion as well as other areas of life. To state it differently, all people live by faith. "Faith means belief in something concerning which doubt is still theoretically possible; and as the test of belief is willingness to act, one may say that faith is the readiness to act in a cause the prosperous issue of which is not certified to us in advance."[42]

The faith of which James speaks is a necessity for several reasons. First, as he tells us above, reason does not provide conclusive evidence on numerous matters, some of which are quite central to our lives. "Objective evidence and certitude are doubtless very fine ideals to play with, but where on this moonlit and dream-visited planet are they found?"[43] Second, even those who claim to assent only to what can be conclusively affirmed are governed by passional elements. *"Our passional nature not only lawfully may, but must, decide an option between propositions, whenever it is a genuine opinion that cannot by its nature be decided on intellectual grounds; for to say, under such circumstances, 'Do not decide, but leave the question open,' is itself a passional decision—just like deciding yes or no—and is attended with the same risk of losing the truth."*[44] Finally, James argues that faith, to some extent, causes things to be true. *"There are then cases where faith creates its own verification.* Believe, and you shall be right, for you shall save yourself; doubt, and you shall again be right, for you shall perish. The only difference is that to believe is greatly to your advantage."[45] What we believe creates our reality. If we believe salvation is available, then our world will include it. If we reject the possibility of salvation, it will not be part of our reality. However, James wants to distinguish the truth-creating function of faith from wishful thinking. Reality has objective existence, and "It is the *inherent relation to reality* of a belief that gives us that specific *truth*-satisfaction, compared with which all other satisfactions are the hollowest humbug."[46]

James's Pragmatism

The means by which we gain a better understanding of reality is through implementation of pragmatic method. Acknowledging his debt to Peirce, James states that no question can be settled in the abstract. Instead, "To attain perfect clearness in our thoughts of an object, then, we need only consider what conceivable effects of a practical kind the object may involve—what sensations we are to expect from it, and what reactions we must prepare."[47] We can determine whether an idea is true by observing whether it makes a difference in actual circumstances. "'Grant an idea or belief to be true,' it [pragmatism] says, 'what concrete difference will its being true make in any one's actual life? How will the truth be realized? What experiences will be different from those which would obtain if the belief were false? What, in short, is the truth's cash-value in experiential terms'?"[48] To state it otherwise, truth is what works.

What this means for James then is that ideas are tools: "All our theories are *instrumental,* are mental modes of *adaption* to reality, rather than revelations or gnostic answers to some divinely instituted world-enigma."[49] With this James shifts the attention from objects about which statements are made to the statements themselves. "The difference is that when the pragmatists speak of truth, they mean exclusively something about the ideas, namely their workableness; whereas when anti-pragmatists speak of truth they seem most often to mean something about the objects."[50] The problem with the latter is that objects do not have the characteristic of being true or false. "The 'facts' themselves meanwhile are not true. They simply are. Truth is the function of the beliefs that start and terminate among them."[51] Only when we enter the realm of beliefs or ideas can we entertain the possibility of true and false. Moreover, these ideas are always someone's beliefs. Therefore, truth has a subjective element; it is true if it works *for us.*

This concept of truth depends on Kant's first *Critique,* which argues that even though a noumenal realm may exist, we are denied direct access. Instead reality is always mediated by our experience. James departs from Kant in two areas, however. First, he refuses to see truth as static. "The truth of an idea is not a stagnant property inherent in it. Truth happens to an idea. It becomes true, is made true by events. Its verity is in fact an event, a process: the process namely of its verifying itself, its veri-*fication.* Its validity is the process of its vali-*dation.*"[52] Second, while traditional epistemology conceived of the knower as passive, James wants a livelier version in which we select from the experience provided by sensation in order to construct our reality.

This process of constructing reality brings us to a pivotal concept in James's philosophy. At all moments of conscious life our mind presents to us a great variety of unformed, disconnected and contradictory ideas. This is what he calls our "stream of consciousness." From this stream of ideas we choose or, as James frequently puts it, give "attention" to certain ideas and disregard others. This process of giving attention is not random. Instead we test an idea by projecting it into the future, thus anticipating its effects. If our expectation is borne out, if the idea works, it has "cash-value" and becomes a guide by which we select future ideas. When our stream of consciousness offers new concepts that are consistent with others that have shown themselves to have cash-value, we pay attention to them and integrate them into our belief system. Or, as James would say, these new ideas *become* true for us because they bring a measure of order and unity to our life.

James frequently sums up the goal of our belief-building process in the term "satisfaction." When a belief unifies our life, proves consistent with existing concepts and is useful for predicting verifiable results, we experience subjective satisfaction. However, empirical verification is a public process, and results are governed by existing structures in the universe. Moreover, when confronted with an idea that has little or no intellectual validity, we do not will to believe it. Therefore, James believes that the will to believe that which is satisfying does not degenerate into subjectivism and irrationality, although these accusations continue to dog him even today.

Determinism

The concept of the will to believe assumes the freedom of the will, and James sees the age-old question of freedom versus determinism as a perfect test case for demonstrating the benefits of pragmatic method. This is one of those incorrigible metaphysical problems for which the intellectual evidence does not compel universal assent on one side or the other. However, pragmatism cuts the Gordian knot by taking the question outside the realm of reason alone. To make his case against determinism James refers to a brutal murder that had occurred in Brockton, a town just outside Boston. In this situation a husband lured his wife to a secluded location and shot her several times. As she lay bleeding, he finished the job by smashing her head with a rock.

James argues that we should simultaneously consider two different things in this case: the murder itself and our response to it. The normal response to a brutal murder is regret: the sentiment that what happened should not have happened. However, to regret the murder puts the determinist in a difficult position. "Regret for the murder must transform itself, if we are determinists and wise, into a larger regret. It is absurd to regret the murder alone. Other things being what they are, it could not be different. What we should regret is that whole frame of things of which the murder is one member."[53] For determinism, the Brockton murder is not isolated from everything else that occurs but is the necessary result of it. Therefore, if our regret of the murder is proper, we must regret everything that has ever happened. This leads to a profoundly pessimistic view of the world.

However, there is also an optimistic version of determinism, which states that in the larger scheme of things the murder was a good thing. We do not understand how such an apparently atrocious act could be positive, but it is a necessary part of a larger picture that is good. This view may make sense of the event, but it renders our regret incomprehensible. Why should we regret that which is good? Therefore, with optimistic determinism, "We have got one foot out of the pessimistic bog, but the other one sinks in all the deeper. We have rescued our actions from the bonds of evil, but our judgments are now held fast. . . . Murder and treachery cannot be good without regret being bad: regret cannot be good without treachery and murder being bad."[54]

On the other hand, indeterminism, the idea that not all events occur from necessity, makes sense of both the event and our reaction to it. The murder was really evil *and* we should feel regret. As James puts it, "I cannot understand the willingness to act, no matter how we feel, without the belief that acts are really good and bad. I cannot understand the belief that an act is bad, without regret at its happening. I cannot understand regret without the admission of real, genuine possibilities in the world. Only *then* is it other than a mockery to feel, after we have failed to do our best, that an irreparable opportunity is gone from the universe, the loss of which it must forever after mourn."[55] Therefore, while a straightforward rational, metaphysical analysis of determinism versus freedom does not settle the question, an indeterminist position creates a way to hold together both the event and our moral evaluation of it, justifying our willingness to believe it. James is aware that this is not an objective proof for human freedom. Instead it relies on passional factors such as our moral sensitivity and the subjective sense of having real choice to decide the question. While determinism violates one or the other of these factors and appears to cut across common sense, including them produces what James calls a "sentiment of rationality."

Metaphysics

James believes that metaphysical pluralism and a melioristic view of the universe are natural implications of his understanding of human freedom. In general, pluralism means that the universe consists of multiple entities rather than existing as an undifferentiated whole. When James interprets it along pragmatic lines, he states that "pluralism or the doctrine that it [the world] is many means only that the sundry parts of reality *may be externally related.* . . . Things are 'with' one another in many ways, but nothing includes everything or dominates over everything. The word 'and' trails along after every sentence. Something always escapes."[56] There is no one thing, idea or system that incorporates and explains everything else. This makes freedom possible.

By speaking of externally related plural realities, James stakes out a middle ground between Hume's empirical atomism and idealism's rationalistic monism. Once again he argues that experience supports this position. In our life we see both unity and disjunction in the world. The problem comes when either is overemphasized. When the rationalist's attention falls exclusively on unity, it generally does so because one aspect of experience is subjectively chosen as the sole reality, and all facts that do not fit the resulting model are ignored or absorbed into it.[57] On the other hand James disagrees with Hume's contention that empiricism requires that we forswear any connection between the plural realities of our experience. "Our 'multiverse' still makes a 'universe'; for every part, tho it may not be in actual or immediate connexion, is nevertheless in some possible or mediated connexion, with every other part however remote, through the fact that each part hangs together with its very next neighbors in inextricable interfusion."[58] In a sense James's model is one of reality increasingly collecting itself. The "many" of the universe is never reduced to the one. Instead there will remain forever a pluralism, but in greater coherence and connection. The analogy suggested by James is a social model, in which communities have both autonomy and interrelationship to other communities.

It is the *possibility* of connections between the world's components that intrigues James. His pluralistic universe is open to novelty, therefore its structure (and its truth) is not final. The tension arises when he attempts to bring two other elements into play. The first is his metaphysical realism, which states that the world possesses structure and order. "This notion of a reality independent of either of us, taken from ordinary social experience, lies at the base of the pragmatist definition of truth. With some such reality any statement, in order to be counted true, must agree."[59] The final element is, as we have seen, James's view that beliefs create our world and make certain things true.

James attempts to hold these three ideas together by stating that beliefs will not work when they violate the structure of the universe, but because the realities of the universe are not absolute, different ways of understanding the world may be true.

The mind, in short, works on the data it receives very much as a sculptor works on his or her block of stone. In a sense the statue stood there from eternity. But there were a thousand different statues beside it, and the sculptor alone is to thank for having extricated this one from the rest. Just so the world of each of us, howsoever different our several views of it may be, all lay embedded in the primordial chaos of sensations, which gave the mere *matter* to the thought of all of us indifferently.[60]

Therefore, from the numerous possibilities open to us, many can bring fulfillment to the extent they are in accord with existing patterns in the universe and to the extent that we act on them.

The second ramification of indeterminism is meliorism. Meliorism says that the world is neither wholly good or wholly evil but can be improved through human activity. Thus meliorism opposes both an optimistic determinism that sees progress as inevitable and independent of human activity as well as pessimist determinisms such as we find in Schopenhauer. In contrast to these worldviews a melioristic outlook involves risk. Salvation is a genuine possibility but is not guaranteed. It depends largely on what we choose to do. However, James believes that "a world with a *chance* in it of being altogether good, even if the chance never comes to pass, is better than a world with no such chance at all. . . . This is the only chance we have any motive for supposing to exist. . . . For its presence is the vital air which lets the world live, and salt which keeps it sweet."[61] Because meliorism makes life worth living, it is expedient for us and thus passes the pragmatic test for truth.

Religion

James finds pragmatism especially advantageous in the religious realm of our life because it is here that reason so frequently fails to find clear and demonstrable conclusions.[62] While some believe their approach provides certain answers to religious questions, James implies that this is because their method determines the conclusions in advance. However, he is confident that pragmatism carries no such baggage: "She has in fact no prejudices whatever, no obstructive dogmas, no rigid canons of what shall count as proof. She is completely genial. She will entertain any hypothesis, she will consider any evidence. It follows that in the religious field she is at a great advantage both over positivistic empiricism, with its anti-theological interest in the remote, the noble, the simple, and the abstract in the way of conception."[63]

Pragmatism's means of testing religious truths remains the same as inquiry in other areas. Its "only test of probable truth is what works best in the way of leading us, what fits every part of life best and combines with the collectivity of experience's demands, nothing being omitted. If theological ideas should do this, if the notion of God, in particular, should prove to do it, how could pragmatism possibly deny God's existence?"[64] In fact, James believes that belief in God passes muster, even if the question cannot be settled intellectually. As he succinctly states it, "God is real since he produces real effects."[65] The real effects to which James refers are especially evident in mystical experience, which he examines in depth in his groundbreaking *Varieties of Religious Experience* (1900).[66] In such events an individual is seized by something that transcends words. This ineffable quality points beyond natural causes. Moreover, these mystical experiences, while themselves transient, transform a person's life and give their entire existence a religious orientation. In addition these experiences possess a noetic quality; they provide the means by which an individual can understand important aspects of their life and world. Finally, they cannot be understood solely in terms of human will. Instead the person is overtaken by something beyond himself or herself and is largely passive in the experience. Therefore, while nowhere in the mystical experience is God apprehended directly, James believes that attribution of these effects to God provides the most satisfactory explanation for the data.[67]

The experiential basis upon which James constructs his religious views puts him at odds with approaches that focus on doctrine. He justifies this on pragmatic grounds. First, "The truth is that in the metaphysical and religious sphere, articulate reasons are cogent for us only when our inarticulate feelings of reality have already been impressed in favor of the same conclusion."[68] Therefore, while doctrinal statements shape the believer's world, such statements depend on religious experience as their source and are impotent without it. Second, because traditional theology does not begin from concrete experience, its conclusions reflect the subjective tastes of the theologian. "This is why it seems to me that the logical understanding, working in abstraction from such specifically religious experiences, will always omit something, and fail to reach completely adequate conclusions."[69]

James argues that dogmatic theology should be replaced by what he calls a science of religion. Even though religious experiences transcend purely rational categories, their effects are still subject to empirical study. And because it is grounded in observation, James argues that a science of religion can gain acceptance in a way traditional theology cannot. "I do not see why a critical Science of Religions of this sort might not eventually command as general a public adhesion as is commanded by a physical science. Even the personally non-religious might accepts its conclusions on trust, much as blind persons now accept the facts of optics— it might appear as foolish to refuse them."[70]

While acknowledging that empiricism has often been hostile to religion, James argues the problem is not empiricism itself but the empiricists' arbitrary limitation of their interest to the natural realm alone. But no one, not even the scientist, lives in a purely natural realm. The scientific person "wants facts; he wants science; but he also wants a religion."[71] Pragmatism gives us the best of both worlds because it "can remain religious like the rationalism, but at the same time, like the empiricisms, it can preserve the richest intimacy with facts."[72] When this science of religion is in place, James optimistically states, "I believe that a new era of religion as well as of philosophy will be ready to begin."[73]

Just as James rejects naturalistic determinism as a hindrance to human freedom, any divinely imposed determinism must be discarded for the same reason. This makes it necessary to abandon certain metaphysical characteristics ascribed to God in orthodox theology, most notably omnipotence and omniscience. First, James believes that these attributes are incompatible with human freedom. Second, if God knows and controls each detail in the universe, he is responsible for evil. Finally, these attributes stress transcendence to such an extent that there is no possibility of a real relationship with humanity: "Orthodox theism has been so jealous of God's glory that it has taken pains to exaggerate everything in the notion of him that could make for isolation and separateness."[74] Therefore, James concludes, "The line of least resistance, then, as it seems to me, both in theology and in philosophy, is to accept, along with the superhuman consciousness, the notion that it is not all-embracing, the notion, in other words, that there is a God, but that he is finite, either in power or in knowledge, or in both at once."[75]

In a famous analogy toward the end of "The Dilemma of Determinism," James compares God to a chess master. God knows all possible moves we may make but not the actual moves we will make. This allows for genuine human freedom. However, God intends to win, and when we "make our moves," God responds to them in a manner that will eventually counteract any negative effects. Thus our actions have real consequences for the world, but at the same time, God assures the ultimate outcome.[76] "So the creator himself would not need to know *all* the details of actuality until they came; and at any time his own view of the world would be a view partly of facts and partly of possibilities, exactly as ours is now. Of one thing, however, he might be certain; and that is that his world was safe, and that no matter how much it might zig-zag he could surely bring it home at last."[77]

Given the open nature of the universe, we should not pretend to have discovered final religious truths. Our knowledge of religious verities can and will grow when tested in the laboratory of pragmatism; therefore, "Pragmatism has to postpone the dogmatic answer, for we do not yet know certainly which type of religion is going to work best in the long run." However, in other places James seems to say that, as long as there are different people in different circumstances, variation in religious practice will always be desirable: "Is the existence of so many religious types and sects and creeds regrettable? To these questions I answer 'No' emphatically. And my reason is that I do not see how it is possible that creatures in such different positions and with such different powers as human individuals are, should have exactly the same functions and duties."[78] Whatever the reason, James seeks to preserve the dynamic nature of faith so we do not fail to gain an ever-deeper religious knowledge and the greater level of satisfaction that results from it.

Pragmatism's Significance

While Peirce laid the foundation from which James constructed his philosophy, he failed to speak directly to the American consciousness in the way his disciple did. Not only does James's definition of truth as "that which works" put philosophy into the vernacular, he also addresses the questions that appealed to his audience. An important component of this appeal is his use of psychological categories to deal with issues that had reached an impasse when approached in traditional ways. For example, James uses the retrospective and prospective powers of the mind as a key to breaking the deadlock on the matter of determinism. Similarly, he submits religious experience to psychological investigation as a means of defining the validity of religious belief.

James's new take on religious belief also provides a plausible means of pulling science and religion together. His pragmatism mitigates the effects of a radical empiricism in that, over against the reductionist tendencies of a Humean approach, it views reality as interconnected and organic. However, it does not limit itself to only the tangible realities. Thus James offers an alternative to the Idealistic monism that seemed so counterintuitive to the empirical mind. One can be scientific and religious without apologies in either area. Related to this, James's emphasis on the passional element of human existence includes the whole of our experience, while, at the same time, its empirical nature appears to provide some protection from the subjectivity of Romanticism or Transcendentalism. To state it otherwise, James moves the boundary lines of what is generally defined as rational to encompass elements that create subjective satisfaction.

No agenda this ambitious survives without criticism, and the most common attacks on James have been aimed at the heart of his pragmatism. Many critics charge that his failure to distinguish between truth and usefulness drags him back into the subjectivism he criticizes in other approaches. Indeed James tends to vacillate on the issue of whether truth is a matter of which ideas generate the most satisfying consequences or if we cause something to be true by the use we make of an idea. There are actually a number of smaller problems included in the charges above. For example, a belief in God's existence creates a wide array of responses in people, not all of which can be described as subjective satisfaction. However, it seems clear that the question of whether God actually exists is surely different from the question of whether belief in God "works" for us. Therefore, how do we determine whether we give primacy to the question of God's objective existence or to the expediency of belief in God's existence? Second, the term *works* is itself a relative term. What works will be subject to differences in individuals and their situations. And if what works is the standard of truth, is not truth subject to the same things? Another way of stating the problem argues that if we use human experience as our point of departure, we ultimately discover only truths that reflect what we want to be a part of our experience. In short, pragmatism eventually terminates in wishful thinking. Finally, while James wants to frame an epistemology amenable to public verification (an assumption of empirical science), the foundation of his pragmatism is highly individualistic. In spite of these questions James's influence continues to extend beyond philosophy into diverse areas such as education, psychology, science and theology.

Anglo-American Idealism

While the influence of Hegel was on the wane in German-speaking countries, in English ones his moon was just beginning to wax luminous. There were several centers and loose affiliation of Idealism in the English-speaking world, including Scotland, England, New England and stretching even to the heartland of America. At the same time Idealism per se, that is, the ontology that argues that the ultimate nature of reality is Mind or Idea, was hardly new to England and America. Bishop George Berkeley (1685-1753) was a famous Idealist in Ireland in the eighteenth century, while in New England Jonathan Edwards (1703-1758), America's greatest philosopher before Peirce, was likewise developing an Idealist worldview.[79] But the impulse of Hegel and the type of philosophical method he represented began a huge push forward for Idealist thought. So great was the impetus of Idealism during the last half of the nineteenth century that it became the dominant school of thought in English-language philosophy.

While Idealism would seem to have little in common with the philosophical pragmatism we have surveyed above, there are some important connections that bring these two schools into conversation. First, while pragmatism was more ardent in its desire to find a philosophy that was amenable to the sciences and scientific methodology, both the pragmatists and the Anglo-American idealists argue that science itself does not have the final word on every type of question. Second, for both schools, growth was not simply a matter of our developing understanding of an essentially static universe. Instead in addition to our intellectual growth, there is a dynamism that occurs outside the mind. Finally, and parallel to the point above, both pragmatism and Idealism envisioned a world that contained tensions and contradictions. Thus while we attempt to untangle mental tensions inwardly, the external realm is also working through its own contradictions. The most important and influential British idealist of this period was F. H. Bradley (1846-1924), while among the Americans Josiah Royce (1855-1916) stands out as the most brilliant spokesman.

F. H. Bradley

Idealism in the English-speaking world began, as with Hegel, through the Romantic movement. Men of letters such as S. T. Coleridge and Thomas Carlyle in Britain and the Transcendentalists in America, created an intellectual environment in which Idealist philosophy could flourish. They were the first to bring the ideas and ideals of German romantic literature and Idealist philosophy to English-speaking culture.[80] The romantic emphasis on spirituality, metaphysics and a holistic conception of the universe, opened the door for professional philosophers to develop Idealist systems. Another source of Idealistic philosophy, on the British side, was the classical education of the English schools. This allowed for a powerful influence of Platonic thought on British philosophy.[81] These movements and flows joined into a powerful current of English-speaking Idealism that became the dominant philosophical school. While British Idealism was stimulated by Plato, Kant and Hegel, it was not a monolithic movement embracing a single system. Rather, a number of philosophers adopted a generally Idealist approach to questions of truth, meaning and reality, questions that prior British philosophers like Locke and Hume had pondered. Among these British Idealists, by all accounts, the most important and impressive was Francis Herbert Bradley (1846-1924).

Bradley was born in London to an evangelical Anglican pastor.[82] Sent to all the proper schools such as Marlborough and Oxford, he received a classical English education, culminating in a First Class degree in classics and a Second Class in Lit. Hum. (philosophy at Oxford comes under Lit. Hum., *literae humaniores*). Despite a less than stellar showing in philosophy, Bradley was offered a fellowship at Merton College in 1870, a lifetime position that could only be terminated if one married. Bradley lived in College the rest of his life. The Fellowship was a generous one and did not require him to lecture or teach at Oxford: and he never did lecture there. He soon developed a serious kidney infection, however. For this reason he usually spent the cold winters in warmer parts but always returned for official College meetings. Bradley published a number of significant philosophical works during his fifty-four years at Oxford.[83] This *oeuvre* pushed him to the forefront of British philosophy, and he was honored with several awards, including the Order of Merit in 1924, the year he died.

Bradley's first philosophical work was stimulated by his Christian background. The historical-critical work of David F. Strauss and F. C. Baur in the Tübingen School prompted him to compose *The Presuppositions of Critical History* (1874).[84] Already in this early work we see some of the moves characteristic of his thought. He is interested in the presuppositions that make historical knowledge possible, declaring that "it is when history becomes aware of its presupposition that it first becomes truly critical."[85] Bradley argues that for historical science, the uniformity of nature and principle of analogy with present experience are foundational principles. Here we also find the seed of his later metaphysical system in his argument that testimony must be examined in the light of a connected, rational system. "Every part here must live, and live in the life of the whole."[86] The connection to Hegel is obvious. Like Hegel and indeed much of European culture, Bradley also reveals himself in the last part of this essay to be a firm believer in human cultural progress.

The early essay by Bradley is of some historical interest, but his greatest works were his *Principles of Logic* (1883) and especially his famous book *Appearance and Reality* (1893). Bradley was a consistent critic of empiricism, utilitarianism and scientism typical of English-speaking philosophy. Utilitarian ethics comes under serious attack in *Ethical Studies* (1876), while his *Principles of Logic* takes aim at the various dogmas of empiricism. Here Bradley anticipates the contemporary view that logical truths cannot be derived from inner, psychological experience. Clearly he is reacting in both books to the views of J. S. Mill, the giant of British philosophy in the generation preceding Bradley's.

While these were important works, Bradley was a man with a magnus opus, and that work was his *Appearance and Reality,* devoted to metaphysics. Bradley attacked both a common sense view of the world, as Idealists had been doing since Plato, but also a naive scientism that accepts the doctrines of the special sciences as the ultimate truth about reality. A whole host of our common sense verities about the world—including the existence of independent facts of time, space, causation and even of our own self—are shot through with philosophical problems and contradictions according to Bradley. Such everyday assumptions and scientific presumptions give us mere appearance and not truth, not the correct understanding of reality (hence the title of the book). After undermining our faith in the world of appearance, book two outlines Bradley's reconstruction of the true nature of reality.

For Bradley, the ultimate criterion by which we can judge between truth and illusion is contradiction: "Ultimate reality is such that it does not contradict itself."[87] Based on this notion Bradley develops a view of the Absolute as a harmonious Whole in which all appearances are both included and reconciled with each other. Bradley lays out a hierarchy of knowledge sources (not unlike Plato), moving from feeling or direct experience at the lowest level, to relational thinking about "independent" facts, to a knowledge where all things are interdependent and interrelated, to finally his conception of the Absolute. For Bradley, at the fullest and highest level of knowledge, reality is One. Although it may appear that there are independent things—rocks, trees, people, cars— they are all unified and reconciled in the Absolute.

Bradley's Absolute is the one true whole World, but it is not God. "If you identify the Absolute with God, that is not the God of religion."[88] He found religious doctrines, like all discursive thinking, to be full of contradictions. Our theological picture of God, according to Bradley, is not ultimately real. "God is but an aspect, and that must mean but an appearance, of the Absolute."[89] Bradley's Absolute is not God and in fact is not even personal. Rather it represents the whole of true reality, the unification and reconciliation of all appearances. "There is nothing in the Whole beside appearance, and every fragment of appearance qualifies the Whole; while on the other hand, so taken together, appearances, as such, cease."[90]

Bradley was the last great Idealist thinker in British philosophy (at least so far!). There is little doubt that *Appearance and Reality* represents the most sustained and brilliant essay in dialectical thinking ever written in English. It remains a monument to a way of thought that has now passed into history. Ironically, even while Bradley was adding additional notes and correcting new editions of his works, his philosophical method was on the wane. By the time of his death in 1924 the Cambridge trio of Bertrand Russell, G. E. Moore and Ludwig Wittgenstein would begin a revolution in philosophical method and in logic that would overthrow the vast systems of Idealism the previous generation had built with such intellectual energy.

And yet even in the creation of a new method, the young generation would rely upon Bradley as a source of concepts and arguments against which they would test themselves. Even the very name of this new movement, "analytic" philosophy, takes its name from a section of Bradley's *Logic* on analysis and synthesis. Perhaps British Idealism has indeed passed into the pages of history, but its concerns and questions should not be so casually dismissed, as once they were. The impulse toward metaphysics, which such philosophy represents, will not long lay dormant under the anesthetic of "analysis."

Josiah Royce
Royce is the first Californian of any import in the history of Western

thought. Born of forty-niner parents in a mining camp at Grass Valley, California, Royce was first educated by his mother, Sarah.[91] At the age of eleven he was ready for more formal education, and his intellectual gifts were already apparent. His parents sent him to San Francisco to school, and at the age of sixteen he entered the new University of California. He so distinguished himself that five years later he earned a scholarship to study in Germany, where he came under the influence of Idealist thought and romantic poetry. In 1876 he returned to America and entered Johns Hopkins where he received his Ph.D. in 1878. There he also heard the famous philosopher William James. After a brief stint back at the University of California where he taught English and logic, the young philosopher joined the faculty at Harvard in 1882, where he spent the rest of his professional life.

Although he wrote history and even a novel, most of Royce's publications were in areas of technical philosophy.[92] The first philosophical tome to win widespread approval was *The Religious Aspect of Philosophy* (1885), which he wrote soon after joining the Harvard faculty as a *temporary* replacement for William James. Royce was at Harvard during the "golden age" of its philosophy department. While holding some views similar to the growing philosophical school of pragmatism (Peirce and James), Royce was always enamored with the work of Kant and went to Harvard already convinced that pragmatism on its own was inadequate.[93] He went his own way as a thinker and was not a slavish follower of Idealism any more than he bought into American pragmatism. Rather his mature philosophy is a blend of both schools, which he called "absolute pragmatism."[94] Like James and Kant, Royce wished to begin with experience. From Peirce he took a number of important philosophical ideas, including the insistence that truth is public, his theory of signs, the importance of interpretation and the idea of a community of inquiry as the ultimate means of philosophical advance.[95] He also accepted the notion "Ideas are tools. They are there for an end."[96]

While Royce was no doubt influenced by Peirce and James, the heart of his philosophy was an Absolute Idealism. In his most important work, his Gifford Lectures for 1899-1900, Royce begins with a full-blown metaphysics of Being. Since ideas are tools having some end or purpose, they have an internal meaning (the purpose of the idea) and an external meaning (the actual object the idea represents). Knowledge of reality is possible because ideas seek their objects through their own internal volition. "What is, or what is real, is as such the complete embodiment, in individual form and in final fulfillment, of the internal meaning of finite ideas."[97] Because of this emphasis on will or volition in knowledge of reality, Royce also called his philosophy voluntaristic idealism.

For Royce, to exist is to embody a concrete idea, the fulfillment of a purpose. From this it is but a short step to seeing the need for an Infinite Mind. His Gifford lectures were entitled *The World and the Individual*, because Royce was most interested in the relationship between the world, the individual and the Absolute. He developed his concepts of idea, truth and Being into a comprehensive system of thought concerning human being, ethics, nature and God.

By attending to particular things the will comes to know, in part, the object of its ideas. But we come to know not only nature but others, that is, the rest of human society, as well. Nature thus functions as an intermediary between myself and my fellows. But the whole of nature and society is known only in part; a fully definite reality demands an Absolute, an infinite individual Mind. This is the ultimate source of nature, society and the individual. For Royce, each person is a partial fulfillment of the divine will, lived out in time. As early as 1892 he was arguing that there exists one infinite Self of which all the finite selves are moments or organic parts.[98] Individual selves work out their destiny in communion with others and as expressions of the Absolute Will.

The community of human selves is knit together both ontologically and morally in Royce's philosophy. His ethical theory focused upon the virtue of loyalty. For him, the first ethical principle was loyalty to the principle of loyalty. In his ethical works the term loyalty takes on a powerful meaning, approaching the Christian idea of love.[99] In fact, of the famous American philosophers of his time, Royce was the one most obviously indebted to Christian ideas. For Royce, in contrast with Bradley, the Absolute is a personal-infinite God.[100]

In his last important work, *The Problem of Christianity* (1913), Royce specifically takes up three Christian themes and gives them philosophical interpretation. Loyalty he defines there as the willing and thoroughgoing devotion of a self to a cause, when the cause is something which united many selves into one, and which is therefore the interest of a community. For a loyal human being the interest of the community to which he belongs is superior to every merely individual interest of his own.[101]

His ethical views lead Royce into a consideration of the Pauline notion of the church. This Royce reinterprets as the beloved community, an ideal human community that embodies the highest virtue, namely, loyalty. Loyalty to this community, which in the end equals loyalty to God, is our highest task on earth.[102] Royce also takes up the ideas of sin and atonement in this work, which he uses to further develop his ethic of loyalty. Sin is for him the loss of loyalty, treason to the highest good we know. Thus atonement is the work of the beloved community, calling back and opening its arms to the "sinner" in a new and creative act. "The triumph of the spirit of the community over the treason which was its enemy, [and] the rewinning of the value of the traitor's own life."[103]

In Josiah Royce, America had found its own best Idealistic philosopher.[104] Like Hegel, Royce believed he had captured the essence of Christian ideas in his metaphysical and ethical translation of them. He gave philosophical interpretations of key Christian concepts, usually making strong philosophical reinterpretations so as to fit the ideas into his own system. He accepted key concepts from pragmatism too, which was and remains a powerful American school of thought. Like Christian concepts, the ideas of Peirce and James underwent significant transformation in the hands of Royce. Royce borrowed from many sources but was no slavish follower of any. He created his own unique synthesis. Despite his powerful mind and willingness to learn from others, Royce left little philosophical legacy. During his own lifetime the death toll of Idealism had already begun to ring.

10. CONFESSIONALISM AND LIBERALISM: REASON AND RELIGION

S urveys of a period's intellectual life rarely provide much insight into popular spirituality. Often ideas at the cutting edge only find their way into most people's religious lives after the movement is past its apex and then only in attenuated form after new concepts are filtered through the structures and institutions that have the most direct influence on popular life. While it is not our intent to offer a full-orbed outline of popular religion in the nineteenth century, a general introduction will put our overview of confessionalism in context.

Nineteenth Century Confessionalism and Related Movements
The nineteenth century was a time of social changes that had snatched power from traditional institutions—political, social, economic as well as religious. This power shift contributed to a belief that religious ideas and practices no longer needed approval from ecclesiastical leaders. Thus we see a proliferation of revivals and renewals outside established denominations that were often viewed with suspicion or actively opposed by traditional church powers: the "New Measures" revivalism of Finney in America, neopietism in Germany, the Wesleyan movement in England (later exported to the United States) and the Quakers. These and numerous other groups often grew out of a conviction that existing denominations, doctrines and practices stifled Christian vitality. Though not always explicitly stated, the twin concerns that drove these movements are faith in individual judgment (or stated in the negative, distrust of institutions)

and a belief that the past stands in the way of the future.

While often envious of the massive appeal of such movements, the guardians of tradition pointed to dangers inherent in revivalism. First, these movements placed heavy emphasis on the experiential aspects of faith. Therefore, church practices such as catechetical instruction, reliance on an educated pastorate and the sacraments were downplayed, redefined or eliminated. Doctrine, creed and confession were given little attention. Second, such movements led to a proliferation of new sects. To the traditionalists, sectarianism was one of the major problems faced by the church universal and was the natural outcome of abandoning practices and doctrines that formerly provided some level of unity. A third danger was individualism, in which a person's private experience of the divine became the grid through which religious doctrine and practice was judged, rather than the other way round.

The response to these concerns is a movement that can be broadly labeled confessionalism. Such a name is problematic because it encompasses many groups that occupy significantly different theological territory. What the confessionalists hold in common, however, is their opposition to religious subjectivism and individualism and an antidote that provides an objective foundation for Christianity in the past, whether this be apostolic succession, confession, Scripture, the sacraments or some combination of these. The Oxford Movement under the leadership of John Henry Newman will be used as a prototype of confessionalism, and related groups will be briefly described to indicate the various forms confessionalism takes as it responds to changes in the religious life of the mid-nineteenth century.[1]

The Oxford Movement

As the name implies, the Oxford Movement (or Tractarians) sprang from a collection of Anglican divines and lay intellectuals in residence at the colleges of Oxford. They were part of the Anglo-Catholic party within Anglicanism that attempted to maintain both Catholic and Protestant credentials. To many Roman Catholics and Protestants, Anglo-Catholicism was an oxymoron; to be both meant they were neither. The Anglo-Catholics, however, viewed themselves as the proper balance between excesses on either side. The Oxford Movement's goal was to demonstrate the *via media* (middle way) as the solution to problems that bedeviled popular Christianity.

The members of the Oxford Movement took up the fight against the elements of Catholicism it saw as a perversion of true Christianity: the papacy, transubstantiation, the system of penance, and the view that an individual's obedience precedes justification. Efforts on this front simply reiterated Anglican attempts over a three-hundred-year period to differentiate themselves from Roman Catholicism and thus lacked a sense of newness and urgency. Greater immediacy came from the Protestant challenge as these groups established their presence in England, and the Oxford Movement tended to focus their strongest criticism here.

Specific criticisms will be considered later; however, the general charge against Protestantism was innovation, a dirty word for Anglo-Catholicism. Most Protestant groups ignored the church fathers, downplayed the ancient creeds and councils, and generally disregarded church tradition between the early patristic period until the Reformation. This led to such novelties in Protestant groups as believer baptism, neglect of catechesis and improper redefinition of the sacraments. In contrast, Anglicanism considers unbroken apostolic succession as a mark of the true church. Since Christianity is established by Christ and sustained by those ordained by him, proper theology and praxis is rooted in antiquity, not new ideas. Therefore, many in the Oxford Movement, seeking to distance themselves from theological novelty, rejected the label of Protestant.

This conservative approach to religion was paralleled by a political conservatism that also helps explain the emergence of the movement. One important impetus for the Oxford Movement was the French Revolution, in which the close association between church and state in France was almost completely destroyed, followed by social and political disarray and suppression of religion. Many Anglicans saw England drifting in the same direction. In their own country the Test and Corporations Act that kept dissenters from public office was repealed in 1828, and in 1832 the Reform Bill was passed, giving greater power to the middle classes. The final straw was the Church Temporalities Bill (1833), which reduced the number of bishoprics in Ireland and redistributed the money from these regions. Those who would become the leaders in the Oxford Movement saw this bill as a direct encroachment of the state on church authority (even if a long overdue reform) and moved quickly to stem the momentum against them.[2]

The first response to the Church Temporalities Bill was a sermon entitled "National Apostasy" by John Keble (1792-1866), preached on July 14 from the Oxford University pulpit at St. Mary's Church. Keble's sermon blasted the shift in the traditional partnership between the Anglican hierarchy and the secular government. Of this, John Henry Newman (1801-1890) says, "I have ever considered and kept the day, as the start of the religious movement of 1833."[3] Along with Keble and Newman, Anglo-Catholic leaders such as Richard Hurrell Froude (1803-1836) and Robert Isaac Wilberforce (1802-1857) joined forces to launch a full attack against state interference in ecclesiastical affairs that broadened into a call for a return to Anglican tradition. The main vehicle for their views was a series entitled *Tracts for the Times* (thus the name Tractarians), under the editorship of Newman. Newman also authored the first tract, which traces episcopal authority to Jesus' commission of the apostles. Since Jesus founded the church and gave authority over it to the bishops, the state has no right to intervene in clergy affairs. Those who do are labeled "enemies of Christ."[4] Subsequent tracts expanded on the theme of tradition by addressing the necessity of catechetical instruction, liturgy, the centrality of the sacraments and the authority of the church fathers.

A major coup for the Oxford Movement was the involvement of Edward B. Pusey (1800-1882). Pusey, the Regius Professor of Hebrew at Oxford, joined the movement four years after its beginning and provided a heightened element of intellectual and institutional respectability. Newman says of Pusey, "Without him we should have had no chance, especially at the early date of 1834, of making any serious resistance to the Liberal aggression."[5] However, there was something of a loss with his involvement as well. The tracts increasingly relinquished their popular flavor and became more lengthy and academic. Nonetheless, the Oxford Movement was by all accounts on a very successful course during the middle and late 1830s. The *Tracts for the Times*, eventually reaching ninety in number, were collected into six volumes and enjoyed broad circulation. Many conservatives in the Anglican Church were reenergized by the call to action in the tracts. Newman's sermons from the university pulpit sold well in print form and drew new members to the cause.

With increased popularity came resistance, and questions about the Tractarians' relation to Protestantism came to the fore, especially with two events. First, Froude's journals, published shortly after his death, enraged many with their negative references to Protestantism. Second, and more significantly, was the publication of Tract 90 (1841) by Newman. In this he sought to demonstrate that, in large part, several disputed doctrines of Roman Catholicism are in accord with the Thirty-nine Articles of the Anglican Church. The outcry over what many took as an unambiguous endorsement of the Roman Church was immediate and severe. Newman says of it, "I saw indeed clearly that my place in the Movement was lost; public confidence was at an end; my occupation was gone."[6]

Indeed Newman's sympathies were moving increasingly in the direction of the Roman Church. To bolster their claims to conformity with church tradition, the Oxford Movement authorized a translation of the Catholic fathers under the title of *A Library of the Fathers of the Holy Catholic Church*. The effect on Newman was the opposite of that intended. He came to believe that Anglicanism did not stand the test of tradition but was instead a modern parallel to a heretical position condemned by the very tradition upon which he claimed to rely. "My stronghold was Antiquity; now here, in the middle of the fifth century, I found, as it seemed to me, Christendom of the sixteenth and the nineteenth centuries reflected. I saw my face in that mirror, and I was a Monophysite. The Church of the *Via Media* was in the position of the Oriental communion; Rome was, where she now is; and the Protestants were the Eutychians."[7] In short, he concluded that the Anglican claim to apostolic succession could not be sustained. In 1845 Newman became a Roman Catholic, eventually rising through the ranks to become Cardinal.[8] Some members of the Oxford Movement followed Newman to Catholicism, most notably Robert Wilberforce. Keble and Pusey did their best to keep the movement on course, but with the loss of Newman much of the initial momentum went out of the group.

Characteristic Doctrines of the Oxford Movement

An overarching theme in Tractarian writings is the church. Newman writes that one of his two lifelong principles is "that there was a visible Church with sacraments and rites which are the channels of invisible grace."[9] This seemingly simple statement has profound implications for every aspect of theology. Apostolic succession, a tenet moved to center stage in the Oxford Movement, defined the church. "We [the Anglican Church] have been born, not of blood, nor of the will of the flesh, nor of the will of man, but of God. The lord Jesus Christ gave His Spirit to these Apostles; they in turn laid their hands on those who should succeed them; and these again on others; and so the sacred gift has been handed down to our present Bishops."[10] The efficacy of the sacraments is dependent on administration by those within the line of bishops going back to Christ. Since the means through which God provides grace is the sacraments, salvation cannot be divorced from the visible church. In general, members of the Oxford Movement believed the Protestant principle of "justification by faith came to be opposed in men's minds to Baptism, the means ordained by Christ Himself for the remission of sin or for justification."[11] Therefore, the Protestants wrongly emphasized the individual's role in their salvation and undermined the sacraments as the channels of grace. Instead most Tractarians followed Pusey in his view that baptism is efficacious for salvation so long as disbelief is not present.[12]

The Oxford Movement's strongest criticism of Protestantism was on the matter of Scripture. There was agreement between the two groups that the Bible is the only standard of doctrine. At issue, however, is who is the proper interpreter of Scripture. The Oxford Movement considered the Protestant principle of *sola Scriptura* dangerously individualistic because it leaves interpretation to "private judgment." This leads inevitably to subjectivism and sectarianism. As Newman states, "No two Protestant sects can agree together whose interpretation of the Bible is to be received; and under such circumstances each naturally prefers his own;—his own 'interpretation,' his own 'doctrine,' his own 'tongue,' his own 'revelation'."[13]

The inevitable disagreement that follows from allowing individual interpretation is due in part to Scripture itself. "It is in point to notice also the structure and style of Scripture, a structure so unsystematic and various, and a style so figurative and indirect, that no one would presume at first sight to say what is in it and what is not."[14] Not only does lack of systematization make interpretation problematic, Scripture itself does not fully explicate Christian truths. Instead, "Scripture . . . begins a series of developments which it does not finish; that is to say, in other words, it is a mistake to look for every separate proposition of the catholic doctrine in Scripture."[15]

Newman argues that Scripture's lack of clarity and incompleteness is not something to be lamented because God makes allowance not only for inspired revelation in Scripture but also for a proper unfolding of its complete meaning. "Whereas Revelation is a heavenly gift, He who gave it virtually has not given it, unless He has also secured it from perversion and corruption, in all such development as comes upon it by the necessity of its nature, or, in other words, that that intellectual action through successive generations, which is the organ of development, must, so far forth as it can claim to have been put in charge of the Revelation, be in its determinations infallible."[16] The infallible interpreter given by God is church tradition.

It is obvious that the church fathers are not consistent in all they teach. For the *Via Media* the test of proper doctrine is apostolicity, more commonly referred to as "Antiquity": "Whatever doctrine the primitive ages unanimously attest, whether by consent of Fathers, or by Councils, or by the events of history, or by controversies, or in whatever way, whatever may fairly and reasonably be considered to be the universal belief of those ages, is to be received as coming from the Apostles."[17] Frequently Newman refers to Vincent of Lerins's view that true doctrine is that which has been taught "always, everywhere, and by all."[18] When church tradition is uniform on a matter, it is authoritative.

Since the Protestants do not accord antiquity the same place as the Anglicans, Newman argues that controversies within Protestantism will never get beyond the stage of opinion. On the other hand, since Roman Catholics accept the fathers as authoritative, doctrinal disputes "with Rome are arduous, but instructive, as relating rather to matters of fact."[19] Therefore, Newman states, where the Oxford Movement disputed the doctrines of Roman Catholicism, it must do so by demonstrating they did not have the catholicity, antiquity and consent of the fathers required by the Vincentian Canon.

While both revivalist and liberal movements of the time downplayed the role of doctrine, the Tractarians argued that true Christianity depends on correct dogma.[20] Newman's statement is indicative of the general feeling of the movement: "From the age of fifteen, dogma has been the fundamental principle of my religion: I know no other religion; I cannot enter into the idea of any other sort of religion; religion, as a mere sentiment, is to me a dream and a mockery."[21] For the Oxford theologians, dogma provides the moorings that prevent us from being swept away by transient human philosophies, individual experience and theological novelty. Thus the purpose of proper doctrine is not just to achieve intellectual victory over competing denominations; doctrinal truth has practical effects. "No one, I say, will die for his own calculations: he dies for realities. This is why a literary religion is so little to be depended upon; it looks well in fair weather; but its doctrines are opinions, and when called to suffer for them it slips them between its folios, or burns them at its hearth."[22]

An additional overarching theme of Oxford confessionalism is the necessity of faith and inner renewal. On this aim they were very much in accord with the revivalist schools of the day. But they disagreed on the means by which authentic renewal is gained. The revivalists often contrasted inner religion with external institutions, viewing the latter as hindrances to faith. The Oxford Movement, on the other hand, stressed the necessary connection between them. The sacraments, catechism and doctrines of the church are the path to spiritual fulfillment. To forsake the means of grace Christ offers through his church opens the door to individualism, unchecked enthusiasm and error.

A different form of individualism is presented by rationalism, or what is often called *liberalism*. "Liberalism, is the mistake of subjecting to human judgment those revealed doctrines which are in their nature beyond and independent of it; and claiming to determine on intrinsic grounds the truth and value of propositions which rest for their reception on the external authority of the Divine Word."[23] Similarities with the views of Coleridge and Romanticism are clear in the idea that spiritual realities cannot be known through unaided human reason.[24] The problem is that the divine transcends human faculties, therefore rational argumentation can never lead one to the faith. Instead rational religion makes people indifferent to Christianity since it creates the impression that divine truths can be discussed in the same way as any other subject. Stated otherwise, rationalism makes us the judge of what is true. In contrast, Newman argues that religious truth must be the judge of our reason. Therefore, faith precedes reason.[25]

At the heart of rational religion's error is a misunderstanding of human nature. "After all, man is *not* a reasoning animal; he is a seeing, feeling, contemplating, acting animal."[26] Since rationality is not at the core of our nature, it can never provide the religious impulse. Instead the basis of spirituality is moral action; faith is rooted in volition. "Faith is a principle of action, and action does not allow time for minute and finished investigations."[27] Therefore, Newman argues that faith—real, not notional, assent—depends on moral temperament.[28] Those callous of spirit will never find an acceptable foundation for belief because "to be in earnest in seeking the truth is an indispensable requisite for finding it."[29]

A final characteristic of the Oxford Movement, which also exhibits affinities with Romanticism, is the desire to maintain the mystery in religion. The attempt to avoid the accusation that Christianity is irrational, Newman believes, results from misplaced fear. "We are in danger of unbelief more than of superstition."[30] In the attempt to eradicate superstition, rationalism removed the supernatural element of religion. Instead Newman argues that we need a greater emphasis on the mystery and divine in religion. Reverence and holy fear, not reason, light the path to divine truth. We can only know God when we are properly receptive. The role of the church, through its doctrine, liturgy and sacraments, is to maintain the mystery that creates a healthy sense of humility in us.

Significance of the Oxford Movement

Perhaps the most enduring influence of the Oxford Movement is not its appeal to antiquity or its ecclesiology but its pastoral and devotional influence. Anglicanism, in general, had increasingly directed its message toward the highly educated as it rationalized Christianity. However, by identifying the will as the moral and spiritual center of human nature, the Tractarians made faith once again accessible to the common person. Moreover, they demonstrated to many that a powerful inner religion was not incompatible with a high church ecclesiology. Liturgy, tradition, doctrine and the sacraments do not hinder spiritual life but are the means by which it is attained.

The theological position of the Oxford Movement was not new, although stated quite ably by respected individuals who arose at a time when circumstances in England aroused greater receptivity. However, while the Oxford Movement may have expressed many fears of the English people—spiritual indifference in many quarters, religious anarchy, the breakdown of tradition, the encroachment of secular power on ecclesiastical affairs—it was less equipped to address its hopes. One growing hope in this day was for a world where ideals such as freedom and equality would be realized in greater measure. The Oxford Movement, which by nature relied on a hierarchical model, was out of step with this trend. In a sense they were attempting to "unring the bell" that brought an end to the religious and cultural uniformity of England's past as well as the partnership that gave the established church broad influence over secular government. Moreover, because appeal to tradition secured their place at the top of the power structure, the ideas of the Anglican clergy who constituted the core of the Oxford Movement appeared to many to be self-serving and paternalistic.

Another problematic issue is the precritical approach to history assumed in the theology of the Oxford Movement. They insulated themselves from the discussions of biblical criticism that raised the question of historical development, both within church tradition and Scripture. Thus while Newman has some awareness of movement within doctrine and praxis, he falls into the same trap we see in religious liberalism: the historians of the day assumed that they were able to free themselves of their historical circumstances to provide an objective view. The only difference in Newman is that he takes the historian's claims to objectivity and vests them in the church fathers, without any argument as to how they escape the relativity of their own historical situation.

Neo-Lutheranism

On the tercentenary of Martin Luther's Ninety-Five Theses in 1817, a joint communion between leaders from German Lutheran and Reformed churches took place as part of the effort to bring the two groups together under the Prussian Union Church. On the same day

Claus Harms, an influential Lutheran pastor, reissued Luther's Theses and upped the ante with ninety-five of his own. Many of Harm's theses directly opposed the Prussian Union Church but also supplied warnings about other perceived threats to traditional Lutheranism—theological and social liberalism, religious subjectivism, pietism and the presence of the nonorthodox in the academy. These concerns struck a chord with many like-minded individuals and provided the impetus for the Lutheran confessional movement, often called neo-Lutheranism. Neo-Lutheranism was characterized by renewed interest in Luther and his ideas, a heightened sense of Lutheran identity and stress on unification behind the Lutheran confessions.

In addition to Harms a number of prominent figures lent their support to the neo-Lutheran cause: August Vilmar (1800-1868), professor of theology at Marburg, Theodor Kleifoth (1810-1895), superintendent of the Lutheran Church in Mecklenburg, and F. A. Philippi (1809-1892), also in Mecklenburg. One of the most important was Ernst Wilhelm Hengstenberg (1802-1869), who received a professorship at Berlin at age twenty-six. A highly polemical individual, he used *Evangelische Kirchen-Zeitung*, of which he was editor from 1827 until his death, as a tool for his attacks on those who opposed neo-Lutheranism. He had particular disdain for the historical-critical approach to biblical interpretation. God's work in history cannot be conditioned by anything circumstantial or temporal. The presence of historically contingent material in Scripture compromises the doctrine of inspiration, upon which everything else in Christian doctrine depends.[31]

Perhaps the clearest and best popular expression of neo-Lutheran views is presented in Wilhelm Löhe's (1808-1872) *Three Books About the Church* (1845). While Löhe and most neo-Lutherans did not adopt Hengstenberg's dictation theory, his view that theology's foundation is a divinely inspired Bible is the thread that runs through the entire movement. *Sola Scriptura* was the principle on which they parted ways with Roman Catholicism and the Oxford Movement. Löhe argues that both groups misunderstand the concept of apostolicity. True apostolicity has nothing to do with an unbroken line of ordination reaching back to the Twelve but refers to a denomination's faithfulness to the word of the apostles as contained in Scripture. "A congregation can be apostolic even if no apostle ever entered its territory if only it holds to the Word of the apostles and, vice versa, it can be unapostolic, unchristian, even anti-christian, though it itself may have been founded by apostles and may dwell above the graves of apostles."[32] Similarly, Löhe argues that the true test of Antiquity is not determined by concordance with the church fathers but with Scripture, since this predates the Fathers. "The doctrine and the confession which have the Holy Scriptures on their side certainly have antiquity in their favor. We must never let ourselves be driven from the truth that the Scriptures are clear, for here we have a valid norm for distinguishing between the contradictory teachings of the fathers as well as between the contradictory confessions of our day."[33]

At the heart of the controversy between Lutheran and Anglo-Catholic confessionalism was the relationship between the church and Scripture. To allow tradition to function as the interpreter of Scripture is to subordi-nate the Bible to the church. In contrast, Löhe states, "The church is the child of God's Word and can never, never stand above the Word."[34] Therefore, what creates and unites the church is not tradition and an appeal to antiquity grounded in the fathers. Instead, "The church is one in truth; it is the truth which draws all its children into one community."[35] This truth is derived from Scripture alone by those who accurately inter-pret it. This search for the Bible's proper interpretation is the rallying point of neo-Lutheranism. "If the differences among the various denom-inations consisted only of external matters such as, for example, liturgical forms and formulas or vestments and the like, we could overlook them in favor of what might be common to all groups and let each one live according to his pleasure. But this is not the case. The things which divide them are doctrines, expressions of divine truth. They teach differ-ent things, and this is a serious matter."[36]

The defining teachings of any group are encapsulated in its confes-sions. Thus in order to know which denomination is in greatest confor-mity with Scripture, and most truly the church, we must look to these documents. From this point Löhe asserts, "The greatest treasure of the Lutheran Church is the pure doctrine which flows from a pure confes-sion."[37] Therefore, he allows that "the Augsburg Confession may be refuted by the writings of the fathers, which do not always agree, but it can never be refuted by God's Word."[38] The Lutheran Church is "the one

among all [denominations] which has the mark of the pure denomination, the church par excellence."[39]

Using the Augsburg Confession as its benchmark, the Lutheran confessionalists placed increased stress on the sacraments and church discipline. This set them at odds with the Pietists, who relied more heavily on
Luther's idea of the priesthood of all believers to assert individual freedom over against church authority. However, part of the success of neo-
Lutheranism resulted from its ability to co-opt the Pietists' call for inner
renewal and put it in the context of Scripture, confession and sacrament.
Neo-Lutheranism also had greater success than confessional movements
in England and America because German national unity had not
reached the level achieved elsewhere, and regional identity was still
closely connected with religious tradition. Finally, the proliferation of
dissenting religious groups was not as great in Germany as elsewhere.
The long-standing equilibrium between Roman Catholic, Reformed and
Lutheran groups was maintained without significant interference from
other denominations.

However, several factors eventually converged to weaken the influence of neo-Lutheranism. Gradually, growing political unity between the
German states replaced the regional character that encouraged traditional religious identification. Second, critical methods undermined
many claims of the neo-Lutherans, and theological liberalism demonstrated that themes in Luther's writings were open to new definition.
Related to this, the neo-Lutheran case is constructed on premises about
the congruity of its confessions with Scripture, the role of church tradition and the primacy of Luther's view of doctrine. Since these premises
were held only by those who were already Lutheran, the movement
tended to preach to the choir. As the trends mentioned above chipped
away at the traditional Lutheran foundation, the neo-Lutheran message
moved to the margins.

Mercersburg Theology

That a small German Reformed Seminary in Mercersburg, Pennsylvania,
would find a place in the history of theological ideas would appear
unlikely. However, the school was saved from obscurity by the convergence of two very able scholars, whose works were influential far beyond

the narrow confines of the German Reformed Church. John Williamson Nevin (1803-1886), who studied under Charles Hodge at Princeton, came to the school in 1840 as professor of theology. He was joined from Germany by Philip Schaff (1819-1893) in 1844, who studied under theological luminaries such as Isaac Dorner (1809-1884), F. C. Baur, Neander, Tholuck and E. W. Hengstenberg. Together they formed the foundation of what became known as the Mercersburg Theology.[40]

Schaff's welcome to America was less than positive. His inaugural address, *The Principle of Protestantism* (later expanded and published with an introductory essay by Nevin), led to heresy charges. He was decisively cleared the following year with the support of Nevin, who was in broad agreement with Schaff's ideas. Both believed that the major problem facing the church was disunity born of a rejection of doctrine, catechism and sacrament, and the embrace of revivalist methods and rationalistic theology. Nevin's influence was less widespread, but Schaff became recognized as one of the leading church historians of the day, finishing an illustrious career at Union Theological Seminary.

While renewal movements were present in England and the Continent, certain trends in these groups were intensified in America. First, early dominance of denominational groups in some regions was quickly diluted with rapid immigration of those with different or no religious sympathies. Second, the spirit of individualism was much stronger in this country, which weakened the appeal to tradition and institution that was very much part of the mindset across the Atlantic. Therefore, confessionalism had a more difficult task in establishing its claims. This led to a tendency toward sectarianism that is not uniquely American but much stronger here. Separation of church and state made the cost of affiliating with a new denomination less severe. Moreover, because mother churches in Europe were often slow in sending their pastors to the New World, many new immigrants who would have preferred to maintain connections with their confessions were unable to do so, and many found refuge in the new denominations. Finally, the American spirit tended to be pragmatic in orientation. Therefore, the issue of a tradition's pedigree often carried less weight than the usefulness of an idea or method.

The question of pragmatism forms an important element in the background of Mercersburg Theology. Finney's "New Measures" were extremely successful in attracting converts. This success caused many groups that were initially wary of such methods, including congregations within Mercersburg's sphere of influence, to reconsider their positions. These New Measures featured fiery preaching, protracted meetings and methods geared to evoking emotional responses in the hearer. The symbolic center of these methods was the anxious bench, at which sinners would publicly repent of their sins, often in a highly emotional manner. In general, this and related movements argued that the unifying element in Christianity was not doctrinal or ecclesiastical but the experience and evidence of spiritual rebirth.

Like most confessional movements the Mercersburg theologians were suspicious of reliance on emotion and experience. This is most clearly revealed in Nevin's *The Anxious Bench* (1843, expanded second edition 1844), a direct critique of the New Measures revivalism. One problem is the disorderly nature of services in these groups. Strong emotional response is not necessarily an indication of spiritual maturity and progress but may be a counterfeit spirituality. "As the spirit of the Anxious Bench tends to disorder, so it connects itself also naturally and readily with a certain vulgarism of feeling in religion, that is always injurious to the worship of God, and often shows itself absolutely irreverent and profane. True religious feeling is inward and deep; shrinks from show; forms the mind to a subdued humble habit."[41] At the heart of this criticism is the belief that emotional disarray in revival movements separates the subjective element of faith from its objective basis.

The corrective for religious subjectivism is found in the worship structures provided by the church. These forms provide a check on emotionalism and allow faith to become sober, steadfast and informed. Therefore, to the revivalists' charge that traditional church structures lead to mere formalism, Nevin responds, "To rely upon the Anxious Bench, to be under the necessity of having recourse to new measures of any sort to enlist attention or produce effect, in the work of the gospel, shows a want of inward spiritual force. If it be true that old forms are dead and powerless in a minister's hands, the fault is not in the forms, but in the minister himself; and it is the very impotence of quackery, to think of mending the case essentially by the introduction of new forms."[42] In short, it is not the forms themselves that are wanting but the inability of the minister to properly employ them to bring about their proper ends.

Behind the appeal of the New Measures, Nevin and Schaff saw an arrogant individualism unwilling to submit to established church discipline and practices. This pride led to sectarianism, as individuals moved by their conversion experiences separated from existing denominations, certain they now discerned the truth missed by all existing groups. Although it appears to fall at the opposite end of the theological spectrum from revivalism, the Mercersburg theologians saw rationalism as a manifestation of the same problem. "Protestant rationalism holds the *isolated* will and reason of the *individual* sufficient for the purposes of salvation, and in this way is altogether *subjective and unchurchly* in its nature."[43] Both sectarianism and rationalism are two sides of the same subjectivistic coin. *"Rationalism is theoretic sectarism; sectarism is practical rationalism."*[44]

Nevin and Schaff recognized that the evangelistic movements often brought together people from different communions in their services. However, they argued that this was a false unity achieved on a purely pragmatic and experiential foundation. "The union of the Church, in any case, is not to be established by stratagen or force."[45] The means by which revivalism brought Christians together were external. In contrast, Nevin argues, "If the evil [of sectarianism] is ever to be effectually surmounted, it must be by the growth of Christian charity in the bosom of the Church itself. No union can be of any account at last, that is not produced by inward sympathy and agreement between the parties it brings together."[46]

Inward sympathy only springs from proper understanding of and submission to doctrine and sacrament. It is especially the latter that Nevin emphasizes in *The Mystical Presence,* a protest to the trend in many Reformed churches to downplay the doctrine of Christ's real presence in the Eucharist. Nevin argues that, while Christ is not corporeally present in the elements of communion, the reality of his full divinity and humanity is available to the recipient. Thus through the Lord's Supper, the communicant experiences union with Christ. "The union indeed is not natural but sacramental. The grace is not comprehended *in* the elements, as its depository and vehicle outwardly considered. But the union is none the less real and firm."[47]

Nevin's concept of Christ's real presence in the sacrament provides the foundation upon which Schaff identifies Christology as the core of Christian unity. Just as Christ is God in the flesh, so the church is the divine presence in history. This is the result of the union that exists between Christ and his people. "They are inserted into his life, through faith, by the power of the Holy Ghost, and become thus incorporated with it, as fully as they were before with that corrupt life they had by their natural birth."[48] The mystical union of Christ and his church prompts Schaff to describe Christianity in an organic paradigm. The emergence of various denominations is seen from the perspective of continuity and development rather than as discontinuous movements. The church as organism implies "development, evolution, progress. . . . It is not as though the knowledge of some truths had been absolutely complete, and so stationary from the beginning, while the knowledge of other truths has been numerically added to it from time to time. But the whole, in all its parts, is comprehended more or less in the same law; since no truth can be absolutely complete separately from the rest."[49]

Schaff, in a manner that reflects the influence of Baur, understands the organic growth of the church dialectically. "We must distinguish in the Church accordingly between Idea and manifestation. As to her Idea, or as comprehended in Christ, she is already complete; in the way of manifestation, however, she passes—like every one of her members—outwardly and inwardly, through different stages of life, until the Ideal enclosed in Christ shall be fully actualized in humanity and his body appear thus in the ripeness of complete manhood."[50] Under this approach all denominations are expressions of Christianity to the extent that they reflect the ideal of Christ. This allows a more charitable understanding of other denominations than is common during this time. For example, the Reformation is not to be seen as a radical break from Catholicism but as "the fruit of all the better tendencies of the Catholic Church itself."[51] Nor does any part of the Reformation tradition represent Christianity in its complete expression. "The Reformation must be regarded as still incomplete. It needs yet its concluding act to unite what has fallen asunder, to bring the subjective to a reconciliation with the objective."[52] The theologians of Mercersburg are confident, however, that the highest current expression of Christian truth is contained in the Reformed Church.

Nevin and Schaff do not speculate on the form the church would assume in its perfected unity, but they are clear that an individualistic movement built on pragmatic methods is counterproductive. "It is a different system altogether [from the New Measures] that is required, to build up the interests of Christianity in a firm and sure way. A ministry apt to teach; sermons full of unction and light; faithful, systematic instruction; zeal for the interests of holiness; pastoral visitation; catechetical training; due attention to order and discipline; patient perseverance in the details of the ministerial work; these are the agencies, by which alone the kingdom of God may be expected to go steadily forward, among any people."[53] This forward movement of the kingdom requires that the church reject individualism and the sectarian spirit in order to realize its unity in Christ.

Princeton Theology

The Old Princeton School shares a great deal with the Mercersburg theology. Both have a common Reformed heritage, a desire for intellectual rigor in theology and a distrust of religious emotionalism. There are differences, however, that set the two schools apart. Most importantly, the Mercersburg school put greater emphasis on tradition and the submission of the individual to the collective body of Christ. This was largely the result of Mercersburg's closer tie to Germany.[54] By contrast, the Princeton theologians were more indicative of the American frame of mind. While wary of religious emotionalism, they displayed a greater trust in the individual. As a result, the center of gravity shifts from the church to Scripture in the Princeton theology. It remains a form of confessionalism in its emphasis on the doctrinal purity of classical Calvinism, its appeal to the Westminster Confession and its grounding of Christianity in Scripture.

The strength of the Princeton theology can be attributed in large part to the presence of powerful intellects who provided an almost seamless continuity of theological thought over an extended period of time.[55] The first and for a time the only faculty member of Princeton Seminary (founded 1812) was Archibald Alexander (1772-1851). Entering Princeton as a student in this same year was Charles Hodge (1797-1878), who was to become the most famous of the Princeton theologians. Hodge graduated from the seminary in 1819 and joined the faculty as professor of Oriental and biblical literature in 1822. When Alexander died in 1858, Hodge became professor of polemic theology. He remained on the faculty until his death, a tenure of fifty-six years. Hodge's son, Archibald Alexander Hodge (1823-1886), succeeded his father and carried on his theological positions but did not distinguish himself as a scholar. At the younger Hodge's death the task of theological instruction fell to Benjamin Breckinridge Warfield (1851-1921), a scholar of broad knowledge and dialectical skill, who remained in the position until his death.

For almost 110 years these four theologians, supported by other very able Princeton faculty members, defended Calvinist distinctives—divine sovereignty, the total depravity of humanity and election—against the opposing forces of the day. Their influence reached far since Princeton Seminary was the largest theological institution in America. Moreover, they drew the cream of the crop, with their graduates occupying many prominent church pulpits as well as ascending to positions of ecclesiastical and academic influence.[56] The amazing continuity of the Princeton theology came to an end when J. Gresham Machen (1881-1937), professor of New Testament at the school, determined that the trend toward liberalism at the school was irreversible and left to help found Westminster Seminary in 1929.

Hodge's statement "I am not afraid to say that a new idea never originated in this Seminary"[57] has created the perception in some circles that the Princeton theologians thrust their heads into the sand and ignored the ideas of the day. Although they were committed to holding back the tide of liberalism, which in their view included almost all new ideas, it is incorrect to see them as theological anachronisms. They were well-informed about the ideas of the age. Hodge had firsthand knowledge of theological developments in Germany, spending 1826-1828 in the country. Warfield's early training was in natural science and mathematics. The issues they engaged—Mercersburg theology, Finney's revivalism, New England Unitarianism, Darwinism—were the pressing questions of American religion. Similarly, while Hodge is famous for fighting the scientism of his day, he embraced the inductive method of science and argued that our interpretation of Scripture should change when science brings new facts to light. Ultimately, he argues that true science and Scripture are fully compatible. "If geologists finally prove that it [the earth] has existed for myriads of ages, it will be found that the first chapter of Genesis is in full accord with the facts, and that the last results of science are embodied on the first page of the Bible."[58] His well-known dispute with Darwinism did not result from a rejection of evolution per se but evolutionary theories that devalued human worth and left no room for divine purpose or involvement in the world.[59] In fact, Hodge's successor, Warfield, embraced theistic evolution.

While the Princeton theologians did engage contemporary issues more frequently than most recognize, they did so with the tools of the past. The first of these tools was the Westminster Confession (1646), to which all professors at Princeton were required to subscribe. Of it Warfield says, "It is our special felicity, that as Reformed Christians, and heirs of the richest and fullest formulation of Reformed thought, we possess in that precious heritage, the Westminster Confession, the most complete, the most admirable, and most perfect statement of the essential Christian doctrine of Holy Scripture which has ever been formed by man. Here the vital faith of the church is brought to full expression."[60] While the Westminster Confession is the ballast that holds Calvinism firm against novelty and the errors of other groups, the means by which it is interpreted was filtered through the early Reformed theologian Francis Turretin (1623-1687). His *Institutio theologiae elencticae* (1679-1685), viewed by the early Princetonians as the most faithful expression of Calvin's thought, was the theological text used (in Latin) at Princeton until replaced by Hodge's *Systematic Theology* (1872-1873).

Systematization of truth is essential to human nature, and the process by which we do this is a central concern for Hodge. "The Bible is to the theologian what nature is to the man of science. It is his store-house of facts; and his method of ascertaining what the Bible teaches, is the same as that which the natural philosopher adopts to ascertain what nature teaches."[61] In the latter part of this quote Hodge argues that the theologian should employ a method analogous to that of the natural scientist. "The true method of theology is, therefore, the inductive, which assumes that the Bible contains all the facts or truths which form the contents of theology, just as the facts of nature are the contents of the natural sciences."[62] While many theological conservatives of the age had abandoned inductive approaches to theology, the Princeton theologians built on the empiricism of Scottish Common Sense Realism.[63] This provides the foundation to Hodge's evidentialist approach to scriptural inspiration.

Christianity rests on the objective basis provided by an infallible Scripture: "All the books of Scripture are equally inspired. All alike are infallible in what they teach."[64] The effect of the Spirit on the authors is such that "the inspired penmen wrote out of the fulness of their own thoughts and feelings, and employed the language and modes of expression which to them were the most natural and appropriate. Nevertheless, and none the less, they spoke as they were moved by the Holy Ghost, and their words were his words."[65] While maintaining verbal inspiration Hodge moves away from the dictation theory, stating that, "The sacred writers were not machines. Their self-consciousness was not suspended; nor were their intellectual powers superseded."[66] Instead the Spirit's inspiration means that the authors were not infallible "except for the special purpose for which they were employed. . . . As to all matter of science, philosophy, and history, they stood on the same level with their contemporaries. They were infallible only as teachers, and when acting as the spokesmen of God. Their inspiration no more made them astronomers than it made them agriculturists."[67]

While Hodge was a champion of a propositional approach to doctrine, he does state that spiritual experience plays a role in our interpretation of Scripture. "Although the inward teaching of the Spirit, or religious experience, is no substitute for an external revelation, and is no part of the rule of faith, it is, nevertheless, an invaluable guide in determining what the rule of faith teaches."[68] Moreover, the essential message of Scripture is open and clear to every person. Therefore, no one should be required to bow to any authority on their interpretation of Scripture. "The Bible is a plain book. It is intelligible by the people. And they have the right, and are bound to read and interpret it for themselves; so that their faith may rest on the testimony of the Scriptures, and not on that of the Church."[69]

The Influence of the Princeton Theology

While the Princeton theologians were, by all accounts, men of personal piety and respect for Scripture, a recurring criticism is that their attempts to bring together their views of Scripture and experience were hardly successful. Both are present in their theology (although the emphasis is clearly on Scripture), but little is done to integrate them into a whole.[70] A second common criticism concerns the inductive approach upon which much of Hodge's theology is built. Even during its day Scottish Common Sense Realism was seen as a questionable foundation for theological conclusions. Unless we can demonstrate that induction can be free of cultural, moral and religious assumptions, and that such an assumption-free method can result in knowledge of God, the theology Hodge builds on this Baconian method lacks a convincing epistemological foundation.

These issues notwithstanding, the influence of the old Princeton School was profound during its day. It provided a third way between liberalism and revivalist experientialism. For most of the nineteenth century it was the main voice in Reformed thought in America. Its influence has also extended into this century, originally through Westminster Theological Seminary and later through other institutions seeking to preserve Calvinism against liberalizing tendencies. The Princeton Theology has also been highly influential for many conservative and fundamentalist Christians who have endeavored to maintain the propositional nature of doctrine and evidentialist apologetics. It is probably fair to say, however, that few heirs of the Princeton School have been as skilled as Hodge and company, and as a result, they have often continued the fights of the nineteenth century long after others have moved beyond them.

The Rise of Theological Liberalism

The confessional theologies had the weight of tradition behind them, and this made them an important force through the middle of the nineteenth century, especially in Continental Europe and England. However, tradition's strength was progressively eroded during this time when newness and progress were so frequently seen as equivalents. Moreover, while religious diversity had been a reality in America from its beginning, the religious homogeneity so common to Europe's various regions began breaking down, reducing the power of the previously dominant confessions. Thus while new and minority religious groups had earlier faced an uphill battle with academic, ecclesiastical or political powers, tolerance toward them grew when it became apparent they would not go away.

In some ways, the church's institutional power in the past contributed to its erosion. State churches played a key role in the development of national identity, and as secular power and religious diversity increased, governments felt more secure in using newly acquired power against ecclesiastical authorities. This was often the case as new measures of status came into being and the old hereditary structures, often sanctioned by the church, were cast off. Confessionalist systems tended to be hierarchical, and the democratizing forces of the age diminished the clout of these groups. As increasing education and political privileges became available to the populace, it was very difficult to sell the idea that they were incapable of properly interpreting Scripture themselves and must rely on tradition or institutional pronouncements.

Perhaps the greatest cause of confessionalism's diminished strength was its reliance on the past. Even though none of the theologies considered above are simple restatements of older systems, they found their grounding in past realities that were themselves static and unchanging. In contrast, theological liberalism saw the future as destiny. Its optimism about human nature and the progressive realization of the kingdom of God through social forces resonated with the *Zeitgeist*. Therefore, as theological liberalism reaches its ascendancy, it puts ethics, not doctrine, at the center of Christianity and radically reconstructs traditional understandings of human sinfulness, divine activity in the world, and the nature and message of Jesus.[71]

Albrecht Ritschl

Despite Karl Barth's negative assessment that "Ritschl has the significance of an episode in more recent theology; and not, indeed not, that of an epoch,"[72] it is difficult to see Albrecht Ritschl (1822-1889) as anything but the most influential theologian between Schleiermacher and Barth.[73] He synthesizes ideas from disparate sources—Luther, Schleiermacher, Hegelian thought, Kant—into a theological approach that gives a fresh expression of the spirit of the age. In doing so, his theology sets the theological agenda for his numerous disciples as well as his opponents until World War I.

Ritschl's father, a bishop in the Prussian Reformed Union Church, was concerned about the Hegelian influence at Tübingen and only reluctantly gave permission for his son to study there after time at Bonn, Halle and Heidelberg. His fears were well-founded. At Tübingen, Ritschl came under the spell of Baur's theology. However, while he remained indebted to Baur's groundbreaking work in historical method, the younger Ritschl eventually broke with Baur's Hegelian theology in favor of a more Kantian ethical approach. Throughout his mature work his ideas reflect the dual influence of a moral theology constructed through historical investigation. Ritschl began his teaching career at Bonn (1846) as Privatdozent, lecturing in the history of dogma. He became professor of dogmatics there in 1852 and moved to Göttingen in 1864, where he remained until retirement in 1889. The final volume of his three-volume magnum opus, *The Christian Doctrine of Justification and Reconciliation* (1870-1874), became the defining text for theological liberalism.

Doctrine as Value Judgment

While Ritschl is rightly referred to as the father of liberal Christianity, in comparison to the Hegelian theologians he represents a conservative turn in his view that theology must always return to Scripture for its bearings: "It stands as the fundamental principle of the Protestant church that Christian doctrine is to be obtained from the Bible alone."[74] Contrary to the Hegelian theologians, Ritschl argues that speculative philosophy does not correct theology but distorts it. The problem with metaphysics is that "natural and spiritual phenomena concern metaphysics only in so far as they may be conceived as things in general."[75] In other words, metaphysics levels off all realities, so that the divine, human and natural are explored in the same manner.

The negative implications of metaphysical theology are twofold. First, speculative metaphysics turns God into an abstraction, stripped of all attributes. Therefore, "the idea of God does not belong to metaphysics since metaphysical knowledge is indifferent toward the distinctions of kind and value that exist between spirit and nature."[76] Second, Hegelian thought, in Ritschl's opinion, makes no room for the spiritual aspect of humanity. When the natural and spiritual are viewed as two poles of the same reality, speculative philosophy becomes simply a variation on scientism, which absorbs human freedom into a materialistic nexus of cause and effect. In contrast, Ritschl states that "the religious view of the world, in all its species, rests on the fact that man in some degree distinguishes himself in worth from the phenomena which surround him and from the influences of nature which press in upon him."[77]

Its reduction of humanity to mere nature and its implicit determinism is a major reason Ritschl views metaphysics as a false start for theology. Even as we experience subjection to certain natural forces, we still have awareness of our dignity and value. Thus only a specifically theological approach gives due attention to our moral will, which is the foundation of our spirituality. This reflects the Kantian influence, which argues that religion is essentially practical and moral.[78] However, he only follows Kant so far. Unlike his predecessor, who allows religion to remain the handmaiden to ethics, Ritschl argues that religion always illuminates our need for justification and reconciliation and creates the recognition that these cannot be attained through the natural realm.

Because the quest for salvation is personal in nature, its resolution must be found through a personal power. This realization draws Ritschl away from the arid ethical theology of Kant and back to revelation given through Christ. "Personality is the form in which the idea of God is given through Revelation. As theology has to do with the God revealed in Christ, this is justified scientifically as the only practicable form of the conception of God."[79] Thus in opposition to the Hegelian Absolute and the Kantian moral Arbiter, Ritschl insists on a God whose essence is love and who cannot be seen except as personal. Only such a God can resolve our need for salvation. "The compassion for men in the midst of the difficulties of life . . . is excluded in the unmoved *actus purus* which the philosopher conceives of as the destiny and ordering ground of the world in general. No veneration of God can attach itself to this idea."[80]

The personality of God contributes to a key principle in Ritschl's theology. Since we cannot find the divine through metaphysics, knowledge of God comes via our experience of sin and redemption. Such knowledge has personal and religious significance for us, therefore it can only be described as what Ritschl calls value judgments. "But if Christ by what He has done and suffered for my salvation is my Lord, and if, by trusting for my salvation to the power of what He has done for me, I honour Him as my God, then that is a value-judgment of a direct kind. It is not a judgment which belongs to the sphere of disinterested scientific knowledge, like the formula of Chalcedon."[81]

Ritschl's assertion that "every cognition of a religious sort is a direct judgment of value"[82] means that religious doctrines are not factual propositions. Instead statements about God only take on meaning in the context of our own salvation; theology only has validity from within faith. Ritschl credits Luther with recovering this view.

> Knowledge of God can be demonstrated as religious knowledge only when He is conceived as securing to the believer such a position in the world as more than counter-balances its restrictions. Apart from this value-judgment of faith, there exists no knowledge of God worthy of this content. So that we ought not to strive after a purely theoretical and "disinterested" knowledge of God, as an indispensable preliminary to the knowledge of faith. To be sure, people say that we must first know the nature of God and Christ ere we can ascertain their worth for us. But Luther's insight perceived the incorrectness of such a view. The truth rather is that we know the nature of God and Christ only in their worth for us. For God and faith are inseparable conceptions.[83]

Thus rather than looking to speculative proofs to bolster religious truth, Ritschl employs a form of practical proof, in which God's being and activity on our behalf gives value to human being.

Ritschl acknowledges that defining doctrine as value judgment leaves him open to the accusation of subjectivism, a charge he desires to avoid. His first line of defense is that even methods that appear objective involve value judgments. "Value-judgments therefore are determinative in the case of all connected knowledge of the world, even when carried out in the most objective fashion. Attention during scientific observation and the impartial examination of the matter observed always denote that such knowledge has a value for him who employs it."[84] To the extent that science and philosophy engage in statements of value, they enter the realm of religion.

It is, however, Ritschl's second response to the charge of subjectivism that receives the most attention. The fact that theological doctrine is value judgment rather than literal truth does not mean it is arbitrary or subjectively derived. The anchor for these value-laden claims is God's revelation through the life of Jesus. If Jesus reveals God's nature and plan, this revelation can only be recovered through historical inquiry. The historical factuality of Jesus' life is the objective touchstone necessary for Christianity. This purely historical approach is a decisive rejection of the Hegelians' assertion that we can see reality through the divine eyes. Ritschl argues that we do not begin from the super-historical Idea but from the historical life of Jesus. All theology commences "from below," from historical research. Thus unlike Baur, who sought to synthesize metaphysics and history, Ritschl *replaced* metaphysics with historical research.

Although Ritschl rejects the metaphysical point of departure in Baur, his dialectical model is retained. Ritschl, however, modifies it into a dialectic of form and message. On the one hand, Christianity must adapt its forms and expressions to address the issues and developments of history. On the other hand, the pristine message of Christ is always in danger of being obscured by its response to historical circumstances. Christianity must speak in new ways to preserve itself in the midst of change but must also avoid confusion between what is historically contingent and what is essential. For example, early Christianity was forced to assume Greek categories of thought to ward off threats from gnosticism. However, without benefit of historical method these metaphysical ideas, which are alien to the gospel, eventually became confused with the gospel. The historian's role is to isolate historically contingent forms and to assure that these and not the Christian message are discarded when new circumstances arise.

The Kingdom of God

With this method in place Ritschl, the historian, moves forward to recover the essence of the gospel. This core, in Ritschl's view, is Jesus' proclamation of the kingdom of God. God's kingdom consists in his lordship over us and our fellowship with others. As Ritschl is fond of describing it, "Christianity, so to speak, resembles not a circle described from a single centre, but an ellipse which is determined by two foci."[85] Corresponding to these dual foci are the great themes of salvation in Jesus' message: justification and reconciliation. At one end of the ellipse is Christ, who mediates our salvation. At the other pole is the community that participates in this salvation. As such, the gospel is simultaneously redemptive word and ethical imperative. "The kingdom of God is the divinely ordained highest good of the community founded through God's revelation in Christ; but it is the highest good only in the sense that it forms at the same time the ethical ideal for whose attainment the members of the community bind themselves to each other through a definite type of reciprocal actions. This meaning of the concept 'kingdom of God' becomes clear through the imperative which is simultaneously expressed in it."[86] Thus Christianity is a specifically ethical religion in which neither the religious nor the ethical can be overlooked.

However, Jesus does not simply proclaim the kingdom as God's goal for humanity; he also establishes it as a reality. "By making the aim of His own life the aim of mankind, who are to be called into the fellowship of His community, He is before all else the Founder of a religion and the Redeemer of men from the dominion of the world."[87] Jesus' special status as Redeemer is not derived from any ontological uniqueness in his person but is based "on the fact that he was the only one qualified for his special vocation—bringing in the kingdom of God; that he devoted himself to the exercise of this highest conceivable vocation in the preaching of the truth and in loving action without break or deviation."[88]

As the archetype and mediator of the kingdom he sought to found, Jesus' perfect love and obedience to his vocation is the source of the church's valuation of him as divine. This moral interpretation of Jesus' divinity is radically different from traditional formulations that begin from an analysis of the two natures. However, Ritschl argues that the traditional approach goes beyond historical warrant. "The origin of the Person of Christ—how His Person attained the form in which it presents itself to our ethical and religious apprehension—is not a subject for theological inquiry, because the problem transcends all inquiry."[89] Christologies that begin from metaphysical statements of Jesus' Person are holdovers from Christianity's encounter with Greek culture, in which it was forced to state the significance of Christ in ontological categories. Now, however, the idea of Christ as both fully human and fully divine must be abandoned as outmoded metaphysical speculation.[90] Similarly, since preexistence, resurrection and ascension are not part of the historical experience of Jesus, they have no place in Christology.[91] Not only are such claims inaccessible to historical investigation, they have no concrete significance for the Christian. "The estimation of Christ as God, involved in the act of putting our trust in Him, implies also a change in, or at least a new interpretation of, those attributes which directly or indirectly are ascribed to Christ in the Creed. Christ cannot be the object of our trust if the description of Him in the Creed is meant to be understood in a sense purely objective."[92] Instead, as in all other doctrinal statements, the assertion of Jesus' divinity refers to the value we place on Christ for us as the one who conquers the limitations of the world.

Ritschl's substitution of historical investigation for metaphysical analysis in Christology is paralleled by his restatement of sin and atonement. He rejects the idea of divine retributive justice as a holdover from Greek thought. "Such a moral order, which is based upon the Hellenic juridical conception of divine justice, and which, moreover, in virtue of our first parents' sin issues in the condemnation of the whole human race, leaves no room for the possibility of the reconciliation of man with God."[93] While he does not deny the universality of sin, he does argue, "In so far as men, regarded as sinners both in their individual capacity and as a whole, are objects of the redemption and reconciliation made possible by the love of God, sin is estimated by God, not as the final purpose of opposition to the known will of God, but as ignorance."[94] Given this definition of sin as ignorance, Ritschl also rejects the forensic model of atonement. "For Christ had no sense of guilt in His sufferings, consequently He cannot have regarded them as punishment, nor even as punishment accepted in the place of the guilty, or in order to deter men from sin."[95] In its place he establishes an educational model in which human institutions such as state and family prepare us for inclusion in the kingdom, though they only dimly reflect this reality.

Against what he sees as a dangerous individualism and subjectivism in pietism and mysticism, Ritschl hastens to add that Christ's mediation "for us" is known only through the church.[96] "Authentic and complete knowledge of Jesus' religious significance—His significance, that is, as a Founder of religion—depends, then, on one's reckoning oneself part of the community which He founded, and this precisely in so far as it believes itself to have received the forgiveness of sins as His peculiar gift."[97] The reason for this is our dependence on the church's evaluation of Christ. "Here also is the explanation of the fact that the conception of Christ's Divinity, or the application to Christ of the Old Testament Divine name, first arose in the Christian community; Christ Himself was never in the position thus to describe Himself. Therefore this attribute can be rightly appraised by theology only when Christ is conceived as the living Head of the community of God's Kingdom. For we must bring Christ into relation to His people, before we are in a position to recognize that in His own order He is unique."[98] Christ is Christ only in relation to his church. Therefore, only through the church can Christ be Christ for us.

Significance and Remaining Issues
Ritschl's followers included many of theology's bright lights in the later nineteenth and early twentieth centuries. Most prominent among them are Adolf Harnack, Wilhelm Herrmann and Ernst Troeltsch, all of whom will be considered later. Also strongly influenced by his thought are Martin Kähler (1835-1912) in Germany, P. T. Forsyth (1824-1921) in the United Kingdom, and proponents of the Social Gospel in the United States, and the French Catholic theologian, A. F. Loisy (1857-1940). His reach also extended to the students of those who trained under him. Even though two of the most famous theological grandchildren, Emil Brunner (1889-1966) and Karl Barth (1886-1968), had little positive regard for him, Ritschl's impact is evident in their work. A more positive evaluation is provided by Rudolf Bultmann (1884-1976), who develops Ritschl's idea of theological doctrine as value judgment.

Because Ritschl's work touches so many areas, his legacy is substantial. He adds a significant chapter in the discussion of the role of metaphysics in theology. By identifying the kingdom of God as the primary theme of Jesus' message, he rekindled the question of the historical Jesus and the nature of his teaching. With his emphasis on the church, Ritschl contributes to the debate of the community's role as mediator of the gospel. Finally, he adds new fuel to the discussion concerning the relationship between historical fact and theological significance.

Ritschl's tremendous scope leaves him open to criticism from a number of different directions. Only two broad areas will be considered here. First, many have noted that despite his stress on the church, his theology contains the seeds of the individualism he disliked so intensely. At the core of this is his definition of doctrine as value judgment. It is difficult to maintain an objective basis for theology when the question of value is divorced from fact. If the faithful valuations of the community must be grounded in historical research, an objective foundation is possible only to the extent that we are certain our conclusions about the historical Jesus are not clouded by subjectivity or cultural setting. But if the latter is questioned, as was increasingly the case, judgments of Jesus' worth are cut loose from their moorings. This tendency toward individualism becomes more explicit in Ritschl's disciples, as we will see.

The second area in which Ritschl's conclusions have been challenged is in his moral interpretation of Christianity. While he explicitly maintains that the religious and the moral must be maintained as the twin foci of the theological ellipse, it is not without reason that some suspect that Ritschl has simply dressed Kant in Jesus' robes. The eschatological element in Jesus' kingdom teachings are reduced to statements of ethical urgency, sin becomes ignorance and its residual effects on all, and salvation is interpreted as a matter of progressive education in which society will increasingly reflect kingdom ideals. Thus many question whether Ritschl has been shaped more by a cultural confidence in moral progress than by Luther and Scripture, as he claims.

Adolf von Harnack

Two of Ritschl's earliest and most influential followers were Adolf von Harnack (1851-1930) and Wilhelm Herrmann (1846-1922). Their views overlap with Ritschl's in a number of central areas: the necessity of the historical approach in recovering the gospel, denial of metaphysics's place in theological method, and the life and work of Jesus as the basis of Christology. We will not rehearse their ideas where they parallel Ritschl's but will instead focus on significant developments and unique aspects in their thought. Adolf von Harnack became the most prominent church historian of his day, practicing the discipline at universities in Leipzig, Giessen, Marburg and Berlin.[99] His *History of Dogma* (1st ed. 1885, 3rd ed. 1893) set the standard for the field, and *What Is Christianity?* (1900) established new directions for liberal works on the historical Jesus. While Harnack received tremendous respect from academic and political authorities,[100] he was viewed with suspicion by church leaders, not only because of his theological positions but also because he proposed that a creed constructed on Reformation ideas replace the Apostles' Creed in worship.

Harnack is famous for his assertion that only historical investigation of Christian dogma allows us "to grasp what is essential in the phenomena, and to distinguish kernel and husk."[101] The kernel, Christianity's essence, is always encased in the husk of cultural expression. Since Christianity "contains something which, under differing historical forms, is of permanent validity,"[102] the historian's role is to blow away the accumulated chaff and identify its timeless truth. In his search for the eternally valid in Christianity, Harnack reminds us that "Jesus Christ and his disciples were situated in their day just as we are situated in ours; that is to say, their feelings, their thoughts, their judgments and their efforts were bounded by the horizon and the framework in which their own nation was set and by its condition at the time."[103] Because of this, theology should not attempt a return to the forms and ideas of the primitive church, as some had urged. "The history of the Church shows us in its very commencement that 'primitive Christianity' had to disappear in order that 'Christianity' might remain; and in the same way in later ages one metamorphosis followed upon another."[104]

The first element of primitive Christianity to be abandoned was the Jewish apocalyptic husk in which Jesus had wrapped his teaching. Paul takes the critical step of restating the faith outside its original Jewish confines and in doing so saves Christianity. "Without doing violence to the inner and essential feature of the Gospel—unconditional trust in God as the Father of Jesus Christ, confidence in the Lord, forgiveness of sins, certainty of eternal life, purity and brotherly fellowship—Paul transformed it into the universal religion, and laid the ground for the great Church."[105]

The next major challenge for the church was Gnosticism. Harnack states, *"The struggle with Gnosticism compelled the Church to put its teaching, its worship, and its discipline, into fixed forms and ordinances, and to exclude everyone who would not yield them obedience."*[106] To do this, theology was wedded to metaphysical ideas, particularly in the identification of Jesus with the Logos. Harnack is of two minds about this development. On the one hand, he argues that this fusion of Jesus with the Logos concept led thoughtful Greeks to adopt Christianity and that "a man must be blind not to see that for that age the appropriate formula for uniting the Christian religion with Greek thought was the Logos."[107] On the other hand, he says in the same paragraph, "Most of us regard this identification as inadmissible, because the way in which we conceive the world and ethics does not point to the existence of any logos at all."[108]

Eventually Greek metaphysics displaced the gospel's kernel. This adulteration was compounded by institutionalization of the church in medieval Catholicism, in which the Christian faith itself was identified with the hierarchical structure and practices of the church. Only with the Reformation do we get the corrective. "Protestantism must be understood, first and foremost, by the contrast which it offers to Catholicism, and here there is a double direction which any estimate of it must take, first as *Reformation* and secondly as *Revolution*."[109] Reform came in the area of soteriology, in which the saving message of Christianity was restored to its pristine form. Protestantism was revolutionary in that it separated institutional superstructure from the Christian message.

The kernel of revelation rediscovered by Protestantism is really quite simple.

If, however, we take a general view of Jesus' teaching, we shall see that it may be grouped under three heads. They are each of such a nature as to contain the whole, and hence it can be exhibited in its entirety under any one of them.

Firstly, the kingdom of God and its coming.

Secondly, God the Father and the infinite value of the human soul.

Thirdly, the higher righteousness and the commandment of love."[110]

This is the gospel gleaned from its dogmatic and institutional husk. *"Protestantism reckons . . . upon the Gospel being something so simple, so divine, and therefore so truly human, as to be most certain of being understood when it is left entirely free, and also as to produce essentially the same experience and convictions in individual souls."*[111]

Two elements should be noted in this. First, Harnack asserts that the experience of entering the kingdom validates its truth. No institutional, theoretical or dogmatic systems are required. Second, Harnack greatly reduces Ritschl's emphasis on the believing community's role. "Individual religious life is what he [Jesus] wanted to kindle and what he did kindle; it is, as we shall see, his peculiar greatness to have led men to God, so that they may thenceforth live their own life with Him."[112] Harnack does exhibit confidence that all people in whom religious life is kindled arrive at similar convictions, but this is only a shadow of the emphasis Ritschl places on the church.

Harnack's reconstruction of the gospel also removes Jesus farther from the center of Christology than does Ritschl. In his much quoted statement Harnack claims, *"The gospel, as Jesus proclaimed it, has to do with the Father only and not with the Son."*[113] Now it is not so much the work and obedience of Jesus that leads to the claim of his divinity but his *message* of the Fatherhood of God. To be sure, this message is revealed only through Jesus, but his role is essentially reduced to that of a conduit. Doctrinal formulae focused on Jesus' Person arise as a capitulation to the demands made on the gospel as it enters Greek soil. Through the service of the historian, we can now relieve ourselves of this husk.[114] By extension we can also be rid of all ponderous theological, social or political systems that have formed around the gospel. In the end, Harnack tells us, "It [the kingdom of God] is not a question of angels and devils, thrones and principalities, but of God and the soul, the soul and its God."[115]

Harnack's idea that cultural forms of expression are, in large part, the enemy of religion, had a profound impact on the direction of liberal theology. Theology's objective anchor is found in the historian's reconstruction of Jesus' message by removing the potentially dangerous elements of transient husks. However, the difficulty of this endeavor is transparent to George Tyrrell, who states, "The Christ that Harnack sees, looking back through nineteen centuries of Catholic darkness, is only the reflection of a Liberal Protestant face, seen at the bottom of a deep well."[116] In other words, what Harnack isolates as the kernel of the faith may say much more about the inclinations of the historian than the essence of Christianity.

Wilhelm Herrmann

Wilhelm Herrmann was professor of dogmatic theology at Marburg from 1889-1916.[117] He is in solidarity with Ritschl and Harnack in what he rejects. Natural theology is impossible because nature is not humanity's true counterpart. "God is hidden from us in nature because we do not find our whole selves there."[118] Although he makes more allowance for a christocentric form of mysticism than his liberal predecessors, in most forms it bypasses Christ in its search for oneness of God and thus falls under his condemnation. He opposes confessionalism because it failed to address current scholarship and rested in the traditions of the past.

A major breech between Herrmann and theological conservatives concerns the role and status of Scripture. Herrmann believed that reliance on Scripture's infallibility does not provide the objective foundation for faith but instead throws Christianity into uncertainty. "If men will imagine that the reliability of the sacred records is the proper ground of religious faith, then they must necessarily be rendered in the highest degree uneasy by faithful attempts to estimate the historical probability of what is narrated in those records."[119] If one examines the biblical materials as historical documents, "No one can still hold to the idea that all the words of scripture, being the word of God, are infallible expressions of the truth."[120] In this Herrmann went even further than many of his liberal brethren to argue that historical limitations in Scripture are not limited to secondary facts but doctrine as well.

The root problem in most theology is its contention that Scripture provides certain propositions that are to be synthesized into a coherent body of doctrine. However, Herrmann believes this turns living Scripture into dead letter. Instead the objective pole of theology "rests on *two objective facts, the first of which is the historical fact of the Person of Jesus . . . The second objective ground* of the Christian's consciousness that God communes with him *is that we hear within ourselves the demand of the moral law.*"[121] While the internal demands of the moral law confirm our need for communion with God and testify to its reality, Herrmann clearly puts emphasis on the first foundation. "The true confession is that Jesus is the Christ. Rightly understood, however, it means nothing else than this: that through the man Jesus we are first lifted into a true fellowship with God."[122]

When Herrmann speaks of Christ's role in creating our unity with God, it takes on a different meaning than in Ritschl. It is not the events of Jesus' life or even his message that has finality for Christianity. These are only historically probable. Certainty is available only when we look to the inner life of Christ: "Jesus Himself becomes a real power to us when He reveals His inner life to us; a power which we recognize as the best thing our life contains."[123] The power that arises from Jesus' inner life, however, is apparent only from within faith, since "the inner content of any such personality is laid open only to those who become personally alive to it, and feel themselves aroused by contact with it and see their horizon widened."[124]

In the statements above we find the basis from which Herrmann broadened two concerns dear to Ritschl. First, he built on Ritschl's idea of theological claims as value statements. To a greater extent than in his theological father, it is the existential meaning of Jesus and not the activity or teaching that represents the core of Christianity. Second, like Ritschl he returned to Luther's work as a touchstone for reshaping Christian doctrine. However, he draws our attention to the Reformer's antithesis of gospel and law. Taken apart from his inner life, the teachings of Jesus degenerate into law. The irony, by Herrmann's account, is that Paul's teaching against justification by the law has been turned back into law by those who seek to tease an exhaustive system of doctrine from Scripture: "They evidently imagine that the sum of doctrine constructed in this way by them ceases to be law when it gets the name 'gospel'."[125]

The vitality of faith can only be maintained by directing theology back to the inner life of Jesus. However, Jesus' inner consciousness is always mediated through the community. In this he attempted to bring a corrective to Harnack's individualism by appealing to the role of the Christian community as the creators of Scripture. The community and its experience with Christ is the source of doctrine, not the other way around. Only within the community of faith can the word arise that brings others to fellowship with God. However, the community is only the medium and thus is not infallible. Its proclamation of "the sovereignty of God in the inner life of personal beings and in their communion one with another"[126] must constantly be renewed by theology to keep it from degenerating into law.

Herrmann attempted to maintain the community's necessity, but this remained in uneasy tension with the implications of Jesus' inner life as the heart of Christianity. First, while the community is the source of Scripture, its place is diminished in Herrmann's contention, "No human being can so help another by the information he may give him that the latter shall be put in possession of what is best in religion. Each individual must experience it for himself as a gift from above."[127] Even if we rely on the church's witness for initiation into the community, its ongoing significance is blunted by Herrmann's claim, "If we have experienced His power over us, we need no longer look for the testimony of others to enable us to hold fast to His life as a real thing."[128] The implicit individualism of Herrmann's theology is increased by his admission that common experience of fellowship with Christ does not lead to a unified witness to that experience. "But since that reality is infinite, therefore the doctrine in which one Christian seeks to express what his faith sees, cannot be laid down as the limit for other believers. Different men see differently, and therefore, since they ought to be truthful, they must express themselves differently."[129] These factors lead many to believe that Herrmann's work does not escape the subjectivism he finds so offensive.

Related to these concerns is Herrmann's inclination to want history both ways. He abandons Ritschl's confidence that we can recover the events of Jesus' life but on the other hand argues that Jesus' inner life can be known with certainty. Since both are the subject matter of the same documents, why should we trust Scripture on one and not the other? Herrmann's answer seems to be that Scripture's testimony to the inner life of Christ is rendered certain by the believer's experience. However, this makes experience the gatekeeper of what is valid in Scripture, which seems to revert to the individualism and subjectivism he wants to avoid. These tendencies prompt others who fall within the liberal camp to continue the search for an objective basis for theology. Two such variations are found in Catholic modernism and the Social Gospel.

Alfred Loisy and Roman Catholic Modernism

A combination of factors had brought Catholic theology and biblical studies almost to a standstill in the mid-nineteenth century. The *Syllabus Errorum* (1864), which identified almost all of the philosophical and social ideas of the day as heretical, the strong affirmation of papal doctrinal authority at Vatican I and the conservatism of Pope Pius IX had a chilling effect on any attempt to question or modify traditional views. Moreover, with the exception of Germany, Roman Catholic academic institutions were on the ropes. This was particularly the case in France, where the Catholic universities had been shut down during the Revolution and were only allowed to reopen late in the nineteenth century. As the church circled the wagons around its precritical theology, there was a feeling that Catholic scholarship had been left behind by recent developments in biblical inquiry, held back by limits imposed by institutional authorities. To those within Catholicism who lamented this situation, two items provided a glimmer of hope. The first was the ascent of Leo XIII to the papacy. His first encyclical, *Inscrutabile Deo consilio* (1878), which encouraged scholarly pursuits in philosophy and biblical criticism, was perceived as an attempt to pull Catholicism back into the contemporary world. Second, Newman's *Essay on the Development of Christian Doctrine* (1843) seemed an invitation to give new consideration to doctrinal change.

It is in this context that the movement known as Roman Catholic modernism arose.[130] It would be a mistake to think of the modernists as a group that advocated a unified set of ideas. There was more uniformity in what they rejected, namely naïve biblicism and dogmatics backed by ecclesiastical authority. The positive principle of the movement was an expression of Catholic faith that addressed current social and intellectual developments, but how this was done allowed for significant variation. Three names deserve mention in association with the movement. Baron Friedrich von Hügel (1852-1925) encouraged many in the group but was careful to remain at the edge of the fray. Less temperate was George Tyrrell (1861-1909), the Anglican turned Jesuit. Tyrrell viewed himself as a reformer calling the Roman Catholic Church out of its medieval past and was eventually excluded from the sacraments for his views. However, the point person for Catholic modernism was Alfred Loisy (1857-1940).

Loisy had been influenced as a student by Ernst Renan's (1823-1892) use of historical criticism in biblical study and attempted to translate this into an updating of Roman Catholic apologetics. While a biblical scholar at the Institut Catholique in Paris, Loisy questioned the historicity of early chapters in Genesis. In the ensuing furor he was relieved of his position and moved to a position at a girl's school. He later moved to the Sorbonne's Ecole des hautes Etudes. While there he wrote his most enduring work, *The Gospel and the Church* (1902).[131] On the surface this was a response to Harnack's *What Is Christianity?* but it also offered Loisy the occasion to recast more traditional Catholic views of Scripture, doctrine and Christology using historical-criticism methods.

The central issue of *Gospel and the Church* is whether doctrinal development is, as Harnack claimed, a concealment of a timeless essence or a necessary process of growth. Loisy advocates the latter, stating that the church's role is to insure the gospel's survival by constantly expanding the truth implicit in the biblical witness. "The gospel has not entered the world as an unconditioned absolute doctrine, summed up in a unique and steadfast truth, but as a living faith, concrete and complex, whose evolution proceeds without doubt from the internal force which has made it enduring, but none the less has been, in everything and from the beginning, influenced by the surroundings wherein the faith was born and has since developed."[132] Both the church and the message must adapt to meet new challenges; doctrine cannot remain static. Therefore, the Hellenization of the gospel that Harnack found so distasteful is seen by Loisy as positive evolution. However, the process does not end there. Even the formulae that grew out of the christological and trinitarian controversies of the early church must be open to change because "though the dogmas may be Divine in origin and substance, they are human in structure and composition."[133]

The vehicle through which faith's vitality is preserved is the Church. Loisy is famous for his dictum, "Jesus foretold the kingdom, and it was the Church that came; she came, enlarging the form of the gospel, which it was impossible to preserve as it was."[134] In this way Loisy draws a closer tie between the message of the kingdom and the church than does Harnack. While the latter views the visible church and its doctrinal claims as a temporal husk to be distinguished from the kernel of the gospel (and discarded), Loisy urges that "he [Harnack] should return to the parable of the mustard seed, comparing the new-born Christianity to a little grain. . . . This grain . . . enclosed the germ of the tree that we now see."[135] The grain of primitive church doctrine has been nourished and preserved by the Church and has grown to encompass the doctrinal extensions embedded in its creeds and councils. Therefore, while the two can never be identified, since this growth is an ongoing process, "the Church is as necessary to the gospel as the gospel to the Church."[136]

From our current vantage point Loisy's position may seem very compatible with Catholic doctrine. *Gospel and the Church* defends the creeds and councils, apostolic succession, the papacy and Catholicism's position as guardian of Christianity. However, Loisy crosses an important line, going beyond Newman's assertion that the eternal truths of Scripture require explication by the church to state that the truths themselves evolve. Moreover, in their evolution a human element is inescapably present, and the historical form in which an idea is communicated must be distinguished from the idea itself.

Since the historical approach used by Loisy was rejected by the ecclesiastical hierarchy, his attempts to defend himself were frustrated from the outset. *Gospel and the Church* and four of his other works were put on the *Index* by Rome in 1903. When he refused to recant his ideas, he was excommunicated (1908). Firm steps were also taken against modernism as a whole. Pius X, who followed Leo XIII, was even less tolerant than his predecessor. He issued twin encyclicals in 1907 entitled *Pascendi,* which gave broad definition to the error of modernism and established the line for acceptable scholarship within Catholicism, and *Lamentabili Sane Exitu,* which listed sixty-five specific errors, most of which were taken directly from the writings of Loisy and Tyrrell. Beginning in 1910 all university teachers were required to take an oath repudiating modernism. With this Catholicism returned to the defensive stance it had taken through most of the previous century.

Walter Rauschenbusch and the Social Gospel

The primary goal of the Social Gospel Movement was to restate the gospel in a manner that would express Christianity's social character and allow it to resolve problems that are essentially corporate in nature. The name most often associated with the Social Gospel is Walter Rauschenbusch (1868-1918).[137] Before moving to a position in church history at Rochester Seminary, Rauschenbusch had pastored in New York's notorious "Hell's Kitchen." This experience heightened his awareness of the plight of the dispossessed and led to the belief that their problems were not individual in the making nor could solutions be provided on an individual level. Thus while he is in broad agreement with, and strongly influenced by, the German liberals on several matters—the ethical nature of religion, the centrality afforded to Jesus' proclamation of the kingdom and the human capacity to advance the kingdom—he believes they and theologians of other stripes have blunted the social facet of

Christianity. "My own conviction is that the professional theologians of Europe, who all belong by kinship and sympathy to the bourgeois classes and are constitutionally incapacitated for understanding any revolutionary ideas, past or present, have overemphasized the ascetic and eschatological elements in the teachings of Jesus."[138]

Unlike many of his European counterparts, Rauschenbush did not believe that current social structures are the means by which the kingdom will reach greater fulfillment but that they are obstacles. Only through a radical reformation of economic, political and ecclesiastical systems can the disenfranchised find the salvation envisioned by Jesus. Abolition of militarism, penal reform and reshaping industrialism are all tasks of the kingdom and are implicit in Jesus' teaching on the subject. However, the church has identified itself with and acquiesced to destructive social forces because it replaced the kingdom ideal with institutional values. When this occurred, the church became preoccupied with maintaining the status quo, of which it is a part, rather than being a revolutionary movement. "The Kingdom of God breeds prophets; the Church breeds priests and theologians. The Church runs to tradition and dogma; the Kingdom of God rejoices in forecasts and boundless horizons."[139]

Rauschenbush argues that the church will only regain a sense of its goal and purpose with recovery of the kingdom concept. First, the kingdom of God is an inherently teleological concept. It provides a goal toward which we are to move, and thus it looks forward to the future realization of God's promise, not backward to tradition and dogma. Because no institution, the church included, is the equivalent to the kingdom, "the Kingdom of God is not confined within the limits of the Church and its activities. It embraces the whole of human life. It is the Christian transfiguration of the social order. The Church is one social institution alongside of the family the industrial organization of society, and the State. The Kingdom of God is in all these, and realizes itself through them all."[140] Second, "the Kingdom is a fellowship of righteousness,"[141] thus it is both corporate and ethical in nature. This is a direct attack on Protestantism's tendency to view sin and salvation in an individual manner. By contrast, "The social gospel tries to see the progress of the Kingdom of God in the flow of history; not only in the doings of the Church, but in the clash of economic forces and social classes, in the rise and fall of despotisms and forms of enslavement."[142]

These two factors lead to new definitions of sin and salvation. Rausch-enbush intensifies Ritschl's idea of the kingdom of evil and interprets almost all sin as corporate. Therefore, Rauschenbush tells us, "Those who do their thinking in the light of the Kingdom of God make less of heresy and private sins."[143] Instead we should combat the sins, all social in nature and still present in corporate life, that led to Jesus' death—religious bigotry, graft and political power, corruption of justice, militarism, mob spirit and class contempt.

This corporate definition of sin results in a revised understanding of salvation. Like the German liberals, Rauschenbush argues, "The fundamental terms and ideas [associated with atonement]—'satisfaction,' 'substitution,' 'imputation,' 'merit'—are post-biblical ideas, and are alien from the spirit of the gospel."[144] Instead of debating metaphysical formulations of Christology "the problem of the social gospel is how the divine life of Christ can get control of human society."[145] Rauschenbush answers this question in a manner similar to Herrmann: through the personality of Jesus we become conscious of God's desire for humanity. Because Jesus mediates this consciousness of God and his kingdom, he holds a unique role in Christianity. Through this mediation we become empowered to progressively eliminate the hold of corporate evil. "The consciousness of God which we derive from Jesus is able to establish centres of spiritual strength and peace which help to break the free sweep of evil in social life."[146]

Postlude to Theological Liberalism

Because the spirit of the latter-nineteenth century was on the side of theological liberalism, success in combating its views at the ideological level were limited at best. However, the *Zeitgeist* changed dramatically with the First World War, and only then was liberalism's ascendancy challenged. With the war, liberalism's fundamental tenets of human goodness and inevitable progress were cast into doubt. The illusion that we were somehow able to stand outside the transient and provisional in history through social science, individual communion with Christ or some other means, shattered when the realities of war demonstrated that what had been taken as progress proved unable to keep the world free of massive tragedy and evil. This is heightened in liberalism's birthplace, Germany, where religious aspirations were so closely tied to the political and social institutions held responsible for casting so much of the world into war.[147]

One predictable result of world-wide war was a reexamination of liberalism's doctrine of human sinfulness and its optimism that sin's power would be increasingly diminished by human efforts. At another level, however, is the question of theological method. Liberalism found its starting point in human experience. But when it was revealed that our experiences continued to be tainted by sinfulness and cultural circumstances, it became difficult to see how theological endeavor can begin from the human side. The person at the cutting edge of the emerging revolt against theology approached from the human experience was an obscure thirty-year-old pastor named Karl Barth (1886-1968), whose *Commentary on the Epistle to the Romans* (1918), as has been said, "fell like a bomb on the playground of the theologians." While liberalism's influence lingered, Barth's return to a theology in which human efforts are always under the judgment of God's revelation increasingly displaced it.

11. DARWIN AND THE RISE OF THE SOCIAL SCIENCES

Our final chapter, which consists of an examination of figures such as Charles Darwin and a bevy of early social scientists, may seem out of place in a survey devoted to philosophy and its theological trajectories. In fact, they are very much at home here since they stand at the intersection of some important transitions in the intellectual world. First, we have seen that the concept of evolutionary movement was very much in vogue from the beginning of the century, and it was only a matter of time before different disciplines would adopt this paradigm. The difference in these cases is that we do not find grand Hegelian-like schemes that attempt to explain everything at once but less ambitious programs that look at the process of change within restricted spheres such as sociology or biology.

Second, while social scientists such as Marx and Comte applied evolutionary models to their conclusions, the figures in this chapter depart from these earlier thinkers in an important way. Rather than employ history as a prescription for the future, as Marx and Comte did, the tendency in people such as Darwin, Weber and Freud is to avoid teleology. Absent are the utopian dreams. Instead, like many within the natural sciences, they consider the world a logical realm open to analysis and discovery, but they believed that true scientists should limit their statements to description (even if they were not always consistent about this).

A third important transition is found in methodology. Idealism and its intellectual ancestors tended to rely on an a priori or intuitive approach.

However, the movements considered below are unanimous in adapting the empirical approach. Thus while the notion of improvement, growth and discovery that is so prevalent in nineteenth-century philosophy and theology is maintained, the means by which this occurs more closely approximates those of the physical sciences.

Finally, the individuals in this chapter mark an important intersection in the intellectual realm because they represent the emergence of the social sciences as distinct disciplines rather than aspects of philosophy. On the one hand, it is possible to view their espousal of scientific methods and attitudes as part of the youthful rebellion of children to their philosophical parent. On the other hand, the direction they take is prophetic. The social sciences, less encumbered by history, tradition and size, were more nimble in following the lead of the physical sciences. However, much of philosophy later adopted the same approach.

The Impact of Darwin

The popular perception is that Charles Darwin originated the idea of biological evolution. The reality is that Erasmus Darwin (1731-1802), Charles's grandfather, was an evolutionist, and some form of organic evolution was accepted by many within the scientific community before *The Origin of Species* was published in 1859. The burning question for most scientists was not whether biological evolution was true but the nature, mechanism and implications of biological change. Therefore, Darwin's views did not create a stir both within and outside the scientific community because he argued for evolution. The primary reason for controversy was his argument that evolution was directed by natural selection (or survival of the fittest).

An evolutionary process guided by natural selection was inflammatory for several reasons. First, it assumed a process in which variations within a species appear unpredictably, with few such variations being beneficial to the survival of the organism. The randomness and wastefulness of nature raises questions about whether natural selection left room for divine governance and direction, which many earlier evolutionary theories accommodated. Second, Darwin's view of the survival of the fittest interpreted fitness in terms of adaptation to a specific environment. This tends to relativize existence in a way that makes it difficult to declare any species higher or lower in an absolute sense. Thus humanity's supremacy in the hierarchy of being was merely a result of the fortuitous convergence of adaptations within circumstances that could easily have been different. Third, Darwin's theory boldly states that neither the human race nor any other species results from a special act of creation. Instead existing species have evolved *from* other species, some quite dissimilar and inferior, at least as measured by traditional standards of classification. Fourth, Darwin's natural selection offers a unitary theory for change with profound implications, not only for organic evolution but for interpreting transition in all other realms as well. Finally, Darwin's views captured the attention of scholars outside the natural sciences as well as the general public because he built his case in a new way. Earlier evolutionary theories were derived deductively. In contrast, Darwin defended his position by marshaling vast amounts of empirical evidence. This empirical support, combined with an elegant theory that promised to interpret data that had puzzled scientists for generations, brought almost instant prominence and notoriety, depending on the audience.

Charles Darwin

Charles Darwin (1809-1882) was born into a wealthy and respected family.[1] His mother was a child of the prominent Wedgwood family, his father a physician. It was assumed that young Charles would, like his father and grandfather, become a doctor. He began medical studies at Edinburgh but had little interest and soon dropped the subject. From there he moved to Cambridge where he briefly pursued a degree in theology. However, his real interests resided in the natural sciences. When the opportunity arose to join the crew of the *Beagle* on a six-year exploratory voyage to South America and the Pacific Islands, his career direction was sealed. As the expedition's recorder he proved to have impressive powers of discernment, and he dutifully filled numerous notebooks with his observations during the trip. These observations were published in 1839 under the title *The Voyage of the Beagle*.

The question that vexed Darwin during and after the *Beagle's* expedition was how variations arose that allowed specific plants and animals to survive in different environments. A critical piece of the puzzle fell into place when Darwin read Thomas Malthus's (1766-1834) *An Essay on the*

Principle of Population in 1838.[2] Malthus noted that human population grows at a rate that cannot be sustained by available resources. Struggle for these scarce resources reduces the number of humans to a level that can be maintained within an environment. Darwin married this idea to observations made while on the *Beagle,* and his theory of natural selection began taking shape. However, Darwin was a very cautious scientist and refused to go public with his views until he was confident that he had data sufficient to make a case within the scientific community. He planned a multivolume work with extensive examples to support his position, but a situation arose that forced his hand. In 1858 an essay was received from A. R. Wallace (1823-1913) proposing very similar conclusions about natural selection. Darwin decided he must act quickly to receive credit for the theory. Therefore, when Wallace's essay was presented to the Linnean Society, a summary of Darwin's views were appended, and both were published together in the *Linnean Journal.* Darwin then expanded his summary and published it the following year under the title *The Origin of Species.* Controversy came quickly in the wake of *Origin,* but Darwin, desirous of continuing his own work without distraction, preferred the eye of the hurricane. He rarely ventured from his countryside home and let his supporters, particularly Thomas H. Huxley (1825-1895), argue his case. Darwin remained active in research until his death in 1882 and was honored by his country with a funeral in Westminster Abbey.

Natural Selection

Darwin's theory of natural selection is rather simple. It begins with the observation that small variations occur in the offspring of the same parents. In domestic husbandry these variations have been exploited for generations in order to increase production and quality. Given this, Darwin asks, "If man can by patience select variations useful to him, why, under changing and complex conditions of life, should not variations useful to nature's living products often arise, and be preserved or selected?"[3] In the latter case, then, selection of beneficial attributes is not determined by human agency but by the environment in which a species lives.

At this point the key provided by Malthus's work on population becomes important. "There is no exception to the rule that every organic being naturally increases at so high a rate, that, if not destroyed, the earth would soon be covered by the progeny of a single pair. Even slow-breeding man has doubled in twenty-five years, and at this rate, in less than a thousand years, there would literally not be standing-room for his progeny."[4] Because of the limits of an environment, nature selects those most capable of existing within the available resources. If a random variation in an individual organism renders its possessor better suited to its environment, it is more likely to survive and pass on this beneficial attribute to its offspring. No organism is exempt from the ceaseless sifting process of natural selection. As Darwin puts it, "It may metaphorically be said that natural selection is daily and hourly scrutinising, throughout the world, the slightest variation; rejecting those that are bad, preserving and adding up all that are good; silently and insensibly working, *wherever and whenever opportunity offers,* at the conditions of life."[5] While the language here suggests a conscious and intentional process, Darwin elsewhere expresses misgivings about the idea that "selection" is purposeful and for this reason occasionally expresses a preference for Herbert Spencer's phrase, "survival of the fittest."

Variation within species is only half of the story. The other side of the equation is the dynamic and multifaceted environment in which a particular species exists. "Let it also be borne in mind how infinitely complex and close-fitting are the mutual relations of all organic beings to each other and to their physical conditions of life; and consequently what infinitely varied diversities of structure might be of use to each being under changing conditions of life."[6] No single variation or attribute is advantageous in an absolute sense because each environment is different. Therefore, "any being, if it vary however slightly in any manner profitable to itself, under the complex and sometimes varying conditions of life, will have a better chance of surviving, and thus be *naturally selected.*"[7]

This process of environmental circumstances selecting the fittest individuals within a species for survival and propagation eventually leads to the creation of new species. Slight variations, which Darwin refers to as "incipient species," might be more pronounced in offspring and eventually would develop to the degree that a new species emerges, sometimes displacing that from which it originated, sometimes existing alongside it.

Because environments change and the process of natural selection is continuous, variations within these new species might further give birth to yet other species. Darwin speaks of current species as the twigs at the end the branches from which they have emerged. These branches have grown out of a few main trunks, from which they themselves have originated.

Darwin viewed variation within species as a random process in which the environment only determines which mutations have survival value but does not create the variations themselves. This randomness was problematic for those who were willing to accept an evolutionary scheme that included divine control and direction. However, Darwin argues that if variations within species are divinely willed, we must ask why few variations are useful and why nature is so wasteful that most mutations doom their possessors to early death. The apparent capriciousness of nature seems contrary to divine governance and caused Darwin to become increasingly agnostic about the existence of a purposeful God.

> That there is much suffering in the world no one disputes. Some have attempted to explain this with reference to man by imagining that it serves for his moral improvement. But the number of men in the world is as nothing compared with that of all other sentient beings, and they often suffer greatly without any moral improvement. This very old argument from the existence of suffering against the existence of an intelligent First Cause seems to me a strong one; whereas . . . the presence of much suffering agrees well with the view that all organic beings have been developed through variation and natural selection.[8]

The Descent of Man

Darwin was aware that natural selection had implications beyond biology,[9] but it would be twelve years after *Origin* before he made a significant foray into this area with his *Descent of Man* (1871). Although it did not generate the public outcry elicited by his earlier work, *Descent* is at least as philosophically and theologically significant as *Origin*. Perhaps of greatest impact is that Darwin here states what was only implicit before: "He who is not content to look, like a savage, at the phenomena of nature as disconnected, cannot any longer believe that man is the work of a separate act of creation."[10] Instead the human race has descended from non-human species. The implication for Darwin is that no basis exists upon which we can set ourselves apart from the animal world qualitatively. "The difference in mind between man and the higher animals, great as it is, is certainly one of degree and not of kind."[11]

To explain why the human race emerged with significantly greater intelligence than the species from which it originated, Darwin appeals once again to natural selection. First, he argues that intelligence in any species is a survival-enhancing attribute. As he puts it, "The more intelligent members within the same community will succeed better in the long run than the inferior, and leave a more numerous progeny, and this is a form of natural selection."[12] Second, he states that all the ingredients necessary for the development of the human mind are present, although in primitive form, in the animal realm. "It is generally admitted that the higher animals possess memory, attention, association, and even some imagination and reason. If these powers, which differ much in different animals, are capable of improvement, there seems no great improbability in more complex faculties, such as the higher forms of abstraction, and self-consciousness, etc., having been evolved through the development and combination of the simpler ones."[13] Therefore, he concludes that homo sapiens evolved from lower species as more mentally adept variations within these earlier forms survived and bred, and even more intelligent progeny were preserved by the hand of nature.

Like intelligence, the highly complex social structures of the human race are also magnified versions of survival devices present in the animal world. In general, communal life provides greater protection than solitary existence. "With those animals which were benefited by living in close association, the individuals which took the greatest pleasure in society would best escape various dangers, while those that cared least for their comrades, and lived solitary, would perish in greater numbers."[14] For any social system to work, group members must be bonded through sympathy for purposes of nurture and protection. The sympathetic tendencies necessary for human society have their antecedents in lower forms of life. "Every one has seen how jealous a dog is of his master's affection if lavished on any other creature; and I have observed the same fact with monkeys. This shows that animals not only love, but have a desire to be loved."[15] However, humans have climbed to the top of the food chain because, by combining their inherited sympathetic tendencies with intellect, their sense of obligation includes those outside the immediate tribe or group. "But as man gradually advanced in intellectual power and was enabled to trace the more remote consequences of his actions . . . his sympathies become more tender and widely diffused, extending to men of all races, to the imbecile, maimed, and other useless members of society, and finally to the lower animals."[16]

The last part of the quote above points to one of the most significant elements of Darwin's social interpretation of natural selection. Morality is a product of evolution. Stated otherwise, morality emerges from biological traits that equip individuals for survival by drawing them under the protection of the group and allowing them to benefit from the skills of others within the group.[17] Thus as natural selection performs its duties, morality emerges: "The social instincts—the prime principle of man's moral constitution—with the aid of active intellectual powers and the effects of habit, naturally lead to the golden rule. 'As ye would that men should do to you, do ye to them likewise'; and this lies at the foundation of morality."[18] Darwin finds moral sentiment the most distinctive characteristic of the human species and has faith that increased virtue, because of its utility for survival, is in the evolutionary cards. "Looking to future generations, there is no cause to fear that the social instincts will grow weaker, and we may expect that virtuous habits will grow stronger, becoming perhaps fixed by inheritance. In this case the struggle between our higher and lower impulses will be less severe, and virtue will be triumphant."[19]

Finally, Darwin situates religious sentiment at the pinnacle of evolutionary development. Spiritual impulses are indicative of and result from advanced intellectual, social and moral development. "The feeling of religious devotion is a highly complex one, consisting of love, complete submission to an exalted and mysterious superior, a strong sense of dependence, fear, reverence, gratitude, hope for the future, and perhaps other elements. No being could experience so complex an emotion until advanced in his intellectual and moral faculties to at least a moderately high level."[20] However, Darwin immediately makes it clear that human religious sensibilities are not categorically unique from qualities found in lower species: "Nevertheless, we see some distant approach to this state of mind in the deep love of a dog for his master, associated with complete submission, some fear, and perhaps other feelings."[21] While Darwin views religious sentiment as a sign of evolutionary superiority, he keeps his distance on any conjecture concerning whether these sentiments correspond to any ultimate reality or creator. Such questions are beyond the reach of science, and he therefore concludes that agnosticism is the proper response.

Darwin's Significance

Darwin cannot be credited with (or blamed for) giving birth to the idea of evolutionary development. We have seen in previous chapters that the idea of inevitable social, religious, political and intellectual growth was strongly characteristic of the age. However, Darwin did give broad credence to natural selection by the vast amount of empirical evidence he draws on in support of his theory. His success in using an empirical approach to explain phenomena lends new luster to the biological sciences and encourages many to abandon earlier mathematical and deductive approaches. This in particular was strongly influential for the social sciences, which increasingly looked to the physical sciences rather than philosophy for their methodology.

A second significant influence concerns the place human beings occupy in explorations in both the physical and social sciences. If Darwin is correct, human beings do not occupy a categorically distinct place in the universe but are unique only in the extent of their development. All the characteristics once considered exclusively the domain of human existence—rationality, social responsibility, moral sensitivity and even religious consciousness—are attributed also to nonhuman species, albeit in lesser degrees. Therefore, we share in the relativity characteristic of all other animals. Our position in the universe is not a matter of absolute superiority in our distinction from other species but results from beneficial adaptation to a specific environment. For many in the social sciences this relativity opens the door to abandon the search for *Truth* in favor of a quest for *truths* that hold only for a given situation, period or environment. A result is that, while many early social scientists felt compelled to approach their disciplines metaphysically, the trend in the post-Darwinian period is away from a normative approach to one that seeks to be neutral and descriptive. John Dewey (1859-1952) credits this departure from metaphysics to Darwin. Concerning metaphysical questions he states, "We do not solve them: we get over them. Old questions are solved by disappearing, evaporating, while new questions corresponding to the changed attitude of endeavor and preference take their place."[22]

Finally, Darwin's impact is profound in its implications for understanding the nature of evolution. Most evolutionary paradigms before natural selection considered change teleologically. In other words, there was direction, purpose and growth in transition. However, natural selection does not comfortably accommodate a teleological model since adaptation is always relative to a specific environment. Therefore, the discussion shifts from one that looks toward the end or goals of change to the question of antecedent causes. This is a formative idea for the social sciences, which become increasingly oriented toward viewing their task as descriptive, focusing their attention on the process of social change, and less interested in making normative statements that require some universal standard of measurement or concept of purpose.

Reflections on Darwinism

Darwin's impact upon Western thought can hardly be overrated. His biological explanation for diversity, based upon inherited mutation plus adaptation, is a true scientific advance. However, the negative impact of his ideas surfaced in areas like racism and "eugenics" in the movement we now call social Darwinism.[23] In this view one race (some European one) was considered "naturally" superior to the others because it was more technologically dominant. War was welcomed as the "natural selection" of superior nations. Other races were "naturally" inferior. For the eugenics movement, "inferior" men and women should be neutered so that their genes could not be passed on. Such conceptions were and are morally odious. But intelligent, morally deluded men believed that Darwin had sanctioned such understandings of society, politics and economics.

Ironically, Darwin had in fact proven no such thing. Darwin used words like evolution, natural selection and survival of the fittest far beyond the meanings his own theory warranted. The concept of evolution contains within it an idea of progress, not merely of change. Yet Darwin had only accounted for biological change or variation, not the biological progress that we find in the fossil record. The "descent of man" is assumed rather than explained by Darwin—his biological theories have no explanation of the development of higher organisms, other than random chance (which, of course, is no explanation at all). This failure to explain progress in the development of life means that, *a fortiori*, Darwin had no basis for assuming his theory accounted for ethics, beauty or freedom.

As far as "natural selection" goes, the meaning of this term for Darwin is simply that of inherited mutation plus adaptation to environment. While the process is indeed natural, there is no "selection" going on; Darwin uses a bad metaphor for this process, and biologists today perpetuate this unfortunate language with talk of the environment "selecting" certain genotypes. Finally, survival of the "fittest" turns out to contain a circular definition, since "fittest" means that a species or organism survives. "Survival of the fittest," when clarified, only means "survival of those with survival-enhancing characteristics," which is circular.[24] Much of the rhetoric of Darwinism, then, which had such a powerful influence upon social Darwinism, is illegitimate in the writings of Darwin himself. Darwin's biological science, considered as science, may have been a real advance yet it was still incomplete as a full scientific explanation of the origin of intelligent life.[25] What Darwin did discover was the mechanism for biodiversity, which is no mean feat—but social Darwinists are interested in superiority, not diversity![26]

Herbert Spencer

While Darwin was reluctant to develop the implications of natural selection for social thought, his hesitancy was not shared by Herbert Spencer (1820-1902).[27] Intellectual history has tended to consign Spencer to the second tier of sociology, excluding him from the founding trinity of Karl Marx, Émile Durkheim and Max Weber.[28] However, his contribution was significant. Spencer was a forerunner of Durkheim's famous premise that social realities should be approached as things.[29] He is also an early advocate of the view, adopted by most sociologists who came later, that the function of elements within social structures account for their origin and survival, not the part they play within a divine plan or a metaphysical system. Moreover, it is difficult to underestimate his importance in boosting the status of the social sciences in America, which found his empiricism, his idea of progress and his individualism highly attractive.[30] His works were often standard texts in English and American universities, and he managed to accumulate a modest fortune through the sale of his books in these countries.

Similarly, Spencer's role as an originator of evolutionary thought has been downplayed by the "social Darwinist" label generally assigned to him. However, it could be persuasively argued that the movement from the direction of Spencer to Darwin is more fundamental. Spencer's early writings predate Darwin's, whose own works are sprinkled with words of admiration for Spencer's ideas and an acknowledgment of his debt to the fellow Englishman for the idea of the "survival of the fittest." Moreover, Spencer applies evolutionary ideas on a broader scope than Darwin, who rarely ventures beyond the biological arena.[31]

Several reasons might be cited for Spencer's secondary position in the intellectual world. He held no university position and as a result left no disciples to perpetuate his legacy within the academy. Also, while he vigorously rejects the deductive approach of the Idealist predecessors of the social sciences, he maintains the Idealist tendency to bring the whole of reality into his compass in an era when sociology was moving toward specialization and investigation of discrete problems. This has led to the charge that he was not scientific enough in his method and failed to differentiate between philosophy and science. Many later sociologists find his extreme political individualism unacceptable and believe that it undercuts the entire sociological enterprise. If the individual is the ultimate category, as his political philosophy argues, how does this fit with sociology's assertion of the primacy of interactive systems? Finally, many of his ideas promote a view of racial superiority that later sociologists wanted to put at arm's length. In any case, many within the social sciences are taking a second look at Spencer's work and reevaluating his place in the history of social and evolutionary thought.

Spencer's father was a school teacher who was, ironically, self-educated and a dedicated advocate of self-education. As a result of the latter, the younger Spencer's formal schooling lasted for three months, and he received most of his education from his father and an uncle. He credits his father's encouragement of intellectual self-help with shaping his scientific orientation.

A constant question with him was,—"I wonder what is the cause of so-and-so"; or again, putting it directly to me,—"Can you tell the cause of this?" Always the tendency in himself, and the tendency strengthened in me, was to regard everything as naturally caused; and I doubt not that while the notion of causation was thus rendered much more definite in me than in most of my age, there was established a habit of seeking for causes, as well as a tacit belief in the universality of causation.[32]

Spencer began his career as a civil engineer. However, because of a considerable inheritance from an uncle he was able to leave this work and spend most of his adult life writing. His output was impressive, ranging from articles for science periodicals to the magnum opus that occupied thirty years of his life, *Synthetic Philosophy* (1862-1893). A lifelong bachelor, he preferred the reclusive existence of an author, even more so as his health began to fail, and rarely lectured or ventured out to defend his views publicly. He suffered from frequent bouts of depression and insomnia, and though he had many admirers, he maintained few close friendships.

Evolutionary Method
Spencer's philosophy builds on Comte's idea that the world and the movements of its various components can be described in terms of law and that these laws become increasingly apparent as we evolve. "Rightly understood, the progress from deepest ignorance to highest enlightenment, is a progress from entire unconsciousness of law, to the conviction that law is universal and inevitable."[33] Similarly, he adopts Comte's conclusion that scientific thought is unable to pierce the veil of metaphysics. "Thinking being relationing, no thought can ever express more than relations."[34] However, while Spencer believes that all true knowledge is derived through a scientific method, he also argues that some aspects of the world are outside the grasp of science. "Ultimate Scientific Ideas [e.g., time, space, force, consciousness], then, are all representative of realities that cannot be comprehended. After no matter how great a

progress in the colligation of facts and the establishment of generalizations ever wider and wider; after the merging of limited and derivative
truths in truths that are larger and deeper has been carried no matter
how far, the fundamental truth remains as much beyond reach as ever."[35]
This throws all metaphysical statements, whether derived from science,
philosophy or religion, into the same category. "Ultimate religious ideas
and ultimate scientific ideas alike turn out to be merely symbols of the
actual, not cognitions of it."[36]

The reality behind these symbolic expressions is what Spencer rel-
egates to the category of the "Unknowable." "By continually seeking
to know and being continually thrown back with a deepened conviction of the impossibility of knowing, we may keep alive the consciousness that it is alike our highest wisdom and our highest duty to regard
that through which all things exist as The Unknowable."[37] This means
that while he is keenly aware of the pitfalls of using religion to
address scientific concerns, he also does not believe that science
answers the questions that have occupied the theologians and metaphysicians. Therefore, the wisest course is to remain agnostic about
the realm of metaphysics and religion. Knowledge, properly defined,
is limited to the sphere of experience. Our task, then, is to seek out
the laws governing phenomena.

Even though he dismisses the possibility of metaphysical truth, Spencer argues that science should not divorce itself from philosophy. "Science means merely the family of the Sciences—stands for nothing more
than the sum of knowledge formed of their contributions, and ignores
the knowledge constituted by the *fusion* of all these contributions into a
whole."[38] Each individual science includes only a small portion of phenomena within its domain. However, the parts are understood only if we
have a vision of the whole. Philosophy, which seeks *"knowledge of the highest degree of generality"*[39] is the discipline within which the contributions of
the individual sciences are fused into a comprehensive system. Therefore, Spencer does not follow many later social scientists who deny any
role to philosophy. At the same time he radically redefines and limits its
domain, making philosophy a discipline within which scientific ideas are
collected and synthesized, not a field that searches for the truths behind
observable entities and their relations.

Spencerian Evolution

In his first book, *Social Statics* (1850), published almost a decade before Darwin's *Origin of Species,* Spencer speaks of nature's gleaning process in seeking members of a species that are adapted to an environment. "A plant, for instance, produces thousands of seeds. The greater part of these are destroyed by creatures that live upon them, or fall into places where they cannot germinate. . . . and *in the average of cases,* only one of them produces a perfect specimen of its species, which, escaping all dangers, brings to maturity seeds enough to continue the race. Thus is it also with every kind of creature."[40] Spencer's previous sentence makes clear what is only implied in Darwin's work: evolution is a single process that includes all things in its scope. "There are not several kinds of Evolution having certain traits in common, but one Evolution going on everywhere after the same manner. We have repeatedly observed that while any whole is evolving, there is always going on an evolution of the parts into which it divides itself."[41]

Spencer's concept of universal evolution is highly complex, in which individual entities are drawn into small systems that evolve within themselves while at the same time striving to adapt to the larger systems within which they must function. For example, evolving circulatory systems exist within evolving human individuals, who inhabit evolving social groups, that reside within an ever-shifting cosmos. He formulates this elaborate evolutionary dance in several steps. At the earliest stage inchoate individual elements are brought together into a process or system. Following this concentration phase is a stage within which differentiation occurs. At differentiation the previously diverse entities become specialized around various functions within a system. The last step is called determination. In this advanced stage of evolution, "The same process is exhibited by the whole and by its members. The entire mass is integrating, and simultaneously differentiating from other masses; and each member of it is also integrating and simultaneously differentiating from other members."[42] The direction in this evolutionary process is from homogeneity to heterogeneity. As systems grow by including more members, greater differentiation is necessary to maintain the integrity of the system. "Evolution then, under its primary aspect, is a change from a less coherent form to a more coherent form, consequent on the dissipation of motion and integration of matter."[43]

This general evolutionary model applies to all facets of the cosmos—geological, biological and astrological systems manifest the same process, though some systems evolve over a much greater span of time than others. An example of the steps of this process may be found in the social realm. In the early stage, individuals attach themselves to tribes. When the tribe reaches critical mass, a division of labor is necessary to provide a diversity of specialized skills that contribute to the survival of the whole. However, this small system moves toward unity within greater systems in which, for example, tribes may unify into a confederation so that the specific abilities of one tribe complement those of other tribes.

Though this evolutionary paradigm, as outlined thus far, seems to point toward unilinear and inevitable progress, Spencer's view is more nuanced. The equlibrium achieved between various components in the later stages of the evolutionary process is not, once achieved, a static one. Change is continuous, and equilibrium breaks down as the environment continues to change. Evolutionary growth is then followed by a process Spencer refers to as dissolution. "The processes thus everywhere in antagonism, and everywhere gaining now a temporary and now a more or less permanent triumph the one over the other, we call Evolution and Dissolution. Evolution under its simplest and most general aspect is the integration of matter and concomitant dissipation of motion; while Dissolution is the absorption of motion and concomitant disintegration of matter."[44] Dissolution represents a new scattering of the elements within a system and is followed by a new process of evolution in which systems are reconstructed to meet the new demands of a transitory environment.

The dissolution aspect of his evolutionary model distinguishes Spencer's view from the simple unilinear approaches often characteristic of evolutionary thought. However, the concept of dissolution is often overlooked because Spencer subsumes the cycles of evolution (in the more narrow sense defined above) and dissolution under the general category of evolution in most of his work. Also, while Spencer's philosophy of change includes these periods of disintegration, his attention is largely focused on the constructive, evolutionary side of the process.[45]

Social Evolution

Spencer's social thought departs from that of many of his contemporaries by rejecting the belief that societies are created by human activity, ideology or contractual agreement. "Instead of civilization being artificial it is a part of nature; all of a piece with the development of an embryo or the unfolding of a flower. The modifications mankind have undergone, and are still undergoing, result from a law underlying the whole organic creation."[46] Since evolutionary pressures allow no species to remain the same, Spencer argues that social thought must abandon the idea that human nature is static. "Strange indeed would it be, if, in the midst of this universal mutation, man alone were constant, unchangeable. But it is not so. He also obeys the law of indefinite variation. . . . Between the naked houseless savage, and the Shakespeares and Newtons of a civilized state, lie unnumbered degrees of difference."[47]

The transition from naked savage to Newton has significant implications for ethics. Since the laws of evolution dictate that all things—species, beliefs, abilities and institutions—arise only when they fulfill a needed function, ethics must also be analyzed in a functionalistic manner. As Spencer tells us, "The notion of goodness can be framed only in relation to ends."[48] These ends are not simple in nature since our moral obligations arise in a complex environment. Therefore, morality is a matter of attaining a balance between duties to ourselves, our offspring, and society as a whole. When equilibrium exists between all these actors and the environment in which they exist, moral perfection will reign.[49] If good refers to a balance of forces in which means are adapted to ends, then evil is simply an evolutionary maladjustment. "All evil results from the non-adaptation of constitution to conditions. This is true of everything that lives."[50] Whether an act is good or evil is just another way of inquiring as to the degree of evolutionary progress manifested in an act.

While Spencer, when discussing the evolutionary process in the abstract, seems to move away from the idea of inevitable development and growth, his social thought generally envisions unimpeded forward progress from barbarism to industrial society, the latter of which is seen favorably by Spencer. As expected, movement toward the higher is guided by selection of social structures according to their fitness to the current environment. In this process "the more-evolved societies drive the less-evolved societies into unfavourable habitats; and so entail on them decrease of size, or decay of structure."[51] The most common mechanism by which this selection of advanced societies over inferior groups has occurred is warfare. However, he believes that military combat is destined to be eradicated by the forward evolution of human nature. "From war has been gained all that it had to give. The peopling of the Earth by the more powerful and intelligent races, is a benefit in great measure achieved; and what remains to be done, calls for no other agency than the quiet pressure of a spreading industrial civilization on a barbarism which slowly dwindles."[52]

While Spencer envisions the end of military warfare, struggle within the "spreading industrial civilization" continues on a different level. At every stage of development, nature rewards the strong and punishes the weak. "Partly by weeding out those of lowest development and partly by subjecting those who remain to the never-ceasing discipline of experience, nature secures the growth of a race who shall both understand the conditions of existence and be able to act up to them."[53] As this reveals, Spencer believes that attributes like strong and weak are as applicable to groups as they are to individuals. Thus his insistence that some societies are less fit for their environment than others and are destined for extinction leads many to condemn his ideas as racist. His response is that even casual observation exposes differences between groups in their knowledge of nature and its laws, and these differences correspond with their relative ability to survive. "Inconvenience, suffering, and death are the penalties attached by nature to ignorance, as well as to incompetence— are also the means of remedying these. And whoso thinks he can mend matters by dissociating ignorance and its penalties lays claim to more than Divine wisdom and more than Divine benevolence."[54]

While the law of evolution seems heartless when applied to social structures, Spencer argues that its actions are the spur to our betterment. "If to be ignorant were as safe as to be wise, no one would become wise. And all measures which tend to put ignorance upon a par with wisdom inevitably check the growth of wisdom."[55] Only scientific wisdom, attained on the competitive field of evolutionary fitness, allows for the improvement and eventual perfection of humankind. Any attempt to ignore or circumvent it runs counter to progress and survival.

This concept of competition stands behind Spencer's ardent support of the individual's priority over the state. Governmental control, according to Spencer, represents interference with the iron laws of nature. Even government involvement born of sympathy for the plight of individuals within the state is ultimately harmful because "it defeats its own end. Instead of diminishing suffering, it eventually increases it. It favors the multiplication of those worst fitted for existence, and, by consequence, hinders the multiplication of those best fitted for existence—leaving, as it does, less room for them."[56]

Spencer sees individualism as a necessary adjunct of his overarching evolutionary model, which envisions, as we have seen above, a movement from homogeneity to diversity. When societies are homogeneous, the tendency is to suppress and combat that which is different. However, as societies adapt to their environment through specialization and diversity, suspicion of the different gives way to a recognition of heterogeneity's benefits. And since heterogeneity relies on the freedom to be different, evolutionary progress in the social realm requires individual liberty. Thus within advanced societies the rule should be, *"Every man has freedom to do all that he wills, provided he infringes not the equal freedom of any other man."*[57]

In what is perhaps the strongest indicator of Spencer's faith in evolution, he believed that human progress would render government all but superfluous because the primary role of government—protecting the person's rights and properties—would become part of the voluntary actions of individuals. This is because evolution demands that

a society in which life, liberty, and property, are secure, and all interests justly regarded, must prosper more than one in which they are not; and, consequently, among competing industrial societies, there must be a gradual replacing of those in which personal rights are imperfectly maintained, by those in which they are perfectly maintained. So that by survival of the fittest must be produced a social type in which individual claims, considered as sacred, are trenched on by the State no further than is requisite to pay the cost of maintaining them, or rather, of arbitrating among them.[58]

Spencer's Religious Views

Spencer locates the original impetus for religion in dreams: "Dream-life in general is at first undistinguished from waking life."[59] Those who died were remembered by their primitive descendants, and since many of these memories occurred in dreams, the idea arose that these ancestors inhabited a different world. Gradually, beliefs and doctrine about the powers of these departed relatives arose as explanations for events in this realm. As society became more complex, the hierarchy of gods did also, and the highest members of the divine pantheon became identified with cosmic bodies and natural forces. In the next step of religion's evolution, these gods were combined into a single God, in a manner that reflected a society with monarchical political and ecclesiastical systems.

Once the evolutionary process had brought these formerly disparate powers together into a solitary divinity (just as evolution in general pulls individual entities into ever more complex systems), the concept of God continued to evolve. "While in proportion as there arises the consequent conception of an omnipotent and omnipresent deity, there is a gradual fading of his alleged human attributes: dissolution begins to affect the supreme personality in respect of ascribed form and nature."[60] Spencer argues the more impersonal picture of the divine will ultimately evolve into a synthesis of all powers within the universe. "Consequently, the final outcome of that speculation commenced by the primitive man, is that the Power manifested throughout the Universe distinguished as material, is the same Power which in ourselves wells up under the form of consciousness."[61] Like Idealism, Spencer refuses to accept a dualism of independent powers. However, unlike Idealism, he attempts to support his unity of the forces of the universe empirically.

This unity of the powers that are now viewed as distinct by religion and science will, Spencer believes, bring about a fusion of the two realms in the future. "It behooves each party [religion and science] to strive to understand the other, with the conviction that the other has something worthy to be understood; and with the conviction that when mutually recognized this something will be the basis of a complete reconciliation."[62] However, it is clear that Spencer anticipates that the more highly evolved religion of the future will owe a greater debt to science than its religious ancensors. Primitive religious practitioners constrict their sense of wonder to narrow bits of the world, while "science under its concrete forms enlarges the sphere for religious sentiment."[63] As the insights of the various sciences become unified under philosophy, this will bring the enlightened person to the conclusion "that he is ever in presence of an Infinite and Eternal Energy, from which all things proceed."[64]

Critique of Spencer

Since we considered the impact and significance of Spencer's work at the beginning of this section, we will not cover that ground again. Instead we will examine some areas where his ideas are vulnerable to criticism. First, any philosophical paradigm that seeks a universal explanation for all things encounters problems that arise because of the scope of such a project. However, these problems are magnified when one attempts such an endeavor through empirical means. While Spencer offers many examples from widely diverse areas of science to bolster his points, such examples can encompass only a very small slice of the phenomena of the universe. This leaves him open to the charge that he seeks out only anecdotal evidence that mistake illustration for proof. In other words, his empirical orientation leaves open the question of when we can determine that his examples amount to generalized evidence that supports his conclusions.

Spencer also invites criticism by the uneasy tension created by evolution and dissolution. While the latter is an important tool for explaining what causes a previous state of equilibrium to break down, he maintains the attitude that what follows will offer an advance over the old. However, his general theory of evolution (which includes both evolution and dissolution) gives no reason we should expect this process to be progressive rather than cyclical. It is true that his paradigm supports the idea that systems of all types are destined to become more complex and diverse. But, as noted in the discussion of Darwinism, complexity and progress are very different matters.

Finally, many find a contradiction between Spencer's general view of evolution and his political individualism. The former dictates that as systems become more complex greater centralization and interdependence is necessary. This requires that the individual's role is service to the whole. However, when dealing with social and political structures, the purpose of the whole is to benefit the individual. This seems to introduce a difficult tension to Spencer's philosophy, and his attempts to bring his political ideas into conformity with his overall evolutionary model appear to many critics to be contrived. One such critic is Émile Durkheim, who draws on Spencer's empirical and functionalistic approach but attempts to provide a more consistent picture of the relationship between the individual and society.

Émile Durkheim

Émile Durkheim's (1858-1917) sociology stands on the shoulders of pioneers such as Comte and Spencer, who argued that our sociological horizon was distinct from and at least as important as the psychological realm.[65] Durkheim represents a step forward in that he decisively removes sociology from the ideological realm and transforms it into a discipline grounded in empirical research. "Instead of contenting himself with metaphysical reflection on social themes, the sociologist must take as the object of his research groups of facts clearly circumscribed, capable of ready definition, with definite limits, and adhere strictly to them."[66] Thus Durkheim does not seek a comprehensive system that draws everything under a single program. Instead he applies sociological investigation to specific groups and issues.

To some degree, Durkheim's attempt to move from religious and metaphysical models to a more scientific approach to understanding society parallels a transition is his own life. His father was a rabbi, and Durkheim himself spent time in rabbinical school. However, he came to reject Jewish religious beliefs, for reasons that he never fully explains, and advocated science as the only means by which modern society could advance. Although he was not an outstanding student, his first book, *The Division of Labor in Society* (1885), gained the attention of the academic community and led to an appointment at the University of Bordeaux in 1896. In 1902 he went to the Sorbonne as part of the education faculty. He taught sociology while there, but since the discipline was still suspect, it was not until eleven years later that the word sociology was added to his title. Durkheim displayed missionary zeal in his desire to bring sociology to a place of academic respectability, founding France's first journal of sociology, gathering around him a group of talented scholars and demanding rigor in the research produced by himself and his associates. As part of that effort many of his early works focus on methodology and its specific application. However, his final major work, *The Elementary*

Forms of Religious Life, pulls the various strands of his groundbreaking thought together as a prototype for a structuralist approach to sociology.

Sociological Method

The Sorbonne's reluctance to formally recognize sociology as an academic discipline brings into focus Durkheim's sense of creating a new discipline with its own methodology.

> Sociology appears destined to open a new way to the science of man. Up to the present, thinkers were placed before this double alternative: either explain the superior and specific faculties of men by connecting them to the inferior forms of his being, the reason to the sense, or the mind to matter, which is equivalent to denying their uniqueness; or else attach them to some super-experimental reality which was postulated, but whose existence could be established by no observation.[67]

On the one hand, he wants to avoid reduction of human social activity to analysis of individual biological or psychological functions. On the other hand, he believes that metaphysics, which acknowledges the uniqueness of human activities, cannot satisfy the demands of science. Durkheim, therefore, seeks to stake out sociology's territory as a science with its own subject matter and methods.

The attempt to find a way between biology and psychology on the one side and metaphysics and religion on the other is clear in *The Rules of Sociological Method* (1895). He argues, "The first and most fundamental rule is: *Consider social facts as things.*"[68] Durkheim defines a social fact as *"every way of acting, fixed or not, capable of exercising on the individual an external constraint;* or again, *every way of acting which is general throughout a given society, while at the same time existing in its own right independent of its individual manifestations.*"[69] Behind this definition stands his belief that social facts differ from facts about individual consciousness and belief. The social realm into which we are born provides the lens through which we understand ourselves and the world in which we interact. As an example Durkheim points out that church members do not create the universe of beliefs and practices into which they are born, but these will shape and govern the devotee's spiritual life. Such beliefs and practices preexist the individual, which indicates their existence external to the church member. Furthermore, these social realities have a life of their own and are largely beyond the capacities of any individual to change them. Because these social powers are external to us and independent of our control, they meet the definition of fact.

Not only are these social facts of a different species than individual facts, they are open to scientific investigation and are thus "things." "All that is given, all that is subject to observation, has thereby the character of a thing. To treat phenomena as things is to treat them as data, and these constitute the point of departure of science."[70] While ideas are not directly accessible to observation, the practices of social groups are and can be studied scientifically.[71] Therefore, just as we look for the causes of physical entities and activities in antecedent physical causes, if we correctly observe and analyze prevailing social practices (or facts), we can determine how and why these social "things" originate.

Durkheim's treatment of social facts as things is exemplified in *Suicide* (1897), which is the first attempt to deal with a sociological issue in a strictly empirical manner. *Suicide's* enduring influence is due, in large part, to the fact that it takes a phenomenon that seems highly individual—suicide—and demonstrates how it fits into sociological categories. The study begins by looking at the usual explanations for suicide— heredity, climate, poverty, place of residence, alcoholism—and debunks them. In keeping with his belief that individual well-being cannot be reduced to a simple description of an individual's psychology, Durkheim seeks to demonstrate that the relative prevalence of suicide can be correlated to one's social context. The salient factor he identifies is the relative strength or weakness of the community surrounding those who killed themselves. And since the sense of community is largely derived through one's religious connection, Durkheim finds significant correlations between suicide rates and religious affiliation.

The religious group with the highest rate of suicide was Protestantism. Durkheim finds it significant that, of the three major religious groups he considers, Protestantism has fewer ritualistic means through which the adherent might establish solidarity with a group. Moreover, Durkheim states, "The proclivity of Protestantism for suicide must relate to the spirit of free inquiry that animates this religion."[72] While Protestants may celebrate their freedom from the explicit ritualism of other religions and the ability to explore new ideas and forms of worship, this individualism also reduces their sense of community. And this feeling of isolation weakens the Protestant's attachment to life.

Catholicism, with a higher level of ritual, has a lesser incidence of suicide than Protestantism. "Because the Catholic religion imposes on its faithful a vast system of dogmas and practices, and so penetrates all the details of even their earthly life, it attaches them to this life with greater force than Protestantism. The Catholic is much less likely to lose sight of the ties binding him to the confessional group of which he is part, because at every moment this group is recalled to him in the shape of imperative precepts applying to different circumstances of life."[73] Thus while Catholicism and Protestantism share similar doctrines about the inadmissibility of suicide, these doctrines are more effectively internalized in Catholics by ritual reinforcement.

Durkheim's study found the lowest suicide rates among Jews, even though their doctrines are less restrictive concerning suicide than those of Protestantism and Catholicism. However, Jewish people have the strongest sense of group identity, reinforced not only through ritual but also through persecution. "Indeed, the reproach to which the Jews have for so long been exposed by Christianity has created feelings of unusual solidarity among them. Their need of resisting a general hostility, the very impossibility of free communication with the rest of the population, has forced them to strict union among themselves."[74]

In short, Durkheim discovered that a higher level of incorporation into a community correlates with a reduced tendency toward suicide. To put it otherwise, an individual believes his or her life has meaning when part of a society. Without the moral center provided by a community into which one can be integrated, an individual has difficulty finding a purpose for his or her life and thus less reason to continue living. Moreover, as we see above, Durkheim stresses the role that practices and rituals play in cementing the sense of integration into a group. Therefore, Durkheim argues that the beliefs of a particular religion regarding suicide are secondary in importance to the effectiveness of the objective mechanisms by which it produces a sense of community.

> If religion protects man against the desire for self-destruction, it is not that it preaches the respect for his own person to him with arguments *sui generis;* but because it is a society. What constitutes this society is the exist-

ence of a certain number of beliefs and practices common to all the faithful, traditional and thus obligatory. The more numerous and strong these collective states of mind are, the stronger the integration of the religious community and also the greater its preservative value.[75]

Society and the Collective Consciousness

Many social theories of this age gave temporal and logical priority to the individual over the community. Followers of Hobbes argued that society was created by a social contract between consenting individuals. Spencer views a sense of social belonging as the natural result of pursuits that furthered the interests of individuals. In contrast, Durkheim argues that social solidarity exists on the moral underpinnings present prior to social agreements. Unless we have faith in others to hold up their end of the bargain, we cannot live together. The feeling of mutual trust that forms the basis of society rests on what Durkheim calls the *conscience collective,* usually translated as "collective consciousness." He defines the collective consciousness as "the totality of beliefs and sentiments common to average citizens of the same society [that] forms a determinate system which has its own life."[76]

The French *conscience* means both conscience and consciousness, and Durkheim's use of *conscience collective* embraces both meanings. The collective consciousness tells us what society views as important, true, real and morally right. In other words, "The collective consciousness is the highest form of the psychic life, since it is the consciousness of the consciousnesses."[77] Because this common consciousness permeates an individual's social horizon, it generates the feeling of obligation to others that is foundational to any society. Therefore, like an individual conscience, the collective consciousness encourages and inhibits certain behaviors among members.

In order for this collective consciousness to govern the behavior of a community, Durkheim argues that this phenomenon shapes the member's ideas of self, the divine, ethics, time and space. Thus in contrast to traditional metaphysics, Durkheim argues that such ideas are not realities that exist independently of our collective consciousness but are products of it. For example, right and wrong is not a violation of metaphysical truths embedded in the structure of the universe. Against this view

Durkheim points out that "there are many acts which have been and still are regarded as criminal without in themselves being harmful to society. What social danger is there in touching a tabooed object, an impure animal or man, in letting the sacred fire die down."[78] Moreover, he states, "Even when a criminal act is certainly harmful to society, it is not true that the amount of harm that it does is regularly related to the intensity of the repression which it calls forth."[79] Therefore, Durkheim concludes that "an act is criminal when it offends strong and defined states of the collective conscience. . . . In other words, we must not say that an action shocks the common conscience because it is criminal, but rather that it is criminal because it shocks the common conscience."[80]

Because society cannot exist without the foundations provided by the common conscience, punishment of crime, consciously or not, represents an attempt to preserve society. "It [vengeance] consists, then, in a veritable act of defense, although an instinctive and unreflective one. We avenge ourselves only upon what has done us evil, and what has done us evil is always dangerous."[81] Moreover, given Durkheim's definition of crime as violation of the community consciousness, social transgression is not just a danger to individuals within a society but "is an offense against an authority in some way transcendent."[82] When society's rules are violated, it is an affront to all that society relies on. Vengeance therefore is a renewal of social bonds, a ritual by which society remembers what holds it together. "Wherever a directive power is established, its primary and principal function is to create respect for the beliefs, traditions, and collective practices; that is, to defend the common conscience against all enemies within and without."[83] Since those outside the community also stand outside the circle of moral sympathy, societies can tolerate brutal treatment for those considered rebels, infidels and heretics.

As is the case with ethics, Durkheim views time and space as social constructs rather than metaphysical realities. The Christian tradition enumerates the years in relation to the birth of Christ (A.D. = anno Domini). Jews observe the seventh day (sabbath) as a day of worship or sunset as a time of prayer. In these cases, the idea of time reflects views central to those communities. However, there are few references to precise measurements of time in the sacred writings of Jews and Christians since primitive cultures had no need for them. In contrast, our current

complex exchange systems require exact means of measuring time, so
Western societies set their watches to the minute and have a keen awareness of the time of day (as we measure it). Similarly, certain places are
designated as sacred according to the collective consciousness of a society, whether such a space be a temple, a football stadium or a capital
building. Durkheim's point is that beliefs about ethics, space and temporal cycles, taken as grounded in reality itself, are actually socially relative
and will change as the collective consciousness goes through transition.
That they appear so fixed and objective to us only reflects the extent to
which our ideas are shaped by this community consciousness.

Creation of the Collective Consciousness

If the collective consciousness shapes our view of the world and even the
categories through which we understand the world, we need to understand how it comes into being. However, we must be careful how we raise
this question lest we revert to metaphysics, which assumes we are capable
of a neutral observation of the universe. Durkheim argues, "The individual would never have risen to the conception of forces which so immea-
surably surpass him and all his surroundings, had he known nothing but
himself and the physical universe."[84] Metaphysics, by starting from the
individual and moving to the collective consciousness, begins from the
wrong end of the "chicken and egg" question. Instead community ideals
preexist the individual, who is born into a collective consciousness, and
create in that individual the potential for idealizing the world.

> It is in assimilating the ideals elaborated by society that he has become
> capable of conceiving the ideal. It is society, which by leading him
> within its sphere of action, has made him acquire the need of raising
> himself above the world of experience and has at the same time fur-
> nished him with the means of conceiving another. For society has
> constructed this new world in constructing itself, since it is society that
> this expresses. Thus both with the individual and in the group, the fac-
> ulty of idealizing has nothing mysterious about it. It is not a sort of lux-
> ury that a man could get along without but a condition of his very
> existence.[85]

With this Durkheim presents the human being as constitutionally
social, and our ability to create transcendents—God, the soul, moral truth

or time and space—is a natural function of our social nature.

The mechanism of idealization is the individual's internalization of the collective consciousness. When internalization occurs, it leads to the belief that the contents of the collective consciousness are of higher genesis than ourselves. "In a word, above the real world where his profane life passes he has placed another which, in one sense, does not exist except in thought, but to which he attributes a higher sort of dignity than to the first."[86] By this means we can understand how the idea of the sacred originated. "For our definition of the sacred is that it is something added to and above the real: now the ideal answers to this same definition; we cannot explain one without explaining the other. In fact, we have seen that if collective life awakens religious thought on reaching a certain degree of intensity, it is because it brings about a state of effervescence which changes the conditions of psychic activity."[87] In other words, this sense of the sacred that grows out of the internalization of the collective consciousness assumes a life of its own and shapes our view of the world, becoming more than simply the sum of all individual beliefs.[88] Now a new creature external to the members of society—the collective consciousness—exerts directive force on the lives of those immersed in it.

Durkheim's view that the collective consciousness creates our sense of the divine helps explain his intense interest in religion, even though he has no personal religious commitments. "If religion has given birth to all that is essential in society, it is because the idea of society is the soul of religion."[89] The belief that religion is a manifestation of social solidarity allows Durkheim to shift the question of truth from the *content* of a particular religion, a matter outside the realm of sociological investigation, to the *function* of these beliefs in all religions. With this functionalistic perspective, Durkheim can then argue that no religion is false. "It is an essential postulate of sociology that a human institution cannot rest upon an error and a lie, without which it could not exist. If it were not founded in the nature of things, it would have encountered in the facts a resistance over which it could never have triumphed. So when we commence the study of primitive religions, it is with the assurance that they hold to reality and express it."[90] He quickly adds, however, that "one must know how to go underneath the symbol to the reality which it represents and which gives it its meaning."[91] While the believer's understanding of the reality behind his or her religion's beliefs and practices may be mistaken, social phenomena do not lie. Thus it is possible that "the reasons with which the faithful justify them [religious beliefs] may be, and generally are, erroneous; but the true reasons do not cease to exist, and it is the duty of science to discover them."[92]

Durkheim's aim in *Elementary Forms of the Religious Life,* his most complete examination of human spirituality, is to use the science of sociology to peel back erroneous tenets of religious beliefs to discern "the ever-present causes upon which the most essential forms of religious thought and practice depend."[93] Behind the variations in religious belief and ritual he finds a common function. "Religion is in a word the system of symbols by means of which society becomes conscious of itself; it is the characteristic way of thinking of collective existence."[94] In other words, religion provides a means of propagating the collective consciousness. Therefore, Durkheim does not find it important to fix attention on the elements that distinguish one religion from another. All perform the task of binding members of a society to each other.

The unifying power of religion is the secret to its longevity. The sense of unity experienced by adherents, which they call salvation, fulfills an essential human need. However, while it seems to believers that it is the God and the beliefs contained in their religion that generate their sense of well-being, Durkheim says, "In fact, whoever has really practiced a religion knows very well that it is the cult which gives rise to these impressions of joy, of interior peace, of serenity, of enthusiasm which are, for the believer, an experimental proof of his beliefs."[95] What the believer considers to be a divinely given salvation is, in reality, the acceptance of the community. Human beings need a sense of salvation that is possible only when they are bound to others by a collective consciousness, and religion has traditionally provided this.

The Transition to Modern Society

In Durkheim's time, traditional religious communities, which rely on authorities for their beliefs and generally require a high degree of homogeneity, were giving way to communities characterized by a complex division of labor. As modern society became more intertwined and diverse, people's sphere of identification grew because a complex division of labor demands cooperation with those outside their own religious group. Moreover, since each had his or her own specific role in the community, an increasingly diverse society required greater individual freedom. As a result of these profound social changes the collective consciousness constructed on a traditional social model was insufficient for the emerging modern, secular society.

This rapid social transformation created what Durkheim calls "anomie." The institutional structures had changed, but people still had an inherent need for a sense of community. The latter had previously been satisfied by religion and its rituals, but religion was being replaced by secular social structures before new vehicles for the collective consciousness were in place. This creates anomie, a state of disequilibrium in which social values are thrown into disarray. Therefore, Durkheim believes that society's pressing need was to create new ritual media through which the lagging collective consciousness could catch up with social structures. Until then, people would experience rootlessness and a loss of their sense of salvation and well-being.

While these anomic circumstances created a difficult time of transition, Durkheim saw movement toward a secular society as positive. In his view the moral foundation facilitated by a complex division of labor provides greater tolerance of others and a more rational and efficient basis for interaction than religion. Thus the structures of modern industrial society will progressively displace religion as the bearer of the collective consciousness. In other words, Durkheim believes that the social sciences point in the direction of democracy. "Just as the ideal of lower societies was to create or maintain as intense a common life as possible, in which the individual was absorbed, so our ideal is to make social relations always more equitable, so as to assure the free development of all our social useful forces."[96]

This development of socially useful forces, according to Durkheim, is most effectively guided by science, not religion. However, that does not require that we do away with religion altogether. "That which science refuses to grant to religion is not its right to exist, but its right to dogmatize upon the nature of things and the special competence which it claims for itself for knowing man and the world."[97] While science is the route to knowledge, Durkheim reminds us that we cannot eradicate that in human nature that gives rise to religion:

> There is something eternal in religion which is destined to survive all the particular symbols in which religious thought has successively enveloped itself. There can be no society which does not feel the need of upholding and reaffirming at regular intervals the collective sentiments and the collective ideas which make its unity and its personality. Now this moral remaking cannot be achieved except by the means of reunions, assemblies and meetings where the individuals, being closely united to one another, reaffirm in common their common sentiments; hence come ceremonies which do not differ from regular religious ceremonies, either in the object, the results which they produce, or the processes employed to attain these results. What essential difference is there between an assembly of Christians celebrating the principal dates of the life of Christ, or of Jews remembering the exodus from Egypt or the promulgation of the decalogue, and a reunion of citizens commemorating the promulgation of a new moral or legal system or some great event in the national life?[98]

With this Durkheim signals his agreement with Comte that social reality cannot exclude the sacred as the vehicle for creating and communicating moral beliefs and communal solidarity. Society will always need ritual, with its sacred times and places, in order to create a sense of wholeness in its members. However, as society becomes more complex and all-encompassing, religious symbols must be replaced by secular symbols such as flags and national anthems as the means by which we gain a sense of the higher and holy.

Durkheim's Significance

There are several reasons Durkheim can rightly lay claim to the prominence he enjoys as a founder of sociology. First, he provides a model for a scientific approach to the study of society and is one of the first to advocate a shift from an ideological method that uses social science as a means of advocacy to a more descriptive model that attempts to establish conclusions apart from personal preferences. Stated otherwise, his support of a sociological method that focuses on the function of beliefs instead of their metaphysical verity is an important benchmark in the discipline.

Second, while he parallels Comte in his view that society requires a moral core and that ritual is a necessary means for reinforcing these unifying sentiments, Durkheim goes beyond his predecessor. Comte tends to simply assert the necessity of these social requirements, while Durkheim grounds them by demonstrating their role in creating our collective consciousness. Moreover, Comte's tendency to portray religious sentiments as the most effective means of appealing to the unsophisticated implies that such sentiments might be dispensed with—at least by the scientific elite. Durkheim, on the other hand, represents humanity as inherently religious, even if this sense of the transcendent does not need religion as traditionally defined.

This understanding of the human as a religious being stands as an important contribution in its own right. Many social thinkers in Durkheim's day thought that science would and should entirely displace religion. However, they were confounded by the fact that, while science challenged the basic beliefs of traditional religion on a number of different fronts, people remained very religious, even many who abandoned long-held dogmas. Durkheim's recognition that sensitivity to the transcendent is not something that can be eradicated generated great interest in his time and is perhaps even more influential in the post-World War II period when many have lost faith in science as the sole answer to all human problems. Durkheim's argument that we cannot put aside our idea of the transcendent without losing something of ourselves reopens the question of what the reality of human spirituality means and where it originates.

Finally, Durkheim's concept of the sociology of knowledge has had tremendous impact in the way differences in belief and practice are viewed. Under the metaphysical model, variations in belief were measured against a standard that was unchanging and beyond observation. This, of course, led to unending wrangling about what this standard was and how it was discovered. Durkheim's attempt to explain categories such as God, ethics or time from the perspective of collective consciousness is seen by many as a useful way of cutting the Gordian knot of metaphysics. Even if he overstates his case by implying that such categories are nothing beyond a given society's means of speaking of itself, he makes it impossible to deny the profound impact our social horizon exerts on our outlook on life.

Durkheim's understanding of the human capacity for creating the transcendent parallels that of Feuerbach in some important ways. Both see a social origin for our ideas of the transcendent and metaphysical and contend that the true source of these concepts are not transparent to the believer. Likewise, both argue, though in somewhat different ways, for a replacement of the divine with the secular and anthropological.[99] The linchpin of the arguments presented by both Feuerbach and Durkheim is the same: if we can isolate a valid human need and show how a society's beliefs and practices attempt to satisfy the need, we can conclude that the origin of these beliefs and practices is the need itself. This makes Durkheim's functional explanation of social phenomena susceptible to the same criticisms leveled at Feuerbach's. Both seem to confuse an answer to the question of "what does it do?" for an answer to (or a reason to ignore) the question "what is it?" In other words, to demonstrate that ideas about certain realities traditionally thought to exist outside society (e.g., God, right and wrong, time) have social functions does not necessitate that such realities have no existence apart from social beliefs. Durkheim may argue that the metaphysical reality of God or time are not sociological questions, but he provides no basis to say they are not valid questions for other disciplines.

Second, in his zeal to set sociology apart from psychology, Durkheim fixes his attention on the unifying elements of society to the neglect of disunifying aspects and disparate factions within society. For example, there is much in religion that is countercultural. While a faith community may indeed absorb a large amount of the collective consciousness of a given society within which it exists, it often defines itself in opposition to the social norms of that society. Furthermore, these religions themselves have actors that are not easily accommodated by Durkheim's views, such as the religious hermit or the prophetic figure, functioning as a gadfly who chastises believers for compromises with social norms.

Finally, Durkheim attempts to walk a difficult line in his optimistic vision for a new secularism. He will not be sorry to see traditional religious beliefs, structures and institutions fade away, but he believes that the social solidarity facilitated by religion is fundamental to human nature. What he fails to convincingly demonstrate is that the sense of community formerly provided by religious doctrine and ritual can be replicated by secular rituals. This is further complicated by the fact that he views his own period as anomic, one in which people lacked this feeling of communal solidarity because secular rituals had not fully supplanted religion mechanisms. Given this situation, he has little evidence from his own experience of secular society to bolster his argument that secular symbols, beliefs and practices can provide the social glue that religion once did.

Max Weber

Max Weber (1864-1920) takes his place alongside Émile Durkheim as one of the founders of modern sociology, but even though there was significant overlap in their years of activity and their professional interests, their ideas differ in some important ways.[100] First, Weber brings to sociology a consciousness of history that was lacking in Durkheim, whose analytical categories tended to be static. Also, as we have seen, Durkheim believed that religious doctrines are relatively unimportant in understanding the actions of religious people. However, Weber argues that beliefs are the necessary beginning point since differences in doctrine lead to variations in action. Thus rather than viewing all religions as mere elaborations on the same impulse, as Durkheim did, for Weber differences in beliefs *are* the object of sociological interest. While Durkheim went to great lengths to show that social activities differ from the actions of individuals, Weber makes individual motive a centerpiece of sociological investigation. Finally, we find little of the unbounded optimism about the movements of society in Weber that permeated much of the social science of his day.

Weber was born to parents of opposite temperaments. His mother was warm and giving, possessing a principled sense of duty from her Calvinist upbringing. Weber's father had worked himself up through minor political offices to becomes a member of the German Reichstag. While his prestigious position allowed young Max the opportunity to meet many of Germany's intelligentsia, his father's ascent in the political world involved the type of opportunistic compromises the younger Weber came to despise. At home the older Weber was demanding and authoritarian, and his abusiveness to his wife and children was a sore point that only worsened as time went on.

During Weber's time at the University of Heidelberg he manifested tendencies of both parents. He occupied much of his time in beer consumption and dueling but balanced this with avid dedication to his studies. Before he completed his degree, Weber was required to go to Strasbourg for military service. While there, he developed a close relationship with an uncle, the historian Hermann Baumgarten, and his wife. Baumgarten became a formative figure in Weber's interest in history and, with his consistent political principles, also shaped his nephew's approach to politics. Weber's aunt exemplified the ideal of the Protestant ethic that figured prominently in his later analysis of Western culture.

After his military obligations ended, Weber returned to live with his parents for the next eight years and grew increasingly resentful of his father's domineering ways and his financial dependence on his father. During this time he completed his Ph.D., produced his *Habilitationsschrift* on Roman agrarian history and began his teaching career as lecturer in law at Berlin. In 1893 Weber was awarded a chair in economics at Freiburg, which also allowed him to leave his parents' home. His star rose quickly, and he received a call to Heidelberg in 1896. However, a career that appeared to have unlimited potential came to an abrupt halt the next year during a visit from his parents. Weber had his fill of his father's mistreatment of his mother, the two had a harsh confrontation, and Weber demanded that his father leave. A month later the elder Weber died of a massive stroke.

This death precipitated a mental breakdown from which Weber did not recover for five years. During this time he traveled extensively and sought help from numerous doctors. After he had given up on finding a medical solution, he mysteriously began to recover in 1903 and was once again able to function intellectually. In 1904 he gave a public lecture in St. Louis, his first since his breakdown, and spent the next three months touring the United States. His observations of the American spirit helped crystallize his ideas about the influence of the Protestant worldview on the capitalist economics and Western political structures.

Following his return to Europe he embarked on a decade of feverish and fruitful writing. This productive period was interrupted by the beginning of World War I, during which Weber supervised nine military hospitals. When war ended, he immersed himself in German political life to help rebuild the country and correct the problems that had led Germany into war. A founder of the German Democratic Party, Weber believed that he would be advanced as the party's candidate for president. However, he refused to develop the political connections necessary for the nomination, believing it required the type of compromise his father engaged in, and was passed over. Before he had a second chance to run for the party head, he contracted pneumonia and died in 1920.

Weber's Sociological Method

Weber defines sociology as "that science which aims at the interpretive understanding of social behavior in order to gain an explanation of its causes, its course, and its effects."[101] As he expands on this seemingly innocuous definition, however, Weber sets himself at odds with other sociologists. First, Weber dismisses the assumption that the methods of social science should be the same as those of the natural sciences. The subject matter of the natural scientist does not talk back; it attributes no meaning to its actions but simply follows laws that can be defined impersonally and abstractly. The subjects of social science (i.e., human beings), on the other hand, attach meaning to their activities. Moreover, even when humans consider the workings of inanimate objects, purpose and meaning are ascribed to the artifact. "Without reference to this meaning such an object remains wholly unintelligible. That which is intelligible or understandable about it is thus its relation to human action in the role either of means or of end; a relation of which the actor or actors can be said to have been aware and to which their action has been oriented. Only in terms of such categories is it possible to 'understand' objects of this kind."[102] Finally, the subjective interests and values of researchers will determine which facets of human behavior they will consider worthy of investigation. Because the realm within which the sociologist operates is value-laden, sociology cannot simply duplicate the methods of the natural science.

A second important methodological departure from current wisdom was Weber's understanding of the basic components of sociological interest. While Durkheim argues that social realities can be explained only by appeal to groups, Weber argues that sociological method must begin from the individual. "There is no such thing as a collective personality which 'acts'. When reference is made in a sociological context to a state, a nation, a corporation, a family, or any army corps, or to similar collectivities, what is meant is, on the contrary, *only* a certain kind of development of actual or possible social actions of individual persons."[103] Sociology begins with the individual because only individuals act from motives and give reasons for what they do. "We shall speak of 'action' insofar as the acting individual attaches a subjective meaning to his behavior—be it overt or covert, omission or acquiescence. Action is 'social' insofar as its subjective meaning takes account of the behavior of others and is thereby oriented in its course."[104]

Since Weber has told us that social action is inextricably bound up in subjective motives and meanings, some explanation is necessary to show how sociology is a science. In an interesting turn he argues that sociology is a science precisely *because* human activities depend on underlying values and motives. Motives are *reasons* for actions. This means that anything humans pursue is, in some sense, rational. It is clear that this definition of rationality differs radically from the Enlightenment concept, in which rationality is an objective ideal to which we align our thought process. For Weber, rationality refers to the reasons for which we do something, even if those reasons appear irrational to others. Therefore, in order to understand the activities of a subject group, we must first comprehend the worldview from which it emanates: "For a science which is concerned with the subjective meaning of action, explanation requires a grasp of the complex of meaning in which an actual course of understandable action thus interpreted belongs."[105] Once this "complex of meaning" is understood, we can analyze the actions of a group by comparison and generalization and express our findings in terms of law. Therefore, even though the activities under consideration may not be rational according to our definition, our interpretation of these phenomena is still subject to rules of scientific demonstration and can be publicly tested.

The process by which we grasp the motivations of a subject group involves what Weber calls *verstehen,* which means something like "sympathetic understanding." Through *verstehen* we project ourselves into the world of those we are investigating in order to experience life as they experience it. We cannot do this through simple observation of external factors because similar activities can result from vastly different motivations. For example, casting a young child into a fire as a religious sacrifice seems to most people to be an irrational act. However, if we can comprehend the thought world and motives of the individuals involved, we can recognize why they believe the sacrifice to be rational, even though it does not conform to our personal canons of logic.

At some points Weber admits to the difficulty of achieving a sympathetic understanding. He states that "our ability to share the feelings of primitive men is not very much greater . . . [than the ability to know the] subjective state of mind of an animal."[106] Even when temporal distance is not a factor, "many ultimate ends or values toward which experience shows that human action may be oriented, often cannot be understood completely, though sometimes we are able to grasp them intellectually. The more radically they differ from our own ultimate values, however, the more difficult it is for us to understand them empathically. Depending upon the circumstances of the particular case we must be content either with a purely intellectual understanding of such values or when even that fails, sometimes we must simply accept them as given data."[107] In general, however, Weber is confident that such barriers can be overcome and *verstehen* achieved: "One need not have been Caesar in order to understand Caesar."[108]

An additional problem encountered as we attempt to attain an empathetic understanding of a social group or structure is that attributes that typify the whole may not be true of each individual within the group. Collectivities are comprised of diverse individuals who do not manifest all the characteristics attributed to the group, nor do they manifest these characteristics to the same degree. This leads Weber to offer his concept of the "ideal type." "An ideal type is formed by the one-sided *accentuation* of one or more points of view and by the synthesis of a great many diffuse, discrete, more or less present and occasionally absent *concrete individual* phenomena, which are arranged according to those one-sidedly emphasized viewpoints into a unified *analytical* construct."[109] Thus the ideal type is a theoretical tool that offers a purified composite, not a statistical average, of social realities. It combines certain characteristics into a unified whole as a touchstone of comparison. Therefore, when Weber speaks of Protestantism, he has no Protestant individual or group in mind. As he tells us, "It is probably seldom if ever that a real phenomenon can be found which corresponds exactly to one of these ideally constructed pure types."[110] Instead the ideal type is a conceptual tool that allows us to distinguish Protestantism from other social entities.

Not only do concrete entities fail to perfectly exemplify the ideal type, individuals who are included within the type are frequently unaware of the source of their actions.

> In the great majority of cases actual action goes on in a state of inarticulate half-consciousness or actual unconsciousness of its subjective meaning. The actor is more likely to "be aware" of it in a vague sense than he is to "know" what he is doing or be explicitly self-conscious about it. In most cases his action is governed by impulse or habit. Only occasionally and, in the uniform action of large numbers, often only in the case of a few individuals, is the subjective meaning of the action, whether rational or irrational, brought clearly into consciousness.[111]

Therefore, for example, the majority of those who fit the bureaucratic type about which Weber writes may be only vaguely aware of how the bureaucratic model structures their everyday lives or thought patterns.

The Emergence of Rational Society

The early twentieth century world in which Weber lived was much different from the one inhabited by his ancestors. In a few short generations western Europe, England and the United States had been transformed from agrarian economies based on barter to industrial nations with centralized governments. Such a rapid social, political and economic transformation demanded explanation, especially when even older societies such as those of India or China had not experienced the same revolution in production and social structure. Weber believed the key was the rationalization of society.

We have already seen that Weber believes that all actions have some sort of rationale as their impetus. Thus when Weber refers to rationalization in this context, his more precise meaning is goal oriented or purposeful (*zweckrational*) activity. He contrasts this with three competing types of rationality. One form of rationality is value oriented (*wertra-*

tional). The end *wertrational* seeks does not appear to meet the canons of rationality to outsiders but may be sought through rational means. For example, we may not think it makes sense to devote a life to producing a single work of art, but the steps taken by an artist to achieve this aim would be viewed by others as a rational process. A second type refers to motivations that are based on emotional attachments. If we understand a certain type of sentiment, even if we do not share it, we may be able to understand why an individual engages in a certain type of activity. Thus many of us can comprehend a parent's defense of an obviously guilty child, even while disagreeing with it. A third type of rationality is traditional, in which traditional structures establish the goals to be pursued as well as the means. Purification of the soul through ritual bathings as prescribed in sacred writings may be an example of this.

A central question for Weber is what has driven the transition from the first three models of rationality to the ascendancy of goal-oriented rationality in Western countries. Weber believes that a key is found in the mechanisms of authority and legitimacy within social orders. A basic element of every social system is the existence of some form of authority. While Weber recognizes that sociology must give attention to the individual who holds authority, his unique contribution is the examination of the relationship between the leader and those over whom authority is exercised. Weber argues that "every genuine form of domination implies a minimum of voluntary compliance, that is, an *interest* (based on ulterior motives or genuine acceptance) in obedience."[112] The interest of which Weber speaks legitimates the dominance of those who exercise authority. Therefore, authority cannot be understood without also understanding the legitimacy conferred on leaders by their followers.

Weber identifies three forms of social authority and their corresponding forms of legitimacy. The first is traditional authority, in which power is believed to be vested in an individual by a higher authority. Therefore, the use of lineal descent as a means of selecting monarchs did not rest on the longevity of the practice. Instead it was reinforced by the idea of divine right, in which it was believed that God gave warrant to those who occupy thrones. Similarly, the power of the priestly class arose because they were seen as divine designees. The legitimacy of this structure rested "on an established belief in the sanctity of immemorial traditions and the legitimacy of those exercising authority under them."[113]

The prototypical form of traditional authority, according to Weber, was patrimonialism. In such a system, there was little or no distinction between public and private realms. The kingdom's wealth was accessible to the king for his private benefit, and those who carried out official duties were linked to the ruler through family ties or friendship. The difficulty with patrimonialism is that it is inefficient on a large scale. Since all power comes from the top, the messages and goals are often lost, misinterpreted or subverted by lieutenants by the time they move down the hierarchy.

The second type of domination Weber examines is charismatic authority. "The term 'charisma' will be applied to a certain quality of an individual personality by virtue of which he is considered extraordinary and treated as endowed with supernatural, superhuman, or at least specifically exceptional powers or qualities."[114] In contrast to traditional authority, then, charismatic social structures rely on individuals rather than the past, and this often pits the two structures against each other. "Within the sphere of its claims, charismatic authority repudiates the past, and is in this sense a specifically revolutionary force."[115] Charismatic leaders gain their legitimacy from the faith of followers, which rests on the "follower's devotion to the exceptional sanctity, heroism or exemplary character of an individual person, and of the normative patterns or order revealed or ordained by him (charismatic authority)."[116]

The centrality of a revolutionary, charismatic individual in this model reveals the instability of this model. When the revolution has been completed or the leader stumbles in his pursuits or dies, "his followers abandon him for pure charisma does not recognize any legitimacy other than one which flows from personal strength proven time and again."[117] Furthermore, a charismatic model is less durable than other forms of authority because, by its nature, it lacks institutional infrastructure. "Charisma knows no formal and regulated appointment or dismissal, no career, advancement or salary, no supervisory or appeals body, no local or purely technical jurisdiction, and no permanent institutions in the manner of bureaucratic agencies, which are independent of the incumbents and their personal charisma. Charisma is self-determined and sets its own limits."[118]

The final form of domination is bureaucratic authority. Instead of gaining power through tradition or the ability to inspire, bureaucracy gains power through rules formulated on the basis of rational principles. These rules designate the rights and responsibilities of all within a group and gain legitimacy through "belief in the legality of enacted rules and the right of those elevated to authority under such rules to issue commands (legal authority)."[119] While bureaucracy is fundamentally opposed to the traditional model of authority, both "share *continuity* as one of their most important characteristics. In this sense both are structures of everyday life."[120] Before we consider the characteristics of bureaucracy in greater depth, we need to examine how long-standing traditional social systems were displaced by bureaucracy.

The Protestant Ethic and the Spirit of Capitalism
Increasingly, those who wielded traditional authority were replaced by those who possessed rational-legal authority with its corresponding bureaucratic social structure and capitalist economic system. In order for bureaucracy and capitalism to emerge, however, two ingredients are necessary. First, the proper material conditions must exist: a money economy, widespread literacy and physical infrastructure. Similar circumstances had existed at other points in history, but since this is only one side of the equation, capitalism did not come into being. The proper "spirit" must also be present. By spirit Weber refers to the goal-oriented rationality of bureaucracy that displaces the "magical" doctrines and practices of traditional social orders that were incompatible with a rationality structured society. To explain the transition Weber puts forward his theory of the Protestant ethic.

The first step in creating the spirit from which capitalism emerged was Protestantism's doctrine of the "priesthood of all believers." This doctrine undercut the traditional authority of the priestly class by putting all believers on the same level. Once the traditional leadership structure was challenged, all other elements of the traditional order fell under suspicion. Doctrines that had generally been inculcated in the laity through priestly authority now required a new means of justification. The new basis of grounding the church and its structures was reason, which required that Christianity become rationalized and systematized.

While Lutheran Protestantism gave birth to the doctrine of the priest-hood of all believers, this alone was not sufficient to generate the spirit necessary for capitalism. The reason for this, according to Weber, is that Luther's concept of calling (or vocation) encouraged Christians to be sat-isfied with the status quo in politics, society and economics, and also their position in life. "Thus for Luther the concept of the calling remained tra-ditionalistic. His calling is something which man has to accept as a divine ordinance, to which he must adapt himself."[121] For Calvin, however, this passive view of calling represented an unwillingness to respond to oppor-tunities God provides. Instead the purposeful use of resources provided by God is the route by which the layperson glorifies God. Work directed toward achievement of goals therefore becomes a calling and is inte-grated into the realm of spirituality.

This Calvinist concept of calling is the result of another defining doc-trine of the movement: predestination. Predestination states that one's salvation or damnation is decided by God alone before the creation of the universe. This "makes it impossible for the church to administer sac-raments whose reception can have any significance for eternal salvation. Moreover, the actual behavior of the believer is irrelevant to his fate, which has been determined from eternity through God's inscrutable and immutable will."[122] Because predestination makes all human works insig-nificant for gaining salvation, Weber argues that Calvinism is able to dis-pense with Catholicism's "magical" view of sacramentalism.[123]

At first glance, belief that everyone's salvation or damnation is sealed before the creation of the universe would seem to lead to fatalism, but Weber argues that it produces the opposite effect in Calvinism. Since Cal-vinists believe that we are not privy to our soteriological status, this cre-ates what Weber refers to as "salvation anxiety." "In its extreme inhumanity this doctrine [predestination] must above all have had one consequence for the life of a generation which surrendered to its magnifi-cent consistency. That was a feeling of unprecedented inner loneliness of the single individual. In what was for the man of the age of the Reforma-tion the most important thing in life, his eternal salvation, he was forced to follow his path alone to meet a destiny which had been decreed for him from eternity."[124] Weber asserts that this sense of uncertainty would inevita-bly create a circumstance in which the convinced Calvinist would seek "certain indices *(Symptome)* by which he may determine whether he possesses this incomparable charisma, inasmuch as it is impossible for him to live on in absolute uncertainty regarding his salvation."[125]

What counts as evidence of salvation, according to Weber, is the meaningful pursuit of material success: "For the believer and his community, his own ethical conduct and fate in the secular social order became supremely important as an indication of his state of grace."[126] Since the faithful cannot contribute to their salvation, fruitful activity is viewed as a sign of God's grace as well as evidence of obedience to God's call to service within creation. "For if that God, whose hand the Puritan sees in all the occurrences of life, shows one of His elect a chance of profit, he must do it with a purpose. Hence the faithful Christian must follow the call by taking advantage of the opportunity."[127] This motivated the Puritans to engage in the rational pursuit of material goals.

Interestingly, the quest for tangible signs of God's blessing stands alongside Puritan warnings about wealth. However, Weber argues that these concerns did not prohibit accumulating goods. "The real moral objection is to relaxation in the security of possession, the enjoyment of wealth with the consequence of idleness and the temptations of the flesh, above all of distraction from the pursuit of a righteous life. In fact, it is only because possession involves this danger of relaxation that it is objectionable at all."[128] Therefore, wealth is only a moral danger when it leads to idleness and frivolous enjoyment. Since profits were God's stamp of approval, they must be put to productive use. And since the greater level of productivity came about through a rational pursuit of material ends, the Protestant work ethic represents a challenge to traditional means of domination. When it had taken root, Weber concludes, "The religious valuation of restless, continuous, systematic work in a worldly calling, as the highest means to asceticism, and at the same time the surest and most evident proof of rebirth and genuine faith, must have been the most powerful conceivable lever for the expansion of that attitude toward life which we have here called the spirit of capitalism."[129]

The Transition to Secular Bureaucracy

The next step of the transition toward modern capitalism and bureaucracy involves the replacement of the religious underpinnings with secular rituals. The material success of Calvinists caught the attention of others, who then appropriated the spirit of goal-directed rationality. Once this rational pursuit of ends became broadly diffused throughout society, its influence in the economic, political, interpersonal and even religious realms was no longer apparent to us. "The capitalistic economy of the present day is an immense cosmos into which the individual is born, and which presents itself to him, at least as an individual, as an unalterable order of things in which he must live. It forces the individual, in so far as he is involved in the system of market relationships, to conform to capitalistic rules of actions."[130] When this foothold is achieved in the general social consciousness, capitalism "no longer needs the support of any religious forces, and feels the attempts of religion to influence economic life, in so far as they can still be felt at all, to be as much an unjustified interference as its regulation by the State."[131]

The social structure underlying capitalist economics is bureaucracy, which overtakes and replaces traditional systems because of its superior efficiency.

> The decisive reason for the advance of bureaucratic organization has always been its purely *technical* superiority over any other form of organization. The fully developed bureaucratic apparatus compares with other organizations exactly as does the machine with the non-mechanical modes of production. Precision, speed, unambiguity, knowledge of the files, continuity, discretion, unity, strict subordination, reduction of friction and material and personal costs—these are raised to the optimum point in the strictly bureaucratic administration, and especially in its monocratic form.[132]

What makes bureaucracy's technical superiority possible is enactment of rules and hierarchies that allow the various parts of an institution to work in tandem toward an institutional end. "Bureaucratization offers above all the optimum possibility for carrying through the principle of specializing administrative functions according to purely objective considerations. . . . 'Objective' discharge of business primarily means a discharge of business according to *calculable rules* and 'without regard for persons.'"[133] Organizations utilizing impersonal rules in logical hierarchies are able to undertake and complete large-scale endeavors efficiently and allow society to make use of all its resources. This entails removal of all motivations from an institution that do not further the goals of the institution. Individual interests, emotional attachments, spiritual concerns and the traditions of the past all give way to rational rules, guidelines and procedures that allow us to achieve predictable results. Therefore, while traditional forms of authority seek to unite the spheres of life into a whole, "the modern organization of the civil service separates the bureau from the private domicile of the official and, in general, segregates official activity from the sphere of private life."[134]

Despite its ability to streamline operations, efficiently utilize resources and provide order, Weber sees a number of serious problems with bureaucratic authority. First, he notes, "Once fully established, bureaucracy is among those social structures which are the hardest to destroy. Bureaucracy is *the* means of transforming social action into rationally organized action. Therefore, as an instrument of rationally organizing authority relations, bureaucracy is a power instrument of the first order for one who controls the bureaucratic apparatus."[135] The quantity of power it affords those at the top is especially troubling since "bureaucratic administration always tends to exclude the public, to hide its knowledge and action from criticism as well as it can."[136]

However, Weber's foremost concern about bureaucracy and capitalism is the inverse relationship between efficiency and inclusion of personal elements in bureaucracy. If productivity is to increase, personal and emotional attachments must be eliminated. "Bureaucracy develops the more perfectly, the more it is 'dehumanized,' the more completely it succeeds in eliminating from official business love, hatred, and all purely personal, irrational, and emotional elements which escape calculation. This is appraised as its special virtue by capitalism."[137] Because rules and guidelines are the lifeblood of the bureaucracy, the individuals are replaceable in the same way that machinery is maintained by replacement parts. This is as true for those at the top as it is for those at the lower strata of an organization. For example, if the smooth functioning of government is facilitated by the rules, once these are in place, they tend to take on a life of their own, and the ruler can become superfluous. This is what happened as nineteenth century Europe, with its large-scale political structures governed by bureaucratic guidelines, found it possible to live without a monarch.

While Weber disliked the dehumanizing nature of bureaucracy, he did not see a way out of it. Its effectiveness meant that if a person wants to gain status and engage in activity deemed significant in society, he or she must become part of the rational-legal bureaucracy, even as it threatens to become what he calls an "iron cage" in which the human spirit is trapped and its energies diverted from personal pursuits toward goals dictated by an impersonal system.[138] Therefore, Weber disagrees with his compatriots in the social sciences who find humanity's salvation in the movement away from traditional forms of social structure. Instead we face the danger of losing our humanity in the slick efficiency of impersonal systems.

Evaluation and Criticism of Weber

Weber's sociology has been influential on a number of different levels. One significant contribution is his attempt to distinguish between the natural sciences and the social sciences by his appeal to motive. Since people differ from artifacts by attributing value and meaning to actions, the methods of sociology must reflect this in its method. For this reason Weber's assertion that the social scientist must attempt to empathetically enter the subject's world shaped sociological method for decades.

His attempt to look at political and social authority through the lens of legitimating mechanisms has also been an important contribution. It has recast discussion about the basis and nature of social authority and is a helpful tool in analyzing political transition and social discontent. Closely related to this is Weber's views concerning the nature and problems of bureaucracy. Through his analysis of bureaucracy, we gain important insight into the tensions created in the personal realm by the demands of modern institutional structures and processes, and many elements of his thought still figure prominently in interpreting organizational structures and problems.

Finally, Weber's concept of the Protestant ethic as the trigger for the rationalization of modern secular society has generated discussion that continues into the present. Many find his thesis that we need to look beyond the material circumstances of an age and include also the ideological horizon in our consideration of social change a useful tool for the social sciences. Moreover, the correlation he draws between the rise of Calvinism and the spirit of capitalism is seen as convincing by many.

However, even those who do not agree with his specific conclusions about the relationship between the two have felt compelled to reconsider the broader question about the influence of religious ideas in shaping modern society. Rather than assuming that there is broad discontinuity between earlier religious structures and modern secularism, later social thinkers have rediscovered important links.

Our examination of problem areas in Weber's thought can be divided into concerns about method and challenges to his conclusions. On the methodological level, many have questioned his belief that *verstehen* can be achieved when the values, presuppositions and social background of our subject matter differ significantly from those of the investigator. Since he is clear that a professional interest in a topic is vastly different from existential concern, it is difficult to know how the professional researcher can truly attain the level of empathy necessary for *verstehen*. Weber himself states that "the more radically they [a subject's values] differ from our own ultimate values . . . the more difficult it is for us to understand them empathically" to the point that "sometimes we must simply accept them as given data."[139] However, Weber predicates the sociological endeavor on our ability to get beyond external data and discover the underlying motives and worldviews. Therefore, if *verstehen* is a necessary tool for sociology, we need to ask whether an outsider can effectively understand a worldview that differs extensively from his or her own.

A second methodological criticism comes from the opposite side. Weber asserts that once researchers have stepped into the world of the subject matter, they must step back out into a scientific neutrality to analyze their data and not allow their presuppositions and wishes to shape conclusions. However, he also reminds us that every person, the sociologist included, exists in a value-laden world that is so ingrained in the psyche that the individual is seldom aware of how those values shape his or her actions and ideas. Weber seems to believe that if the sociologist is conscious of how and where personal presuppositions and ideals differ from those of the subject, this has a prophylactic quality that guards against contamination of conclusions. However, even if this is true, it assumes that the investigator can and will be cognizant of his or her assumptions (even though those under investigation are not generally aware of their own and not allow these to guide evaluation.

A third question of method deals with the ideal type. Weber defends his use of this conceptual tool by stating that sociological realities are rarely, if ever, found in pure form in concrete reality. However, if such composites are constructed by the sociologist, it is not difficult to see how different sociologists may create different ideal types of the same entity. The elements Weber views as key to the Protestant ethic, Indian religion, bureaucracy or other entities he studies could easily be moved to the periphery by another sociologist and replaced by other defining attributes. Since the characteristics of the ideal type are selected by the researcher, the type can easily become a reflection of the investigator's interests and his or her conclusions a self-fulfilling prophecy.

Given the extent of Weber's work, scholars have had a vast array of conclusions about which to raise questions. We will confine our comments to just a couple of criticisms concerning his idea of the Protestant ethic. First, while Weber may have found it personally impossible to live with the uncertainty created by predestination, he offers little by way of argument to demonstrate that the average Calvinist experienced the same anxiety. If one was willing to accept a doctrine that contains the inherent uncertainties presented by predestination, why would they not be willing to live with the uncertainties rather than attempt to beat the system and get a look inside? Moreover, Weber does not offer compelling arguments as to why these Calvinists looked to material, industry and success rather than some other external evidence for signs of God's favor. It is not difficult to envision responses other than saving and reinvesting that would grow out of the same impulse, such as giving profits to the church or the poor, success in preparing the best and brightest of their offspring for ministry, scholarship, or government service, size of family or some other external sign of divine blessing. Why material success and asset accumulation would be anointed by Calvinism as the indicator of election rather than other potential candidates is not clear.

Sigmund Freud

Sigmund Freud's (1856-1939) long career allows him to straddle the very different worlds of pre- and post-World War I and makes him an important transitional figure.[140] However, it is not simply his longevity but his ideas that mark him as a hinge between the nineteenth and twentieth centuries. As a fierce advocate of science as the best and only hope for humankind's future, he is a child of the nineteenth-century world. However, his portrayal of human nature as subject to irrational instincts is more characteristic of the twentieth century and allows his psychoanalytic theory to survive the horrors of World War I as a viable theory rather than a historical curiosity.

Freud's father was a well-to-do wool merchant who lost his business in Moravia when the Austrian economy turned sour. Following this reversal the family moved to Vienna in his fourth year. Freud lived in this city for the rest of his life, except for a time of study in France and the last few months of his life when forced to flee the occupying Nazis. There is evidence that Freud, from a young age, was somewhat embarrassed by his father's unremarkable accomplishments and believed himself superior. This self-confidence was cultivated by the indulgence of his mother on her first-born (Freud's father had two children from a previous marriage). The stock example of his mother's favor is her compliance with ten-year-old Sigmund's insistence that the family piano be removed from the home because his sister's practice made him unable to concentrate on his studies.

Freud was intensely proud of his Jewish heritage, although he abandoned any belief in God early in life for reasons about which he is strangely silent. His biographer and close associate for three decades, Ernest Jones (1879-1958), states simply, "He [Freud] grew up devoid of any belief in a God or immortality, and does not appear ever to have felt the need of it."[141] While a Jewish background might have barred an average student from university admission in a time when anti-Semitism permeated Austrian society, Freud showed exceptional promise and entered the University of Vienna as a medical student. However, he tells us in his autobiography, "Neither at that time, nor indeed in my later life, did I feel any particular predilection for the career of a doctor. I was moved, rather, by a sort of curiosity, which was, however, directed more toward human concerns than towards natural objects."[142] Nor did his time at the university incline him any more toward the traditional work of the doctor. However, he found a mentor in a physiology professor named Ernst Brücke (1819-1892) and gained renewed interest in his studies. "At length, in Ernst Brücke's physiological laboratory, I found rest and full satisfaction—and men, too, whom I could respect and take as my models."[143]

Freud finished his medical degree in 1881 and spent the next several years doing neurological research and, beginning in 1885, teaching neuropathology as an unpaid *Privatdozent* at the University of Vienna. He was ambitious and from an early period sought an angle that would establish his prominence in the medical world. His first independent attempt was to test the medical uses of cocaine. This became a dead end, which stymied attempts to attain a salaried professorship at Vienna. A turning point came during work with Josef Breuer (1842-1925). Breuer had experimented with hypnosis as a means of treating hysteria, attempting to eliminate symptoms through suggestion. What he discovered instead was that the subject, under hypnosis, would recall past events she had not been aware of in the waking state. When brought out of hypnosis the symptom would be relieved. Breuer concluded that the patient's hysteria was caused by early traumas that were not consciously remembered. With this Freud received the germ of his theory of the unconscious, which he later expanded and brought into association with other psychological concepts.

Perhaps the decisive benchmark in Freud's shift from physiology to psychology is the publication of *The Interpretation of Dreams* (1900), which Freud considered his best work. Following 1900 Freud's ceaseless writing on new and groundbreaking ideas such as the role of the unconscious, repression, the Oedipus complex, the structure of the self and the nature of human sexuality allowed him to quickly gather a circle of disciples intrigued by the possibilities of psychoanalysis as a therapeutic method. An important indicator of the movement's growing credibility was the establishment of The International Psycho-Analytical Association in 1910. Its first president was Carl Jung (1875-1961), whom Freud had designated as his intellectual heir. As Freud's fame became more firmly established, he demanded unswerving admiration from his disciples, and many early followers were exiled for divergences from Freudian orthodoxy. The most famous was the split between Freud and Jung, which caused the latter to separate himself completely from the Psycho-Analytical Association and the former to engage in a systematic attempt to purge any remaining Jungians from the organization.

With psychoanalysis firmly established as a therapeutic method, Freud increasingly turned his energies toward broader applications of the theory.

My interest, after making a lifelong *detour* through the natural sciences, medicine and psychotherapy, returned to the cultural problems which had fascinated me long before, when I was a youth scarcely old enough for thinking. . . . I perceived ever more clearly that the events of human history, the interactions between human nature, cultural development and the precipitates of primeval experiences (the most prominent example of which is religion) are no more than a reflection of the dynamic conflicts between the ego, the id and the super-ego, which psycho-analysis studies in the individual—are the very same processes repeated upon a wider stage.[144]

In 1938 the Nazis occupied Austria before Freud and his family were able to leave the country. Fearful of the negative public reaction that would follow persecution of such a well-known figure, the Germans allowed him, his family and some close associates to flee to England. Freud continued to write and see patients up until a month before his death in 1939.

Freud's Method

Freud's method rests on two pillars that may, at first glance, seem incompatible. On the one hand, he argues that human beings are driven by irrational urges and instincts. On the other hand, he believes that reason is the key to unraveling our most profound problems. Freud's means of putting these two seemingly contradictory ideas together argues that our irrational (and essentially sexual) impulses cannot be fully eliminated since they provide the raw energy necessary for human life and achievement. However, their potentially destructive powers can be controlled by our reason. Therefore, with his assertion that "we have no other means of controlling our instinctual nature but our intelligence,"[145] Freud agrees with the metaphysicians' belief that reason is the route to freedom. However, while the philosophers had rightly identified the intellect as the tool of liberation, they had not properly identified the force it must tame. Only when we own up to the inherent sexuality of our appetites can we get beyond the illusions that trap us.

The idea our actions have causes that can be reshaped reflects Freud's early training in physiology. What we call "mental" or "psychological" is actually of physical origin. "In the last analysis, all suffering is nothing other than sensation; it only exists in so far as we feel it, and we only feel it in consequence of certain ways in which our organism is regulated."[146] Therefore, when a mental imbalance manifests itself, the psychiatrist must function as a scientist who seeks the origin of a problem in order to correct it. However, when Freud tells us that "the intellect and the mind are objects of scientific research in exactly the same way as any non-human thing,"[147] he assumes one important distinction. While the subject matter of the natural sciences is passive, the psychiatrist's patients actively (but unconsciously) hide the causes of their behavior through repression. This requires that the therapist find a way around the subject's resistance to allowing these thoughts and experiences into the sphere of consciousness. With this qualification in place Freud is completely at ease in putting psychoanalysis on par with the natural sciences and states, "Strictly speaking there are only two sciences: psychology, pure and applied, and natural science."[148]

Freud on Human Nature

Freud clearly recognizes that his concept of human nature was a blow to conventional wisdom's more benign vision of human nature, and he nicely sums up the reasons. Our intellectual prejudice is offended by his assertion that "mental processes are in themselves unconscious and that of all mental life it is only certain individual acts and portions that are conscious."[149] Freud's second challenge to the collective aesthetic and moral self-image is the "assertion that instinctual impulses which can only be described as sexual, both in the narrower and wider sense of the word, play an extremely large and never hitherto appreciated part in the causation of nervous and mental diseases. It asserts further that these same sexual impulses also make contributions that must not be underestimated to the highest cultural, artistic and social creations of the human spirit."[150] While Freud here abstracts these two offenses from each other, in his thought they were closely intertwined, as we will see below.

The working assumption throughout the Western intellectual tradition was that the activities of the mind are transparent to us. While some philosophers, going back to Plato, posited an unconscious element within our psychic processes, this realm was almost completely ignored. In contrast Freud claims that all our mental activities at first, and the vast majority of them later in life, are unconscious. To use a tired but apt analogy, the human psyche is like an iceberg, the vast majority of which is submerged and unseen by us. The connection between this unconscious realm of our mind and sexuality is Freud's belief that elements of the human sexual impulses are so reprehensible that they are censored by the ego before they reach our consciousness and the energy of the instincts are diverted or repressed to the unconscious. The process by which this occurs takes us first through Freud's famous analysis of the structure of the mind.

Like Plato, Freud envisions a threefold division within the psyche, although the functions assigned to the three aspects differ in their expositions.[151] The first facet of the mind is *das Es,* or the id (literally, the "it"). The id refers to the boiling cauldron of instincts, emotions and desires that provide the wild energy of human action. It is the home of the libido, a term Freud says is "properly reserved for the instinctual forces of sexual life."[152] The libido is the source of all attempts to gain pleasure through the body, not just through the genitals. Thus we see that Freud defines sexuality more broadly than is usually the case. The energy possessed by the id is inchoate; thus it "has no means of showing the ego either love or hate. It cannot say what it wants; it has achieved no unified will."[153] Lacking a unified will, these instincts have no contradictions. They all clamor for immediate satisfaction and must be held in check for the individual to survive.

The mental capacity charged with subduing the id is what Freud calls *das Über-Ich:* the superego or ego ideal. The superego "is the outcome of two highly important factors, one of a biological and the other of a historical nature: namely, the lengthy duration in man of his childhood helplessness and dependence, and the fact of his Oedipus complex."[154] We will discuss the Oedipus complex later, but we must note that the offspring of the human species are more dependent for their survival on adults, particularly the parents, than the offspring of nonhuman species. During this period of dependency the father in particular exemplifies authority by restraining the child's pursuits of pleasure by rules, punishments and other forms of restraint. However, the father's authority does not remain external. "It is in keeping with the course of human development that external coercion gradually becomes internalized; for a special mental agency, man's super-ego, takes it over and includes it among its commandments."[155] The superego uses our conscience—an enduring parental voice—to remind us that the pleasure-seeking impulses of the id must be kept in place in order to remain within society's good graces. "As the child was once under a compulsion to obey its parents, so the ego submits to the categorical imperative of its super-ego."[156]

Situated (trapped?) between the id and superego is *das Ich,* or the ego (literally, the "I"). Freud describes the ego as "a coherent organization of mental processes,"[157] the unifying center of the psyche. We might add to this that the ego is our bridge to the external world. As our contact to external reality, its primary tool is perception, which "may be said to have the same significance for the ego as instincts have for the id."[158] The ego shares one goal with the id, that of obtaining pleasure. However, since it is the means by which we relate to the external world,

> the ego discovers that it is inevitable for it to renounce immediate satisfaction, to postpone the obtaining of pleasure, to put up with a little unpleasure and to abandon certain sources of pleasure altogether. An ego thus educated has become "reasonable"; it no longer lets itself be governed by the pleasure principle, but obeys the *reality principle,* which also at bottom seeks to obtain pleasure, but pleasure which is assured through taking account of reality, even though it is pleasure postponed and diminished.[159]

The ego's task of bringing reality to bear on the demands of the id is made difficult because it gets a late start. At birth we enter the world with an extremely weak ego and an id at full force, as evidenced by an infant's desire to gain satisfaction with no regard for others. As the child develops, these narcissistic tendencies are moderated by the parents, who force delays in certain forms of gratification, and are later subdued by the superego's use of the ego to control our instincts. Thus in a passage that echoes Plato's analogy of the proper balance of the soul's functions, Freud states, "In its relation to the id it [the ego] is like a man on horseback, who has to hold in check the superior strength of the horse; with this difference, that the rider tries to do so with his own strength while the ego uses borrowed forces [those of the superego]. . . . Often a rider, if he is not to be parted from his horse, is obliged to guide it where it wants to go; so in the same way the ego is in the habit of transforming the id's will into action as if it were its own."[160]

This exposition provides the background against which Freud understands certain mental complications. If the passions of the id are allowed to run wild, which they will do if not restrained, we place ourselves in danger by not properly accounting for the realities of the external world. In other words the ego is the human's means of self-preservation. However, because the id is the engine that drives life, the ego cannot suppress it completely by applying the suppression of the conscience against it. Therefore, if the superego holds too tight a rein on the id, we turn our aggressions inward. This is the problem of neurosis, in which the superego uses the conscience as a club with which we beat ourselves for entertaining the demands of the id.[161]

Human Sexuality

The process of balancing the various facets of the psyche is complicated by the fact that we are sexual beings from birth. Remembering that Freud defines sexuality as the pursuit of physical pleasure, he states that "sexual development in man shows *two different periods*" interrupted by a period of latency.[162] The earlier stage, infantile sexuality, "makes its appearance to the satisfaction of the major organic needs, and it behaves *auto-erotically*—that is, it seeks and finds its objects in the infant's own body."[163] In this stage sexual feelings are not repressed, and children seek sexual pleasure without a sense of inhibition. Later, as the boundary between the conscious and unconscious is established, children learn from their parents that genital play is unacceptable social practice and gradually engage in behavior that is more in line with societal acceptability. At this point sexuality enters a period of latency. However, Freud tells us, "The influx of this sexuality does not stop even in this latency period, but its energy is deflected either wholly or partially from sexual utilization and conducted to other aims."[164] This deflection, or sublimation, is an important step in preparing the older child for adult responsibilities within society.

Freud traces the bodily locations in which the young child finds sexual pleasure through three stages. "*Oral erotism* stands in the foreground in a first, very early phase; a second of the 'pregenital' organizations is characterized by the predominance of . . . *anal erotism,* and only in the third phase . . . is the sexual life determined also through the participation of the true genital zones."[165] Concurrently with this progression the child, who at birth cannot distinguish between him or herself and others, begins to recognize a world beyond. Awareness of the external world leads the child to seek a sexual object. Since those closest to the child are family members, "A human being's first choice of an object is regularly an incestuous one, aimed, in the case of the male, at his mother and sister; and it calls for the severest prohibitions to deter this persistent infantile tendency from realization."[166]

The son's choice of the mother as the object of libidinal desire encounters a severe obstacle—he has competition. "It is easy to see that the little man wants to have his mother all to himself, that he feels the presence of his father as a nuisance, that he is resentful if his father indulges in any signs of affection towards his mother and that he shows satisfaction when his father has gone on a journey or is absent."[167] This is the basis of the Oedipus complex. Freud states that the story of King Oedipus, who unknowingly murders his father and marries his mother, resonates with us because it is our own. "It may be that we were all destined to direct our first sexual impulses toward our mothers, and our first impulses of hatred and violence toward our fathers."[168] To make the transition to a healthy adult life we must be able to transform these elements of the Oedipus complex. "For the son this task consists in detaching his libidinal wishes from his mother and employing them for the choice of a real outside love-object, and in reconciling himself with his father if he has remained in opposition to him, or in freeing himself from his pressure if, as a reaction to his infantile rebelliousness, he has become subservient to him. These tasks are set to everyone; and it is remarkable how seldom they are dealt with in an ideal manner."[169]

The reason we seldom deal with our Oedipal impulses successfully is that we are unaware of these feelings we have held (and hold) toward our parents. Behind this lack of awareness we find two additional cornerstones of Freudian thought: repression and the unconscious. The mind represses, or pushes into the unconscious, certain memories or thoughts in order to avoid the pain they bring with them. Childhood desire for one's mother and the desire to kill one's father certainly qualify as thoughts a person would want to repress. However, no thought or experience is ever lost, and if these impulses reemerge, they still have the power to create pain. Therefore, those who enter therapy do not, at first, want to be cured because this requires memory of distressing experiences. "A man who has gone to the dentist because of an unbearable toothache will nevertheless try to hold the dentist back when he approaches the sick tooth with a pair of forceps."[170]

Freud compares the mind's repressive activity to the idea of a watchman, who censors painful thoughts that reside in the unconscious realm to keep them from entering the room of consciousness. However, there are certain times when the watchman is less attentive and the contents of the unconscious may slip into our consciousness. One such time is during sleep. "On falling asleep the 'undesired ideas' emerge, owing to the slackening of a certain arbitrary (and, of course, also critical) action, which is allowed to influence the trend of our ideas."[171]

However, Freud makes it clear that dreams do not give an unimpeded view of what is repressed during our waking hours. In dream-formation, there are

> two psychic forces (tendencies or systems), one of which forms the wish expressed by the dream, while the other exercises a censorship over this dream-wish, thereby enforcing on it a distortion. . . . Nothing can reach the consciousness from the first system which has not previously passed the second instance; and the second instance lets nothing pass without exercising its rights, and forcing such modifications as are pleasing to itself upon the candidates for admission to consciousness.[172]

In other words the dream exposes a desire we have, but this desire is distorted by the groggy but still functioning censorship of our consciousness to case it into more acceptable form. *The dream is the (disguised) fulfilment of a (suppressed, repressed) wish.*[173]

Civilization and Its Discontents

The social ramifications of ideas such as superego, the unconscious, the Oedipus complex and sexual instinct are not immediately apparent, and for most of his early career Freud was content to focus his attention on individual issues. However, many of his later writings did attempt to apply these ideas to civilization as a whole.

Civilization, as Freud defines it, "describes the whole sum of the achievements and the regulations which distinguish our lives from those of our animal ancestors and which serve two purposes—namely, to protect men against nature and to adjust their mutual relations."[174] Adjusting the mutual relations of human beings encounters an obstacle, however, when we recall that our id is asocial. Absent civilization's prohibitions, the libido demands that the individual "take any woman one pleases as a sexual object, if one may without hesitation kill one's rival for her love or anyone else who stands in one's way, if too, one can carry off any of the other man's belongings without asking leave—how splendid, what a string of satisfactions one's life would be!"[175] The problem is that ultimately only one person would be able to enjoy such a life, and all competitors would be exterminated or subjugated. Such a winner-take-all contest between competing libidos would be extremely destructive. Therefore, "every civilization must be built up on coercion and renunciation of instinct."[176]

However, the instinctual cannot be completely renounced. Just as the individual cannot function without the energy of the instincts, so also society needs the forces of the libido. "The motive of human society is in the last resort an economic one; since it does not possess enough provisions to keep its members alive unless they work, it must restrict the number of its members and divert their energies from sexual activity to work."[177] This diversion is what Freud calls sublimation. "Sublimation of instinct is an especially conspicuous feature of cultural development; it is what make it possible for higher psychical activities, scientific, artistic or ideological, to play such an important part in civilized life."[178]

As sexual latency ends with the onset of puberty, "society must undertake as one of its most important educative tasks to tame and restrict the sexual instinct when it breaks out as an urge to reproduction, and to subject it to an individual will which is identical with the bidding of society."[179] In other words civilization begins to play the role of the father by impressing on individuals the need to conform to society's demands. "Civilization, therefore, obtains mastery over the individual's dangerous desire for aggression by weakening and disarming it and by setting up an agency within him to watch over it, like a garrison in a conquered city."[180]

Civilization's role as the father surrogate means that the Oedipus complex has a social dimension. Just as the son encounters problems when he is unable to separate himself from the father, societies become neurotic when consumed by the obligations they impose on individuals. "If civilization is a necessary course of development from the family to humanity as a whole, then . . . there is inextricably bound up with it an increase of the sense of guilt, which will perhaps reach heights that the individual finds hard to tolerate."[181] In other words the individual must maintain a sensitive balance between satisfaction of libidinal desires and social demands. We need the moderating and sublimating aspects of civilization, but "the price we pay for our advance in civilization is a loss of happiness through the heightening of the sense of guilt."[182]

While Freud argues that "primitive man was better off in knowing no restrictions of instinct,"[183] he is vague about which social prohibitions should be lessened. The one negative example he cites is the command that we should love all people. Although the intent of this rule is to increase happiness, Freud believes that it creates the opposite effect. "If more is demanded of a man, a revolt will be produced in him or a neurosis, or he will be made unhappy. The commandment, 'Love thy neighbour as thyself,' is the strongest defense against human aggressiveness and an excellent example of the unpsychological proceedings of the cultural superego. The commandment is impossible to fulfill; such an enormous inflation of love can only lower its value, not get rid of the difficulty."[184]

As an antidote, Freud states generally that "we are very often obligated, for therapeutic purposes, to oppose the super-ego, and we endeavour to lower its demands. Exactly the same objections can be made against the ethical demands of the cultural super-ego. It, too, does not trouble itself enough about the facts of the mental constitution of human beings. It issues a command and does not ask whether it is possible for people to obey it."[185] Freud's point is that unrealistic social expectations are responsible for personal unhappiness and psychological maladjustment.

Freud on Religion

What Feuerbach originally put forward as the basis for his atheism and

Marx modified by adding an economic interpretation, Freud also co-opts, while providing a psychological spin: religion is a vain attempt to fulfill our wishes. More specifically, religion "satisfies the human thirst for knowledge, . . . it soothes the fear that men feel of the dangers and vicissitudes of life, . . . it issues precepts and lays down prohibitions and restrictions."[186] If we want to know the origin of these needs, Freud states that all we need to do is look back to our infancy. "The derivation of religious needs from the infant's helplessness and the longing for the father aroused by it seems to me incontrovertible, especially since the feeling is not simply prolonged from childhood days, but is permanently sustained by fear of the superior power of Fate. I cannot think of any need in childhood as strong as the need for a father's protection."[187] However, the father is not simply a source of security; he is also wrathful judge. In the latter role, religion issues commandments and prohibitions that limit our natural inclinations. "Their parents' prohibitions and demands persist within them as a moral conscience. With the help of this same system of rewards and punishments, God rules the world of men."[188] While we might secretly resent religion's control of our behavior, it is a small price to pay for the protection of a benevolent providence "which will not suffer us to become a plaything of the over-mighty and pitiless forces of nature."[189]

Because "the root of every form of religion [is] a longing for the father,"[190] Freud believes that the Oedipus complex helps us understand the shape religion takes. "The hatred of his father that arises in a boy from rivalry for his mother is not able to achieve uninhibited sway over his mind; it has to contend against his old-established affection and admiration for the very same person. The child finds relief from the conflict arising out of this double-sided, this ambivalent emotional attitude toward his father by displacing his hostile and fearful feelings on a *substitute* for his father."[191] This substitute was found in primitive religions in a totem animal. The totem was considered sacred by a tribe and thus was protected. Ironically, though, it was also a sacrificial animal. "Psychoanalysis has revealed that the totem animal is in reality a substitute for the father; and this tallies with the contradictory fact that, though the killing of the animal is as a rule forbidden, yet its killing becomes a festive occasion—the fact that it is killed and yet mourned."[192] Freud finds the same impulse behind the Christian Eucharist, which reflects "the crime by which men were so deeply weighed down [killing the father] but of which they must none the less feel so proud. The Christian communion, however, is essentially a fresh elimination of the father, a repetition of the guilty deed."[193] The fact that the father, represented by God, continues to dominate the life of the religious person reveals, "Religion would thus be the universal obsessional neurosis of humanity; like the obsessional neurosis of children, it arose out of the Oedipus complex, out of the relation to the father."[194]

In Freud's view, then, religious teachings "are not precipitates of experience or end-results of thinking: they are illusions, fulfilments of the oldest, strongest and most urgent wishes of mankind."[195] At its root, religion's illusions represent an infantile attempt to return to the security of a daddy and a failure to face the world's realities in a mature manner. "We shall tell ourselves that it would be very nice if there were a God who created the world and was a benevolent Providence, and if there were a moral order in the universe and an after-life; but it is a very striking fact that all this is exactly as we are bound to wish it to be. And it would be more remarkable still if our wretched, ignorant and downtrodden ancestors had succeeded in solving all these difficult riddles of the universe."[196]

A Freudian View of Salvation

While many of the social scientists of the day were willing to take a "live and let live" view of religion, as long as the latter knew its place, Freud saw this is a dangerous compromise. "It is not permissible to declare that science is one field of human mental activity and that religion and philosophy are others, at least its equal in value, and that science has no business to interfere with the other two. . . . It is simply a fact that the truth cannot be tolerant, that it admits no compromises or limitations, that research regards every sphere of human activity as belonging to it and that it must be relentlessly critical if any other power tries to take over any part of it."[197] Since religion attempts to master the sensory world with tools borrowed from an infantile perspective of the world, "civilization runs a greater risk if we maintain our present attitude to religion than if we give it up."[198]

Only science can provide a sufficient alternative to a religious worldview. "Our best hope for the future is that intellect—the scientific spirit, reason—may in process of time establish a dictatorship in the mental life of man. The nature of reason is a guarantee that afterwards it will not fail to give man's emotional impulses and what is determined by them the position they deserve."[199] Stated somewhat differently, Freud argues that freedom is possible only when we recognize the reality of the world around us. Since our faults, problems and illnesses are rooted in physical reality, they can be corrected only through science.

Like the patient who clings to his or her neurotic symptoms, many resist giving up religion because it means the end of their narcissism. "The scientific view of the universe no longer affords any room for human omnipotence; men have acknowledged their smallness and submitted resignedly to death and to the other necessities of nature."[200] It is clear from this that Freud does not envision any absolute salvation or purpose in life. These disappear with the loss of God. Therefore, rather than asking what the purpose of life may be, Freud suggests that we "turn to the less ambitious question of what men themselves show by their behaviour to be the purpose and intention of their lives." He responds, "The answer to this can hardly be in doubt. They strive after happiness; they want to become happy and to remain so."[201] While psychoanalysis cannot promise the eternal happiness offered by religion, Freud believes that science will take humanity farther than it has been at any point in the past. Ultimately, however, this is only a limited form of salvation: "Our god *Logos* is perhaps not a very almighty one, and he may only be able to fulfil a small part of what his predecessors have promised. If we have to acknowledge this we shall accept it with resignation."[202]

Freud's Significance

It is common in some circles to view Freud's ideas as extreme, speculative and misguided. However, it is dangerous to so quickly dismiss an individual whose theories have shaped discussion in almost every academic discipline. Moreover, his impact is evident from the number of his concepts that have become part of our accepted wisdom. For example, few doubt the influence of early childhood on our adult life. The extent to which our parents shape our view of the world well beyond childhood is also generally acknowledged. Freud's belief that mental illness could only be resolved by looking for causes rather than treating symptoms, even though not universally accepted in therapeutic practice, strongly influences most psychological approaches today and helped transform a field viewed as an art into a science. And even though his assertion of sexual impulses in children finds more resistance, he notes that "the people who deny the existence of sexuality in children do not on that account become milder in their educational efforts but pursue the manifestations of what they deny exists with the utmost severity—describing them as 'childish naughtinesses.'"[203] The sense that these are conventional truths reveals the influence Freud wields over our understanding of the psyche.

One of Freud's more distressing contributions to contemporary discussion is his belief that humans are not essentially rational beings. While earlier scholars such as Nietzsche and Schopenhauer developed the idea of blind irrational forces as part of the human makeup, it was relatively simple to relegate their formulations to the abstract category of human behavior. In contrast, Freud's psychoanalytic perspective gives the idea more urgency, especially when the confident pronouncements about the progress of human beings in general did not seem to be matched by an increased sense of well-being in individuals in particular. The struggle many experience in bringing their actions under the control of reason seems to be explained by Freud's idea of the id (which many accepted without embracing his view of the id's exclusively sexual nature).

A related area is Freud's investigation of the unconscious. The concept that many of our actions spring from experiences or instincts that lie beneath the conscious level is, in itself, an important contribution. However, Freud's impact was intensified by two additional factors. First, his assertion that this unconscious realm could be subjected to scientific investigation has generated great interest in how access might be gained into this region. A second feature of his concept of the unconscious is that the mental activities that occur in this region of the psyche are highly advanced. Faculties such as conscience and self-criticism, among our most acute mental capacities, often operate beneath the level of consciousness.

Several criticisms of Freud also deserve attention. First, although

Freud claims that "psycho-analysis is a method of research, an impartial instrument, like the infinitesimal calculus, as it were,"[204] most of Freud's intellectual descendants acknowledge the difficulty of claiming this degree of impartiality for psychoanalytic method. When the therapist's task involves stripping away the disguises and decoding the symbols imposed by the mind's subterranean activities, we cannot but acknowledge that interpretations will vary among trained observers considering the same data. Moreover, many have asked the more basic question of whether psychoanalytic theory can be falsified, generally considered a requirement of scientific method. In other words once Freud's analytical filters are in place, everything has to pass through them, even criticisms of the system. This can leave him open to the charge that psychoanalysis is a Procrustean bed that shapes the data before it receives consideration.

In addition to the criticism that psychoanalytic method is not as scientific as Freud claims, he is also open to the charge that his trust in the soteriological value of science is naive. Even during Freud's day there were many who put a great deal of stock in science but recognized that it would not by itself meet the demands of human nature (e.g., Durkheim). Indeed many with strong links to the psychoanalytic movement, such as Carl Jung and Alfred Adler, found that science without religion threatened to exclude basic components of human nature and need. And if his experience in World War I did not shake his view that an exclusively scientific *Weltanschauung* offered the best hope for human existence, his perspective on the eve of World War II should have provided strong evidence that unlimited faith in science was misplaced.

Like many others of his day, while Freud rejected belief in God, he did not find it necessary to offer reasons for disbelief once he recognized a correlation between religion belief and human desire. "To assess the truth-value of religious doctrines does not lie within the scope of the present enquiry. It is enough for us that we have recognized them as being, in their psychological nature, illusions."[205] Illusion, as we have seen above, is defined as anything that fulfills a need or desire. Thus Freud concludes that belief in God is simply a projection of purely human needs into a new realm. However, Hans Küng (1928-) skillfully points out that, "All human believing, hoping, loving—related to a person, a thing, or God—certainly contains an element of projection. But its object need not, for that reason, be a mere projection. Belief in God can certainly be very greatly influenced by the attitude of the child to its father. But this does not mean that God may not exist."[206] To put this in a slightly different manner, we might say that Freud applies his critique of illusion unevenly. He does not classify other ideas as illusions simply because they correspond to human need. Therefore, some explanation needs to be offered as to why religion can be dismissed as illusory simply because it fulfills a widespread human desire.

Finally, few of Freud's followers have defended his Oedipus complex theory of religion's origins because it finds little support in ethnology. His thesis that totemism constituted the earliest form of religion, the pivotal point in his argument, is strongly disputed by most scholars of the history of religion. Thus his critique of religion suffers from an outdated view of religious origins. He is also subject to the criticism that he misunderstands the nature of religion by lumping all into an attempt to gain power over the universe and its forces. At the basis of many religions is an essential acknowledgment of our inability to overcome both external nature and our own inner nature.

EPILOGUE:

RETROSPECT AND PROSPECT

I t is risky business to attempt a summary of any century's intellectual currents. Such enterprises necessarily exclude important threads and are in danger of dissolving into useless generalities. The richness of the nineteenth century makes this hazard even more real. On the other hand, the peril of a survey that treats benchmark movements and individuals in a sequential manner is that we miss the proverbial forest for the trees. There are important trends and trajectories that bring coherence to what otherwise might appear to be a tangle of competing theories. Therefore, we will trace the evolution of four major ideas—optimism, the development of the scientific orientation, the concept of rationality and the paradigm of organic unity—through the nineteenth century, fully aware that selection of these four themes is somewhat arbitrary. However, it is a necessary artifice in order to pull the various threads into some semblance of a whole and to show how these ideas become points of departure for the twentieth century.

The Optimistic Century

The nineteenth century was heir to the optimism of the Enlightenment that preceded. With a few exceptions, from Descartes to the end of the eighteenth century, there was an undercurrent of confidence that the potential of human nature could be realized. If anything, this upbeat mood intensified during the nineteenth century. From Kant's confident assertion that he had birthed an intellectual "Copernican Revolution," to

Hegel's unfolding Spirit, to the utopian social visions of Comte and Marx, to the can-do vitality of James's pragmatism, the general feeling was that any problem could be overcome and that humanity was salvageable or even perfectible. The external evidence also seemed to support this optimism. By almost any standard to which one might appeal—economic well-being, relative freedom from the ravages of military conflict, scientific and medical advances, the growing access of the common person to educational resources and political power—life was getting better.

The scene in the early stages of the twentieth century was more ambiguous, however. In two World Wars the machinery that brought the prospect of progress was no different in kind than the equipment that allowed us to destroy each other with ruthless precision and efficiency. Economic, political, educational, artistic and cultural changes that had earlier been cited as evidence of moral and spiritual improvement had not scrubbed humanity free of its blemishes. Any war tends to dampen national confidence, but the devastation and scope of these World Wars accentuated the impact on the hopefulness of the preceding century. Although the jolt of these events was not felt as keenly in the United States, the darkness experienced in Western Europe in the early twentieth century was a stark contrast to the enthusiasm that characterized the nineteenth century.

The Scientific Century

Freud is symbolic of one tension that marked the transition to the twentieth century: the problems and promise of science. At the end of his life he was forced into exile by a war made increasingly brutal by the fruits of scientific methodology. At the same time he remained convinced that whatever truth was available to us could only be discovered through strictly scientific means. Freud's faith in science has its roots in the nineteenth-century desire to assess problems in a logical manner with full confidence that human resources could provide the solutions. Thus while he toiled to transform psychology into a field where behaviors could be analyzed and modified by understanding underlying causal factors, Freud's contemporaries in sociology—Durkheim and Weber—endeavored to apply similar methods to social phenomena. What distinguishes these three from earlier social scientists such as Comte and Marx is that they adopted a more quantitative approach that narrowed the scope of investigation to more specific problems, while the earlier social thinkers attempted to explain everything at once. The connecting thread between them, however, is that science, with its ironclad rules of cause and effect, allows the astute observer to predict the direction of history (individual and social) and, to some degree, grants the ability to shape it.

The quest of the social sciences to become more scientific has its roots in the philosophy and theology of the earlier part of the nineteenth century. Baur and Strauss attempted to transform theology with a scientific method that envisioned the supernatural as immanent within nature and its processes. Because God's activity is not arbitrarily imposed from outside history, divine activity is manifest not just within the history of the church but in all of life's structures. These theologians were drinking from the Hegelian well, which replaced the Enlightenment's dualistic model of the universe with a monistic paradigm. Therefore, while Hegel's Idealism does not seem to conform to current definitions of science, he provides a foundation for modern science by pulling nature and supernature together. If the spiritual and the natural are not ultimately distinct realms but two facets of the same reality, the door is opened for a unified method as a means to uncovering this reality. Because Hegel's philosophy understood the Absolute as rational, he sets the stage for the scientific method of the later part of the century.

When we retrace the path of science's development from Hegel to the end of his century, we notice that the scope of consideration tends to narrow as we move toward the twentieth century. Hegel's ideas of an Absolute that consumes all reality presents a model that dominated the first part of the century but only limps to the finish line in later Idealists such as Bradley and Royce. It increasingly gives way to an attitude such as that found in Durkheim and Weber, who focus on specific issues such as suicide or the Protestant work ethic. In a general way we may attribute this trend to the difficulty in maintaining a metaphysical basis for the unity of history. While Hegel's work is essentially metaphysical, the nature of the force that is supposed to pull the many into One becomes increasingly murky.

One reason for the gradual loss of a metaphysical foundation for unity is that Hegel's idealistic approach gradually gives way to a more empirical methodology in later thinkers. Thus Feuerbach and Comte attempted to locate the unifying and perfecting power in an abstract humanity, Mill in a cloudy "permanent possibilities of sensation," Spencer and Darwin in an ambiguous force called natural selection that governs nature, and Marx in the unnamed but unswerving economic forces that lead history toward a socialist perfection. They all yield the same result. Each declares the presence of an organic and teleological force behind change but does not make a clear case for why the smaller bits of data they cite as evidence of unity and direction are anything more than a collection of isolated facts. Thus implicit in their systems is a problem that continually bedevils an empirical approach. How do we move from individual facts to a coherent picture of the whole?

It is possible to assert order, direction and purpose when circumstances give the impression of evolution toward the higher. However, the events at the beginning of the twentieth century demolished the illusion of corporate progress and made the organic paradigm that had governed a scientific approach more difficult to maintain. This resulted in an identity crisis for science that was paralleled in philosophy. Should our method be one that seeks to explain the whole, or do we simply deal with individual problems? Stated differently, the question was whether we should retain the teleological orientation of the nineteenth century or abandon the idea of an ultimate goal in history. The latter option, already gaining ascendancy in the physical and social sciences at the end of the nineteenth century, took hold in twentieth century philosophy as well. Those who followed in Peirce and James's pragmatic footsteps saw philosophy's role as that of resolving concrete problems as they arise. Many positivistic and linguistic philosophers limited philosophy's tasks to defining the meaning of single propositions or classifying a statement so it can then be transferred to the proper discipline in order to determine its truth value. Various versions of postmodern philosophy denied even the possibility of referring to problems in general. A problem is always a problem within a context, and the philosopher's aim is simply to define the context within which something is perceived as a problem. This constricting focus of scientific method may properly be linked to the loss of optimism noted above. As confidence in the ability to grasp the whole dissipates, a parallel movement occurs in what we expect from science and philosophy. Both gradually shed the view that they were normative disciplines and increasingly limited their sphere of operation to description and definition.

This picture of the reduction of philosophy's role under the influence of science is oversimplified. To be sure, two contrary voices in the twentieth century can be distinguished. First, there are those such as Henri Bergson and Alfred North Whitehead who attempt sweeping systems that maintain both the unity of experience and a teleological orientation. While they retain the dynamism of the Hegelian approach to which they are indebted, they modified the earlier epistemological underpinnings to make it more amenable to current definitions of science. At the same time they are critical of the growing tendency in science to assume that claims should be limited to external phenomena.

Moving in the opposite direction, however, we find the growing influence of existentialism, which rejects almost everything that characterized the nineteenth century. The individual replaced the whole as the primary metaphysical category (if it is possible to speak of metaphysics at all in existentialism). The hope of universal salvation, however it was defined, was exchanged for a recognition of our capacity for radical evil. Teleology was displaced by randomness. Science and logic gave way to analysis of the irrational human will. The general feeling in existentialism was that science was not our savior but represented a threat of enslavement. The phenomenalism of Edmund Husserl and Martin Heidegger provided the intellectual impetus behind existentialism's rapid rise to prominence in the middle of the twentieth century, while the devastating results of world war furnished the catalyst. However, the true founders of twentieth-century existentialism were Nietzsche and Kierkegaard. Every theme that shaped twentieth century existentialism had been readily available in these two philosophers. They had been overlooked because they were out of step with their own age, but their ideas were surprising contemporary decades later.

The Expansion of Rationality

The two tends we have mentioned—optimism and trust in science—are rooted in the Enlightenment ideal of the rational individual. In the nineteenth century, however, both the concept of rationality and the place of the individual went through significant transitions. The first modification to the Enlightenment's perspective of reason has been mentioned above, so it will only be covered briefly here. With the advent of the organic paradigm in Romantic, Transcendentalist and Idealist movements, the dualisms between nature and supernature and between human and natural collapsed. Reason was no longer seen as exclusively characteristic of the human realm but also permeated the nonhuman world as well. Therefore, whether the engine behind history was understood as an all-encompassing divine spirit (Hegel), purely human economic systems (Marx) or something in between, logic was not just a human tool used to understand the world around us. It was also an attribute of the processes being observed. This belief that natural, historical and human processes were infused with rationality survived in the early philosophers in the twentieth century such as Gottlob Frege, Husserl and Bergson. However, their ideas are largely framed before the advent of world war. The insanity that followed made it more difficult to argue for a logical infrastructure within any of these spheres.

There was, however, a second expansion on the concept of rationality that more easily makes the transition into the twentieth century. With Kant's suggestion in his first *Critique* that the mind does not simply receive knowledge but also shapes it, we possess the raw material for an enlarged definition of human nature. We are not simply rational entities but also creative and volitional beings. This modified concept of the human mind opens new and widely diverse vistas. Let us cite a few examples. While Fichte preserves much of the Kantian connection between reason and ethics, he also argues that the mind does not simply encounter the universe within which moral struggle occurs but *creates* it. Romanticism and Transcendentalism argue that limiting human identity to a lifeless rationalism without acknowledging our creative and imaginative powers severely distorts any attempt to understand human nature. Marx quite consciously rejects the definition of humans as thinkers and describes us primarily in terms of our creative and productive endeavors. Freud makes a strong case that the human psyche cannot be adequately comprehended if we do not include consideration of the untamed id. Schopenhauer, Nietzsche and Kierkegaard react strongly against conventional ideas of reason and move will to the forefront. While their rejection of reason in favor of volition is extreme in comparison to the mainstream in this century, even one as heavily invested in rationality as James argues that we cannot live without faith. The will to believe must come into action when reason reaches its limits. Although we could add to the number of examples noted above to show how reason is not excluded but nudged aside to make room for other facets of human experience, these suffice to demonstrate the broadening concept of human nature within the nineteenth century.

A second modification to the Enlightenment concept of human nature is a decisive rejection of individualism. Abandoning Descartes's model of the solitary thinker, the nineteenth century moves to unpack the idea of humanity as an organic whole. This paradigm is present but undeveloped in Kant's third *Critique*. It is not until Schelling and Hegel that this strand of Kant's philosophy was pursued. Once in place their corporate definition of humanity makes it difficult to return to an individualistic approach to human nature. Ideas of the nature of our social existence vary widely, however. Hegel's paradigm is imported almost wholesale by Baur as a means of interpreting church history. Feuerbach and Marx adopt Hegel's view that history can only be illuminated by looking at human society as a whole, but they turn Hegel upside down. In contrast to Hegel, no abstract Idea creates our collective history. Instead material, historical entities create ideas. Thus individual identities are now determined by the social structures in which they participate. The various confessional movements within Christianity rebel against the individualism of revival movements and attempt to ground Christian solidarity in church tradition and doctrinal formulae. In short, regardless of how the competing theological and philosophical movements defined salvation, the tendency is to understand the realization of our goal in corporate rather than individual terms.

The social sciences, which came into their own beside this philosophical awareness of our social nature, presented a powerful case for the influence of social structures on the life of the individual. Thus even after the earlier metaphysical foundations for corporate humanity were abandoned, twentieth century thought could not revert to a naïve individualism. However, the organic model so common in the earlier century had to adapt to the reality of failed expectations. In the nineteenth century the clash of opposing social forces was believed to lead to higher realizations of latent potential. The dialectical struggle of social powers remains a staple in much of twentieth century philosophy, but, with notable exceptions such as process thought, the prospects for a rosy outcome were muted. Improvement does not inevitably result from conflict.

This disenchantment with corporate salvation expressed itself in various ways. The nineteenth century's enthusiasm for social utopias waned in Western Europe and the United States. Instead social scientists abandoned the activist mentality of its origins and increasingly viewed their work as descriptive rather than prescriptive. Social analysis could account for the forces that created historical movements but could offer little remedy. More radical responses are found in existentialism. The evil that was manifest on the world stage revealed the evil present beneath the veneer of each person. Any resolution of this depravity, if resolution was available at all, was individual and provisional. An equally stiff challenge came from the various strands of postmodern philosophy. The idea of a general human nature was the presupposition that allowed analysis of social entities, activities and ideas under a single paradigm in earlier thought. However, postmodernism argues that it is impossible to speak of humanity as a whole. Instead the diversity of human experience rather than its commonalities became the point of departure.

Theological Transitions into the Twentieth Century

Although we have touched on how various intellectual trends affected Christian thought during the nineteenth century, it will be useful to focus more specifically on the theological transitions into the twentieth century. An important turning point is the "German-Christian" movement of the 1930s. This movement brought Reformed and Lutheran churches in Germany together and proclaimed that the mission of the church was paralleled in the work of Hitler's Nazi government. In protest to what many considered a dangerous capitulation to growing nationalism and anti-Jewish fervor in the German-Christian movement, some Protestant pastors formed the Confessing Church. This group issued what came to be known as the Barmen Confession, written for the most part by Karl Barth. The confession contained the seeds of what would later become neo-orthodoxy. Under Barth's leadership the neo-orthodox movement stressed the difference between the church's mission and the calling of secular institutions. In addition it reasserted many of the Reformation's themes—the primacy of Scripture, Christ as God's self-revelation to the world, salvation by grace alone and the necessity of faith. With this new foundation, neo-orthodoxy captured the spirit of the twentieth century in much the same way that classical theological liberalism had defined the tenor of the previous century.

In hindsight it is easy to see the harmful results of the German-Christian movement's union with Hitler's National Socialism. However, several factors converge in the nineteenth century that make this melding of church and state understandable. A key influence for German-Christianity's belief that the goals of the church would ultimately merge with the activities of the state is Hegel's monistic paradigm. As developed by Strauss and Baur, history was a process through which God worked out his plan of salvation in an incremental way. Moreover, the divine purpose does not simply manifest increasingly greater presence within the church but also brings political, social, educational and economic structures under the umbrella of the kingdom. Sin is eventually resolved through the dialectical process. Corresponding to this gradual conquest of sin is our growing awareness of the good as it unfolds within history. Since the entire process is logical, sin's demise is closely linked with our increasing rationality.

Obviously this summary of Hegelian-influenced theology tells the story of only one facet of Christianity during this period. At the same time, other important theologians use themes present here—reason as the vehicle of revelation, the gradual eradication of sin's power over humanity and the manifestation of God's will in all aspects of life. However, these themes manifest themselves in different ways. For example, while it lacks the strong emphasis on the evolutionary component, the Kantian model of moral self-salvation retains the emphasis on reason's role in freeing ourselves from sin. The essentially ethical view of Christianity found in Kant and Fichte had a profound impact on Ritschl and other liberal theologians. Reason, as reflected in the methods of biblical criticism, allows us to cut through the culturally conditioned "husk" imposed on the teachings of Jesus to discover the enduring ethical "kernel."

For Schleiermacher, the strong rationalistic strain of later liberalism is overshadowed by a more experiential approach, while the organic orientation of Idealism is retained. For example, sin in Schleiermacher's theology is a denial of our dependence on the Infinite. However, one does not sin or suffer the consequences of sin in isolation. The transgressions of the past are borne by the present generation. Like his Idealist counterparts, Schleiermacher is confident that sin will be gradually overcome as our consciousness of the Infinite increases. In short, all these influential strains of theology to some degree define sin as a defect that increasingly loses its power, believe that this conquest will involve substantial human participation, and understand both sin and salvation corporately.

World War II cast serious doubt on the benchmark tendencies of nineteenth-century theology noted above. The confidence that we would learn or evolve our way out of sin was displaced in several ways in the twentieth century. Fundamentalist and conservative confessional movements strengthened their emphasis on original sin. Neo-orthodoxy rejected the literal interpretations of original sin in the more conservative twentieth-century theologies but stressed the idea that human beings always stand before God as sinners. The nineteenth century's synergistic tendencies, in which God works through human means to bring about salvation, are replaced by views in which salvation is solely the result of God's activity, sometimes accompanied by attempts to recover more traditional Calvinist and Lutheran predestinarian views. In the expressions of liberal theology that survived into the twentieth century, events compelled them to adopt the view of their Social Gospel cousins that institutions by nature are steeped in sin and that we are implicated by our involvement in these social structures.

This pessimistic view of human ability to erase sin is paralleled by a loss of confidence in a historical evolution toward the higher. Against the previous century's predisposition to view history as destiny, twentieth-century theology reflects a disenchantment with history. One interesting indicator of this more circumspect perspective on history is found in shifting millennial views. Postmillennialism, with its optimistic view of humanity's role in ushering in the eschaton, is often associated with theological liberalism. However, postmillennialism also had a strong following among very conservative theologians such as Charles Hodge, which is an indicator of the hopefulness of the nineteenth century. Only in the twentieth century, with its historical confusion, did the more pessimistic premillennial eschatology become deeply rooted in churches.

Other examples of this more ambivalent view of history are found in calls to return to the creeds and confessions of the past or neo-orthodoxy's call to return to the Reformation. When hopes for the future are dashed, movements often look to the past to find a "golden age" to help them reestablish their bearings. Theologies that emerged later in the twentieth century—such as liberation, feminist and black theologies—viewed the nineteenth century's analysis of history as merely the interpretation of a small minority of highly educated, politically and economically powerful, white, male Western Europeans and Americans. The histories of oppressed groups, however, did not match the picture they had drawn. Implicit in this criticism is that we cannot, as so many in the nineteenth century did, speak of history as a singular phenomena. Instead, there are *histories,* all of which tell different stories.

The final shift in theological perspective concerns the relationship of reason and revelation. In many cases in nineteenth century, biblical criticism was the means by which the divine message in Scripture was separated from what were considered culturally conditioned and, therefore, dispensable elements. By this means, revelation was essentially placed under the judgment of reason. In reaction many of the more conservative Christian movements of the twentieth century rejected critical methodology in the examination of Scripture. Groups like neo-orthodoxy and theologies influenced by existentialism staked out the middle ground. They accepted critical methods but did not see these as the final word. The validity of God's Word is not determined by historical or factual accuracy. These standards put finite humans in the position of judgment. Instead neo-orthodoxy presents Scripture as the means through which we encounter God. In this encounter God's Word confronts us, judges us and calls for a decision.

So many of the nineteenth-century philosophies viewed their immediate intellectual precedents as part of an adolescent stage that would soon give way to a mature, adult grasp of the world. These expectations proved hollow when they crashed into the gritty realities of world war. Although these nineteenth century philosophers were wrong about their era as the penultimate stage of history's fulfillment, this period does, in another way, embody the spirit of adolescence. Like adolescence, it was confident in its abilities and possibilities, perhaps more self-assured than any century. Even in the most technical material of this century, an energetic and hopeful quality frequently comes through. In its youthful exuberance, its willingness to experiment with the new and untried is both invigorating and frightening. The thinkers of the nineteenth century were prepared in a way that earlier ages were not to stop tinkering with the paradigms of their intellectual parents. When these ideas proved problematic, they simply discarded the old and moved on to different models. While this sense of freedom from the past can be refreshing, there is also the feeling that they were working without a net. In hindsight, the "all or nothing" mentality may seem naïve and reckless. However, we may also look at the nineteenth century's optimistic and energetic spirit as we do our own adolescence. The time came when it had to end, but it was fun and exciting while it lasted.

Notes

Chapter 1: A Century of Transition

[1]For general surveys of the philosophy of the nineteenth century, see Frederick Copleston, *A History of Philosophy*, vol. 7 (Garden City, N.J.: Image, 1963); Henry D. Aiken, *The Age of Ideology: The Nineteenth Century Philosophers* (Boston: Houghton Mifflin, 1957); Maurice Mandelbaum, *History, Man, and Reason: A Study in Nineteenth-Century Thought* (Baltimore: Johns Hopkins Press, 1971); W. T. Jones, *Kant and the Nineteenth Century*, 2nd ed. (Fort Worth, Tex.: Harcourt Brace Jovanovich, 1969); John Herman Randall, *The Career of Philosophy*, vol. 2 (New York: Columbia University Press, 1965); Karl Löwith, *From Hegel to Nietzsche: The Revolution in Nineteenth Century Thought*, trans. David E. Green (New York: Columbia University Press, 1991); C. L. Ten, ed., *The Nineteenth Century*, vol. 7 of *Routledge History of Philosophy* (New York: Routledge, 1994); A. Robert Caponigri, *Philosophy from the Romantic Age to the Age of Positivism*, vol. 4 of *A History of Western Philosophy* (Notre Dame: University of Notre Dame Press, 1971); Etienne Gilson et al., *Recent Philosophy: Hegel to the Present* (New York: Random House, 1966). Although they overlap into both earlier and later periods than those under consideration here, much of Robert C. Solomon, *Continental Philosophy Since 1750: The Rise and Fall of the Self* (Oxford: Oxford University Press, 1988) and Roland N. Stromberg, *European Intellectual History Since 1789*, 2nd ed. (Englewood Cliffs, N.J.: Prentice-Hall, 1975) provide nice summaries of many philosophers covered here. Anthologies of readings in nineteenth century philosophy are available in Patrick L. Gardiner, ed., *19th-Century Philosophy* (New York: Free Press, 1969); Richard L. Schoenwald, ed., *Nineteenth-Century Thought: The Discovery of Change* (Englewood Cliffs, N.J.: Prentice-Hall, 1965); Henry D. Aiken, ed., *The Age of Ideology* (New York: Mentor, 1956). Basil Willey, *Nineteenth Century Studies: Coleridge to Matthew Arnold* (New York: Columbia University Press, 1949) covers English thought during this period. An anthology that covers the century, but provides more attention to Romanticism than is customary, is Bruce Wilshire, ed., *Romanticism and Evolution*, vol. 4 of *The Spirit of Western Civilization* (New York: G. P. Putnam's Sons, 1968). Sources for the theological thought of this century are Claude Welch, *Protestant Thought in the Nineteenth Century*, 2 vols. (New Haven, Conn.: Yale University Press, 1985); Ninian Smart, ed., *Nineteenth Century Religious Thought in the West*, 3 vols. (Cambridge: Cambridge University Press, 1985); Paul Tillich, "Perspectives on 19th and 20th Century Protestant Theology," in *A Complete History of Christian Thought* (New York: Harper & Row, 1968); Otto Pfleiderer, *The Development of Theology in Germany Since Kant and Its Progress in Great Britain Since 1825*, trans. J. Frederick Smith (London: Swant Sonnenschein, 1890); Hugh Ross Mackintosh, *Types of Modern Theology: Schleiermacher to Barth* (New York: Charles Scribner's Sons, 1964).

[2]The vitality of Christianity in this century is illustrated in Kenneth Scott Latourette, *A History of the Expansion of Christianity* (New York: Harper & Brothers, 1937-1945). Of his seven volume series, three of the volumes, collectively entitled *The Great Century* (vols. 4-6) are devoted to the nineteenth century alone.

[3]Of interest on this topic is Owen Chadwick, *The Secularization of the European Mind in the Nineteenth Century* (Cambridge: Cambridge University Press, 1975).

[4]The extent to which this optimism characterized the age is seen in the fact that most scholars place the intellectual conclusion of the nineteenth century at 1914, the beginning of World War I. We will use this general delineation in this volume.

⁵The most notable "Kantian" philosopher was Karl Leonhard Reinhold (1743-1819), who was instrumental in popularizing Kant's writings. However, toward the end of his career he sought to distance himself from Kant and moved toward the views of Fichte.

⁶See Colin Brown, *Christianity and Western Thought* [hereafter, Brown], vol. 1 (Downers Grove, Ill.: InterVarsity Press, 1990), pp. 309-28. Since the publication of volume 1 by Colin Brown, several scholars have begun the definitive, critical English translation of Kant's works: *The Cambridge Edition of the Works of Immanuel Kant*, 14 vols., ed. P. Guyer and A. Wood (Cambridge: Cambridge University Press, 1992-). Students should consult this set whenever possible.

⁷Brown, pp. 203-14.

⁸In a sense, it may be said that the nineteenth century was the period when history was discovered. Toward the end of the century, few scholars remained who supposed that ideas were independent of external events and movements in the world. For a survey of views on history in Germany, see George G. Iggers, *The German Conception of History: The National Tradition of Historical Thought from Herder to the Present* (Middletown, Conn.: Wesleyan University Press, 1968).

⁹Several helpful surveys of nineteenth century theology are available. See Claude Welch, *Protestant Thought in the Nineteenth Century*, 2 vols. (New Haven, Conn.: Yale University Press, 1972, 1985); Ninian Smart et al., eds., *Nineteenth Century Religious Thought in the West*, 3 vols. (Cambridge: Cambridge University Press, 1985). Stephen Sykes, *The Identity of Christianity: Theologians and the Essence of Christianity from Schleiermacher to Barth* (Philadelphia: Fortress, 1984) looks at the debate over what constitutes the heart of the Christian faith. Bernard M. G. Reardon, *From Coleridge to Gore: A Century of Religious Thought in Britain* (London: Longman, 1971) surveys theology in England during this period. An older treatment of German theology in this century is Friedrich Lichtenberger, *History of German Theology in the Nineteenth Century*, trans. and ed. W. Hastie (Edinburgh: T & T Clark, 1889); James C. Livingston, *Modern Christian Thought* (New York: Macmillan, 1971) extends beyond the nineteenth century but covers this period in a highly readable manner.

Chapter 2: Expanding Rationality

¹For general sources on Romanticism, see Peter L. Thorslev, *Romantic Contraries: Freedom Versus Destiny* (New Haven, Conn.: Yale University Press, 1984); Ernst Benz, *The Mystical Sources of German Romantic Philosophy*, trans. Blair R. Reynolds and Eunice M. Paul (Allison Park, Penn.: Pickwick, 1983); Gerald NcNiece, *The Knowledge that Endures: Coleridge, German Philosophy and the Logic of Romantic Thought* (New York: St. Martin's, 1992); Rene Wellek, *Confrontations: Studies in the Intellectual and Literary Relations Between Germany, England, and the United States During the Nineteenth Century* (Princeton, N.J.: Princeton University Press, 1965). Sources that deal more specifically with Romanticism and religious thought include: Bernard M. G. Reardon, *Religion in the Age of Romanticism: Studies in Early Nineteenth Century Thought* (Cambridge: Cambridge University Press, 1985). Anthologies that contain readings from Romantic authors are: Bruce Wilshire, ed., *Romanticism and Evolution: The Nineteenth Century* (New York: G. P. Putnam's Sons, 1968); Ronald Taylor, ed., *The Romantic Tradition in Germany: An Anthology* (London: Methuen, 1970); and Brian Hepworth, ed., *The Rise of Romanticism* (Manchester, U.K.: Carcanet, 1978). The latter deals primarily with Romanticism's predecessors.

²Perhaps one of the strongest influences on early Romanticism was Hamann's *Socratic Memoribilia*, trans. James C. O'Flaherty (Baltimore: Johns Hopkins Press, 1967), which focuses on faith as the path to truth.

³Frederick Copleston, *Modern Philosophy*, vol. 7, pt. 1 of *A History of Philosophy* (Garden

City, N.Y.: Image, 1963), p. 34.

[4]Paul Tillich, *Perspectives on 19th and 20th Century Protestant Theology*, ed. Carl E. Braaten (New York: Harper & Row, 1967), p. 83.

[5]Novalis, "Christendom or Europe," in *Hymns to the Night and Other Selected Writing*, trans. Charles E. Passage (New York: Liberal Arts Press, 1960), p. 54.

[6]Friedrich Schlegel, *The Philosophy of Life, and Philosophy of Language*, trans. A. J. W. Morrison (London: Henry G. Bohn, 1847), p. 188.

[7]Friedrich Heinrich Jacobi, "David Hume on Faith," in *The Main Philosophical Writings and the Novel Allwil*, trans. George di Giovanni (Montreal: McGill-Queen's University Press, 1994), p. 328.

[8]Novalis, "Aphorisms," in *Hymns to the Night and Other Selected Writing*, trans. Charles E. Passage (New York: Liberal Arts Press, 1960), 2:18.

[9]An often overlooked contribution to the discussion is Romanticism's challenge to the Enlightenment on the issue of language. Hamann is one of the first to put forward an interpretation of language as symbolic, and it is of significance that both "fathers" of Romanticism—Hamann's disciple, Herder, and Rousseau—produced essays on the nature of language. Both are presented together in John H. Moran and Alexander Gode, eds., *On the Origin of Language* (New York: Frederick Ungar, 1966). Particularly relevant to the Romantic view of the world is Herder's claim that human language originates in music and poetry.

[10]Johann Georg Hamann, *Socratic Memoribilia*, trans. James C. O'Flaherty (Baltimore: Johns Hopkins Press, 1967), p. 169.

[11]Novalis, "Aphorisms," 1:23; 2:12.

[12]Orestes A. Brownson, "Transcendentalism," in George Hochfield, ed. *Selected Writings of the American Transcendentalists* (New York: New American Library, 1966), p. 400. In addition to Hochfield, see Perry Miller, ed., *The Transcendentalists: An Anthology* (Cambridge, Mass: Harvard University Press, 1966) provides a collection of major Transcendentalist works. The classic treatment of Transcendentalism is Octavius Brooks Frothingham, *Transcendentalism in New England: A History* (Philadelphia: University of Pennsylvania Press, 1959). Other works on Transcendentalism and its influence are Anne C. Rose, *Transcendentalism as a Social Movement 1830-1850* (New Haven, Conn.: Yale University Press, 1981); Catherine L. Albanese, *Corresponding Motion: Transcendental Religion and the New America* (Philadelphia: Temple University Press, 1977); William R. Hutchison, *The Transcendentalist Ministers: Church Reform in the New England Renaissance* (New Haven, Conn.: Yale University Press, 1959).

[13]Ralph Waldo Emerson, "The American Scholar" in *The Works of Ralph Waldo Emerson*, ed. Edward Waldo Emerson (Boston: Houghton Mifflin, 1889), 1:109. All quotes from Emerson are cited by volume and page from *Works*.

[14]For Emerson's thought, see *The Works of Ralph Waldo Emerson*, 12 vols., ed. Edward Waldo Emerson (Boston: Houghton Mifflin, 1889); and *Journals and Miscellaneous Notebooks*, 14 vols., ed. William H. Gilman et al.,(Cambridge: Belknap Press, 1960-1982). For intellectual biographies of Emerson, consult Ralph Leslie Rusk, *The Life of Ralph Waldo Emerson* (New York: Columbia University Press, 1949); Stephen E. Whicher, *Freedom and Fate: An Inner Life of Ralph Waldo Emerson* (Philadelphia: University of Pennsylvania Press, 1953); Joel Porte, *Representative Man: Ralph Waldo Emerson in His Time* (New York: Oxford University Press, 1979). An anthology of Emerson's works is *Selections from Ralph Waldo Emerson*, ed. Stephen E. Whicher (Boston: Houghton Mifflin, 1957).

[15]The lyceum circuit began in the 1830s to provide social, political and cultural education for adults through lectures and cultures. Many of the most influential American artists, commentators, social critics and politicians were active on this circuit.

[16]William Ellery Channing, "Likeness to God," in Hochfield, *Selected Writings*, p. 57.

[17]Emerson, *Nature*, 1:68.

[18]Emerson, *Nature*, 1:33.

[19]Emerson, *Nature*, 1:16.

[20]Emerson, "Self-Reliance," 2:58.

[21]Emerson, "The American Scholar" 1:88. While the Transcendentalists had great interest in nature, they could not make it a matter of scientific inquiry. This is to misunderstand it. Scientific study begins with the assumption that nature must be approached as mere matter and attempts to know the whole by examination of the parts. Transcendentalism argues that to begin with the particulars and external appearances of nature distorts the entire process. "It [Transcendentalism] respects the end too much to immerse itself in the means" (Emerson, *Nature*, 1:64).

[22]Emerson, "Address," 1:123.

[23]Emerson, *Nature*, 1:31.

[24]Emerson, *Nature*, 1:32.

[25]Emerson, *Nature*, 1:38.

[26]Emerson, *Nature*, 1:9.

[27]Emerson, "Address," 1:142.

[28]Emerson, *Nature*, 1:9-10.

[29]Emerson, *Nature*, 1:40. A similar sentiment is found in the words of Channing. "In proportion as we approach and resemble the mind of God, we are brought into harmony with the creation; for in that proportion we possess the principles from which the universe sprang; we carry within ourselves the perfections of which its beauty, magnificence, order, benevolent adaptations, and boundless purposes are the results and manifestations. God unfolds Himself in His works to a kindred mind" (Channing, "Likeness to God," p. 55).

[30]Coleridge had a significant impact on Transcendentalism in this area. His *Aids to Reflection*, available in an American edition in 1829, distinguished between "understanding," which is knowledge derived empirically, and "reason," by which he means intuitive knowledge. Like Coleridge, the Transcendentalists argued that understanding cannot move us to the supersensible realm. Any god that could be derived from observation of the natural world could be no more than the sum of all contained within this world. Only by means of intuitive reason can the divine be apprehended. See chapter three for exposition of this point.

[31]Emerson, "Self-Reliance, 2:65.

[32]Emerson, *Nature*, 1:47.

[33]Emerson, *Nature*, 1:46.

[34]Emerson, "Address," 1:122.

[35]Theodore Parker, "The Transient and Permanent in Christianity," in Hochfield, *Selected Writings*, p. 285.

[36]Emerson, "Address," 1:129. The objection to grounding Christianity in the person of Jesus is a corollary to their rejection of all dualisms. The traditional means of establishing the authority of Jesus is to stress his difference from us, while Transcendentalist doctrine focuses on the continuity. "But still was he [Jesus] not our brother; the son of man, as we are; the Son of God, like ourselves? His excellence—was it not human excellence? His wisdom, love, piety—sweet and celestial as they were—are they not what we also may attain? In him, as in a mirror, we may see the image of God and go on from glory to glory, till we are changed into the same image, led by the spirit which enlightens the humble. Viewed in this way, how beautiful is the life of Jesus! Heaven has come down to earth, or rather, earth has become heaven" (Parker, "Transient and Permanent in Christianity," pp. 284-85).

[37]Parker, "The Transient and Permanent in Christianity," p. 283.

[38]Emerson, "Address," 1:128.

[39]Emerson, "Address," 1:131. Identifying the divine and human also leads Emerson to offer a different perspective on prayer. "Prayer that craves a particular commodity,—any thing less than all good,—is vicious. Prayer is the contemplation of the facts of life from the highest point of view. It is the soliloquy of a beholding and jubilant soul. It is the spirit of God pronouncing his works good. But prayer as a means to effect a private end is meanness and theft. It supposes dualism and not unity in nature and consciousness. As soon as the man is at one with God, he will not beg. He will then see prayer in all action" (Emerson, "Self-Reliance," 2:76-77).

[40]Emerson, "The Over-Soul," 2:265-66.

[41]Emerson, "The American Scholar" 1:86.

[42]Henry David Thoreau, *Walden and Civil Disobedience*, ed. Owen Thomas (New York: W. W. Norton, 1966), p. 243. Because of the strong individualistic streak in Transcendentalism, the idea of *society's* evolution toward the better, frequently found in Romanticism and Idealism, is only a minor theme. While secondary to the role given individual development, however, it may well be implied in the opening paragraph of "Civil Disobedience": "I heartily accept the motto,—'Therefore government is best which governs least'; and I should like to see it acted up to more rapidly and systematically. Carried out, it finally amounts to this, which also I believe,—'Therefore government is best which governs not at all'; and when men are prepared for it, that will be the kind of government which they will have" ("Civil Disobedience," p. 224).

[43]Thoreau, *Civil Disobedience*, p. 243.

[44]Emerson, *Nature*, 1:75.

[45]Emerson, *Nature*, 1:61. In places, Emerson argues that this apprehension of the absolute makes the external world subject to the will of those most attuned to God. "Build therefore your own world. As fast as you conform your life to the pure idea in your mind, that will unfold its great proportions. A correspondent revolution in things will attend the influx of the spirit. So fast will disagreeable appearances, swine, spider, snakes, pests, mad-houses, prisons, enemies, vanish. They are temporary and shall be no more seen" (Emerson, *Nature*, 1:79.22).

Chapter 3: Romanticism Christianized/Christianity Romanticized

[1]Coleridge's writings are collected in *The Complete Works of Samuel Taylor Coleridge*, ed. W. G. T. Sheed, 7 vols. (New York: Harper, 1853). His correspondence is available in *Letters of Samuel Taylor Coleridge* 2 vols., ed. Ernest Hartley Coleridge (Boston: Houghton, Mifflin, 1895). Individual works of philosophical and theological importance are *Confessions of an Inquiring Spirit* (Philadelphia: Fortress, 1988); *Aids to Reflection*, ed. Thomas Fenby (Liverpool, U.K.: Edward Howell, 1874); *Biographia Literaria, or Biographical Sketches of My Literary Life and Opinions*, ed. George Watson (New York: Everyman's Library, 1965); *The Friend* (Burlington, Vt.: Chauncey Goodrich, 1831); *The Statesman's Manual* (Burlington, Vt.: Chauncey Goodrich, 1832). A general anthology is *The Portable Coleridge*, ed. I. A. Richards (New York: Viking, 1950). An anthology of mostly literary works is *Samuel Taylor Coleridge: Selected Poetry and Prose*, ed. Elisabeth Schneider (New York: Holt, Rinehart & Winston, 1951). This includes extensive portions of *Biographia Literaria*. A topical arrangement of selections by Coleridge can be found in Kathleen Coburn, ed., *Inquiring Spirit: A Coleridge Reader* (Saarbruchen: Minerva Press, 1951). For biographies of Coleridge, see Basil Willey, *Samuel Taylor Coleridge* (London: Chatto & Windus, 1972); James Dykes Campbell, *Samuel Taylor Coleridge: A Narrative of the Events of His Life* (London: Macmillan, 1894); and E. K. Chambers, *Samuel Taylor Coleridge: A Biographical Study* (Oxford:

Clarendon Press, 1938). Secondary sources that deal with Coleridge's philosophical and theological ideas are James D. Boulger, *Coleridge as Religious Thinker* (New Haven, Conn.: Yale University Press, 1961); Anthony John Harding, *Coleridge and the Inspired Word* (Kingston, Ont.: McGill-Queen's University Press, 1985); Mary Anne Perkins, *Coleridge's Philosophy: The Logos as Unifying Principle* (Oxford: Clarendon, 1994); Alois Brandl, *Samuel Taylor Coleridge and the English Romantic School* (New York: Haskell, 1966); G. N. G. Orsini, *Coleridge and German Idealism: A Study in the History of Philosophy with Unpublished Materials from Coleridge's Manuscripts* (Carbondale, Ill.: Southern Illinois University Press, 1969); John H. Muirhead, *Coleridge as Philosopher* (London: Allen & Unwin, 1930); Owen Barfield, *What Coleridge Thought* (Middletown, Conn.: Wesleyan University Press, 1971); J. Robert Barth, *Coleridge and Christian Doctrine* (Cambridge, Mass: Harvard University Press, 1969); Thomas McFarland, *Coleridge and the Pantheist Tradition* (Oxford: Clarendon Press, 1969); David Jasper, *Coleridge as Poet and Religious Thinker* (Allison Park, Penn.: Pickwick, 1985). A source that considers the influence of Romanticism on the religious views of several English figures, including Coleridge, is Stephen Prickett, *Romanticism and Religion: The Tradition of Coleridge and Wordsworth in the Victorian Church* (Cambridge: Cambridge University Press, 1976).

[2]A generation after his death, J. S. Mill, no proponent of Coleridge's ideas himself, saw Coleridge's thought as the only real alternative to the Benthamite school. For a survey of nineteenth century theology in England, see Bernard M. G. Reardon, *From Coleridge to Gore: A Century of Religious Thought in Britain* (London: Longman, 1971).

[3]For more information about the relationship between the two men, see H. M. Margoliouth, *Wordsworth and Coleridge 1795-1834* (Hamden, Conn.: Archon, 1966).

[4]*Aids to Reflection*, ed. Thomas Fenby (Liverpool: Edward Howell, 1874), p. 365.

[5]*Aids to Reflection*, p. 191.

[6]*Aids to Reflection*, pp. 189-90.

[7]*Aids to Reflection*, pp. 152-53.

[8]One of Coleridge's objections to natural theology is that it reduces sin to a physical defect. This runs contrary to our experience that the struggle against sin involves the entirety of our person. "Man was and is a *fallen* Creature, not by accidents of bodily constitution, or any other cause, which *human* Wisdom in a course of ages might be supposed capable of removing; but diseased in his *will*, in that Will which is the true and only strict synonym of the word, I, or the intelligent Self" (*Aids to Reflection*, p. 122).

[9]*Aids to Reflection*, p. 159.

[10]For a brief study on Coleridge's view on this topic, see R. L. Brett, *Fancy and Imagination* (London: Methuen, 1969).

[11]*Biographia Literaria*, p. 167.

[12]*Letters of Samuel Taylor Coleridge* 2 vols., ed. Ernest Hartley Coleridge (Boston: Houghton Mifflin, 1895), 1.352.

[13]*Biographia Literaria*, p. 167.

[14]The theme of unity with God is a constant in Coleridge's writings. His early literary works expressed this in a panentheistic manner, which is common to Romanticism. Later, however, he concludes that ontological unity between ourselves and God is the practical equivalent of naturalism: it strips God of the personality and makes it impossible for us to enter into relationship with him. For God to meet the needs of persons, he must own the attributes of personality himself. Similarly, he returned to trinitarianism after determining that it did have practical implications for the life of the believer (the doubt of which seems to have been his major reason for embracing Unitarianism) because it presents to us a God whose very nature is relational.

[15]*Confessions of an Inquiring Spirit*, p. 48.

[16]*Confessions of an Inquiring Spirit*, p. 26.

[17]*Aids to Reflection*, p. 144.

[18]*Confessions of an Inquiring Spirit*, p. 63.

[19]While Coleridge directs his criticism toward the natural theology of his own day, he believed that neglect of the subjective reached back to the church's early days. "Too soon did the Doctors of the Church forget that the heart, the Moral Nature, was the beginning and the end; and that Truth, Knowledge, and Insight were comprehended in its expansion. This was the true and first apostasy—when in Council and Synod the Divine Humanities of the Gospel gave way to speculative Systems, and Religion became a Science of Shadows under the name of Theology, or at best a bare Skeleton of Truth, without life or interest, alike inaccessible and unintelligible to the majority of Christians." See *Aids to Reflection*, pp. 167-68. Coleridge sees himself as a reformer who is directing the church back to its original balance.

[20]*Biographia Literaria*, p. 287. Coleridge goes so far as to state that "it is my conviction that in all ordinary cases the knowledge and belief of the Christian Religion should precede the study of the Hebrew Canon. Indeed, with regard to both Testaments, I consider oral and catechismal instruction as the preparative provided by Christ himself in the establishment of a visible Church" (*Confessions of an Inquiring Spirit*, pp. 49-50).

[21]*Confessions of an Inquiring Spirit*, p. 50. While Coleridge gives priority to the existential facet of reason, he has no sympathy with those who rely on the subjective aspect exclusively. "First, it defaces and makes useless that part of the Image of God in us, which we call REASON: and secondly, it takes away that advantage, which raises Christianity above all other Religions, that she dare appeal to so solid a faculty" (*Aids to Reflection*, pp. 129-30).

[22]*Aids to Reflection*, p. 183.

[23]*Biographia Literaria*, p. 289.

[24]*Aids to Reflection*, p. 147.

[25]Of intellectual proofs Coleridge says, "I hold then, it is true, that all the (so called) Demonstrations of a God either prove too little, as that from the Order and apparent Purpose in Nature; or too much, *viz.*, that the World is itself God: or they clandestinely involve the conclusion in the premisses, passing off the mere analysis or explication of an Assertion the Proof of it." See *Aids to Reflection*, p. 160. When the evidence is drawn from empirical evidence, we are either trapped within the empirical realm and do not get beyond it, or we radicalize what is in the world to conclude that all contained in the sensible realm is God himself, or we simply beg the question.

[26]*Aids to Reflection*, p. 363.

[27]Elsewhere, Coleridge appears willing to take a somewhat more charitable view toward more traditional evidences but still clearly gives priority to his experiential approach. "I shall merely state what my belief is concerning the true evidences of Christianity. 1. Its consistency with right reason I consider as the outer court of the temple—the common area within which it stands. 2. The miracles with and through which the religion was first revealed and attested I regard as the steps, the vestibule and the portal of the temple. 3. The sense, the inward feeling, in the soul of each believer of its exceeding desirableness—the experience that he needs something, joined with the strong foretokening that the redemption and the graces propounded to us in Christ are what he needs—this I hold to be the true foundation of the spiritual edifice. . . . But 4, it is the experience derived from a practical conformity to the conditions of the Gospel—it is the opening eye; the dawning light; the terrors and the promises of spiritual growth; the blessedness of loving God as God, the nascent sense of sin hated as sin, and of the incapability of attaining to either without Christ" (*Biographia Literaria*, p. 286).

[28]*Confessions of an Inquiring Spirit*, p. 29.

[29] *Confessions of an Inquiring Spirit,* pp. 48-49.

[30] *Confessions of an Inquiring Spirit,* p. 27.

[31] *Confessions of an Inquiring Spirit,* p. 31.

[32] *Confessions of an Inquiring Spirit,* p. 27.

[33] *Confessions of an Inquiring Spirit,* p. 41.

[34] *Confessions of an Inquiring Spirit,* p. 52.

[35] *Confessions of an Inquiring Spirit,* pp. 35-36.

[36] *Confessions of an Inquiring Spirit,* p. 45.

[37] "But the case is quite different with a Christian, who accepts the Scriptures as the Word of God, yet refuses his assent to the plainest declarations of these Scriptures, and explains away the most express texts into metaphor and hyperbole, *because* the literal and obvious interpretation is (according to *his* notions) absurd and contrary to reason." See *Aids to Reflection,* p. 162.

[38] *Aids to Reflection,* p. 303.

[39] Works of Schleiermacher translated into English are *On Religion: Speeches to Its Cultured Despisers,* trans. John Oman (New York: Harper, 1958); *Brief Outline of Theology as a Field of Study,* trans. Terrence N. Tice (Lewiston, N.Y.: Mellen Press, 1988); *The Christian Faith,* 2 vols., trans. H. R. Mackintosh and J. S. Stewart (New York: Harper & Row, 1963); *Christmas Eve,* trans. Terrence N. Tice (Richmond, Va.: John Knox Press, 1967); *Hermeneutics: The Handwritten Manuscripts,* trans. James Duke and Jack Forstman (Missoula, Mont.: Scholars Press, 1977); *The Life of Jesus,* ed. Jack C. Verheyden (Philadelphia: Fortress, 1975); *Introduction to Christian Ethics,* trans. John C. Shelley (Nashville: Abingdon Press, 1989); *Luke: A Critical Study,* trans. Connop Thirlwall (Lewiston, N.Y.: Mellen Press, 1993); *On Freedom,* trans. Albert L. Blackwell (Lewiston, N.Y.: Mellen Press, 1992); *On the Glaubenslehre: Two Letters to Dr. Lücke,* trans. James Duke and Francis Fiorenza (Chico, Calif.: Scholars Press, 1981); *On the Highest Good,* trans. H. Victor Froese (Lewiston, N.Y.: Mellen Press, 1992); *Schleiermacher's Soliloquies,* trans. Horace Leland Friess (Chicago: Open Court, 1926); *Servant of the Word: Selected Sermons of Friedrich Schleiermacher,* trans. Dawn De Vries (Philadelphia: Fortress, 1987). Martin Redeker's *Schleiermacher: Life and Thought,* trans. John Wallhausser (Philadelphia: Fortress, 1973) is the standard text on Schleiermacher's theology. See also Albert L. Blackwell, *Schleiermacher's Early Philosophy of Life: Determinism, Freedom, and Phantasy* (Chico, Calif.: Scholars Press, 1982); Richard B. Brandt, *The Philosophy of Schleiermacher: The Development of His Theory of Scientific and Religious Knowledge* (Westport, Conn.: Greenwood Press, 1971); C. W. Christian, *Friedrich Schleiermacher* (Waco, Tex.: Word, 1979); Jackson Forstman, *A Romantic Triangle: Schleiermacher and Early German Romanticism* (Missoula: Scholars Press, 1977); B. A. Gerrish, *A Prince of the Church: Schleiermacher and the Beginnings of Modern Theology* (Philadelphia: Fortress, 1984); Richard R. Niebuhr, *Schleiermacher on Christ and Religion* (New York: Scribners, 1964); Sergio Sorrentino, ed. *Schleiermacher's Philosophy and the Philosophical Tradition,* (Lewiston, N.Y.: Mellen Press, 1992); Stephen Sykes, *Friedrich Schleiermacher* (Richmond, Va.: John Knox Press, 1971); Robert R. Williams, *Schleiermacher the Theologian: The Construction of the Doctrine of God* (Philadelphia: Fortress, 1978). A nice summary and critique of Schleiermacher can be found in Hugh Ross Mackintosh, *Types of Modern Theology* (New York: Scribner's Sons, 1937). A helpful bibliography of Schleiermacher is Terrence N. Tice, *Schleiermacher Bibliography (1784-1984)* (Princeton, N.J.: Princeton Theological Seminary, 1985). K. W. Clements, *Friedrich Schleiermacher: Pioneer of Modern Theology,* (London: Collins, 1987) contains a brief anthology of Schleiermacher's writing on various topics.

[40] Dilthey's *Leben Schleiermachers* is unavailable in English.

[41] See Karl Barth, *Protestant Thought: From Rousseau to Ritschl,* trans. Brian Cozens (New York: Harper, 1959) and *The Theology of Schleiermacher: Lectures at Gottingen,* ed. Dietrich

Ritschl, trans. Geoffrey W. Bromiley (Grand Rapids, Mich.: Eerdmans, 1982). Unfortunately, Emil Brunner's criticism of Schleiermacher in *Die Mystik und das Wort* is unavailable in English translation.

[42]Freidrich Schleiermacher, *On Religion: Speeches to Its Cultured Despisers,* trans. John Oman (New York: Harper, 1958), p. 14.

[43]*Speeches,* p. 14.

[44]*Speeches,* p. 18.

[45]*Speeches,* pp. 15-16.

[46]*Speeches,* p. 54.

[47]*The Christian Faith,* 2 vols., trans. H. R. Mackintosh and J. S. Stewart (New York: Harper & Row, 1963), #4, p. 12.

[48]C. W. Christian, *Friedrich Schleiermacher* (Waco, Tex.: Word, 1979), p. 60.

[49]*The Christian Faith,* #33, p. 13.

[50]*Speeches,* p. 31.

[51]*Speeches,* pp. 37-38.

[52]*Speeches,* p. 122.

[53]*Speeches,* p. 48.

[54]*Speeches,* p. 161.

[55]*Speeches,* p. 214.

[56]*Speeches,* p. 216.

[57]*Speeches,* p. 245.

[58]*Speeches,* p. 246.

[59]*Speeches,* p. 248.

[60]*Christian Faith,* #30, p. 125.

[61]*Christian Faith,* #15, p. 76.

[62]See *Christian Faith,* #29 for his explanation of this procedure.

[63]*Christian Faith,* #50, p. 194.

[64]As a result of this understanding of Scripture, Schleiermacher refuses to grant any finality to it. While he notes that many confessions delineate what is to be considered canon, "This ought not to prevent further unrestricted investigation of the matter; critical inquiry must ever anew test the individual writings of Scripture with a view to decide whether they rightly keep their place in the sacred collection" (*Christian Faith,* #130.4, p. 603).

[65]*Christian Faith,* #97.2, p. 405. Some may puzzle over Schleiermacher's insistence on a supernatural means of birth for Jesus while rejecting traditional formulations of the virgin birth. However, the former is necessary as a means of explaining the perfection of Jesus in view of the power of sin over the whole of the human race prior to his birth.

[66]*Christian Faith,* #99, p. 417. For Schleiermacher's view of the relevance of Christ's miracles and prophecies, see #14.3, p. 71.

[67]*Christian Faith,* #94, p. 385. The ambiguity concerning the divinity of Christ is even more pronounced in his definition of the Holy Spirit, described as "the vital unity of the Christian fellowship as a moral personality" or "the *common spirit*" of the church. See *The Christian Faith,* #116.3, p. 535; #121.2, p. 562; #123, p. 569.

[68]*Christian Faith,* #88, p. 361.

[69]*Christian Faith,* #100, p. 425.

[70]*Christian Faith,* #94.2, pp. 387, 388.

[71]*Christian Faith,* #40.1, p. 150.

[72]*Christian Faith,* #41.1, p. 153.

[73]*Christian Faith,* #97.2, p. 404. See *Christian Faith,* #69, #77 for a more complete exposition of this idea.

[74]*Christian Faith,* #72, p. 291.
[75]*Christian Faith,* #72.4, p. 299.
[76]*Christian Faith,* #72.2, p. 292.

Chapter 4: Idealism and the End of Dichotomy

[1]G. W. F. Hegel, *The Difference Between Fichte's and Schelling's System of Philosophy,* trans. H. S. Harris and Walter Cerf (Albany, N.Y.: State University of New York Press, 1977), p. 89.

[2]For general overviews of Absolute Idealism, see Frederick Copleston, *Modern Philosophy,* vol. 7, pt. 1, of *A History of Philosophy,* (Garden City, N.Y.: Image, 1963); Robert C. Solomon and Kathleen M. Higgins, eds., *The Age of German Idealism,* vol. 6 of *Routledge History of Philosophy* (London: Routledge, 1993); Justus Hartnack, *From Radical Empiricism and Absolute Idealism* (Lewiston, N.Y.: Mellen, 1986); Franz Gabriel Nauen, *Revolution, Idealism and Human Freedom: Schelling, Hölderlin and Hegel and the Crisis of Early German Idealism* (The Hague: Nijhoff, 1971); George J. Seidel, *Activity and Ground: Fichte, Schelling, and Hegel* (Hildesheim: G. Olms, 1976). Josiah Royce, *Lectures on Modern Idealism* (New Haven, Conn.: Yale University Press, 1919). A rather unique, entertaining and highly readable introduction to this movement is Robert Solomon, *Introducing the German Idealists* (Indianapolis: Hackett, 1981), which presents various views in the form of mock interviews with the leading figures. A study of the legacy of Hegel and other Idealists is Herbert Schnädelbach, *Philosophy in Germany: 1831-1933,* trans. Eric Matthews (Cambridge: Cambridge University Press, 1984). A reader with representative samples of Idealist philosophers is Henry David Aiken, ed., *The Age of Ideology: The 19th Century Philosophers* (New York: New American Library, 1956). Godfrey Vesey, *Idealism: Past and Present,* ed. (Cambridge: Cambridge University Press, 1982) contains a number of helpful articles on both German Idealists as well as later forms of Idealism. A survey that provides an overview of Idealism against the backdrop of Hume and Kant is Justus Hartnack, *From Radical Empiricism to Absolute Idealism* (Lewiston, N.Y.: Mellen Press, 1986).

[3]F. W. J. Schelling, *System of Transcendental Idealism,* trans. Peter Heath (Charlottesville, Va.: University Press of Virginia, 1978), p. 74.

[4]Claude Welch, *Protestant Thought in the Nineteenth Century* (New Haven, Conn.: Yale University Press, 1972), 1:88.

[5]The emphasis placed on Idealism and Romanticism should not lead the reader to conclude that these are the only two philosophical schools of the day. For a helpful survey of the various philosophical options, see Frederick C. Beiser, *The Fate of Reason: German Philosophy from Kant to Fichte* (Cambridge, Mass: Harvard University Press, 1987). A source of post-Kantian readings through Hegel is George di Giovanni and H. S. Harris, eds., *Between Kant and Hegel: Texts in the Development of Post-Kantian Idealism* (Albany: State University of New York Press, 1985).

[6]Texts of Fichte that have been translated into English are: *The Science of Rights,* trans. A. E. Kroeger (New York: Harper & Row, 1970); *Addresses to the German Nation,* ed. George Armstrong Kelly (New York: Harper, 1968); *Attempt at a Critique of All Revelation,* trans. Garrett Green (New York: Cambridge University Press, 1978); *Characteristics of the Present Age; The Way Towards the Blessed Life: Or, the Doctrine of Religion,* ed. Daniel N. Robinson, (Washington, D.C.: University Publications of America, 1977); *Foundations of Transcendental Philosophy,* trans. and ed. Daniel Breazeale (Ithaca, N.Y.: Cornell University Press, 1992); *New Exposition of the Science of Knowledge,* trans. A. E. Kroeger, (St. Louis: n.p., 1869); *On the Nature of the Scholar and its Manifestations,* trans. William Smith, (London: J. Chapman, 1845); *Science of Knowledge; With the First and Second Introductions,* trans. and ed. Peter Heath and John Lachs (New York: Appleton-Century-Crofts, 1970); *The Vocation of Man,* ed. Roderick M. Chisholm (Indianapolis: Bobbs-Merrill, 1956). Collections of Fichte's

writings are *Fichte, Early Philosophical Writings,* trans. and ed. Daniel Breazeale (Ithaca, N.Y.: Cornell University Press, 1988) and *The Popular Works of Johann Gottlieb Fichte,* trans. William Smith, 4th ed. (London: Trubner, 1889). For general works on Fichte's life and thought, see Robert Adamson, *Fichte* (Freeport, N.Y.: Books for Libraries Press, 1903) [reprinted 1969]; Daniel Breazeale and Tom Rockmore, eds., *Fichte,* (Atlantic Highlands, N.J.: Humanities Press, 1994); Frederick Neuhouser, *Fichte's Theory of Subjectivity* (Cambridge: Cambridge University Press, 1990).

[7]While Fichte rejected Spinoza's determinism, his view of the universe as a comprehensive whole exerted a continuing influence on Fichte. Although it may be somewhat surprising that a view that tends toward pantheism such as we find in Fichte's identification of God with the moral order of the world was described as atheism, this was not uncommon at the time.

[8]To add insult to injury, Fichte also lost support from Schelling and Hölderlin, who had been earlier admirers, and was publicly put at arm's length by Kant's repudiation of his philosophy.

[9]*Science of Knowledge: With the First and Second Introductions,* trans. and ed. Peter Heath and John Lachs (New York: Appleton-Century-Crofts, 1970), p. 4. All references to the *First Introduction* and *Second Introduction* are also drawn from this source. In his *Second Introduction* he argues that his presentation "is perfectly in accordance with the teaching of Kant, and is nothing other than Kantianism properly understood." p. 43

[10]*First Introduction,* p. 10.

[11]*Science of Knowledge,* p. 97.

[12]*First Introduction,* p. 17.

[13]*The Vocation of Man,* ed. Roderick M. Chisholm (Indianapolis: Bobbs-Merrill, 1956), p. 64.

[14]This process of positing the nonego and the necessity of the dialectic between the two is influential for Hegel's thought.

[15]*Vocation,* p. 96.

[16]J. Royce, *Lectures on Modern Idealism* (New Haven, Conn.: Yale University Press, 1919), p. 71.

[17]*First Introduction,* p. 21.

[18]*Science of Knowledge,* p. 198.

[19]In a passage that demonstrates the influence of Kant as well as his Idealism, Fichte states, "It [moral law] makes this claim on that holy being: to promote eternally the highest good in all rational natures, and to establish eternally the balance between morality and happiness. That being must thus be eternal himself, to correspond to an eternal moral law; and he must, in conformity with this law, give eternity to all rational being, to whom this law applies and from whom it demands eternity. There must therefore be an *eternal God,* and every moral being must endure eternally, if the final purpose of the moral law is not to be impossible." *Attempt at a Critique of All Revelation,* trans. Garrett Green (New York: Cambridge University Press, 1978), p. 61.

[20]For Fichte's view of God, see chapter one in Joseph Alexander Leighton, *Typical Modern Conceptions of God or The Absolute of German Romantic Idealism and of English Evolutionary Agnosticism* (New York: Longmans, Green, 1901) and Russell Warren Stine, *The Doctrine of God in the Philosophy of Fichte,* (Philadelphia: University of Pennsylvania, 1945).

[21]*Vocation,* p. 140.

[22]Works by Schelling in English are *Bruno, or, On the Natural and the Divine Principle of Things,* ed. and trans. Michael G. Vater (Albany, N.Y.: SUNY Press, 1984); *System of Transcendental Idealism,* trans. Peter Heath (Charlottesville, Va.: University Press of Virginia, 1978); *On the History of Modern Philosophy,* trans. Andrew Bowie (Cambridge: Cambridge University Press, 1994); *Schelling's Treatise on "The Deities of Samothrace,"* trans. Robert F.

Brown (Missoula, Mont: Scholars Press, 1974); *The Unconditional in Human Knowledge: Four Early Essays (1794-1976)*, trans. Fritz Marti (Lewisburg, Penn.: Bucknell University Press, 1980); *On University Studies*, trans. E. S. Morgan, ed. Norbert Guterman (Athens, Ohio: Ohio University Press, 1966); *Schelling: Of Human Freedom*, trans. James Gutmann (Chicago: Open Court, 1936); *The Ages of the World*, trans. Frederick de Wolfe Bolman Jr. (New York: AMS, 1967). For works about Schelling's philosophy, see Robert F. Brown, *The Later Philosophy of Schelling: The Influence of Boehme on the Works of 1809-1815* (Lewisburg, Penn.: Bucknell University Press, 1977); Paul Collins Hayner, *Reason and Existence* (Leiden: E. J. Brill, 1967); Werner Marx, *The Philosophy of F. W. J. Schelling: History, System, and Freedom*, trans. Thomas Nenon (Bloomington: Indiana University Press, 1984); Joseph L. Esposito, *Schelling's Idealism and Philosophy of Nature* (Lewisburg, Penn.: Bucknell University Press, 1977).

[23]For the influence of Schelling on Catholic thought, see Thomas Franklin O'Meara, *Romantic Idealism and Roman Catholicism: Schelling and the Theologians* (Notre Dame, Ind.: University of Notre Dame Press, 1982).

[24]See Paul Tillich, *The Construction of the History of Religion in Schelling's Positive Philosophy*, trans. Victor Nuovo (Lewisburg, Penn.: Bucknell University Press, 1974); Paul Tillich, *Mysticism and Guilt Consciousness in Schelling's Philosophical Development*, trans. Victor Nuovo (Lewisburg, Penn.: Bucknell University Press, 1974); Martin Heidegger, *Schelling's Treatise on the Essence of Human Freedom*, trans. Joan Stambaugh (Athens: Ohio University Press, 1985).

[25]*Bruno*, p. 136.

[26]*System of Transcendental Idealism*, trans. Peter Heath (Charlottesville: University Press of Virginia, 1978), p. 27.

[27]*System of Transcendental Idealism*, p. 231. It is at this point that Schopenhauer's thought comes into closest proximity with Schelling's form of Idealism, although, as we will see in chapter seven, Schopenhauer paints it in terms of his will to life.

[28]Schelling's criticism of Scripture is not limited to its use but the material itself. "One cannot help thinking that full understanding of it [Christianity] has been hampered by the so-called Biblical literature, which in terms of genuine religious ideas is not even remotely comparable to many other works, old and new, especially the Hindu books" (*On University Studies*, ed. Norbert Guterman and trans. E. S. Morgan, [Athens: Ohio University Press, 1966], p. 97).

[29]*On University Studies*, p. 95.

[30]*On University Studies*, p. 94

[31]*On University Studies*, p. 95.

[32]*System of Transcendental Idealism*, p. 212.

[33]The literature by and about Hegel is enormous. A very helpful slim introduction to Hegel is provided by Peter Singer, *Hegel* (Oxford University Press, 1983). Among the numerous expositions of Hegel's system, the best single volume in English is Charles Taylor, *Hegel* (Cambridge University Press, 1975). The present writer has been influenced by the unpublished M. Litt. thesis of Claudia Kuchenbauer, "The Spirit of Hegel in Contemporary Theology" (University of Oxford, 1990). Further bibliography is provided in the next note.

[34]In addition to the books in the previous note, the following expositions of Hegel's philosophical system are recommended. F. C. Beiser, ed., *The Cambridge Companion to Hegel* (Cambridge University Press, 1993), which contains a good selective bibliography; Emil Fackenheim, *The Religious Dimension in Hegel's Thought* (Bloomington: Indiana University Press, 1967); J. N. Findlay, *Hegel: A Re-Examination* (New York: Macmillan, 1958); Michael J. Inwood, *Hegel* (London: Routledge & Kegan Paul, 1983); W. Kaufmann, *Hegel: Reinter-*

pretation, Texts, and Commentary (New York: Doubleday, 1965); Quentin Lauer, *Hegel's Concept of God* (Albany: State University of New York Press, 1982); H. Marcuse, *Reason and Revolution,* 2nd ed. (New York: Humanities Press, 1954); G. R. G. Mure, *The Philosophy of Hegel* (Oxford University Press, 1965); Raymond Plant, *Hegel* (Bloomington: Indiana University Press, 1973); W. T. Stace, *The Philosophy of Hegel* (1924; reprint, New York: Dover, 1955). Further bibliography is provided in the notes below.

[35]On Hegel's life see F. Wiedmann, *Hegel: An Illustrated Biography* (New York: Pegasus, 1968), and on his intellectual growth, H. S. Harris, *Hegel's Development,* 2 vols. (Oxford University Press, 1972, 1983). Important material on Hegel's life is translated in Kaufmann, *Hegel,* and in Hegel, *Letters,* trans. C. Butler and C. Seiler (Bloomington: Indiana University Press, 1984).

[36]Hegel, *Early Theological Writings,* trans. T. M. Knox (Chicago: University of Chicago Press, 1948).

[37]Two fine translations of this book exist: *The Phenomenology of Mind,* trans. J. B. Ballie (1931; reprint, New York: Harper & Row, 1967), and *The Phenomenology of Spirit,* trans. A.V. Miller (Oxford University Press, 1977). My references are to the paragraph numbers in the Miller translation.

[38]This book has been translated in three parts: *The Encyclopaedia Logic,* trans. T. F. Geraets et al. (Indianapolis: Hackett, 1991), also called the "Lesser Logic"; *Philosophy of Nature,* trans. A. V. Miller (Oxford: Oxford University Press, 1970); and *Philosophy of Mind,* trans. W. Wallance and A. V. Miller, rev. ed. (Oxford: Oxford University Press, 1971). References to the *Encyclopaedia* will be to the numbered sections which run throughout the whole set.

[39]Translated by A. V. Miller (New York: Humanities Press, 1969).

[40]Translated as *Philosophy of Right* by T. M. Knox (Oxford: Oxford University Press, 1952). References to this book will be to the numbered sections in the text (excepting the preface).

[41]Newer translations (such as those already cited) have replaced the older nineteenth century ones, which are sometimes unreliable. Modern English translations of the lectures include *Aesthetics,* trans. T. M. Knox, 2 vols. (Oxford: Oxford University Press, 1975), *Lectures on the History of Philosophy,* trans. R. Brown et al., 3 vols. (Berkeley: University of California Press, 1990-); and *Lectures on the Philosophy of Religion,* ed. and trans. P. C. Hodgson, 3 vols. (Berkeley: University of California Press, 1984-1987). For the *Philosophy of History* we must still rely on the older translation of J. Sibree (1857; reprint, New York: Dover, 1956), but the important *Introduction to the Philosophy of History* has been recently translated by L. Rauch (Indianapolis: Hackett, 1988).

[42]From Hegel's own lecture manuscript, in *Lectures on the Philosophy of Religion,* 1.105.

[43]*Phenomenology,* pars. 5 and 10.

[44]From the translation by Stephen Mitchell (San Francisco: Harper, 1988).

[45]*Phenomenology,* pars. 114 and 126.

[46]Hegel did believe that his "contradiction" included logical contradiction; my point is that it is not *limited* to logical contradiction. See his *Science of Logic,* pp. 438-43.

[47]*Phenomenology,* par. 20

[48]*The Philosophy of Right,* § 346.

[49]On Berkeley, see *Christianity and Western Thought,* 1:227-33.

[50]*Phenomenology,* par. 25.

[51]Preface to *The Philosophy of Right,* pp. 10-11.

[52]*Phenomenology,* par. 29.

[53]*Science of Logic,* 50.

[54]*Encyclopaedia,* § 24 (addition 2).

[55]*Encyclopaedia,* § 24.

[56]*Philosophy of Right,* §§ 257 and 260.
[57]*Philosophy of Right,* §§ 257 and 260.
[58]*Science of Logic,* p. 48.
[59]Two excellent discussions of this topic are: Lauer, *Hegel's Concept of God;* and R. K. Williamson, *Introduction to Hegel's Philosophy of Religion* (Albany: State University of New York Press, 1984).
[60]The atheist bias of Kaufmann's *Hegel* mars an otherwise fine introduction.
[61]This is the view of Williamson, *Introduction.*
[62]*Phenomenology,* par. 765.

Chapter 5: Humanity as Divine Incarnation

[1]The standard source on Left Hegelianism is Karl Löwith, *From Hegel to Nietzsche,* trans. David E. Green (New York: Columbia University Press, 1991). Other valuable references on left-wing Hegelianism are Herbert Marcuse, *Reason and Revolution: Hegel and the Rise of Social Theory* (New York: Humanities Press, 1954); William I. Brazill, *The Young Hegelians* (New Haven, Conn.: Yale University Press, 1970); Sidney Hook *From Hegel to Marx: Studies in the Intellectual Development of Karl Marx* (New York: Reynal and Hitchcock, 1936); John Edward Toews, *Hegelianism: The Path Toward Dialectical Humanism, 1805-1841* (Cambridge: Cambridge University Press, 1980); and Harold Mah, *The End of Philosophy and the Origin of "Ideology"* (Berkeley: University of California Press, 1987).
[2]A notable exception to this is David Strauss, who was elected to parliament, primarily on the support of political radicals. To their consternation, Strauss generally aligned himself with the Prussian monarchy once in office.
[3]Major works of Strauss in English translation are *The Life of Jesus Critically Examined,* ed. Peter C. Hodgson and trans. George Eliot, 4th ed. (Philadelphia: Fortress, 1972); *The Christ of Faith and the Jesus of History: A Critique of Schleiermacher's The Life of Jesus,* trans. Leander E. Keck (Philadelphia: Fortress, 1977); *In Defense of My Life of Jesus Against the Hegelians,* ed. and trans. Marilyn Chapin Massey (Hamden, Conn.: Archon, 1983); *The Old Faith and the New,* trans. Mathilde Blind (New York: Henry Holt, 1873); *A New Life of Jesus,* 2nd ed., 2 vols. (London: Williams & Norgate, 1879). For secondary literature on Strauss, see Horton Harris, *David Friedrich Strauss and His Theology* (Cambridge: Cambridge University Press, 1973); Richard S. Cromwell, *David Friedrich Strauss and His Place in Modern Thought* (Fair Lawn, N.J.: R. E. Burdick, 1974); Hans Frei, "David Friedrich Strauss," in *Nineteenth Century Religious Thought in the West,* 1:215-60. Extended treatments of Strauss are available in Albert Schweitzer, *The Quest of the Historical Jesus,* trans. W. Montgomery (New York: Macmillan, 1968), pp. 68-120; and Colin Brown, *Jesus in European Protestant Thought* (Durham, N.C.: Labyrinth, 1985), pp. 183-204.
[4]A study of the criticism that followed publication of *Life of Jesus* is Edwina G. Lawler, *David Friedrich Strauss and His Critics: The Life of Jesus Debate in Early Nineteenth-Century German Journals* (New York: Peter Lang, 1986).
[5]To some degree, Strauss downplayed the difference between his old Idealism and his newfound adherence to materialism, stating that both were monistic and were probably the same thing seen from different perspectives. "If this be considered pure unmitigated materialism, I will not dispute it. In fact, I have always tacitly regarded the contrast so loudly proclaimed between materialism and idealism (or by whatever term one may designate the view opposed to the former), as a mere quarrel about words" (*The Old Faith and the New,* trans. Mathilde Blind [New York: Henry Holt, 1873], #62).
[6]William Baird, *History of New Testament Research,* (Minneapolis: Fortress, 1992), 1: 246.
[7]Albert Schweitzer, *The Quest of the Historical Jesus,* trans. W. Montgomery (New York: Mac-

Millan, 1968), p. 78.

[8]*In Defense of My Life of Jesus*, p. 7.

[9]*The Life of Jesus Critically Examined*, ed. Peter C. Hodgson and trans. George Eliot, 4th ed. (Philadelphia: Fortress, 1972), #14, p. 79.

[10]Much of *In Defense* must be seen in light of this political context. In it, Strauss attempts to refute Hegelians who disavowed the link between Hegelian philosophy and the conclusions of the *Life of Jesus*.

[11]*Life of Jesus*, #16, p. 88.

[12]*Life of Jesus*, #8, pp. 56-57.

[13]*Life of Jesus*, #16, p. 88.

[14]*Life of Jesus*, #16, p. 88.

[15]*Life of Jesus*, #15, p. 86.

[16]*Life of Jesus*, #15, p. 86. The category of pure myth raised the greatest ire among Strauss's critics. While many were comfortable with the idea that certain historical events were embellished to highlight a theological point, they were troubled by the assertion that stories of events were freely created to advance a theological position.

[17]*Life of Jesus*, #15, p. 87.

[18]*Life of Jesus*, #14, p. 86.

[19]*Life of Jesus*, #14, p. 83

[20]While Jesus' acquaintance with John the Baptist sparked his messianic consciousness, Strauss believes that "it is inconceivable that John should ever have held and pronounced Jesus to be the Messiah" (*Life of Jesus*, #46, p. 228).

[21]See *Life of Jesus*, #66, p. 296; #115, pp. 589-90.

[22]Strauss argues that the link between the Messiah and the Suffering Servant originates with Jesus. "Although . . . it cannot be proved, and is even not probable that the idea of a suffering Messiah already existed among the Jews in the time of Jesus: it is still possible that, even without such a precedent, Jesus himself, by an observation of circumstances, and a comparison of them with Old Testament narratives and prophecies, might come to entertain the belief that suffering and death were a part of the office and destination of the Messiah" (*Life of Jesus*, #112, 573).

[23]*Life of Jesus*, #60, p. 279.

[24]*Life of Jesus*, #83, p. 386. Some of the sayings that have parallels in the Synoptics are considered authentic. The effect of this verdict on John's historical value is significant because it robs Schleiermacher of his strongest source.

[25]*Life of Jesus*, #76, p. 342.

[26]*Life of Jesus*, p. 757.

[27]*Life of Jesus*, p. 757.

[28]*In Defense*, p. 3.

[29]*Life of Jesus*, #151, p. 780.

[30]*Life of Jesus*, #151, p. 780.

[31]While Strauss grants this element of priority to Jesus, there is still the possibility that others greater than Jesus will emerge. "Christ would have merely a comparatively highest rank, because, on the one hand, he could be differentiated only by degree from all the other great persons and, on the other, it would always remain uncertain whether, even after such a long interval, someone else would still transcend him" (*In Defense of My Life of Jesus*, p. 18) Strauss argues that we cannot isolate the idea of incarnation to religious genius alone. True divine consciousness encompasses all areas of life. "Nevertheless, the divine, while concentrated, to be sure in the realm of immediate consciousness, is not articulated there as it is in its dispersion in the more peripheral fields of art, science, and so forth. As a consequence, the so-called principal incarnation of God in Jesus must

always be completed by the revelation of the divine life in all these other realms" (*In Defense*, p. 19). Also relevant to Strauss's evaluation is that Jesus erred in his belief that he would return as the victorious Son of Man after his death.

[32]This is an important difference between Strauss and Schleiermacher. While Strauss believes the mythological should be transcended by a conceptual restatement of the essence of the Christian faith, Schleiermacher considers the symbols of the religious imagination a necessary part of religious expression that must be interpreted. This position is seen by Strauss as an unacceptable halfway measure that results in theological schizophrenia. "Schleiermacher, we can say, is a supernaturalist in Christology but in criticism and exegesis a rationalist" (*The Christ of Faith and the Jesus of History: A Critique of Schleiermacher's "The Life of Jesus,"* trans. Leander E. Keck [Philadelphia: Fortress, 1977], p. 160).

[33]*Life of Jesus*, #151, pp. 780-81.

[34]*Christ of Faith*, p. 162.

[35]Only later in his life does Strauss attempt to address the criticism that he had not accounted for the disciples' devotion. In an interesting move he adopted a position similar to the type he so often criticized his rationalist opponents for. Based on a desire to believe in the resurrection of Jesus from the dead, the disciples began to experience hallucinations in which they saw the risen Christ. See *A New Life of Jesus*, 2nd ed., 2 vols. (London: Williams & Norgate, 1879), 1:432.

[36]English translations of Baur's works include *Paul, The Apostle of Jesus Christ*, ed. Eduard Zeller and trans. Allan Menzies, 2 vols. (London: Williams & Norgate, 1875); *The Epochs of Church Historiography* and *Lectures on the History of Christian Dogma*. In *Ferdinand Christian Baur on the Writing of Church History*, ed. and trans. Peter C. Hodgson (New York: Oxford University Press, 1968); *The Church History of the First Three Centuries*, trans. Allan Menzies, 2 vols. (London: Williams & Norgate, 1878).

[37]Most of the secondary literature on F. C. Baur considers him in the context of the Tübingen School. See Horton Harris, *The Tübingen School: A Historical and Theological Investigation of the School of F. C. Baur* (Grand Rapids, Mich.: Baker, 1990); Peter C. Hodgson, *The Formation of Historical Theology: A Study of Ferdinand Christian Baur* (New York: Harper & Row, 1966). An older and generally favorable treatment of Baur, the Tübingen School and its forerunners is R. W. Mackay, *The Tübingen School and Its Antecedents* (London: Williams and Norgate, 1863). Frank Kaufmann, *Foundations of Modern Church History* (New York: Peter Lang, 1992) provides a comparison of Neander and Baur as the initiators of modern church historiography.

[38]In spite of early references that are critical of Hegel, the influence of the older scholar became increasingly clear as Baur's interests turned to church history in the latter part of his career. However, this can be stressed too much. Baur's early monism, inspired primarily by Schelling, is evident before he was introduced to Hegel's philosophy.

[39]While it is Baur's name that is generally associated with the Tübingen School, the member of the circle who was perhaps as instrumental in its establishment was Eduard Zeller, the founder and editor of *Theologishe Jahrbücher*. This journal was the primary vehicle by which the ideas of the Tübingen faculty were transmitted.

[40]"Lectures on the History of Christian Dogma," in *Ferdinand Christian Baur on the Writing of Church History*, ed. and trans. Peter C. Hodgson (New York: Oxford University Press, 1968), p. 362.

[41]*Lectures*, p. 354.

[42]*The Church History of the First Three Centuries*, trans. Allan Menzies, 2 vols. (London: Williams & Norgate, 1878), 1:39.

[43]"The Epochs of Church Historiography," in *Ferdinand Christian Baur on the Writing of*

Church History, p. 46.

[44]"Epochs," p. 212.

[45]"Lectures," p. 270-71.

[46]"Epochs," p. 167. The problem of subjectivism arises in a somewhat different way with Schleiermacher and his disciple, Neander, both of whom Baur categorizes as rationalists. If we follow their lead in analyzing church history in terms of the religious consciousness of individuals, we lose again the Spirit as the objective basis of history. By this method, we may know something of the believer's subjective experience but can know nothing of Christianity per se, whose content is objectively given in history, and so it collapses into subjectivism. Without the objective touchstone of the Spirit, Baur states, we will be unable to transcend our own religious consciousness and will therefore superimpose our subjectivity on the past.

[47]"Lectures," p. 261.

[48]In typical dialectical fashion, he argues that philosophy and theology must be balanced. The problem encountered in autonomous philosophy is the temptation to sever the bond between revelation and the Absolute, taking our consciousness to be the product of our own speculation, rather than something objectively given by the divine. On the other hand, for philosophical speculation to have the freedom it needs, its investigations cannot be determined beforehand by the assumptions of faith. The importance of these two disciplines relative to each other is also subject to dialectical movement. "Just as at an earlier time the history of dogma allowed the history of philosophy to be submerged within itself, and spirit movement could proceed only from a dogmatic interest, so now the reverse prevails, and the philosophical element so predominates in the history of the development of dogma that it is by and large the moving principle" ("Lectures," p. 334).

[49]"Lectures," p. 364.

[50]"Epochs," p. 241.

[51]"Epochs," p. 257.

[52]*Paul, The Apostle of Jesus Christ,* ed. Eduard Zeller and trans. Allan Menzies, 2 vols. (London: Williams and Norgate, 1875), 1:97.

[53]"Lectures," p. 275.

[54]"Lectures," p. 307.

[55]"Lectures," p. 298.

[56]"Lectures," pp. 297-98.

[57]"Lectures," p. 306.

[58]"Epochs," p. 48.

[59]Baur sees this as a gap in Strauss's historical method. While his former student incorporated literary criticism into his analysis of the Gospels, he failed to examine the theological biases of the various authors.

[60]*Church History,* 1:48. Baur expresses a similar idea in *Paul.* "With this [Jesus'] death everything that the Messiah might have been as a Jewish Messiah disappeared; through his death, Jesus, as the Messiah, had died to Judaism, had been removed beyond his national connexion with it, and placed in a freer, more universal, and purely spiritual sphere, where the absolute importance which Judaism had claimed [for Paul] then was at once obliterated" (*Paul,* 2:125).

[61]*Paul,* 2:128.

[62]*Church History,* 1:50. Baur's view of Christ's significance is summed up in his statement, "Christ is thus essentially man, the archetypal man in whom the higher principle of human nature appears" (*Paul,* 2:247). While the idea of Jesus as archetype sounds quite similar to Schleiermacher's view, there is a difference. For Schleiermacher, the arche-

type refers to Jesus' perfect sense of dependence on the Father. For Baur, Jesus is one who recognizes the ultimate unity of all things. He disputes the idea that Paul would be able to consider Christ coequal with God, however.

[63]"Epochs," p. 244.

[64]"Lectures," p. 300.

[65]"Lectures," p. 301.

[66]"Lectures," p. 304. A comparison of Baur's understanding of the significance of the Reformation and that of Johann Adam Möhler, the Church historian on the Catholic faculty at Tübingen, is found in Joseph Fitzer, *Moehler and Baur in Controversy, 1832-1838: Romantic-Idealist Assessment of the Reformation and Counter Reformation* (Tallahassee: American Academy of Religion, 1974). The difference in perspective is particularly interesting because Moehler, like Baur, was influenced by both Schleiermacher and Hegel.

[67]"Epochs," p. 241.

Chapter 6: Hegel Inverted

[1]Works of Feuerbach in English are *The Essence of Christianity*, trans. George Eliot (New York: Harper, 1957); *Lectures on the Essence of Religion*, trans. Ralph Manheim (New York: Harper & Row, 1967); *Principles of the Philosophy of the Future*, trans. Manfred H. Vogel (Indianapolis: Hackett, 1986); *The Fiery Brook: Selected Writings of Ludwig Feuerbach*, trans. Zawar Hanfi (Garden City, N.J.: Anchor, 1972); *Thoughts on Death and Immortality*, trans. James Massey (Berkeley: University of California, 1980). Since Feuerbach's philosophy is most often viewed as a prologue to Marx's thought, there have been few works devoted specifically to an examination of his views. However, see Van A. Harvey, *Feuerbach and the Interpretation of Religion* (Cambridge: Cambridge University Press, 1995); Eugene Kamenka, *The Philosophy of Ludwig Feuerbach* (New York: Praeger, 1970); Marx W. Wartofsky, *Feuerbach* (Cambridge: Cambridge University Press, 1977); William B. Chamberlain, *Heaven Wasn't His Destination* (New York: Norton, 1941); Van A. Harvey, "Ludwig Feuerbach and Karl Marx," in *Nineteenth Century Religious Thought in the West*, ed. Ninian Smart, vol. 1 (Cambridge: Cambridge University Press, 1985).

[2]Feuerbach sent a copy of his dissertation to Hegel with a less-than-humble letter arguing that Christianity encourages selfishness and that belief in immortality is the chief manifestation of this egoism. In place of this, philosophy needs to recognize our connection with nature. The underlying message, which Feuerbach later develops, is that Hegel's philosophy, which sunders the rational from the natural, does not allow us to get beyond subjectivism. A study of this theme in Feuerbach's early writings is Charles A. Wilson, *Feuerbach and the Search for Otherness* (New York: Peter Lang, 1989).

[3]Although *Thoughts on Death and Immortality* was published anonymously, Feuerbach was recognized as the author.

[4]Although he was urged by Arnold Ruge and Karl Marx to assume editorship of the influential *Hallische Jahrbücher*, at this time the literary organ of the political left, he greatly enjoyed his solitude and remained out of the limelight.

[5]See, for example, Friedrich Engels, *Ludwig Feuerbach and the Outcome of Classical German Philosophy*, trans. L. Rudas (New York: International, 1981); and Friedrich Engels, *Feuerbach: The Roots of Socialist Philosophy*, trans. Austin Lewis (Chicago: Charles H. Kerr, 1912).

[6]*Lectures on the Essence of Religion*, trans. Ralph Manheim (New York: Harper & Row, 1967), p. 187.

[7]This is also the essence of Feuerbach's criticism of Schleiermacher's anthropological beginning point for theology. If we take religious experience to be the proper point of departure, how are we to determine the source of this experience? To attribute our experiences to a nonhuman object is a category mistake. We cannot work from human experi-

ence to the divine.

[8]*Principles of the Philosophy of the Future,* trans. Manfred H. Vogel (Indianapolis: Hackett, 1986), #1, p. 5.

[9]*Essence,* p. 1.

[10]*Essence,* p. 2.

[11]*Essence,* p. 159.

[12]*Essence,* p. 3.

[13]*Principles,* #60, p. 71.

[14]*Essence,* p. 153.

[15]*Lectures,* p. 187.

[16]*Lectures,* p. 200.

[17]*Essence,* p. 50.

[18]*Thoughts on Death and Immortality,* trans. James Massey (Berkeley: University of California, 1980), p. 12.

[19]*Thoughts on Death,* pp. 18-19.

[20]*Lectures,* p. 274.

[21]*Essence,* p. 65.

[22]*Principles,* #63, p. 72. In *Essence,* chapter six, Feuerbach gives a more complete analysis of the role of the Trinity. The "I" of the Father requires the "Thou" of the Son. The Holy Spirit is not a person but the bond of love between Father and Son.

[23]*Essence,* p. 14.

[24]*Essence,* p. 13.

[25]*Essence,* p. 20.

[26]*Lectures,* pp. 17-18. The same dialectical energy that moves us from religion to philosophy and then to atheism is at work within each stage as well. In the religious epoch, polytheism precedes monotheism in the development of religion because it reflects an earlier stage of awareness. In times past we were more directly connected with nature and divinized the creatures and natural forces we relied on for continued existence. However, monotheism gradually emerges and puts the forces of the physical order under a single God. Feuerbach understands this as an advance because, in it, we bow down before what is universal in humanity, represented by a single God rather than a multiplicity of divine entities.

[27]*Principles,* #17, p. 30.

[28]"Preliminary Theses," in *The Fiery Brook: Selected Writings of Ludwig Feuerbach,* trans. Zawar Hanfi (Garden City, N.J.: Anchor, 1972), p. 156.

[29]*Lectures,* p. 281.

[30]*Essence,* p. 26.

[31]*Lectures,* p. 282.

[32]*Principles,* #43, p. 60.

[33]*Lectures,* p. 257-58.

[34]"The Necessity of the Reform of Philosophy," in *The Fiery Brook: Selected Writings of Ludwig Feuerbach,* trans. Zawar Hanfi (Garden City, N.J.: Anchor, 1972), p. 148.

[35]"Reform of Philosophy," p. 149.

[36]*Essence,* p. 271.

[37]*Lectures,* pp. 284-85.

[38]Frederick Copleston, *A History of Philosophy,* vol. 7/2, *Modern Philosophy,* p. 67.

[39]Frederick Engels, *Ludwig Feuerbach and the Outcome of Classical German Philosophy,* trans. L. Rudas (1934; reprint, New York: AMS, n.d.), p. 28.

[40]See chapter six in *Essence* for his analysis of the virgin birth.

[41]A collection of Marx's and Engels's works and letters is currently in progress, with 43 vol-

umes currently in publication. See *Karl Marx, Frederick Engels: Collected Works,* trans. Richard Dixon et al., (New York: International, 1975-1995). For individual volumes of Marx's works (including some written with Engels), see *Capital: A Critique of Political Economy,* ed. Frederick Engels, trans. Samuel Moore and Edward Aveling (New York: Kerr, 1906); *The German Ideology,* trans. S. Ryazanskaya (Moscow: Progress Publishers, 1968); *A Contribution to the Critique of Political Economy,* trans. N. I. Stone (Chicago: Kerr, 1904); *The Holy Family,* trans. R. Dixon (Moscow: Foreign Languages Publishing House, 1956). Many of Marx's most significant works are found in collections, and a number of such anthologies exist. Helpful editions are *Karl Marx and Frederick Engels: Selected Works,* 2 vols. (Moscow: Foreign Languages Publishing House, 1958); *Karl Marx: Selected Writings,* ed. David McLellan (Oxford: Oxford University Press, 1977); *Writings of the Young Marx on Philosophy and Society,* ed. and trans. Loyd Easton and Kurt H. Guddat (Garden City, N.J.: Doubleday, 1967); and *Karl Marx: Early Writings,* ed. and trans. T. B. Bottomore (New York: McGraw-Hill, 1964). A mountain of research has been done on the works of Marx, and it is impossible to touch on more than a few of the secondary sources. A good overview is David McLellan, *The Thought of Karl Marx: An Introduction* (New York: Harper & Row, 1971). Saul Padover, *Karl Marx: An Intimate Biography* (New York: McGraw-Hill, 1978); Werner Blumenberg, *Karl Marx: An Illustrated Biography,* trans. Douglas Scott (New York: Herder & Herder, 1972); and David McLellan, *Karl Marx: His Life and Thought* (New York: Harper & Row, 1973) offer treatments of Marx's life. Secondary sources on specific topics include Shlomo Avineri, *The Social and Political Thought of Karl Marx* (Cambridge: Cambridge University Press, 1968); Bertell Ollman, *Alienation: Marx's Conception of Man in Capitalist Society,* 2nd ed. (Cambridge: Cambridge University Press, 1971); John Plamenatz, *Karl Marx's Philosophy of Man* (Oxford: Clarendon Press, 1975); Louis K. Dupre, *The Philosophical Foundations of Marxism* (New York: Harcourt Brace & World, 1966); Henri Lefebvre, *The Sociology of Marx,* trans. Norbert Guterman (London: Penguin, 1968).

[42]For the text of the letter, see *Writings of the Young Marx on Philosophy and Society,* ed. and trans. Loyd Easton and Kurt H. Guddat (Garden City, N.J.: Doubleday, 1967), pp. 40-50.

[43]It is often wrongly assumed that communism originates in the works of Marx and Lenin. While they did give modern communism its current intellectual underpinnings, communistic theories and proponents were present in every Western European country at this time.

[44]*The German Ideology,* trans. S. Ryazanskaya (Moscow: Progress Publishers, 1968), p. 32.

[45]"Economic and Philosophical Manuscripts," in *Karl Marx: Early Writings,* 1:128.

[46]"Economic and Philosophical Manuscripts," 1:127.

[47]*Communist Manifesto,* in *Karl Marx and Frederick Engels: Selected Works,* 2 vols. (Moscow: Foreign Languages Publishing House, 1958), 1:46.

[48]*Theses on Feuerbach* 11, in *Karl Marx: Selected Writings,* ed. David McLellan (Oxford: Oxford University Press, 1977), 2:405.

[49]*Capital: A Critique of Political Economy,* ed. Frederick Engels, trans. Samuel Moore and Edward Aveling (New York: Kerr, 1906), p. 25.

[50]*Capital,* p. 25.

[51]*Theses on Feuerbach* 6, 2:404. It seems clear that Feuerbach is in view when Marx states elsewhere that, "It is above all necessary to avoid postulating 'society' once again as an abstraction confronting the individual. The individual *is the social being*" ("Economic and Philosophical Manuscripts," 3:158).

[52]Marx himself did not use this phrase (it belongs to Engels) but instead refers to his approach as naturalism. However, dialectical materialism is a more precise description of his method.

[53]*German Ideology,* in *The Marx-Engels Reader,* ed. Robert Tucker, 2nd ed. (New York: Norton,

1978), pp. 155-56.

[54]"Economic and Philosophical Manuscripts," 3:164.

[55]*Communist Manifesto,* 1:34.

[56]*Communist Manifesto,* 1:52.

[57]*A Contribution to the Critique of Political Economy,* trans. N. I. Stone (Chicago: Kerr, 1904), pp. 11-12.

[58]For a compilation of Marx and Engels's writings on religious matters see *Karl Marx and Friedrich Engels: On Religion,* ed. Reinhold Niebuhr (New York: Schocken, 1964.)

[59]"Contribution to the Critique of Hegel's Philosophy of Right," in *Karl Marx: Early Writings,* ed. and trans. T. B. Bottomore (New York: McGraw-Hill, 1964), p. 43.

[60]"Contribution to the Critique of Hegel's Philosophy," pp. 43-44.

[61]*Capital,* pp. 91-92.

[62]"Contribution to the Critique of Hegel's Philosophy," p. 44.

[63]"Economic and Philosophical Manuscripts," 3:156.

[64]*Communist Manifesto,* in *Selected Works,* 1:34.

[65]"Economic and Philosophical Manuscripts," 3:191.

[66]"Economic and Philosophical Manuscripts," 3:192.

[67]"Economic and Philosophical Manuscripts," 1:122.

[68]*Capital,* p. 470.

[69]"Economic and Philosophical Manuscripts," 1:121.

[70]*Capital,* p. 470.

[71]"Economic and Philosophical Manuscripts," 1:122.

[72]"Economic and Philosophical Manuscripts," 1:123.

[73]"Economic and Philosophical Manuscripts," 1:124-25.

[74]"Economic and Philosophical Manuscripts," 1:129.

[75]"Economic and Philosophical Manuscripts," 3:178.

[76]*Communist Manifesto,* 1:42.

[77]*Communist Manifesto,* 1:45.

[78]*Communist Manifesto,* 1:65.

[79]*Communist Manifesto,* 1:44.

[80]*Communist Manifesto,* 1:47. Again it is unclear whether the abolition of private property is the result of a new awareness of the labor class or its cause. Marx argues that, since the bourgeoisie are not as firmly entrenched in some countries as others, the coming revolution may not occur as soon in nonindustrialized regions. However, Marx argues that, "The country that is more developed industrially only shows, to the less developed, the image of its own future" (*Capital,* p. 13). He is not of one mind on this matter, however. In places, he seems to believe that industrialization must reach a certain level of development before the proletariat rebels. At other times he speculates that some less-developed regions may skip over full-blown capitalism altogether and move directly to communism.

[81]*German Ideology,* p. 45.

[82]Bertrand Russell, *A History of Western Philosophy* (New York: Simon & Schuster, 1945), pp. 788-89.

Chapter 7: Rebellion Against Rationality

[1]Primary sources of Schopenhauer in English translation are *The World as Will and Idea,* trans. E. F. J. Payne, 2 vols. (New York: Dover, 1958); *Manuscript Remains in Four Volumes,* ed. Arthur Hubscher and E. F. J. Payne (New York: St. Martin's Press, 1988); *On the Four-fold Root of the Principle of Sufficient Reason,* trans. E. F. J. Payne (LaSalle, Ill.: Open Court, 1974); *On Vision and Colors,* trans. E. F. J. Payne and David E. Cartwright (Providence, R.I.:

Berg, 1994); *On the Will in Nature* (New York: St. Martin's Press, 1992); *Parerga and Paralipomena,* trans. E. F. J. Payne (Oxford: Clarendon, 1974); *The Art of Controversy, and Other Posthumous Papers,* trans. T. Bailey Saunders (London: G. Allen & Unwin, 1921); *The Art of Literature,* trans. T. Bailey Saunders (New York: Macmillan, 1915); *On the Basis of Morality,* trans. E. F. J. Payne (Indianapolis: Bobbs-Merrill, 1965); *Counsels and Maxims,* trans. T. Bailey Saunders (New York: Macmillan, 1899); *Essay on the Freedom of the Will,* trans. Konstantin Kolenda (New York: Blackwell, 1985); *Religion: A Dialogue, and Other Essays,* trans. T. Bailey Saunders (New York: Books for Libraries Press, 1972). There are a number of compilations of essays and selections from Schopenhauer's work available, including *The Pessimist's Handbook,* trans. T. Bailey Saunders (Lincoln: University of Nebraska, 1964); *The Will to Live: Selected Writings,* trans. Richard Taylor (Garden City, N.J.: Doubleday, 1962); *The Wisdom of Life, and Other Essays,* trans. T. Bailey Saunders and Ernest Belfort Bax (New York & London: M. W. Dunne, 1901); *Works,* trans. Will Durant (New York: F. Ungar, 1955); *Complete Essays of Schopenhauer,* trans. T. Bailey Saunders (New York, Willey, 1942); *Essays and Aphorisms,* trans. R. J. Hollingdale (London: Penguin, 1970); *The Essential Schopenhauer* (New York: Barnes & Noble, 1962); *The Living Thoughts of Schopenhauer,* trans. Thomas Mann (Philadelphia: D. McKay, 1939); *On Human Nature: Essays (Partly Posthumous) in Ethics and Politics,* trans. T. Bailey Saunders (New York: Macmillan, 1897); *Philosophical Writings,* trans. Wolfgang Schirmacher (New York: Continuum, 1994). Older biographies of Schopenhauer are William Wallace, *Life of Schopenhauer* (London: W. Scott, 1890); Helen Zimmern, *Schopenhauer: His Life and Philosophy* (London: Allen & Unwin, 1932); and Margrieta Beer, *Schopenhauer* (New York: Dodge, 1914). A newer text that puts Schopenhauer's life in the broader context of his age is Rüdiger Safranski, *Schopenhauer and the Wild Years of Philosophy,* trans. Ewald Osers (Cambridge, Mass: Harvard University Press, 1990). A nice brief introduction to Schopenhauer is Christopher Janaway, *Schopenhauer* (Oxford: Oxford University Press, 1994). Other general texts on Schopenhauer's thought are Patrick Gardiner, *Schopenhauer* (Baltimore: Penguin, 1971); D. W. Hamlyn, *Schopenhauer* (London: Routledge & Kegan Paul, 1980); Frederick Copleston, *Arthur Schopenhauer* (New York: Barnes & Noble, 1975); Arthur Hübscher, *The Philosophy of Schopenhauer in Its Intellectual Context: Thinker Against the Tide,* trans. Joachim T. Baer and David E. Cartwright (Lewiston, N.Y.: Mellen, 1989); Bryan Magee, *The Philosophy of Schopenhauer* (Oxford: Clarendon Press, 1983); Christopher Janaway, *Self and World in Schopenhauer's Philosophy* (Oxford: Clarendon, 1989); John E. Atwell, *Schopenhauer: The Human Character* (Philadelphia: Temple University Press, 1990); John E. Atwell, *Schopenhauer on the Character of the World* (Berkeley: University of California Press, 1995).

[2]"Criticism of the Kantian Philosopher," *World as Will and Idea,* 1:429.

[3]*World as Will,* #1, 1:3. I have used here the translation of *Vorstellung* as "idea" since this is the traditional rendering. However, the edition of the text used here actually translates *Vorstellung* as "representation," which is less misleading.

[4]*World as Will,* #1, 1:3.

[5]"On Death and Its Relation to the Indestructibility of Our Inner Nature," *World as Will and Idea,* 2:495.

[6]*World as Will,* #21, 1:110.

[7]"True philosophy must at all costs be idealistic; indeed, it must be so merely to be honest. For nothing is more certain than that no one ever came out of himself in order to identify himself immediately with things different from him; but everything of which he has certain, sure, and hence immediate knowledge, lies within his consciousness." See "On the Fundamental View of Idealism," *World as Will,* 2:4.

[8]*World as Will,* #25, 1:127.

[9]"On Death," p. 493.

[10]*World as Will,* #21, 1:110.

[11]*World as Will,* #28, 1:156.

[12]"On the Vanity and Suffering of Life," *World as Will,* 2:581.

[13]"Characterization of the Will-to-Live," *World as Will,* 2:377.

[14]*World as Will,* #54, 1:275.

[15]*World as Will,* #57, 1:312.

[16]*World as Will,* #57, 1:313-14.

[17]*World as Will,* #58, 1:319.

[18]"On the Vanity," 2:583.

[19]For a more extensive treatment of this subject, see B. V. Kishan, *Schopenhauer's Conception of Salvation* (Andhra: Andhra University Press, 1978.)

[20]*World as Will,* #36, 1:185.

[21]*World as Will,* #68, 1:378-9.

[22]*World as Will,* #38, 1:198.

[23]*World as Will,* #58, 1:320.

[24]*World as Will,* #59, 1:325.

[25]In spite of this view of death Schopenhauer rejects suicide. Suicide is not an escape from the will to live but capitulation to it. "Far from being denial of the will, suicide is a phenomenon of the will's strong affirmation. For denial has its essential nature in the fact that the pleasures of life, not its sorrow, are shunned. The suicide wills life, and is dissatisfied merely with the conditions on which it has come to him. Therefore he gives up by no means the will-to-live, but merely life, since he destroys the individual phenomenon" (*World as Will,* #69, p. 398).

[26]"On Death," p. 507. One apparent contradiction that Schopenhauer does not adequately address is how, given that we *are* the will to live, we can deny the will to live.

[27]Schopenhauer's argument for immortality is a modification of Plato's. Plato argues that since the soul is the principle of life, by definition it is immortal. It is contradictory to speak of the death of the principle of life. For Schopenhauer, Plato is wrong in the failure to recognize that the soul itself is merely a phenomenon, a concrete manifestation of the will to live. However, the will to live is existence itself and by definition cannot not exist. "Consequently, everyone has to conceive himself as a necessary being, in other words, as a being whose existence would follow from its true and exhaustive definition" ("On Death," p. 489).

[28]*World as Will,* #71, 1:411.

[29]*World as Will,* #71, 1:412.

[30]*World as Will,* #68, 1:389.

[31]"Man's Need for Metaphysics," *World as Will,* 2:161.

[32]"On Death," p. 463.

[33]"Man's Need," p. 167.

[34]"Man's Need," p. 165.

[35]"The Road to Salvation,"*World as Will,* 2:634.

[36]"On the Vanity," p. 584.

[37]"Man's Need," p. 170.

[38]"On the Doctrine of the Denial of the Will-to-Life,"*World as Will,* 2:625.

[39]*World as Will,* #63, 1:355.

[40]*World as Will,* #70, 1:405.

[41]Princeton University Press has been publishing new translations of Kierkegaard's works, and many cited below are products of that effort. Major works include *Concluding Unscien-*

tific Postscript to Philosophical Fragments, ed. and trans. Howard V. Hong and Edna H.
Hong (Princeton, N.J.: Princeton University Press, 1992); *Fear and Trembling,* trans.
Alastair Hannay (New York: Penguin, 1985); *The Point of View, etc., Including The Point of
View for My Work as an Author, Two Notes about 'The Individual' and On My Work as an
Author,* trans. Walter Lowrie (London: Oxford University Press, 1939); *Kierkegaard's
Attack upon "Christendom,"* trans. Walter Lowrie (Princeton, N.J.: Princeton University
Press, 1968); *Philosophical Fragments,* ed. and trans. Howard V. Hong and Edna H. Hong
(Princeton, N.J.: Princeton University Press, 1985); *Either/Or,* trans. David F. Swenson
and Lillian Marvin Swenson (Princeton, N.J.: Princeton University Press, 1971); *The
Sickness unto Death: A Christian Psychological Exposition for Upbuilding and Awakening,* ed.
and trans. Howard V. Hong and Edna H. Hong (Princeton, N.J.: Princeton University
Press, 1980); *The Concept of Dread,* trans. Walter Lowrie, 2d ed. (Princeton, N.J.: Princeton University Press, 1957); *Works of Love,* ed. and trans. Howard V. Hong and Edna H.
Hong (Princeton, N.J.: Princeton University Press, 1995); *The Concept of Irony, with Constant Reference to Socrates,* trans. Lee M. Capel (Bloomington: Indiana University Press,
1965); *Eighteen Upbuilding Discourses,* ed. and trans. Howard V. Hong and Edna H. Hong
(Princeton, N.J.: Princeton University Press, 1990); *For Self-Examination: Judge for Yourself*
ed. and trans. Howard V. Hong and Edna H. Hong (Princeton, N.J.: Princeton Univer-
sity Press, 1990); *Repetition: An Essay in Experimental Psychology,* trans. Walter Lowrie
(Princeton, N.J.: Princeton University Press, 1941); *Stages on Life's Way: Studies by Various
Persons,* ed. and trans. Howard V. Hong and Edna H. Hong (Princeton, N.J.: Princeton
University Press, 1988); *Training in Christianity,* trans. Walter Lowrie (Princeton, N.J.:
Princeton University Press, 1944). Of interest also is *Søren Kierkegaard's Journals and
Papers,* ed. and trans. Howard V. Hong and Edna H. Hong, 7 vols. (Bloomington: Indi-
ana University Press, 1967-1978). A shorter version with selections from Kierkegaard's
journals is *Journals,* trans. Alexander Dru (New York: Harper & Row, 1959). For selections of Kierkegaard's writings, see *A Kierkegaard Anthology,* trans. Robert Bretall (Princeton, N.J.: Princeton University Press, 1951); and *A Kierkegaard Reader: Texts and
Narratives,* trans. Roger Poole and Henrik Stangerup (London: Fourth Estate, 1989). An
interesting volume that compiles a number of Kierkegaard's thought-provoking parables is *Parables of Kierkegaard,* trans. Thomas C. Oden and illus. Lonni Sue Johnson
(Princeton, N.J.: Princeton University Press, 1978). The amount of material written
about Kierkegaard in recent years has been enormous, and a number of good studies
exist in his thought. See Louis P. Pojman, *The Logic of Subjectivity: Kierkegaard's Philosophy of Religion* (University: University of Alabama Press, 1984); C. Stephen Evans, *Passionate Reason: Making Sense of Kierkegaard's Philosophical Fragments* (Bloomington:
Indiana University Press, 1992); Merold Westphal, *Becoming a Self: A Reading of Kierkegaard's Concluding Unscientific Postscript* (Lafayette, Ind.: Purdue University Press, 1996);
John W. Elrod, *Kierkegaard and Christendom* (Princeton, N.J.: Princeton University Press,
1981); George J. Stack, *Kierkegaard's Existential Ethics,* (University: University of Alabama
Press, 1977); Josiah Thompson, ed., *Kierkegaard: A Collection of Critical Essays* (Garden
City, N.J.: Doubleday Anchor, 1972); James Daniel Collins *The Mind of Kierkegaard* (Chi-
cago: Henry Regnery, 1953); Paul L. Holmer, *The Grammar of Faith* (San Francisco:
Harper & Row, 1978).

[42]*Journals,* trans. Alexander Dru (New York: Harper & Row, 1959), p. 96.

[43]*Point of View,* p. 76.

[44]*Point of View,* p. 76.

[45]*Journals,* pp. 50-51.

[46]Criticism of Christendom is a common feature of Kierkegaard's writings throughout his
career. However, out of respect for his father's friendship with Bishop Mynster, head of

the Danish Lutheran Church, he was somewhat restrained in his attacks until after the bishop's death. After this, Kierkegaard mounted a full-out assault that continued unabated for the last two years of his life. A study of Kierkegaard's writings during this period is available in John W. Elrod, *Kierkegaard and Christendom* (Princeton, N.J.: Princeton University Press, 1981).

[47]*Journals*, p. 53.

[48]*Kierkegaard's Attack upon "Christendom,"* trans. Walter Lowrie (Princeton, N.J.: Princeton University Press, 1968), p. 164. Kierkegaard goes on to ridicule the enculturation of Christianity by noting that, while Christianity desires chastity, the Danish Lutheran Church "christianizes" prostitution in its requirement that brothels be owned only by Christians.

[49]*Concluding Unscientific Postscript*, p. 23.

[50]*Point of View*, p. 24.

[51]There is considerable debate about the extent to which the pseudonymous works of Kierkegaard reflect his position. Much of the problem arises from statements like the following: "So in the pseudonymous works there is not a single word which is mine, I have no opinion about these works except as third person, no knowledge of their meaning except as a reader, not the remotest private relation to them, since such a thing is impossible in the case of a doubly reflected communication" ("A First and Last Declaration," *Concluding Unscientific Postscript*, p. 551). However, while the pseudonymous "authors" of Kierkegaard's works do not fully express his concept of Christianity, they reveal his understanding of existence within various perspectives on life.

[52]*Sickness Unto Death*, pp. 176-77.

[53]*Journals*, p. 44.

[54]*Philosophical Fragments*, ed. and trans. Howard V. Hong and Edna H. Hong (Princeton, N.J.: Princeton University Press, 1985), p. 91 n.

[55]*Concluding Unscientific Postscript*, p. 79.

[56]*Concluding Unscientific Postscript*, p. 85.

[57]*Either/Or*, trans. David F. Swenson and Lillian Marvin Swenson (Princeton, N.J.: Princeton University Press, 1971), p. 171.

[58]*Sickness Unto Death*, p. 191.

[59]*Either/Or*, p. 163.

[60]*Concluding Unscientific Postscript*, p. 412.

[61]*Fear and Trembling*, p. 83. Because of the centrality of *Fear and Trembling* in Kierkegaard's writings, the reader may want to consult R. L. Perkins, trans., *Kierkegaard's "Fear and Trembling": Critical Appraisals* (Birmingham: University of Alabama, 1981).

[62]*Concluding Unscientific Postscript*, p. 51.

[63]*Concluding Unscientific Postscript*, p. 182.

[64]*Fear and Trembling*, p. 96.

[65]*Fear and Trembling*, p. 139.

[66]*Fear and Trembling*, pp. 87-88.

[67]*Fear and Trembling*, p. 72.

[68]*Fear and Trembling*, 55.

[69]*Fear and Trembling*, p. 60.

[70]It is for this reason that Kierkegaard rejects attempts to prove God's existence. "Faith does not need it [proof]: aye, it must even regard the proof as its enemy. But when faith begins to feel embarrassed and ashamed, like a young woman for whom her love is no longer sufficient, but who secretly feels ashamed of her lover and must therefore have it established that there is something remarkable about him—when faith thus begins to lose its passion, when faith begins to cease to be faith, then a proof becomes necessary so as to command respect from the side of unbelief" (*Concluding Unscientific Postscript*, p. 31).

[71]*Concluding Unscientific Postscript,* p. 178.

[72]*Concluding Unscientific Postscript,* p. 187. For a thorough examination of Kierkegaard's understanding of subjectivity as truth, see Louis P. Pojman, *The Logic of Subjectivity: Kierkegaard's Philosophy of Religion* (University: University of Alabama Press, 1984).

[73]A useful article for evaluating Kierkegaard's view of objective knowledge is Robert Adams's, "Kierkegaard's Argument against Objective Reasoning in Religion," in *The Virtue of Faith and Other Essays in Philosophical Theology* (New York: Oxford University Press, 1987).

[74]*Concluding Unscientific Postscript,* p. 188.

[75]Kierkegaard's language about the absurdity of Christianity should not be understood as meaning that it is per se irrational. Instead the absurdity is the result of human limitation. As he tells us, "An existential system cannot be formulated. Does this mean that no such system exists? By no means; nor is this implied in our assertion. Reality itself is a system— for God; but it cannot be a system for any existing spirit" (*Concluding Unscientific Postscript,* p. 107).

[76]*Sickness Unto Death,* p. 213.

[77]"But the highest passion in a human being is faith, and here no generation begins other than where its predecessor did, every generation begins from the beginning, the succeeding generation comes no further than the previous one, providing the latter was true to its task and didn't betray it" (*Fear and Trembling,* pp. 145-46).

[78]*Fear and Trembling,* p. 102.

[79]The full works of Nietzsche are available in a complete collection, but the translations are notoriously unreliable. See *The Complete Works of Friedrich Nietzsche,* ed. and trans. Oscar Levy (New York: Russell & Russell, 1964). Major writings of Nietzsche include *Beyond Good and Evil,* trans. R. J. Hollingdale (Harmondsworth: Penguin, 1972); *The Birth of Tragedy* and *The Genealogy of Morals,* trans. Francis Golffing (Garden City, N.J.: Doubleday, 1956); *The Will to Power,* trans. Walter Kaufmann and R. J. Hollingdale (New York: Vintage, 1968); *Twilight of the Idols* and *The Anti-Christ,* trans. R. J. Hollingdale (London: Penguin, 1990); *Thus Spoke Zarathustra,* trans. R. J. Hollingdale (London: Penguin, 1961); *The Gay Science,* trans. Walter Kaufmann (New York: Random House, 1974); *Human, All Too Human,* trans. Marion Faber and Stephen Lehmann (Lincoln: University of Nebraska Press, 1984). Useful anthologies are *Basic Writings of Nietzsche,* trans. Walter Kaufmann (New York: Modern Library, 1968); *A Nietzsche Reader,* trans. R. J. Hollingdale (New York: Penguin, 1977); and the immensely popular *The Portable Nietzsche,* trans. Walter Kaufmann (New York: Viking Press, 1954). A sampling of Nietzsche's correspondence is found in *Selected Letters of Friedrich Nietzsche,* trans. Christopher Middleton (Chicago: University of Chicago Press, 1969). Helpful sources on Nietzsche's philosophy are Bernd Magnus and Kathleen M. Higgins, eds., *The Cambridge Companion to Nietzsche* (Cambridge: Cambridge University Press, 1996); Frederick Charles Copleston, *Friedrich Nietzsche: Philosopher of Culture* (New York: Barnes & Noble Books, 1975); Walter Arnold Kaufmann, *Nietzsche: Philosopher, Psychologist, Antichrist* (Princeton, N.J.: Princeton University Press, 1950); John T. Wilcox, *Truth and Value in Nietzsche: A Study of His Metaethics and Epistemology* (Ann Arbor: University of Michigan Press, 1974); Arthur Coleman Danto, *Nietzsche as Philosopher* (New York: Columbia University Press, 1980); Robert John Ackermann, *Nietzsche: A Frenzied Look* (Amherst: University of Massachusetts Press, 1990). A short biography is supplied by Gerald Abraham, *Nietzsche* (New York: Macmillan, 1933).

[80]For the text of this letter of recommendation from Ritschl, see Walter Kaufmann, *The Portable Nietzsche* (New York: Viking Press, 1968), pp. 7-8.

[81]T. V. Morris, *The Bluffer's Guide to Philosophy* (South Bend, Ind.: Diamond Communica-

tions, 1989), p. 64.

[82]Following Nietzsche's collapse his sister gained custody of his unpublished works and notebooks and turned his writings into a personal business. This held two advantages to her. First, small portions of previously unpublished works were bound with already released writings of Nietzsche, forcing readers to purchase an entire collection to obtain a small portion of new material. Second, it allowed her unassailable claim as the authoritative interpreter of her brother's thought since only she had access to the entire corpus of his work.

[83]"Maxims and Arrows" 26, *Twilight of the Idols,* p. 35.

[84]"Expeditions of an Untimely Man" 21, *Twilight of the Idols,* p. 89.

[85]"Expeditions" 14, p. 85.

[86]*Beyond Good and Evil* 9, #259.

[87]*Genealogy of Morals* 2/12.

[88]*Anti-Christ* 7, p. 128.

[89]*Anti-Christ* 7, p. 129.

[90]" 'Reason' in Philosophy" 2, *Twilight of the Idols,* p. 46. Heraclitus was a presocratic Greek philosopher credited with the statement that "we never step into the same river twice." Reality is dynamic. Thus it is not objects (being) but processes (becoming) that form the foundation of reality.

[91]"How the 'Real World' at last Became a Myth" 5, *Twilight of the Idols,* p. 50.

[92]*The Will to Power,* trans. Walter Kaufmann and R. J. Hollingdale, (New York: Vintage, 1968), #521, pp. 282-83.

[93]*Genealogy* 3/24. While there is some material in Nietzsche's early writings that might lead us to classify him as an empiricist, this disappears in later writing. There are also points in his work when Nietzsche seems to take an existential approach to metaphysics, allowing for the possibility of some metaphysical reality behind nature, but he dismisses it as irrelevant. "It is true, there might be a metaphysical world; one can hardly dispute the absolute possibility of it. . . . but we cannot begin to do anything with it, let alone allow our happiness, salvation, and life to depend on the spider webs of such a possibility. For there is nothing at all we could state the metaphysical world except its differentness, a differentness inaccessible and incomprehensible to us. It would be a thing with negative qualities. No matter how well proven the existence of such a world might be, it would still hold true that the knowledge of it would be the most inconsequential of all knowledge" (*Human, All Too Human* #9, p. 18).

[94]Although Nietzsche had earlier entertained the possibility that art and tragedy might provide access into Kant's noumenal world, all vestiges of this early romanticism disappeared by the time Nietzsche wrote *Human, All Too Human.* The arts do not provide access to the transcendent truth we desire, for they are themselves "human, all too human."

[95]"Expeditions of an Untimely Man" 19, p. 88.

[96]*Genealogy* 2/12, p. 209.

[97]*The Gay Science,* trans. Walter Kaufmann (New York: Random House, 1974), #125, p. 181.

[98]*Anti-Christ* 47, pp. 172-73.

[99]"Why I Am so Clever" 1, *Ecce Homo,* in *Basic Writings of Nietzsche,* trans. Walter Kaufmann (New York: Modern Library, 1968), p. 692.

[100]*Beyond Good and Evil* 3, #46.

[101]"Why I Am so Clever" 1, pp. 692-93.

[102]"The Four Great Errors" 8, *Twilight of the Idols,* p. 64.

[103]*Beyond Good and Evil* 9, #260.

[104]*Beyond Good and Evil* 9, #261.

[105]*Beyond Good and Evil* 9, #257.

[106]*Beyond Good and Evil* 9, #260.

[107]*Beyond Good and Evil* 9, #260.

[108]*Genealogy* 1/2, p. 160.

[109]According to Nietzsche, this is also the basis of asceticism. By means of the suffering experienced in ascetic practices, we fix certain ideas into the intellect and our nervous system. See *Genealogy* 2/3.

[110]*Genealogy* 2/6, p. 198.

[111]*Genealogy* 2/22, pp. 225-26.

[112]"Of the Priests," *Thus Spoke Zarathustra* 2, p. 115. Nietzsche argues that the idea of the divine is not destructive of human nature in itself. He asserts that the gods of ancient Greece reflected true nobility. Our shortcomings are viewed by these gods as foolishness, not sin. Moreover, these gods are sources of our deeds and misfortunes. They reflect human nature and thus allow us to keep bad conscience at arm's length. See *Genealogy* 2/23.

[113]*Beyond Good and Evil* 5, #201.

[114]*Anti-Christ* 5, p. 126.

[115]*Anti-Christ* 51, p. 178.

[116]*Genealogy* 1/7, p. 167.

[117]*Anti-Christ* 26, p. 148.

[118]*Anti-Christ* 26, pp. 148-49.

[119]*Anti-Christ* 51, p. 177.

[120]*Genealogy* 1/10, p. 110.

[121]*Genealogy* 1/10, p. 110.

[122]"Skirmishes" 37, *Twilight of the Idols,* p. 540. Nietzsche elsewhere links the idea of equal rights and immortality. Both grant to all what should be limited only to the strong. See *Antichrist* 43, p. 619.

[123]*Genealogy* 3/24, p. 287.

[124]"Of the Higher Man," *Thus Spoke Zarathustra,* 4:298.

[125]"Of the Spirit of Gravity," *Thus Spoke Zarathustra,* 3:210.

[126]"Of the Higher Man," 4:297.

[127]"Zarathustra's Prologue" *Thus Spoke Zarathustra,* 1:41-42.

[128]"The time for petty politics is past: the very next century will bring with it the struggle for mastery over the whole earth—the *compulsion* to grand politics" (*Beyond Good and Evil* 6, 208).

Chapter 8: A Rational Society

[1]For a sampling of Saint-Simon's ideas see Henri de Saint-Simon, *Social Organization, The Science of Man and Other Writings,* ed. and trans. Felix Markham (New York: Harper, 1964).

[2]The six volumes of Comte's main philosophical work, *Cours de philosophie positive,* have not been translated into English. A condensed version is available as *The Positive Philosophy,* trans. Harriet Martineau (New York: AMS Press, 1974). Selections from this work are available in *The Essential Comte,* ed., Stanislav Andreski and trans. Margaret Clarke (London: Croom Helm, 1974), which is an abridgement of *Positive Philosophy.* The first two chapters of *Positive Philosophy* have been published as *Introduction to Positive Philosophy,* ed. and trans. Frederick Ferre (Indianapolis: Hackett, 1988). Other works by Comte are *System of Positive Polity,* trans. John Henry Bridges et al., 4 vols. (New York: Burt Franklin, 1973); *A General View of Positivism,* trans. J. H. Bridges (New York: Robert Speller & Sons, 1957); *The Catechism of Positive Religion,* trans. Richard Congreve, 3rd ed. (Clifton: Augustus M. Kelley, 1973). *Auguste Comte and Positivism: The Essential Writings,* ed. Gertrud Len-

zer (New York: Harper & Row, 1975) provides an anthology of Comte's writings. Mary Pickering *Auguste Comte: An Intellectual Biography*, vol. 1 (Cambridge: Cambridge University Press, 1993), seems destined to become the authoritative biography of Comte. However, only the first of a projected two volumes has been published to date. An older biography is Boris Sokoloff, *The "Mad" Philosopher, Auguste Comte* (Westport, Conn.: Greenwood, 1975). For other major works on Comte, see Edward Caird, *The Social Philosophy and Religion of Comte* (New York: Kraus Reprint, 1968); Robert C. Scharff, *Comte After Positivism* (Cambridge: Cambridge University Press, 1995); Arline Reilein Standley, *Auguste Comte* (Boston: Twayne, 1981); E. E. Evans-Pritchard, *The Sociology of Comte: An Appreciation* (Manchester, U.K.: University of Manchester, 1970); Lucien Levy-Bruhl, *The Philosophy of Auguste Comte* (New York: Augustus M. Kelley, 1973); F. S. Marvin, *Comte: The Founder of Sociology* (New York: Russell & Russell, 1965). W. M. Simon, *European Positivism and the Nineteenth Century: An Essay in Intellectual History* (Ithaca, N.Y.: Cornell University Press, 1963) examines the directions taken by positivism after Comte.

[3]See John Stuart Mill, *The Correspondence of John Stuart Mill and Auguste Comte*, trans. and ed. Oscar A. Haac (New Brunswick, N.J.: Transaction Publishers, 1995) for correspondence between these two figures.

[4]Preface to *System of Positive Polity*, trans. John Henry Bridges et al., 4 vols. (New York: Burt Franklin, 1973), 1: xv. For references to Clotilde's influence on his creation of this religion, see the dedication at the beginning of volume 1 of *Positive Polity* (pp. xxxi-xlv) and the afterword at the conclusion of the work (4:472-81). The entirety of Comte's *Catechism* is a series of simulated conversations between Clotilde as the inquirer within the Religion of Humanity and Comte as the instructing priest. In the preface of this work he lavishes credit on her for her role in creating this institution, stating that "Without her I should never have been able practically to make the career of St. Paul follow on that of Aristotle, by founding the universal religion on true philosophy, after I had extracted the latter from real science" (*The Catechism of Positive Religion*, trans. Richard Congreve, 3rd ed. [New York: Augustus M. Kelley, 1973], p. 13).

[5]*The Positive Philosophy*, trans. Harriet Martineau (New York: AMS Press, 1974), p. 838.

[6]*Introduction to Positive Philosophy*, p. 8.

[7]*Positive Polity*, 2:1. This division of sociology into "social statics" and "social dynamics" is behind Comte's motto of positivism: "Order and Progress." See *Positive Polity*, 1:83.

[8]The idea of the three stages was already present in 1822, when Comte and Saint-Simon coauthored an article outlining these historical periods, although Comte denies that the latter had influenced his ideas in any way. This paradigm of historical evolution has rough parallels in the Idealists who, as we have seen, view history as a growth toward a *telos*. However, since positivism relies on empirical methods, Comte formulates his own evolutionary ideas with a more careful eye toward the actual facts of history than do the Idealists. Also, he does not anchor his "Law of the Three Stages" in a metaphysical system, as did the Idealists. Instead he assumes a natural law, discovered by a scientific approach, behind the movements of history and the corresponding developments in our intellectual capacities.

[9]*Introduction*, p. 4.

[10]*Introduction*, p. 2.

[11]*Introduction*, p. 2.

[12]Conspicuously absent from Comte's list of the sciences is psychology. He argues that psychology is not a subject in itself but is rather a hybrid of physiology and sociology. This exclusion has two bases. First, since the mind, which psychology professes to investigate, is not open to phenomenalogical study, the assumption that the mind exists and that

there are laws governing its operations is unscientific speculation. Thus treating psychology as a discipline is a reversion to mysticism. Therefore, the study of the human subject belongs primarily to sociology. Second, Comte argues that human nature is truly understood only from a social perspective. The individual can only be abstracted from his or her social environment once her or she is comprehended as a social being.

[13]Mathematics, Comte's early love, holds something of a unique position among the sciences. "We must, I think, look upon mathematics, not so much as a constituent part of natural philosophy, properly so called, but as having been, since Descartes and Newton, the true fundamental basis of the whole of that philosophy" (*Introduction*, pp. 65-66). Stated otherwise, mathematics is not so much important for the knowledge it contains but because it constitutes "the most powerful instrument that the human mind can employ in investigating the laws of natural phenomena" (*Introduction*, p. 66). Its power arises in that it provides a certain means of expressing the relations between observable entities.

[14]*Introduction*, p. 10. Just as a scientific or positivist approach develops out of the ruins of the earlier theological and metaphysical stages, so also do the individual sciences grow from nonscientific ancestors. "Without the attractive chimeras of astrology, or the powerful deceptions of alchemy, for example, where should we have found the perseverance and ardor necessary for collecting the long series of observations and experiments which later on served as a basis for the first positive theories of these two classes of phenomena?" (*Introduction*, pp. 7-8).

[15]*Positive Polity*, 2:32.

[16]*Positive Philosophy*, p. 399.

[17]While Comte is sometimes identified as a materialist, he staunchly rejects it. "[M]an is dependent on the world, but he is not a consequence of it. All the efforts of materialists to do away with spontaneous vital action by exaggerating the preponderating influence of the inorganic environment of organised beings have ended in nothing but discrediting the inquiry, as useless as it is idle, henceforth abandoned to the unscientific mind" (*Catechism*, p. 114). One of the shortcomings of the science of his day was that it addressed the nonhuman realm but did not consider the laws that applied to the human arena. This one-sided approach leads to materialism, which, he argues, ignores the spiritual nature of humanity. However, in keeping with his positivism, Comte makes no attempt to explain what exists other than material entities and the laws that govern them.

[18]*Introduction*, p. 12.

[19]*Introduction*, p. 38.

[20]*Positive Philosophy*, p. 828.

[21]See *Positive Polity*, 4:xlviii.

[22]*Positive Polity*, 4:7.

[23]*Positive Polity*, 1:281.

[24]*Positive Polity*, 1:271.

[25]*Positive Polity*, 4:27.

[26]For this reason Comte views the hope of personal immortality as a remnant of egoism.

[27]*Positive Polity*, 1:81.

[28]*Positivism*, p. 113. This is to be balanced with "a solemn reprobation of the two principal opponents of progress, Julian and Bonaparte" (*Positivism*, p. 114).

[29]*Positive Polity*, 1:277. For the Positivist Calendar, or "System of Sociolatry," see Lenzer's *Auguste Comte and Positivism*, pp. 472-73; or table A at the end of *Catechism*.

[30]The first of the sacraments is presentation (shortly after birth), followed by initiation. This occurs at the age of fourteen, when one passes "from its unsystematic training under the direction of its mother, to the systematic education given by the priesthood. At twenty-one, one undergoes admission, in which they enter into the service of Humanity."

The fourth sacrament is destination, at twenty-eight, in which one's social function is chosen. Only then can males be married. For women, destination and admission are simultaneous, since the role of the woman is limited to the home. The sacrament of maturity comes when one reaches forty-two. Retirement, at the age of sixty-three, is the seventh. The final sacrament, prior to death, is transformation. See *Catechism*, p. 95.

[31]*Positive Polity*, 4:64.

[32]*Positivism*, p. 361.

[33]*Positive Polity*, 4:56.

[34]*Positive Philosophy*, p. 776.

[35]*Positive Polity*, 1:107.

[36]*Positive Philosophy*, p. 777.

[37]*Positive Polity*, 4:40. Comte believes that the centrality of altruism levels the playing field for the proletariat. Though the intellectual class surpasses them in understanding, this capacity may overshadow their own capacity for the affective skills. "The working class, then, is better qualified than any other for understanding, and still more for sympathising with the highest truths of morality, though it may not be able to give them a systematic form" (*Positive Polity*, 1:109).

[38]*Positive Polity*, 1:285-86.

[39]W. M. Simon, *European Positivism and the Nineteenth Century: An Essay in Intellectual History* (Ithaca, N.Y.: Cornell University Press, 1963), p. 8.

[40]*Autobiography of John Stuart Mill* (New York: Columbia University Press, 1944), p. 194.

[41]*Autobiography*, p. 167.

[42]*Autobiography*, p. 148.

[43]*Autobiography*, p. 149.

[44]In addition to these intellectual parallels there are interesting parallels in their personal lives. First, like Comte, Mill underwent a severe mental crisis while in his early twenties. Second, while Mill's relationship with Harriet Taylor differed in important respects, his worship of Miss Taylor was every bit as obsessive as Comte's devotion to Clotilde de Vaux. As he describes it, "Her memory is to me a religion, and her approbation the standard by which, summing up as it does all worthiness, I endeavour to regulate my life" (*Autobiography*, p. 170).

[45]*Autobiography*, p. 148.

[46]*Autobiography*, p. 149.

[47]Mill's complete writings have been released in *Collected Works*, ed. John M. Robson et al., 33 vols. (Toronto: University of Toronto, 1963-1991). Major individual works are *Principles of Political Economy*, 2 vols. (New York: Co-operative Publication Society, 1900); *A System of Logic, Ratiocinative and Inductive* (London: Longmans, 1965); *Three Essays on Religion* (New York: Greenwood Press, 1969); *Autobiography of John Stuart Mill* (New York: Columbia University Press, 1944); *An Examination of Sir William Hamilton's Philosophy* (London: Longman, 1865); *Auguste Comte and Positivism* (Ann Arbor: University of Michigan Press, 1961). Mill's *The Subjection of Women* is available with other essays by himself and Harriet Taylor on the issue of gender in *Essays on Sex Equality*, ed. Alice S. Rossi (Chicago: University of Chicago Press, 1970). Several Mill anthologies are available, some of which include complete or almost complete versions of major works. A worthwhile Mill reader is found in *John Stuart Mill: A Selection of his Works*, ed. John M. Robson (Indianapolis: Bobbs-Merrill, 1982), which contains complete versions of *Utilitarianism* and *On Liberty*. Mill's three most famous writings in social philosophy are combined in *Utilitar-ianism, Liberty, and Representative Government* (New York: E. P. Dutton, 1947); *Mill's Ethical Writings*, ed. J. B. Schneewind (New York: Collier, 1965) includes the complete text of *Utilitarianism*. *Philosophy of Scientific Method*, ed. Ernest Nagel (New York: Hafner, 1950) contains major portions of

System of Logic and *An Examination of Sir William Hamilton's Philosophy.* A collection of lesser-known writings is found in *Essays on Politics and Culture,* ed. Gertrude Himmelfarb (Garden City, N.J.: Doubleday, 1962). *On Liberty, Representative Government* and *The Subjection of Women* are all contained in complete form in *Three Essays* (London: Oxford, 1912). For secondary resources see William Thomas, *Mill* (Oxford: Oxford University Press, 1985); R. P. Anschutz, *The Philosophy of J. S. Mill* (Oxford: Clarendon, 1963); H. J. McCloskey, *John Stuart Mill: A Critical Study* (London: Macmillan, 1971); Alan Ryan, *John Stuart Mill* (New York: Pantheon, 1970); John Skorupski, "J. S. Mill: Logic and Metaphysics," vol. 7 of *The Nineteenth Century,* ed. C. L. Ten (London: Routledge, 1994); R. F. Khan, "J. S. Mill: Ethics and Politics," in *The Nineteenth Century,* ed. C. L. Ten, vol. 7, (London: Routledge, 1994). The standard Mill biography is Michael St. John Packe, *The Life of John Stuart Mill* (New York: Macmillen, 1954).

[48]James Mill's major works are *The History of British India* (London: J. Madden, 1840-1848), and *Elements of Political Economy* (New York: Augustus M. Kelley, 1963).

[49]For a survey of the younger Mill's most influential predecessors, see Elie Halevy, *The Growth of Philosophic Radicalism,* trans. A. D. Lindsay (London: Faber & Faber, 1934).

[50]*Autobiography,* p. 34.

[51]*Autobiography,* p. 94.

[52]*Autobiography,* p. 103.

[53]For the story of their relationship see F. A. Hayek, *John Stuart Mill and Harriet Taylor: Their Correspondence and Subsequent Marriage* (Chicago: University of Chicago Press, 1951).

[54]*Autobiography,* p. 161. As we might expect, Mill could be counted on to justify his actions in utilitarian terms.

[55]See *Christianity and Western Thought,* 1:259-68.

[56]*System of Logic,* 3:24.4, p. 399.

[57]*System of Logic,* 2:5.4, p. 152.

[58]*System of Logic,* 3:2.1, p. 189.

[59]*System of Logic,* 3:2.1, p. 188.

[60]*System of Logic,* 3:3.1, p. 202.

[61]*Examination of Sir William Hamilton's Philosophy* (London: Longman, 1865), p. 198.

[62]*Examination of Sir William,* p. 197.

[63]*Examination of Sir William,* p. 205.

[64]*Examination of Sir William,* p. 213.

[65]*System of Logic,* 6:3.2, p. 554.

[66]*System of Logic,* 6:3.2, p. 554.

[67]*System of Logic,* 6:2.3, p. 550.

[68]*System of Logic,* 6:2.2, p. 547.

[69]*Liberty,* p. 16.

[70]*Liberty,* p. 15. Mill qualifies his extension of liberty by excluding children and "those backward states of society in which the race itself may be considered as in its nonage." See *Liberty,* p. 15. The exclusion of children from the category of those who should be given freedom from coercion allows Mill to argue for compulsory education.

[71]*Liberty,* p. 15.

[72]"It is proper to state that I forgo any advantage which could be derived to my argument from the idea of abstract right, as a thing independent of utility. I regard utility as the ultimate appeal on all ethical questions; but it must be ultility in the largest sense, grounded on the permanent interests of man as a progressive being" (*Liberty,* p. 16).

[73]*Liberty,* p. 32.

[74]*Liberty,* p. 25.

[75]*Liberty,* p. 23.

[76]*Representative Government,* p. 181.

[77]*Representative Government,* p. 282. Since the continued existence of democracy depends on an educated citizenry, Mill also argues for some level of literacy for those who are involved in voting: "[U]niversal teaching must precede universal enfranchisement" (*Representative Government,* p. 278).

[78]For a survey of utilitarian thought, both before and after Mill, see Ernest Albee, *A History of English Utilitarianism* (New York: Collier, 1962); and John Plamanatz, *Utilitarianism and the English Utilitarians* (Oxford: Blackwell, 1949).

[79]*Utilitarianism,* p. 6.

[80]*Utilitarianism,* p. 29.

[81]There are two additional modifications of note to Benthamite utilitarianism. First, Mill's formulation of the system moves away from Bentham's more individualistic approach. Second, while both Bentham and Mill are confident that the happiness of the individual and that of greatest number would coincide, the older philosopher believed that the juncture between individual and social happiness must be imposed externally. Mill argues that the connection between individual and social interests comes through the internal development of character.

[82]*Utilitarianism,* p. 7.

[83]*Utilitarianism,* p. 8.

[84]*Utilitarianism,* p. 9.

[85]*Utilitarianism,* p. 10.

[86]*Utilitarianism,* pp. 32-33.

[87]This suspicion seems to be confirmed by a rather cryptic statement in his *Autobiography* (p. 100) in which he says, "I never, indeed, wavered in the conviction that happiness is the test of all rules of conduct, and the end of life. But I now thought that this end was only to be attained by not making it the direct end. . . . Ask yourself whether you are happy, and you cease to be so. The only chance is to treat, not happiness, but some end external to it, as the purpose of life."

[88]"Utility of Religion," in *Three Essays on Religion* (New York: Greenwood Press, 1969), p. 69.

[89]"Utility of Religion," p. 99.

[90]"Theism," in *Three Essays on Religion,* p. 174.

[91]"Utility of Religion," p. 116.

[92]"Nature," in *Three Essays on Religion,* p. 65.

[93]*Utilitarianism,* p. 307.

[94]"Nature," pp. 38-39.

[95]"Utility of Religion," p. 109.

[96]*Utilitarianism,* p. 289.

[97]*Liberty,* pp. 54-55.

[98]These are published in Hayek, *John Stuart Mill and Harriet Taylor (op. cit.);* and also John Stuart Mill and Harriet Taylor Mill, *Essays on Sex Equality,* ed. A. S. Rossi (Chicago: University of Chicago Press, 1970).

[99]Both *Subjection* and Taylor's earlier essay "Enfranchisement of Women" are reprinted in *Essays on Sex Equality.*

[100]*What's Right with Feminism* (London: SPCK, 1985), p. 59.

[101]This section picks up the story of women where Colin Brown left it in *Christianity and Western Thought,* 1:426-41. Here he discusses the reformation writings of women, with bibliography.

[102]Fell later married Fox and is sometimes knows as Margaret Fox for this reason. On her life and thought see her *A Sincere and Constant Love,* ed. T. H. S. Wallace (Richmond, Ind.: Friends United Press, 1992); Isabel Ross, *Margaret Fell: Mother of Quakerism* (London:

Longmans, Green, 1949); and Bonnelyn Kunze, *Margaret Fell and the Rise of Quakerism* (Stanford: Stanford University Press, 1994).

[103]This is reprinted in modern English, in Fell, *A Sincere and Constant Love.*

[104]For some representative surveys of this subject see Donald W. Dayton, *Discovering an Evangelical Heritage* (New York: Harper & Row, 1976); *Women and Religion in America, vol 1: The Nineteenth Century*, ed. R. R. Ruether and R. S. Keller (San Francisco: Harper & Row, 1981); Janette Hassey, *No Time for Silence: Evangelical Women in Public Ministry Around the Turn of the Century* (Grand Rapids, Mich.: Zondervan/Academie Books, 1986); Nancy Hardesty, *Women Called to Witness* (Nashville: Abingdon, 1984).

[105]See the reprint, with introduction, in Lee, *Five Sermons and a Tract,* ed. D. W. Dayton (Chicago: Holrad House, 1975).

[106]For more on Willard, see Hardesty, *Women;* Ruth Bordin, *Women and Temperence* (Philadelphia: Temple University Press, 1981), and her *Frances Willard* (Chapel Hill: University of North Carolina Press, 1986).

[107]Harold Raser, *Phoebe Palmer: Her Life and Thought* (Lewiston, N.Y.: Mellen Press, 1987), p. 2. See further, Thomas C. Oden, ed., *Phoebe Palmer: Selected Writings* (New York: Paulist, 1988); Charles E. White, *The Beauty of Holiness* (Grand Rapids, Mich.: Zondervan/Francis Asbury Press, 1986), and a brief introduction by Sally Bruyneel, "Phoebe Palmer: Mother of the Holiness Movement," *Priscilla Papers* 12, no. 1 (spring 1998): 1-3.

[108]For more on the Grimkés, see C. H. Birney, *The Grimké Sisters* (New York: Dillingham, 1885); G. Lerner, *The Grimké Sisters from South Carolina* (Boston: Houghton, Mifflin, 1967); and *Selected Works of Angelina Weld Grimké,* ed. C. Herron (Oxford: Oxford University Press, 1991).

[109]This is found in her *Selected Works.*

[110]For more on these two leaders and their collaboration see E. C. DuBois, ed. *Elizabeth Cady Stanton/Susan B. Anthony* (New York: Schocken, 1981).

[111]See Brown, *Christianity and Western Thought,* 1:431-35 for an overview.

[112]See D. G. Levy, H. B. Applewhite and M. D. Johnson, eds., *Women in Revolutionary Paris* (Urbana: University of Illinois Press, 1980); and Joan W. Scott, *Only Paradoxes to Offer: French Feminists and the Rights of Man* (Cambridge, Mass.: Harvard University Press, 1996).

[113]See *The Works of Mary Wollstonecraft,* ed. J. Todd and M. Butler, 7 vols. (London: Pickering, 1989); and V. Sapiro, *A Vindication of Political Virtue* (Chicago: University of Chicago Press, 1992).

[114]Burke's *Reflections on the Revolution in France* (1790) was very popular in its time, and is a classic of Western political theory, yet Wollstonecraft's rebuttal is almost never discussed alongside it.

[115]See *The Essential Margaret Fuller* (New Brunswick, N.J.: Rutgers University Press, 1992) for a good overview of her work; and see further Margaret Allen, *The Achievement of Margaret Fuller* (University Park: Penn State University Press, 1979); Paula Blanchard, *Margaret Fuller: From Transcendentalism to Revolution* (New York: Delacorte, 1978).

[116]See the modern critical edition, with intro., by L. J. Reynolds (New York: Norton, 1997).

Chapter 9: Act and Idea

[1]The only book Peirce produced during his life was *Photometric Researches,* which grew out of his work with the U.S. Coast and Geodetic Survey. However, he left an extensive set of essays and notes that have been published in two collections. *Collected Papers of Charles Sanders Peirce,* ed. Charles Hartshorne and Paul Weiss (Cambridge, Mass: Harvard University Press, 1931-1960) groups the writings by topic. The more recent collection, *Writings of Charles S. Peirce: A Chronological Edition,* Max H. Fisch, 5 vols. (Bloomington: Indiana University Press, 1985-1993), provides a chronological survey of Peirce's work. Antholo-

gies that contain major philosophical essays are *Selected Writings,* ed. Philip P. Wiener (New York: Dover Publications, 1958); *Charles S. Peirce: The Essential Writings,* ed. Edward C. Moore (New York: Harper & Row, 1972); *Philosophical Writings of Peirce,* ed. Justus Buchler (New York: Dover, 1955); and *Chance, Love, and Logic,* ed. Morris R. Cohen (New York: Barnes & Noble, 1968). The last volume also contains John Dewey's essay "The Pragmatism of Peirce," which brought Peirce's philosophy to the attention of a broader audience. For secondary sources on Peirce's philosophy see Justus Buchler, *Charles Peirce's Empiricism* (New York: Octagon, 1966); Thomas A. Goudge, *The Thought of C. S. Peirce* (New York: Dover, 1960); Thomas S. Knight, *Charles Peirce* (New York: Washington Square Press, 1965); Carl R. Hausman, *Charles S. Peirce's Evolutionary Philosophy* (Cambridge: Cambridge University Press, 1993); W. B. Gallie, *Peirce and Pragmatism* (New York: Dover, 1966); C. J. Misak, *Truth and the End of Inquiry: A Peircean Account of Truth* (Oxford: Clarendon, 1991); Christopher Hookway, *Peirce* (London: Routledge & Kegan Paul, 1985); Manley Thompson, *The Pragmatism Philosophy of C. S. Peirce* (Chicago: University of Chicago, 1963). Since Peirce died before he was able to systematize his ideas, a favorite pursuit of Peirce scholars is the attempt to assemble his architectonic after the fact. Three sources that undertake this venture are Douglas R. Anderson, *Strands of System: The Philosophy of Charles Peirce* (West Lafayette, Ind.: Purdue University Press, 1995); Murray G. Murphey, *The Development of Peirce's Philosophy* (Cambridge, Mass.: Harvard University Press, 1961); and James K. Feibleman, *An Introduction to Peirce's Philosophy: Interpreted as a System* (London: George Allen & Unwin, 1960). A bibliography of primary and secondary sources is available in Laine Ketner et al., eds. *A Comprehensive Bibliography and Index of the Published Works of Charles Sanders Peirce with a Bibliography of Secondary Studies,* 2nd ed. (Bowling Green, Ky.: Bowling Green State University, 1986).

[2]Peirce was a lecturer in logic at John Hopkins from 1879-1884. However, given his great skills, his failure to receive a permanent appointment is surprising. A number of possible reasons can be cited. First, while he was gracious, witty and affectionate with a small circle of close friends, Peirce had a tendency to be arrogant, oversensitive and impatient with those he considered his intellectual inferiors. The latter included almost everyone, including many of his professors at Harvard. He also injected himself into a rather messy battle over Josiah Royce's position at Harvard. This put him at odds with the president of the school and probably precluded a professorship there, even with William James as his advocate. It was also rumored that he was less than moderate in his drinking habits and indiscreet in his romantic affairs. The former is unlikely in view of his tremendous output, although he was a connoisseur of burgundies. It is unclear how much validity the second charge contains. Peirce was married to Harriet Melusina Fay, the daughter of a prominent family. Although they remained together for thirteen years, she left at the end of this period, and Peirce divorced her seven years later on the grounds of desertion. Whether marital indiscretions were responsible for her leaving is not certain, but it should also be stated that divorce itself was sufficient to put one's academic career in jeopardy during this period. Peirce later remarried.

[3]In spite of reluctance to popularize his views, he made some attempt to do so, and it resulted in his two most-often read essays, "The Fixation of Belief" and "How to Make Our Ideas Clear," originally published in *Popular Science Monthly.*

[4]The Geodetic Survey was a government agency that established benchmarks for surveying and mapping.

[5]Good introductions to pragmatic philosophy are A. J. Ayer, *The Origins of Pragmatism: Studies in the Philosophy of Charles Sanders Peirce and William James* (San Francisco: Freeman, Cooper, 1968) and H. S. Thayer, *Meaning and Action: A Critical History of Pragmatism* (Indianapolis: Bobbs-Merrill, 1968).

[6]"The Architectonic Construction of Pragmatism," in *Collected Papers*, ed. Charles Hart-shorne and Paul Weiss (Cambridge, Mass.: Harvard University Press, 1931-1960), 5:9. Because it is a popular edition of Peirce's philosophical works, I will provide references to Philip P. Wiener, ed., *Selected Writings* (New York: Dover, 1958) where parallels exist.

[7]By referring to consequences that "might conceivably result," Peirce makes clear that we do not have to limit knowledge to activities actually performed but can extend it to those things that would conceivably occur if certain conditions are met.

[8]"How to Make Our Ideas Clear," in *Collected Papers*, 5:401; Wiener, p. 124.

[9]"The Fixation of Belief," in *Collected Papers*, 5:377; Wiener, p. 102.

[10]"The Fixation of Belief," 5:378; Wiener, p. 103.

[11]"The Fixation of Belief," 5:378; Wiener, p. 103.

[12]"The Fixation of Belief," 5:380; Wiener, p. 104.

[13]"But in the most priest-ridden states some individuals will be found who are raised above that condition [belief based on authority]. These men possess a wider sort of social feeling; they see that men in other countries and in other ages have held to very different doctrines from those which they themselves have been brought up to believe; and they cannot help seeing that it is the mere accident of their having been taught as they have, and of their having been surrounded with the manners and association they have, that has caused them to believe as they do and not far differently. And their candor cannot resist the reflection that there is no reason to rate their own views at a higher value than those of other nations and other centuries; and this gives rise to doubts in their minds" ("The Fixation of Belief," 5:381; Wiener, p. 105).

[14]"How to Make Our Ideas Clear," 5:392; Wiener, p. 117.

[15]Peirce sees this as the problem with Descartes' concept of a clear idea. "The distinction between an idea *seeming* clear and really being so, never occurred to him [Descartes]. Trusting to introspection, as he did, even for a knowledge of existentialist things, why should he question its testimony in respect to the contents of our own minds?" ("How to Make Our Ideas Clear," 5:391; Wiener, p. 115).

[16]"The Fixation of Belief," 5:386; Wiener, pp.109-10.

[17]"What Pragmatism Is," in *Collected Papers*, 5:413; Wiener, p. 184.

[18]"The Fixation of Belief," 5:373; Wiener, p. 99.

[19]"The Fixation of Belief," 5:372; Wiener, p. 99.

[20]"How to Make Our Ideas Clear," 5:397; Wiener, p. 121. Peirce is careful to define doubt in ways consistent with his pragmatism. True doubt does not originate in an act of the will but in practical experience. This is contrary to Descartes' use of doubt as a hypothetical or methodological tool that stands at the beginning of philosophical or scientific thought. For Peirce, honest inquiry is motivated by actual circumstances that create the need for new beliefs by calling the old into question. "We cannot begin with complete doubt. We must begin with all the prejudices which we actually have when we enter upon the study of philosophy. These prejudices are not to be dispelled by a maxim, for they are things which it does not occur to us *can* be questioned" ("Some Consequences of Four Incapacities," in *Collected Papers*, 5:265; Wiener, p. 40).

[21]"How to Make Our Ideas Clear," 5:398; Wiener, p. 121.

[22]"Science as a Guide to Conduct," in *Collected Papers*, 1:55. While Peirce's writing contain an undercurrent of confidence that humans will eventually discover truths that accurately describe reality, the recurrent theme is that we not give up the pursuit too soon and assume that our answers are final.

[23]"How to Make Our Ideas Clear," 5:410; Wiener, p. 135.

[24]"The Fixation of Belief," 5:384; Wiener, p. 107.

[25]"Three Kinds of Goodness," in *Collected Papers*, 5:121.

[26]"Evolutionary Love," in *Collected Papers*, 6:307.

[27]By means of agapasm, Peirce distinguishes his evolutionary model from the mechanical and nonteleological versions (what he calls tychistic evolution) of Darwin and Herbert Spencer (see chapter eleven). While Peirce's agapastic evolution possesses certain elements of novelty, it is not constructed primarily on chance mutation but is instead controlled by the increasingly powerful pull of love.

[28]Peirce's thoughts on religion are outlined by Michael L. Raposa, *Peirce's Philosophy of Religion* (Bloomington: Indiana University Press, 1989).

[29]"What Is Christian Faith," in *Collected Papers*, 6:441; Wiener, p. 355.

[30]"What Is Christian Faith," 6:443; Wiener, p. 355. It is this practical, or pragmatic, element that Peirce finds to be the distinction between his religious ideal and conceptions that focus on creed or doctrine. "Yet it is absurd to say that religion is a mere belief. You might as well call society a belief, or politics a belief, or civilization a belief. Religion is a life, and can be identified with a belief only provided that belief be a living belief—a thing to be lived rather than said or thought" ("What Is Christian Faith," 6:439; Wiener, p. 354).

[31]"A Neglected Argument for the Reality of God," in *Collected Papers*, 6:465; Wiener, p. 365.

[32]"A Neglected Argument for the Reality of God," 6:466; Wiener, p. 365.

[33]"My Belief in God," in *Collected Papers*, 6:502.

[34]"The Law of Mind," 6:102.

[35]While Peirce and Whitehead appear to have come to their conclusions independently, there are significant similarities in their concepts of evolutionary movement in both God and the world and in the view that chance gradually gives way to order and perfection. Similarities in their views help explain why one of the editors of Peirce's collected works is Charles Hartshorne, Whitehead's most prominent disciple.

[36]An additional contribution, not discussed in this survey, is his theory of semiotics, which is only indirectly related to pragmatism. Peirce's semiotics anticipates the logical positivism of the twentieth century in his call for a more precise understanding and use of language. Just as science had prepared for its advances by adopting a technical vocabulary, so also would philosophy benefit from such a move.

[37]James's major works are *Pragmatism* (Buffalo: Prometheus, 1991); *The Varieties of Religious Experience* (New York: New American Library, 1958); *The Meaning of Truth: A Sequel to Pragmatism* (Ann Arbor: University of Michigan, 1970); *The Principles of Psychology*, 2 vols. (New York: Holt, 1918); *Psychology, Briefer Course* (Cambridge, Mass: Harvard University Press, 1984); *Some Problems of Philosophy*, eds. Frederick H. Burkhardt, Fredson Bowers and Ignas K. Skrupskelis (Cambridge, Mass: Harvard University Press, 1979); *A Pluralistic Universe* (New York: Longmans, Green, 1909); *The Will to Believe and Other Essays in Popular Philosophy*, eds. Frederick H. Burkhardt, Fredson Bowers and Ignas K. Skrupskelis (Cambridge, Mass: Harvard University Press, 1979). See also *The Correspondence of William James*, eds. Ignas K. Skrupskelis and Elizabeth M. Berkeley (Charlottesville: University Press of Virginia, 1992). Several collections of James's essays are available. See *Essays in Pragmatism*, ed. Alburey Castell (New York: Hafner, 1968); *The Moral Philosophy of William James*, ed. John K. Roth (New York: Crowell, 1969); *William James: The Essential Writings*, ed. Bruce Wiltshire (New York: Harper Torchbooks, 1971); *Essays in Religion and Morality*, eds. Frederick H. Burkhardt, Fredson Bowers and Ignas K. Skrupskelis (Cambridge, Mass: Harvard University Press, 1982); *Essays on Faith and Morals*, ed. Ralph Barton Perry (New York: Meridian, 1962). Sources of biographical information about James are Ralph Barton Perry, *The Thought and Character of William James*, 2 vols. (Westport, Conn.: Greenwood Press, 1974); Gerald E. Myers, *William James: His Life and Thought* (New Haven, Conn.: Yale, 1986); Gay Wilson Allen, *William James* (New York: Viking, 1967). For other secondary sources, see Ellen Kappy Suckiel, *The Pragmatic Philosophy of William James*

(Notre Dame: University of Notre Dame Press, 1982); John Wild, *The Radical Empiricism of William James* (New York: Anchor, 1970); Ralph Barton Perry, *In the Spirit of William James* (Bloomington: Indiana University Press, 1958); Gordon Haddon Clark, *William James* (Nutley, N.J.: Presbyterian & Reformed, 1963).

[38]It was not just his insistence on bringing pragmatism into the mainstream but also his interest in psychical research that was largely responsible for raised eyebrows from fellow scholars.

[39]"What Pragmatism Is," 5:414; Wiener, p. 186.

[40]"The Sentiment of Rationality," in *Essays in Pragmatism*, [hereafter *Essays*] ed. Alburey Castell (New York: Hafner, 1968), p. 24.

[41]"Will to Believe," in *Essays*, p. 106.

[42]"Sentiment of Rationality," p. 22.

[43]"Will to Believe," p. 97.

[44]"Will to Believe," p. 95.

[45]"Sentiment of Rationality," p. 27.

[46]*Meaning of Truth*, p. 194.

[47]*Pragmatism*, pp. 23-24.

[48]*Pragmatism*, p. 88.

[49]*Pragmatism*, pp. 85-86.

[50]*Meaning of Truth*, p. xxxv.

[51]*Pragmatism*, p. 99. For this reason, nature is an illegitimate foundation upon which to construct ethics. "Surely there is no *status* for good and evil to exist in, in a purely insentient world. How can one physical fact, considered simply as a physical fact, be better than another? Betterness is not a physical relation. In its mere material capacity, a thing can no more be good or bad than it can be pleasant or painful.... Physical facts simply *are* or are *not;* and neither when present or absent, can they be supposed to make demands" ("The Moral Philosopher and the Moral Life," in *Essays*, p. 69).

[52]*Pragmatism*, p. 89.

[53]"The Dilemma of Determinism," in *Essays*, p. 49.

[54]"Dilemma of Determinism," p. 50. Another way James expresses this idea is in his famous distinction between "healthy-minded" and "sick soul" religious types. The view outlined above is the healthy-minded approach to evil, which considers apparent evil in the framework of the larger context to discover the greater good. James prefers the "sick soul" model, in which evil is a reality that genuinely threatens the good but from which there is the possibility of salvation. Thus he argues, "The completest religions would therefore seem to be those in which the pessimistic elements are best developed. Buddhism, of course, and Christianity are the best known to us of these. They are essentially religions of deliverance: the man must die to an unreal life before he can be born into the real life" (*Varieties of Religious Experience*, p. 139).

[55]"Dilemma of Determinism," p. 59.

[56]*A Pluralistic Universe* (New York: Longmans, Green, 1909), p. 321. Some have wondered whether James is inconsistent with this idea of externally related entities since a few pages earlier he presented a panpsychic model that seems to support an interior relationship of the parts. "We are indeed internal parts of God and not external creations, on any possible reading of the panpsychic system. Yet because God is not the absolute, but is himself a part when the system is conceived pluralistically, his functions can be taken as not wholly dissimilar to those of the other smaller parts,—as similar to our functions consequently" (*Pluralistic Universe*, p. 318).

[57]James's critique of monism echoes Peirce's view that a priori metaphysics is ultimately subjectivistic. "The rationalist's fallacy here is exactly like the sentimentalist's. Both

extract a quality from the muddy particulars of experience, and find it so pure when extracted that they contrast it with each and all its muddy instances as an opposite and higher nature. All the while it is *their* nature." See *Pragmatism*, p. 101.

[58]*Pluralistic Universe*, p. 325.

[59]*Meaning of Truth*, pp. 217-18.

[60]*The Principles of Psychology*, 2 vols. (New York: Holt, 1918), 1:288.

[61]"The Dilemma of Determinism," p. 61.

[62]For James's views on religion, see Henry Samuel Levinson, *The Religious Investigations of William James* (Chapel Hill: University of North Carolina Press, 1981).

[63]*Pragmatism*, p. 38.

[64]*Pragmatism*, p. 38.

[65]*Varieties of Religious Experience*, p. 389.

[66]The influence of James's pragmatic method is especially clear here. He defines religious experience as *"the feelings, acts, and experiences of individual men in their solitude, so far as they apprehend themselves to stand in relation to whatever they may consider the divine"* (*Varieties of Religious Experience*, p. 42). Thus the validity of someone's religious experience or conversion is not determined by correctness of creed or belief but by whether it makes a difference in the person's life.

[67]James is not so naive to believe that everything that passes under the banner of religion necessarily follows from the existence of God. We must continue to apply pragmatic method to sift out impurities in religious belief. But in no field does the presence of mistakes require that we throw out the baby with the bath water. "Now whatever its [belief in God's existence] residual difficulties may be, experience shows that it certainly does work, and that the problem is to build it out and determine it so that it will combine satisfactorily with all the other working truths" (*Pragmatism*, p. 131).

[68]*Varieties of Religious Experience*, p. 73. "What religion reports, you must remember, always purports to be a fact of experience: the divine is actually present, religion says, and between it and ourselves relations of give and take are actual. If definite perceptions of fact like this cannot stand upon their own feet, surely abstract reasoning cannot give them the support they are in need of. Conceptual processes can class facts, define them and interpret them; but they do not produce them, nor can they reproduce their individuality" (*Varieties of Religious Experience*, p. 346). One might note parallels with Mill, to whom James pronounces his debt on this matter.

[69]*Pluralistic Universe*, p. 303.

[70]*Varieties of Religious Experience*, p. 347.

[71]*Pragmatism*, p. 10.

[72]*Pragmatism*, p. 18.

[73]*Pluralistic Universe*, p. 314.

[74]*Pluralistic Universe*, pp. 25-26. While James denies any pragmatic value in metaphysical formulations of God's nature, stating that "the metaphysical monster which they offer to our worship is an absolutely worthless invention of the scholarly mind," the moral attributes "stand on an entirely different footing. They positively determine fear and hope and expectation, and are foundations for the saintly life. It needs but a glance at them to show how great is their significance." See *Varieties of Religious Experience*, pp. 340-41. However, while true religion always has an ethical component, we cannot reduce religion to ethics since the former affects us "in regions where morality strictly so called can at best but bow its head and acquiesce" (*Varieties of Religious Experience*, p. 54).

[75]*Pluralistic Universe*, p. 311.

[76]In this way James believes he has preserved the idea of Providence but in a modified form. "The belief in free will is not in the least incompatible with the belief in Provi-

dence, provided you do not restrict the Providence to fulminating nothing but *fatal decrees*. If you allow him to provide possibilities as well as actualities to the universe, and to carry on his own thinking in those two categories just as we do ours, chances may be there, uncontrolled even by him, and the course of the universe be really ambiguous; and yet the end of all things may be just what he intended it to be from all eternity" ("The Dilemma of Determinism," p. 62).

[77]"The Dilemma of Determinism," p. 64.

[78]*Varieties of Religious Experience,* p. 368.

[79]On Edwards and Berkeley, see Brown, *Christianity and Western Thought,* 1:227-34 and 1:271-80.

[80]See C. F. Harrold, *Carlyle and German Thought, 1819-1834* (New Haven: Yale University Press, 1934); or G. N. G. Orsini, *Coleridge and German Idealism* (Carbondale: Southern Illinois University Press, 1969). See also chapter two above.

[81]See J. H. Muirhead, *The Platonic Tradition in Anglo-Saxon Philosophy* (London: Allen & Unwin, 1931).

[82]The best introduction to Bradley's life and thought is Richard Wollheim, *F. H. Bradley,* rev. ed. (Harmondsworth: Penguin, 1969). For an introduction to his metaphysical work, see W. J. Mander, *An Introduction to Bradley's Metaphysics* (Oxford University Press, 1994).

[83]For a full bibliography, see R. Ingardia, *Bradley: A Research Bibliography* (Bowling Green: Philosophy Documentation Center, 1991). His major philosophical works were: *The Presuppositions of Critical History* (Oxford: J. Parker, 1874); *Ethical Studies* (1876; 2nd ed., Oxford University Press, 1927); *The Principles of Logic,* 2 vols. (1883; 2nd ed., Oxford University Press, 1922); *Appearance and Reality* (1893; 2nd ed.,1897; 9th impression, Oxford University Press, 1930); *Essays on Truth and Reality* (Oxford: Oxford University Press, 1914); and his *Collected Essays,* 2 vols. (Oxford: Oxford University Press, 1935).

[84]This was reprinted in his *Collected Essays,* vol. 1 and in a separate volume with extensive introduction by L. Rubinoff (Chicago: Quadrangle Books, 1968).

[85]*Presuppositions,* 96 (Rubinoff ed.)

[86]*Presuppositions,* 102f.

[87]*Appearance and Reality,* p. 120.

[88]*Appearance and Reality,* p. 395.

[89]*Appearance and Reality,* p. 397.

[90]*Appearance and Reality,* p. 453.

[91]On the life of Royce see Robert V. Hine, *Josiah Royce* (Norman: University of Oklahoma Press, 1992). There is a short autobiographical lecture by Royce printed in *The Hope of the Great Community* (New York: Macmillan, 1916), pp. 122-36, and reprinted in *The Basic Writings of Josiah Royce,* ed. J. J. McDermott, 2 vols. (Chicago: University of Chicago Press, 1969), 1:31-38. A fine intellectual biography is Bruce Kuklick, *Josiah Royce* (Indianapolis: Bobbs-Merril, 1972), while John Clendenning covers both *The Life and Thought of Josiah Royce* (Madison: University of Wisconsin Press, 1985). Also of biographical interest is Clendenning, ed., *The Letters of Josiah Royce* (Chicago: University of Chicago Press, 1970).

[92]Royce's most important philosophical works are: *The Religious Aspect of Philosophy* (1885; reprint, New York: Harper, 1958); *The Spirit of Modern Philosophy* (Boston: Houghton, Mifflin, 1892); *Studies in Good and Evil* (New York: Appleton, 1898); *The World and the Individual,* 2 vols. (1899, 1901; reprint, New York: Dover, 1959); *The Philosophy of Loyalty* (New York: Macmillan, 1908); and *The Problem of Christianity* (1913; reprint, University of Chicago Press, 1968). A fine collection is *The Basic Writings of Josiah Royce,* which also contains a useful bibliography.

[93]An early, quasi-pragmatist essay is "On Purpose in Thought," in *Fugitive Essays,* ed. J. Loewenberg (1880; reprint, Cambridge, Mass.: Harvard University Press, 1920). compare his more idealists essays: "Kant's Relation to Modern Philosophic Thought," *Journal of Speculative*

Philosophy 15 (1881): 360-81, and "Mind and Reality," *Mind* 7 (1882):30-54. The latter essays are incorporated into his fully idealist work of 1885: *The Religious Aspect of Philosophy.*

[94]*Basic Writings,* 2.813, from "The Principles of Logic" § 21, in *Logic: Encyclopedia of the Philosophical Sciences,* trans. B. Ethel Meyer, vol. 1 (London: Macmillan, 1913). This was later published as a separate pamphlet, *The Principles of Logic* (New York: Wisdom Library, 1961); and is also reprinted in *Royce's Logical Essays,* ed. D. S. Robinson (Dubuque, Iowa: Wm. C. Brown, 1951).

[95]The full influence of Peirce came after he was both appreciative and critical of *The World and the Individual* (see the *Collected Papers of Charles Sanders Peirce,* ed. C. Hartshorne and Paul Weiss, 8 vols. [Cambridge, Mass.: Harvard University Press, 1931-1960], 8:100-131). Royce then (1912) read Peirce carefully and was influenced by him especially in Royce's later book, *The Problem of Christianity.* See, e.g., the way he mentions Peirce in the "Author's Introduction," pp. 53f.

[96]*World and the Individual,* 1:308.

[97]*World and the Individual,* 1:339, italics omitted.

[98]This is one major thesis of his book *The Spirit of Modern Philosophy.*

[99]Royce compares his philosophy of loyalty to Christian love in *Problem of Christianity,* pp. 94-98 (1:96-106 of the 1913 ed.)

[100]*World and the Individual,* 2:418-25.

[101]*Problem of Christianity,* p. 83 (1:68 of the 1913 ed.).

[102]For more on the theme of community in Royce, see Gayle Beebe, *The Interpretive Role of the Religious Community in Friedrich Schleiermacher and Josiah Royce* (Lewiston, N.Y.: Edwin Mellen, 1997), and John E. Smith, *Royce's Social Infinite* (New York: Liberal Arts Press, 1950).

[103]*Problem of Christianity,* p. 181 (1:310 of the 1913 ed.).

[104]Royce remains a subject of interest for American philosophers. For some recent fine books on Royce, in addition to those mentioned in the notes above, see John E. Smith, *America's Philosophical Vision* (Chicago: University of Chicago, 1992); Frank M. Oppenheim, *Royce's Mature Philosophy of Religion* (Notre Dame: University of Notre Dame, 1987) and his *Royce's Mature Ethics* (Notre Dame: University of Notre Dame, 1993). Also of interest is the work of the French Catholic existentialist, Gabriel Marcel, in *Royce's Metaphysics,* trans. V. & G. Ringer (Chicago: University of Chicago, 1956).

Chapter 10: Confessionalism and Liberalism

[1]Major works by Newman are *An Essay in Aid of Grammar of Assent,* ed. Charles Frederick Harrold (New York: Longmans, 1947); *Newman's University Sermons* (London: SPCK, 1970); *The Via Media,* 2 vols. (London: Longmans, Green, 1901); *Apologia Pro Vita Sua* (New York: Random House, 1950); *An Essay on the Development of Christian Doctrine,* ed. J. M. Cameron (Harmondsworth: Penguin, 1974). An anthology of Newman's works is Vincent Ferrer Blehl, ed., *The Essential Newman* (New York: New American Library, 1963). For secondary sources on Newman, see John Coulson, *Religion and Imagination* (Oxford: Clarendon, 1981); Louis Bouyer, *Newman's Vision of Faith* (San Francisco: Ignatius, 1986); Thomas J. Norris, *Newman and His Theological Method: A Guide for the Theologian Today* (Leiden: Brill, 1977); Clyde Nabe, *Mystery and Religion: Newman's Epistemology of Religion* (Lanham, Md.: University Press of America, 1988); William R. Fey, *Faith and Doubt: The Unfolding of Newman's Thought on Certainty* (Shepherdstown, W. Va.: Patmos, 1976); Owen Chadwick, *Newman* (Oxford: Oxford University Press, 1983). The main organ for disseminating the ideas of the Oxford Movement was John Newman, ed., *Tracts for the Times,* 6th ed., 6 vols., (New York: AMS Press, 1969). For excerpts from the writings of the Tractari-

ans, catalogued according to topic, see Owen Chadwick, ed., *The Mind of the Oxford Movement* (Stanford, Calif.: Stanford University Press, 1960). More extensive excerpts from pivotal Tractarian writings can be found in Eugene R. Fairweather, ed., *The Oxford Movement* (New York: Oxford University Press, 1964). Secondary works on the Oxford Movement are Christopher Dawson, *The Spirit of the Oxford Movement* (New York: Sheed & Ward, 1934); S. L. Ollard, *A Short History of the Oxford Movement*, 2nd ed. (Oxford: Mowbray, 1963); William George Peck, *The Social Implications of the Oxford Movement* (New York: Charles Scribner's Sons, 1933); Yngve Brilioth, *The Anglican Revival: Studies in the Oxford Movement* (London: Longmans, Green, 1925). Two books of interest on the interaction between Evangelical groups and the Oxford Movement are Elisabeth Jay, ed., *The Evangelical and Oxford Movements* (Oxford: Oxford University Press, 1983); and Peter Toon, *Evangelical Theology: 1833-1856* (Atlanta: John Knox Press, 1979). The former provides readings from both groups on common issues. Toon's book outlines the evangelical response to the positions of the Tractarians.

[2]The urgency felt by the Tractarians is apparent in Newman's closing words in tract 1, in which he warns readers that the conflict is not one from which people can divorce themselves. "To remain neuter much longer will be itself to take part. *Choose* your side; since side you shortly must, with one or other party, even though you do nothing" (*Tracts for the Times*, 6th ed., [New York: AMS Press, 1969], 1:4).

[3]*Apologia Pro Vita Sua* (New York: Random House, 1950], p. 63).

[4]See *Tracts for the Times*, 1:4.

[5]*Apologia Pro Vita Sua*, p. 86.

[6]*Apologia Pro Vita Sua*, p. 110. Newman anticipated such a reaction in tract 90 itself, where he writes in the conclusion, "It may be objected that the tenor of the above explanations is anti-Protestant, whereas it is notorious that the Articles were drawn up by Protestants, and intended for the establishment of Protestantism" ("Remarks on Certain Passages in the Thirty-Nine Articles" [tract 90] in *The Via Media* [London: Longmans, Green, 1901], 2:344).

[7]*Apologia Pro Vita Sua*, p. 132.

[8]There is considerable continuity between Newman's ideas before and after his conversion to Roman Catholicism. Therefore, some of the sources used, when they are consistent with ideas held during his association with the Oxford Movement, were written after 1845.

[9]*Apologia Pro Vita Sua*, p. 76.

[10]*Tracts for the Times*, 1:2.

[11]*Tracts for the Times*, 2:20.

[12]For Pusey's view of baptismal regeneration, see tracts 67-69 in *Tracts for the Times*, 2.

[13]*Via Media*, 1:27.

[14]*Essay on the Development of Christian Doctrine*, 2:1.6.128.

[15]*Newman's University Sermons* (London: SPCK, 1970), p. 335.

[16]*Essay on the Development of Christian Doctrine*, 2:3.133.

[17]*Via Media*, 1:50.

[18]See, for example, *Via Media*, 1:51.

[19]*Via Media*, 1:40.

[20]There is a certain irony in this since revivalists, liberals and confessionalists often gave the same reasons for contradictory positions on the importance of doctrine: the unity of the church. Revivalists generally supported their position pragmatically. Doctrinal positions were secondary to the experience of salvation and should not be made a major issue lest it present a hindrance to one coming to faith. The liberals frequently saw traditional doctrine as a complicated tangle left over from Greek metaphysical debates. They

often believed that Christianity could be boiled down to something as simple as Harnack's "Fatherhood of God and the value of the human soul." Anything else was a unnecessary danger to Christianity unity. The confessionalists, on the other hand, argued that doctrine was the unifying element of Christianity.

[21]*Apologia Pro Vita Sua*, p. 75.

[22]*An Essay in Aid of Grammar of Assent,* ed. Charles Frederick Harrold (New York: Longmans, 1947), p. 71.

[23]*Apologia Pro Vita Sua*, p. 256.

[24]Newman's view that understanding only revealed the exterior of reality and his expansion of reason to include the moral and imaginative faculties has strong parallels to Coleridge's ideas, but the degree of direct influence is unclear. However, Newman rejects Coleridge's idea of the individual's ability to infallibly discern the voice of God. The individual's capacities must always be tested against church doctrine.

[25]Newman is not advocating irrational fideism; reason has its role. First, Christians may encounter times of confusion or doubt. "Under these circumstances the varied proofs of Christianity will be a stay, a refuge, an encouragement, a rallying point for Faith, a gracious economy; and even in the case of the most established Christian they are a source of gratitude and reverent admiration, and a means of confirming faith and hope" (*Newman's University Sermons*, p. 199). Second, Newman states that "unless the doctrines received by Faith are approvable by Reason, they have no claim to be regarded as true." However, "it does not therefore follow that Faith is actually grounded on Reason in the believing mind itself" (*Newman's University Sermons*, pp. 182-83).

[26]*Grammar of Assent*, p. 72.

[27]*Newman's University Sermons*, p. 188. Conclusions derived through empirical or rational means require that we not only provide support for our arguments but that we demonstrate that the ground on which we build support is also valid, and so on to infinity. Given this situation, "Life is not long enough for a religion of inferences; we shall never have done beginning, if we determine to begin with proof. We shall ever be laying our foundations; we shall turn theology into evidences, and divines into textuaries" (*Grammar of Assent*, p. 72).

[28]In places Newman combines the attack on rationalism with his view that faith is only possible with moral willingness. Since rationalists act "not as suppliants, but as judges" (*Grammar of Assent*, pp. 323-24), rationalism represents a moral intransigence toward the divine will.

[29]*Newman's University Sermons*, p. 7. While he rejects rationalistic arguments as a basis for faith, Newman does allow for a form of moral argument. The sense of responsibility and shame that arises from our moral impulse cannot have its source in the natural realm. "These feelings in us are such as require for their exciting cause an intelligent being: we are not affectionate towards a stone, nor do we feel shame before a horse or a dog; we have no remorse or compunction on breaking mere human law" (*Grammar of Assent*, p. 83). Therefore, "If the cause of these emotions does not belong to this visible world, the Object to which his perception is directed must be Supernatural and Divine; and thus the phenomena of Conscience, as a dictate, avail to impress the imagination with the picture of a Supreme Governor, a Judge, holy, just, powerful, all-seeing, retributive, and is the creative principle of religion, as the Moral Sense is the principle of ethics" (*Grammar of Assent*, p. 84).

[30]*Via Media*, p. 33.

[31]On this basis Hengstenberg's three volume *Christology of the Old Testament* argued that the prophecies of the Old Testament should be read in light of the New Testament's Christology. "They [the Old Testament prophets] were not so much *chronological historians* as

describers of pictures" (Christology of the Old Testament [Grand Rapids, Mich.: Kregel, 1970], p. 107). The version cited here is an abridged translation of his three volume German edition.

[32]Wilhelm Löhe, *Three Books About the Church,* ed. and trans. James L. Schaff (Philadelphia: Fortress, 1969), p. 63.

[33]*Three Books,* p. 119.

[34]*Three Books,* p. 73.

[35]*Three Books,* p. 61.

[36]*Three Books,* p. 101.

[37]*Three Books,* p. 162.

[38]*Three Books,* p. 113.

[39]*Three Books,* p. 111.

[40]Major individual works of John Nevin are *The Anxious Bench* (Chambersburg, Penn.: n.p., 1843); and *The Mystical Presence* (Hamden, Conn.: Archon, 1963). For Schaff, see *The Principle of Protestantism,*ed. Bard Thompson and George H. Bricker, trans. John W. Nevin, (Philadelphia: United Church Press, 1964). For selections from the extensive works of Schaff, see Klaus Penzel, *Philip Schaff: Historian and Ambassador of the Universal Church* (Macon, Ga.: Mercer, 1991). For an anthology of the Mercersburg School in general, see James Hastings Nichols, ed., *The Mercersburg Theology* (New York: Oxford University Press, 1966). A short summary of the Mercersburg theology is Luther J. Binkley, *The Mercersburg Theology* (Lancaster, Penn.: Franklin & Marshall College Press, 1953).

[41]*Anxious Bench,* p. 51.

[42]*Anxious Bench,* p. 22.

[43]*Principle of Protestantism,* p. 136.

[44]*Principle of Protestantism,* p. 155.

[45]"Christian Unity," in *The Mercersburg Theology,* ed. James Hastings Nichols (New York: Oxford University Press, 1966), p. 47.

[46]"Christian Unity," p. 47.

[47]*Mystical Presence,* pp. 61-62.

[48]"Christian Unity," pp. 38-39.

[49]Nevin's introduction, *Principle of Protestantism,* pp. 44-45.

[50]"Theses for the Time," #19, p. 222; *Mercersburg Theology,* p. 127. While Schaff has great respect for Baur's dialectical method, he criticizes Baur and Strauss as ultimately ahistorical in their conclusions, stating that their approach absorbed the concrete into the Idea. See "Theses for the Time" #90, p. 230; *Mercersburg Theology,* p. 135. The "Theses" were a synopsis appended to Schaff's *Principle of Protestantism* (1845).

[51]*Principle of Protestantism,* p. 153. The Reformers "have brought into clear consciousness what existed only darkly before in the soul, and have made that to be common property in the church which had belonged previously only to single and highly gifted individuals" (*Principle of Protestantism,* p. 77).

[52]"Theses for the Time" #46, pp. 225-26; *Mercersburg Theology,* p. 130.

[53]*Anxious Bench,* p. 55.

[54]As an example of the cultural ties, one of the burning issues in the day of the Mercersburg theologians was whether services in German Reformed churches should continue to be conducted in German.

[55]Mark A. Noll, ed., *The Princeton Theology 1812-1921: Scripture, Science, and Theological Method from Archibald Alexander to Benjamin Breckinridge Warfield* (Grand Rapids, Mich.: Baker, 1983) presents an anthology of representative writings from the major Princeton theologians. He also supplies a fine introduction to the school. For summaries of the theologies of Hodge, Warfield and Machen, see David F. Wells, *The Princeton Theology* (Grand

Rapids, Mich.: Baker, 1989). The two most significant individual works from this school are Charles Hodge, *Systematic Theology*, 3 vols. (Grand Rapids, Mich.: Eerdmans, 1946); and Benjamin Breckinridge Warfield, *The Inspiration and Authority of the Bible*, ed., Samuel G. Craig (Philadelphia: Presbyterian & Reformed, 1970).

[56]For the influence of Princeton Seminary in the religious life of nineteenth century America, see Noll, ed., *Princeton Theology*, pp. 18-24.

[57]A. A. Hodge, *The Life of Charles Hodge* (New York: Charles Scribner's Sons, 1880), p. 521.

[58]Hodge, *Systematic Theology* (Grand Rapids, Mich.: Eerdmans, 1946), 1:171.

[59]See his *What Is Darwinism? And Other Writing on Science and Religion*, ed. Mark A. Noll and David N. Livingstone (Grand Rapids, Mich.: Baker, 1994). For an analysis of Hodge's view of Darwin, see Jonathan Wells, *Charles Hodge's Critique of Darwinism: An Historical-Critical Analysis of Concepts Basic to the 19th Century Debate* (Lewiston, N.Y.: Mellen, 1988).

[60]Benjamin Breckinridge Warfield, *The Inspiration and Authority of the Bible*, ed. Samuel G. Craig (Philadelphia: Presbyterian & Reformed, 1970), p. 111.

[61]*Systematic Theology*, 1:10. A similar view is found on the opening page of his *Systematic Theology*, in which he states, "The Bible is no more a system of theology, than nature is a system of chemistry or of mechanics. We find in nature the facts which the chemist or the mechanical philosopher has to examine, and from them to ascertain the laws by which they are determined. So the Bible contains the truths which the theologian has to collect, authenticate, arrange, and exhibit in their internal relation to each other" (*Systematic Theology*, 1:1).

[62]*Systematic Theology*, 1:17.

[63]For more information about the philosophical basis of the Princeton theology, see Peter Hicks, *The Philosophy of Charles Hodge: A 19th Century Evangelical Approach to Reason, Knowledge and Truth* (Lewiston, N.Y.: Mellen, 1997).

[64]*Systematic Theology*, 1:163.

[65]*Systematic Theology*, 1:157.

[66]*Systematic Theology*, 1:157.

[67]*Systematic Theology*, 1:165.

[68]*Systematic Theology*, 1:16.

[69]*Systematic Theology*, 1:183.

[70]For a study of the Princeton theologians on this topic and a more favorable conclusion regarding their integration of personal experience and propositional theology than I have proposed, see W. Andrew Hoffecker, *Piety and the Princeton Theologians* (Grand Rapids, Mich.: Baker, 1981).

[71]For a survey of liberal Christianity in America during the nineteenth century, see William R. Hutchison, *The Modernist Impulse in American Protestantism* (Oxford: Oxford University Press, 1982). Post-Ritschlian theology in Germany is considered in George Rupp, *Culture-Protestantism: German Liberal Theology at the Turn of the Twentieth Century* (Missoula, Mont.: Scholars Press, 1977).

[72]Karl Barth, *Protestant Thought: From Rousseau to Ritschl*, trans. Brian Cozens (New York: Harper & Row, 1959), p. 390.

[73]Ritschl's major work is *The Christian Doctrine of Justification and Reconciliation*, trans. H. R. Mackintosh and A. B. Macaulay (Edinburgh: T & T Clark, 1902). *Three Essays*, trans., Philip Hefner (Philadelphia: Fortress, 1972) contains his influential essay on theology and metaphysics, the introduction to his *History of Pietism* and his *Instruction in the Christian Religion*, which was a theology written for use in German secondary schools. For secondary sources on Ritschl, see Robert Mackintosh, *Albrecht Ritschl and His School* (London: Chapman & Hall, 1915); Philip J. Hefner, *Faith and the Vitalities of History: A Theological Study Based on the Work of Albrecht Ritschl* (New York: Harper & Row, 1966);

Albert Temple Swing, *The Theology of Albrecht Ritschl* (New York: Longmans, Green, 1901); Clive Marsh, *Albrecht Ritschl and the Problem of the Historical Jesus* (Lewiston, N.Y.: Mellen, 1992); David W. Lotz, *Ritschl & Luther: A Fresh Perspective on Albrecht Ritschl's Theology in the Light of His Luther Study* (Nashville: Abingdon, 1974); David L. Mueller, *An Introduction to the Theology of Albrecht Ritschl* (Philadelphia: Westminster, 1969); James Orr, *The Ritschlian Theology and the Evangelical Faith,* 2nd ed. (London: Hodder & Stoughton, 1897); James Richmond, *Ritschl, a Reappraisal: A Study in Systematic Theology* (London: Collins, 1978); Darrell Jodock, ed., *Ritschl in Retrospect: History, Community, and Science* (Minneapolis: Fortress, 1995); and the chapters on Ritschl in both Karl Barth, *Protestant Thought: From Rousseau to Ritschl,* trans. Brian Cozens (New York: Harper & Row, 1959); and Hugh Ross Mackintosh, *Types of Modern Theology: Schleiermacher to Barth* (London: Nisbet, 1937).

[74]"Instruction in the Christian Religion," in *Three Essays,* trans. Philip Hefner (Philadelphia: Fortress, 1972), #3, p. 222.

[75]*The Christian Doctrine of Justification and Reconciliation,* trans. H. R. Mackintosh and A. B. Macaulay (Edinburgh: T & T Clark, 1902), p. 16.

[76]"Theology and Metaphysics," in *Three Essays,* p. 157.

[77]*Justification and Reconciliation,* p. 17.

[78]This allows Ritschl to pursue the same course Schleiermacher followed. Once religion is released from the domain of metaphysics, it receives immunity from metaphysical critique. Instead religious truth can only be tested by criteria compatible with religion itself.

[79]*Justification and Reconciliation,* p. 237. While Ritschl occasionally acknowledges that every theological conclusion has metaphysical implications, his point is that we cannot attain proper theological positions by beginning from metaphysics. The life of Christ is the only proper point of departure for theology. This means, among other things, that Ritschl will have no use for arguments derived from natural theology. Theistic proofs beginning from nature cannot bring us to the personal God who justifies and reconciles through Christ and thus are of no use to Christianity.

[80]"Theology and Metaphysics," pp. 156-57.

[81]*Justification and Reconciliation,* p. 398.

[82]*Justification and Reconciliation,* p. 398.

[83]*Justification and Reconciliation,* p. 212. For Ritschl's use of Luther's themes, see Lotz, *Ritschl & Luther.*

[84]*Justification and Reconciliation,* p. 204.

[85]*Justification and Reconciliation,* p. 11.

[86]"Instruction in the Christian Religion" #5, p. 222.

[87]*Justification and Reconciliation,* p. 414.

[88]"Instruction in the Christian Religion" #21, p. 229. Therefore, while Ritschl considers it theoretically possible that another might manifest the same perfect obedience to the kingdom ideal, Jesus would maintain his particular position as the mediator of salvation. "Jesus is therefore unique, for should any other fulfill the same task as perfectly as he, he would be unlike him because of his dependence upon Jesus. Therefore, as the prototype of the humanity to be united into the Kingdom of God, he is the original object of God's love, so that the love of God for the members of his kingdom is also mediated only through him" ("Instruction in the Christian Religion" #22, p. 230).

[89]*Justification and Reconciliation,* p. 451.

[90]Elsewhere Ritschl speaks of focus on Christ's person as a form of mysticism. The idea of the mystical union of the human with God represents an attempt to overcome the limits of time and space. However, the message of Christianity is proclaimed within history.

[91]Ritschl argues that, given God's eternal plan to implement his kingdom, the preexistence of Christ may have validity but only for God. To remain consistent with what is accessible

to us, we cannot make such a claim part of theology. "But if at the same time we discount, in the case of God, the interval between purpose and accomplishment, then we get the formula that Christ exists for God eternally as that which He appears to us under the limitations of time. But only for God, since for us, as pre-existent, Christ is hidden. Inasmuch, then, as God's standpoint is impossible for us, we shall be wise if we content ours with this formal proof of our religious estimate of Christ" (*Justification and Reconciliation*, p. 471).

[92]*Justification and Reconciliation*, p. 392.

[93]*Justification and Reconciliation*, p. 262. Ritschl expands on his reasons for rejecting original sin by stating, first, that sin cannot be divorced from an individual act of the will. "Secondly, education is possible only on the presupposition that existing bad habits or evil inclinations have come to exist as the products of repeated acts of will. . . . [Therefore] from the standpoint of original sin education is quite unthinkable. . . . Thirdly, the assumption we make of distinct degrees of evil in individuals . . . is incompatible with the dogma of original sin, which asserts of all the descendants of Adam an equally high degree of sinful inclination" (*Justification and Reconciliation*, p. 337).

[94]*Justification and Reconciliation*, p. 384. Just as he refuses to define salvation in individual terms, Ritschl also emphasizes the corporate nature of sin. "The cooperation of many individuals in these forms of sin leads to a reinforcement of the same in common customs and principles, in standing immoralities, and even in evil institutions. So there develops an almost irresistible power of temptation for those who with characters yet undeveloped are so much exposed to evil example that they do not see through the network of enticements to evil. Accordingly, the kingdom of sin, or the (immoral, human) world is reinforced in every new generation. Corporate sin, this opposite of the kingdom of God, rests upon all as a power which at the very least limits the freedom of the individual with respect to the good" ("Instruction in the Christian Religion" #30, p. 233).

[95]*Justification and Reconciliation*, p. 479.

[96]Ritschl's well-known opposition to mysticism also grows out of the centrality of history to his theology. He argues that mysticism, in all its permutations, is wrong-headed because it attempts to bypass history in search of unity with God. The form of mysticism Ritschl combats most forcefully is pietism, which he sees as a distortion of Luther's thought. He was in accord with its view that theology has its beginning in the believer's experience of salvation but believed that Christ's mediation was treated as a dispensable means to God. Similarly, Schleiermacher's belief that theology requires an anthropological beginning point and should be kept separate from philosophy is seen as a positive development by Ritschl. However, he rejects Schleiermacher's reliance on *Gefühl* as ahistorical and subjectivistic.

[97]*Justification and Reconciliation*, p. 2.

[98]*Justification and Reconciliation*, pp. 464-65.

[99]The major works of Harnack in translation are *What is Christianity?* trans. Thomas Bailey Saunders (Philadelphia: Fortress, 1986); *Outlines of the History of Dogma,* trans. Edwin Knox Mitchell (Boston: Beacon Press, 1957); *History of Dogma,* trans. Neil Buchanan, 3rd ed., 7 vols. (New York: Dover, 1961); *The Origin of the New Testament,* trans. J. R. Wilkinson (New York: Macmillan, 1925). A selection of Harnack's works is provided by H. Martin Rumscheidt, ed., *Adolf von Harnack: Liberal Theology at Its Height* (San Francisco: Harper & Row, 1989). Additional sources for his thought are Robert T. Voelkel, *The Shape of the Theological Task* (Philadelphia: Westminster Press, 1968); G. Wayne Glick, *The Reality of Christianity: A Study of Adolf von Harnack As Historian and Theologian* (New York: Harper & Row, 1967); H. Martin Rumscheidt, *Revelation and Theology: An Analysis of the Barth-Harnack Correspondence of 1923* (Cambridge: Cambridge University Press, 1972); Wilhelm Pauck, *Har-*

nack and Troeltsch (New York: Oxford University Press, 1968).

[100]Harnack had nobility conferred on him by the monarchy. He was also the first president of the Royal Society, general director of the Royal Libraries and president of the Evangelical-Social Congress.

[101]*What Is Christianity?* trans. Thomas Bailey Saunders (Philadelphia: Fortress, 1986), p. 12.

[102]*What Is Christianity?* p. 14.

[103]*What Is Christianity?* p. 12. In this way Harnack's employment of historical-criticism methods goes farther than most previous historians. He not only subjects Christian doctrine to its investigations but the essence of its message as well.

[104]*What Is Christianity?* p. 14.

[105]*What Is Christianity?* p. 180.

[106]*What Is Christianity?* p. 207.

[107]*What Is Christianity?* p. 205.

[108]*What Is Christianity?* pp. 204-5.

[109]*What Is Christianity?* p. 268.

[110]*What Is Christianity?* p. 51.

[111]*What Is Christianity?* p. 275.

[112]*What Is Christianity?* p. 11.

[113]*What Is Christianity?* p. 144.

[114]Harnack does not see dogmatic Christological statements as innocuous anachronisms but as a positive danger to Christianity. "On the question of 'Christology' men beat their religious doctrines into terrible weapons, and spread fear and intimidation everywhere. This attitude still continues: Christology is treated as though the Gospel had no other problem to offer, and the accompanying fanaticism is still rampant in our own day" (*What Is Christianity?* p. 125).

[115]*What Is Christianity?* p. 56.

[116]George Tyrrell, *Christianity at the Cross-Roads* (London: George Allen & Unwin, 1963), p. 49.

[117]Herrmann's most definitive theological work is his *The Communion of the Christian with God: Described on the Basis of Luther's Statements*, ed. Robert T. Voelkel (Philadelphia: Fortress, 1971). Other major writings in translation are *Faith and Morals,* trans. Donald Matheson and Robert W. Stewart (New York: Putnam's, 1904); *Systematic Theology,* trans. Nathaniel Micklem and Kenneth A. Saunders (New York: Macmillan, 1927). A useful source on Herrmann's theology is Robert T. Voelkel, *The Shape of the Theological Task* (Philadelphia: Westminster, 1968).

[118]*Communion of the Christian,* p. 65.

[119]*Communion of the Christian,* pp. 69-70.

[120]*Communion of the Christian,* p. 52.

[121]*Communion of the Christian,* pp. 102-3.

[122]*Communion of the Christian,* p.60.

[123]*Communion of the Christian,* p. 74.

[124]*Communion of the Christian,* p. 74.

[125]*Communion of the Christian,* p. lxvi.

[126]*Communion of the Christian,* p. 87.

[127]*Communion of the Christian,* p. 19.

[128]*Communion of the Christian,* p. 74.

[129]*Communion of the Christian,* p. 11.

[130]Overviews of Roman Catholic modernism are Alec R. Vidler, *A Variety of Catholic Modernists* (Cambridge: Cambridge University Press, 1970); *The Modernist Movement in the Roman Church* (Cambridge: Cambridge University Press, 1934); Gabriel Daly, *Transcendence and*

Immanence: A Study in Catholic Modernism and Integralism (Oxford: Oxford University Press, 1980); Bernard M. G. Reardon, "Roman Catholic Modernism," in *Nineteenth Century Religious Thought in the West*, vol. 2 (Cambridge: Cambridge University Press, 1985); John Ratte, *Three Modernists* (London: Sheed & Ward, 1968). Thomas Michael Loome, *Liberal Catholicism, Reform Catholicism, Modernism* (Mainz: Matthias-Grünwald-Verlag, 1979), contains not only a survey of the modernist controversy but also extensive bibliographies on several related topics. A good overview of Loisy's thought and his debate with Harnack is found in Bernard B. Scott's introduction to Loisy's *The Gospel and the Church.*

[131] Alfred Loisy, *The Gospel and the Church,* trans. Christopher Home (Philadelphia: Fortress, 1976).

[132] *Gospel and the Church,* p. 87.

[133] *Gospel and the Church,* p. 211.

[134] *Gospel and the Church,* p. 166.

[135] *Gospel and the Church,* p. 17.

[136] *Gospel and the Church,* p. 151.

[137] Rauschenbush's theology is best presented in *A Theology for the Social Gospel* (Nashville: Abingdon, 1978). Other important writings are *Christianity and the Social Crisis,* ed. Robert D. Cross (New York: Harper, 1964); *The Social Principles of Jesus* (New York: Association Press, 1916); *Christianizing the Social Order* (New York: Macmillan, 1912); *The Righteousness of the Kingdom,* ed. Max L. Stackhouse (Nashville: Abingdon, 1968). See also *Walter Rauschenbusch: Selected Writings,* ed. Winthrop S. Hudson (New York: Paulist, 1984) for other major selections. An anthology of three major figures of Social Gospel (including Rauschenbush) is Robert T. Handy, ed., *The Social Gospel in America* (New York: Oxford University Press, 1966). General works on the Social Gospel Movement are Paul A. Carter, *Decline and Revival of the Social Gospel: Social and Political Liberalism in American Protestant Churches, 1920-1940* (Ithaca, N.Y.: Cornell University Press, 1954); Charles Howard Hopkins, *The Rise of the Social Gospel in American Protestantism 1865-1915* (New Haven, Conn.: Yale University Press, 1940); Janet Fishburn, *The Fatherhood of God and the Victorian Family: The Social Gospel in America* (Philadelphia: Fortress, 1981).

[138] *Theology for the Social Gospel,* p. 158.

[139] *Theology for the Social Gospel,* p. 137.

[140] *Theology for the Social Gospel,* p. 145.

[141] *Theology for the Social Gospel,* p. 134.

[142] *Theology for the Social Gospel,* p. 146.

[143] *Theology for the Social Gospel,* pp. 53-54.

[144] *Theology for the Social Gospel,* p. 243.

[145] *Theology for the Social Gospel,* p. 148.

[146] *Theology for the Social Gospel,* p. 154.

[147] While the Social Gospel shared many of liberalism's theological positions, The war's impact on it was less severe. Two reasons can be cited for this. First, its roots were primarily in America, which did not feel the effects of the war as keenly as Europe. Second, since it represented a protest against the social and political institutions, it could escape the charge of complicity in a way impossible for the German theologians.

Chapter 11: Darwinism and the Rise of the Social Sciences

[1] Darwin's two major writings have been combined in *The Origin of Species, By Means of Natural Selection or the Preservation of Favored Races in the Struggle for Life* and *The Descent of Man, and Selection in Relation to Sex* (New York: Modern Library, 1936.). For the latter text, I have used *The Descent of Man, and Selection in Relation to Sex,* 2nd ed. (New York: Burt,

1874). See also *The Autobiography of Charles Darwin and Selected Letters,* ed. Francis Darwin (New York: Dover, 1958). For a short, readable introduction to his life and thought, see Jonathan Howard, *Darwin* (Oxford: Oxford University Press, 1982). For a good selection of his writing, see *The Darwin Reader,* ed. Mark Ridley, 2nd ed. (New York: Norton, 1996). For biography on Darwin's life, see John Bowlby, *Charles Darwin: A New Life* (New York: Norton, 1990); Janet Browne, *Charles Darwin: A Biography* (New York: Knopf, 1995); Michael White and John Gribbin, *Darwin: A Life in Science* (New York: Dutton, 1995); Peter J. Bowler, *Charles Darwin: The Man and His Influence* (Cambridge: Cambridge University Press, 1996). For an anthology of writings on evolution prior to Darwin and responses to his theories after *Origin* see Philip Appleman, ed., *Darwin* (New York: Norton, 1970). For responses to Darwin's theories in different countries and disciplines, see Thomas F. Glick, *The Comparative Reception of Darwinism* (Austin: University of Texas, 1972); David Hull, *Darwin and His Critics* (Chicago: University of Chicago, 1983); and Ernst Mayr, *One Long Argument: Charles Darwin and the Genesis of Modern Evolutionary Thought* (Cambridge, Mass.: Harvard University Press, 1991). For philosophical issues arising from Darwin's work, see David Hull, *The Philosophy of Biological Science* (Englewood Cliffs, N.J.: Prentice-Hall, 1974); Michael Ruse, *The Darwinian Paradigm: Essays on Its History, Philosophy, and Religious Implications* (New York: Routledge, 1989); Suzanne Cunningham, *Philosophy and the Darwinian Legacy* (Rochester, N.Y.: University of Rochester Press, 1996). The religious impact of Darwin is surveyed in James R. Moore, *The Post-Darwinian Controversies: A Study of the Protestant Struggle to Come to Terms with Darwin in Great Britain and America 1870-1900* (Cambridge: Cambridge University Press, 1979); and David N. Livingstone, *Darwin's Forgotten Defenders: The Encounter Between Evangelical Theology and Evolutionary Thought* (Grand Rapids, Mich.: Eerdmans, 1987).

[2]As Darwin describes it in his *Autobiography,* "In October 1838 . . . I happened to read for amusement Malthus on *Population,* and being well prepared to appreciate the struggle for existence which everywhere goes on from long-continued observation of the habits of animals and plants, it at once struck me that under these circumstances favourable variations would tend to be preserved, and unfavourable ones to be destroyed. The result of this would be the formation of new species. Here, then, I had at last got a theory by which to work; but I was so anxious to avoid prejudice, that I determined not for some time to write even the briefest sketch of it" (*Autobiography,* pp. 42-43).

[3]*Origin of Species,* p. 360.

[4]*Origin of Species,* p. 53.

[5]*Origin of Species,* p. 66.

[6]*Origin of Species,* p. 63.

[7]*Origin of Species,* p. 13.

[8]*Autobiography,* p. 64. For a conclusive refutation of the idea that Darwin had a "deathbed conversion" back to theism, see James R. Moore, *The Darwin Legend* (Grand Rapids, Mich.: Baker, 1994).

[9]"In the future I see open field for far more important researches. Psychology will be securely based on the foundation already well laid by Mr. Herbert Spencer, that of the necessary acquirement of each mental power and capacity by gradation. Much light will be thrown on the origin of man and his history" (*Origin,* p. 373).

[10]*Descent,* p. 694.

[11]*Descent,* p. 143.

[12]*Descent,* p. 162.

[13]*Descent,* p. 94.

[14]*Descent,* pp. 119-20.

[15]*Descent,* p. 80. Since Darwin views social sympathy as an indication of advanced evolution,

he cannot appeal to social behavior of lesser species such as bees or ants. Instead to explain the emergence of human beings, Darwin looks to attributes in higher mammals that approximate human love and empathy. Such characteristics, to be antecedents to human moral sensitivities, must result in unselfish concern for the good of another.

[16]*Descent,* p. 141. This indicates that Darwin believes that the breadth of one's sympathies is a measure of evolutionary development. Darwin links variations in moral empathy between human groups with differing levels of intelligence. "The chief causes of the low morality of savages, as judged by our standard, are, firstly, the confinement of sympathy to the same tribe. Second, powers of reasoning insufficient to recognize the bearing of many virtues, especially of the self-regarding virtues, on the general welfare of the tribe" (*Descent,* p. 135).

[17]Darwin does not hesitate to assert that moral tendencies, since they develop from intellectual and communal characteristics, are heritable. "There is not the least inherent improbability, as it seems to me, in virtuous tendencies being more or less strongly inherited" (*Descent,* p. 140).

[18]*Descent,* p. 143.

[19]*Descent,* p. 142.

[20]*Descent,* p. 108.

[21]*Descent,* p. 108.

[22]John Dewey, *The Influence of Darwin on Philosophy: And Other Essays in Contemporary Thought* (Bloomington: Indiana University Press, 1965), p. 19.

[23]For the history of this movement, see Richard Hofstadter and Eric Foner, *Social Darwinism in American Thought,* rev. ed. (Boston: Beacon Press, 1992); Robert C. Bannister, *Social Darwinism* (Philadelphia: Temple University Press, 1989); and Mike Hawkins, *Social Darwinism in European and American Thought, 1860-1945* (Cambridge: Cambridge University Press, 1997).

[24]This problem does not go away (*contra* M. Ruse) with the insistence that certain characteristics of a genotype confer "fitness" since we cannot decide what those characteristics are independent of the survival of the organism in its environment. See the careful discussion in Hull, *Philosophy of Biological Science,* pp. 66-69.

[25]For these and further philosophical criticisms of Darwinism, eugenics and social Darwinism, see Karl Popper, "Natural Selection and the Emergence of Mind," *Dialectica* 32 (1978):339-55; this article was reprinted in *Evolutionary Epistemology, Rationality and the Sociology of Knowledge,* ed. G. Radnitzky and W. W. Bartley (La Salle, Ill.: Open Court, 1987); Phillip Johnson, *Darwin on Trial* (Downers Grove, Ill.: InterVarsity Press, 1991); D. C. Stove, *Darwinian Fairytales* (Aldershot: Avebury, 1996); and Edward Caudill, *Darwinian Myths* (Knoxville: University of Tennessee Press, 1997). We do not suggest, as some critics do, that modern evolutionary biology is unfalsifiable or unscientific. Nor are we saying that evolution is *false.* Our point (like Popper's) is that modern evolutionary biology is *incomplete.* Critics of biological evolution per se (such as Michael J. Behe, *Darwin's Black Box* [New York: Free Press, 1996]) go too far in suggesting that we need to change our science altogether. Rather, his examples point to the incompleteness of evolutionary theory. For a spirited defense of Darwinism, see Michael Ruse, *Darwinism Defended* (Reading, Mass.: Addison-Wesley, 1982).

[26]Social Darwinism is still with us; for just one recent example, see Albert Somit and Steven A. Peterson, *Darwinism, Dominance and Democracy* (New York: Praeger, 1997).

[27]Major works of Spencer are *Social Statics, Or the Conditions Essential to Human Happiness* (New York: Kelley, 1969); *The Man Versus the State* (Caldwell, Idaho: Caxton, 1965); *First Principles* (New York: DeWitt Revolving Fund, 1958); *The Data of Ethics* (New York: Collier, 1901); *The Principles of Sociology,* 3 vols. (New York: Appleton, 1898). Spencer's autobiogra-

phy, published two years after his death, is available as *An Autobiography,* 2 vols. (New York: Appleton, 1904). *The Evolution of Society* (ed. Robert L. Carneiro [Chicago: University of Chicago, 1967]) is a distillation of Spencer's three-volume *Principles of Sociology.* For secondary sources, see Jonathan H. Turner, *Herbert Spencer: A Renewed Appreciation* (Beverly Hills, Calif.: Sage, 1985); J. D. Y. Peel, *Herbert Spencer: The Evolution of a Sociologist* (New York: Basic Books, 1971); Hugh Samuel Roger Elliot, *Herbert Spencer* (Westport, Conn.: Greenwood, 1970); Tim Gray, *The Political Philosophy of Herbert Spencer: Individualism and Organicism* (Brookfield, Vt.: Avebury, 1996); James G. Kennedy, *Herbert Spencer* (Boston: Twayne, 1978). For a bibliography of works by and about Spencer, see Robert G. Perrin, *Herbert Spencer: A Primary and Secondary Bibliography* (New York: Garland, 1993).

[28]Sources that offer historical surveys of sociological theory that include the next three figures as well as other important contributors to the discipline are Robert A. Nisbet, *The Sociological Tradition* (New York: Basic Books, 1966); Randall Collins and Michael Makowsky, *The Discovery of Society,* 5th ed. (New York: McGraw-Hill, 1993); Lewis A. Coser, *Masters of Sociological Thought: Ideas in Historical and Social Context* (New York: Harcourt Brace Jovanovich, 1971); Irvin M. Zeitlin, *Ideology and the Development of Sociological Theory* (Englewood Cliffs, N.J.: Prentice-Hall, 1968); Harry Elmer Barnes, *Social Thought from Lore to Science,* 2nd ed., 3 vols. (Washington: Harren, 1952); Emory Stephen Bogardus, *The Development of Social Thought,* 4th ed. (New York: D. McKay, 1960); H. Stuart Hughes, *Consciousness and Society: The Reorientation of European Social Thought 1890-1930* (New York: Vintage, 1958).

[29]This marks an important departure from Comte, who, according to Spencer, wanted to maintain the older view that social entities were essentially ideas.

[30]For Spencer's influence on social evolutionists in America, such as William Graham Sumner (1840-1910), see Richard Hofstadter, *Social Darwinism in American Thought,* rev. ed. (Boston: Beacon, 1955).

[31]However, it is also true that Darwin's *Origin of Species* exerted a strong influence on Spencer as well. He credits Darwin with providing impetus to proceed with his massive *Synthetic Philosophy* (1862-1893), and is probably responsible for a significant reduction in the teleological orientation of his early *Social Statics* (1850).

[32]*Autobiography,* 1:101.

[33]*Social Statics,* p. 39.

[34]*First Principles,* p. 97.

[35]*First Principles,* pp. 78-79.

[36]*First Principles,* p. 80.

[37]*First Principles,* pp. 123-24.

[38]*First Principles,* pp. 138-39.

[39]*First Principles,* p. 138. This view of the relationship between science and philosophy is a natural outgrowth of his concept of evolution, which argues that the direction of movement is from disunity and simplicity toward unity and interconnectedness.

[40]*Social Statics,* pp. 415.

[41]*First Principles,* p. 537.

[42]*First Principles,* p. 359.

[43]*First Principles,* p. 327.

[44]*First Principles,* p. 288.

[45]These later statements are in contrast to Spencer's more unilinear approach in his early *Social Statics,* in which he argues that change is directional, irreversible and lawful. There he argues, "When it is shown that this advancement is due to the working of a universal law, and that in virtue of that law it must continue until the state we call perfection is reached, then the advent of such a state is removed out of the region of probability into

that of certainty" (*Social Statics*, p. 64). This general statement is applicable to the perfection of human nature as well. "The ultimate development of the ideal man is logically certain—as certain as any conclusion in which we place the most implicit faith; for instance, that all men will die" (*Social Statics*, p. 64).

[46]*Social Statics*, p. 65.

[47]*Social Statics*, p. 33. As an aspect of the upward development of human nature, Spencer argues, as does Darwin, that mind is a creature of evolution. If the powers of the mind had no beneficial function, they could not have emerged.

[48]*The Data of Ethics* (New York: Collier, 1901), p. 36.

[49]Spencer's definition of the ethical ideal is, "That perfect adjustment of acts to ends in maintaining individual life and rearing new individuals, which is effected by each without hindering others from effecting like perfect adjustments" (*Data of Ethics*, p. 20).

[50]*Social Statics*, p. 59. Spencer argues that there is no one single way by which an equilibrium can be satisfied, which adds an element of relativism to his ethics. "A code of perfect personal conduct can never be made definite. Many forms of life, diverging from one another in considerable degrees, may be so carried on in society as entirely to fulfill the conditions to harmonious co-operation" (*Data of Ethics*, p. 327).

[51]*Principles of Sociology*, 1:102.

[52]*Principles of Sociology*, 2:664.

[53]*Social Statics*, p. 378.

[54]*Social Statics*, p. 378.

[55]*Social Statics*, p. 378.

[56]*Social Statics*, p. 380.

[57]*Social Statics*, p. 103. Against the charge that this individualistic emphasis is egoistic, Spencer argues that this assumes a false dilemma. Egoism and altruism are not mutually exclusive but are two parts of the tension necessary in maintaining an evolutionary equilibrium. "From the dawn of life, then, egoism has been dependent upon altruism as altruism has been dependent upon egoism, and in the course of evolution the reciprocal services of the two have been increasing" (*Data of Ethics*, p. 249). One cannot achieve their desires in isolation from society nor can society attain its ends apart from the satisfaction of individual members. Therefore, he concludes that the individual "must become impressed with the salutary truth, that no one can be perfectly free till all are free; no one can be perfectly moral till all are moral; no one can be perfectly happy till all are happy" (*Social Statics*, p. 456).

[58]*Principles of Sociology*, 2:608.

[59]*Principles of Sociology*, 3/1:688. All references to vol. 3 are from the 1886 edition.

[60]*Principles of Sociology*, 3/1:833. Christianity's insistence on the personal attributes of God is one reason Spencer finds it, in its present form, untenable. Perhaps more damaging for him, however, is the particularism of its Jewish background. As he states it, "Astonishing is the supposition that the Cause from which have arisen thirty millions of Suns with their attendant planets, took the form of a man, and made a bargain with Abraham to give him territory in return for allegiance" (*Autobiography*, 1:171).

[61]*Principles of Sociology*, 3/1:839.

[62]*First Principles*, p. 35.

[63]*Principles of Sociology*, 3/1:841.

[64]*Principles of Sociology*, 3/1:843.

[65]Durkheim's major works are *The Division of Labor in Society*, trans. George Simpson (Glencoe, Ill.: Free Press, 1960); *The Rules of Sociological Method*, ed. George E. G. Catlin and trans. Sarah A. Solovay and John H. Mueller, 8th ed. (Glencoe, Ill.: Free Press, 1962.); *Suicide*, ed. George Simpson and trans. John A. Spaulding and George Simpson, (Glencoe, Ill.:

Free Press, 1951); *The Elementary Forms of the Religious Life,* trans. Joseph Ward Swain (New York: Free Press, 1965). A collection of selected writings is *Émile Durkheim: On Morality and Society,* ed. Robert N. Bellah (Chicago: University of Chicago, 1973). The authoritative intellectual biography of Émile Durkheim is Steven Lukes, *Émile Durkheim: His Life and Work* (New York: Harper & Row, 1972). A good brief introduction to Durkheim's major writings is Kenneth Thompson, *Émile Durkheim* (New York: Tavistock, 1982). An older study of Durkheim is Charles Elmer Gehlke, *Émile Durkheim's Contributions to Sociological Theory* (New York: Columbia University, 1915; New York: AMS, 1968). For other secondary sources, see Kurt H. Wolff, ed. *Émile Durkheim, 1858-1917* (Columbus: Ohio State University, 1960); and Robert A. Nisbet, *Émile Durkheim* (Westport, Conn.: Greenwood, 1976), who provides a nice introduction with additional essays that consider specific aspects of Durkheim's thought.

[66]*Suicide,* p. 36.

[67]*Elementary Forms,* p. 495.

[68]*Rules of Sociological Method,* p. 14 (his italics).

[69]*Rules,* p. 13 (his italics).

[70]*Rules,* p. 27.

[71]In this way Durkheim follows Marx in rejecting ideology as the starting point for understanding why social realities spring to existence and how they work. On the other hand, he also distances himself from the functionalist approach of Comte and Spencer. "To show how a fact is useful is not to explain how it originated or why it is what it is. The uses which it serves presuppose the specific properties characterizing it but do not create them" (*Rules,* p. 90).

[72]*Suicide,* p. 158.

[73]*Suicide,* pp. 374-75.

[74]*Suicide,* pp. 159-60. Durkheim goes on to categorize suicide by reference to one's relative integration into society. Egoistic suicide occurs when a social system's ability to incorporate an individual into the collective consciousness is deficient. As Durkheim puts it, "In this case the bond attaching man to life relaxes because that attaching him to society is itself slack" (*Suicide,* pp. 214-15). On the opposite end of the spectrum is altruistic suicide, in which the intensity of group consciousness is so strong that an individual cannot conceive of acting contrary to a group's demands. This leads to suicide for reasons of religious sacrifice or patriotism, for example. In altruistic suicide, "when a person kills himself, . . . it is not because he assumes the right to do so but, on the contrary, *because it is his duty*" (*Suicide,* p. 219). The final form is anomic suicide, in which the individual is in flux in relation to the social order (e.g., divorce, sudden wealth) leaving them bereft of a previous sense of solidarity. "In anomic suicide, society's influence is lacking in the basically individual passions, thus leaving them without a check-rein" (*Suicide,* p. 258).

[75]*Suicide,* p. 170.

[76]*Division of Labor,* p. 79.

[77]*Elementary Forms,* p. 492.

[78]*Division of Labor,* p. 72.

[79]*Division of Labor,* p. 72.

[80]*Division of Labor,* pp. 80-81.

[81]*Division of Labor,* p. 87.

[82]*Division of Labor,* p. 85.

[83]*Division of Labor,* p. 84.

[84]*Suicide,* p. 312.

[85]*Elementary Forms,* pp. 470-71.

[86]*Elementary Forms,* pp. 469-70.

[87]*Elementary Forms*, p. 469.

[88]Just as this collective consciousness gives rise to our sense of the divine, what we call the soul is nothing more than our consciousness of social mores. Since these mores transcend us in our individuality, we have designated the soul as the higher part of our being. "So the individual soul is only a portion of the collective soul of the group; it is the anonymous force at the basis of the cult, but incarnated in an individual whose personality it espouses; it is *mana* individualized" (*Elementary Forms*, p. 299). Our mistake comes in thinking this to be a distinct component existing alongside our physical body.

[89]*Elementary Forms*, p. 466.

[90]*Elementary Forms*, p. 14.

[91]*Elementary Forms*, p. 14.

[92]*Elementary Forms*, pp. 14-15.

[93]*Elementary Forms*, p. 20. *Elementary Forms* uses the totemic religion of Australian aborigines as the foundation of its argument. The idea is that if we begin with a rather elementary religious structure, it allows us to understand the nature of beliefs about the sacred and secular in more complex societies. "It is necessary to commence by going back to its [religion's] most primitive and simple form, to try to account for the characteristics by which it was marked at that time, and then to show how it developed and became complicated little by little, and how it became that which it is at the moment in question" (*Elementary Forms*, p. 15).

[94]*Suicide*, p. 312.

[95]*Elementary Forms*, p. 464.

[96]*Division of Labor*, p. 387. As we have seen above, Spencer believed that individual freedom and democracy were the result of evolutionary forces in nature and that they should be allowed to continue to shape society without external interference. In contrast, Durkheim, following his view that social structures are creations, argues that "liberty itself is the product of regulation. Far from being antagonistic to social action, it results from social action. It is far from being an inherent property of the state of nature. On the contrary, it is a conquest of society over nature" (*Division of Labor*, p. 386). Rather than society acting as a limit to individual freedom, society's institutional framework is the means to greater freedom because it counteracts our inclination to egotism. Moreover, Durkheim argues that democracies based on national identity were simply a temporary stage because the reach of their moral sympathies was limited to fellow citizens. "For just as private conflicts can be regulated only by the action of the society in which the individuals live, so intersocial conflicts can be regulated only by a society which comprises in its scope all others. The only power which can serve to moderate individual egotism is the power of the group; the only power which can serve to moderate the egotism of groups is that of some other group which embraces them" (*Division of Labor*, p. 405).

[97]*Elementary Forms*, p. 478.

[98]*Elementary Forms*, pp. 474-75.

[99]For an exposition of Feuerbach, see chapter six. A difference between these two thinkers is that, while Durkheim views the content of our idealizing process as a mirror of the society within which we reside, Feuerbach attributes idealization of our recognition of humanity as a whole. In the end, however, the differences are not that great since Durkheim clearly believes that, although the doctrines and practices do reflect cultural particularities, the function of these practices is universal.

[100]Weber's major works include *Economy and Society: An Outline of Interpretive Sociology*, ed. Guenther Roth and Claus Wittich, trans. Ephriam Fischoff et al., 3 vols. (New York: Bedminster, 1968); *The Protestant Ethic and the Spirit of Capitalism*, trans. Talcott Parsons (New York: Charles Scribner's Sons, 1958); *Basic Concepts in Sociology*, trans. H. P. Secher (New

York: Citadel, 1964); *General Economic History,* trans. Frank H. Knight (Glencoe, Ill.: Free Press, 1927); *The Religion of China: Confucianism and Taoism,* ed. and trans. Hans H. Gerth (Glencoe, Ill.: Free Press, 1961); *The Religion of India,* ed. and trans. Hans H. Gerth and Don Martindale (Glencoe, Ill.: Free Press, 1958); *Ancient Judaism,* ed. and trans. Hans H. Gerth and Don Martindale (Glencoe, Ill.: Free Press, 1952). Weber's essays on sociological method are compiled in *Max Weber on the Methodology of the Social Sciences,* ed. and trans. Edward A. Shils and Henry A. Finch (Glencoe, Ill.: Free Press, 1949). Selections of Weber's sociology, organized by topic, can be found in *From Max Weber: Essays in Sociology,* ed. and trans. H. H. Gerth and C. Wright Mills (New York: Oxford University Press, 1967). For his political ideas, see *Weber: Political Writings,* ed. Peter Lassman and Ronald Speirs (Cambridge: Cambridge University Press, 1994). Weber's influential section on religion at the beginning of volume two of *Economy and Society* is available as *The Sociology of Religion,* trans. Ephraim Fischoff (Boston: Beacon, 1963). The standard study of Weber's thought is Reinhard Bendix, *Max Weber: An Intellectual Portrait,* rev. ed. (Berkeley: University of California, 1977). A very readable introduction to Weber's ideas is Frank Parkin, *Max Weber* (New York: Tavistock, 1982).

[101]*Basic Concepts in Sociology,* p. 29.
[102]*Economy and Society,* 1:7.
[103]*Economy and Society,* 1:14.
[104]*Economy and Society,* 1:4.
[105]*Economy and Society,* 1:9.
[106]*Economy and Society,* 1:16.
[107]*Economy and Society,* 1:5-6.
[108]*Economy and Society,* 1:5.
[109]*Max Weber on the Methodology of the Social Sciences,* p. 90.
[110]*Economy and Society,* 1:20.
[111]*Economy and Society,* 1:21-22.
[112]*Economy and Society,* 1:212.
[113]*Economy and Society,* 1:215.
[114]*Economy and Society,* 1:241.
[115]*Economy and Society,* 1:244.
[116]*Economy and Society,* 1:215.
[117]*Economy and Society,* 3:1114.
[118]*Economy and Society,* 3:1112.
[119]*Economy and Society,* 1:215.
[120]*Economy and Society,* 3:1111.
[121]*Protestant Ethic and the Spirit of Capitalism,* p. 85. In addition to Lutheranism, Weber's ideal type of Protestantism excludes those groups that disagree with predestination. The closest concrete example of Weber's ideal of Protestantism is seventeenth-century Puritanism. The Puritan divine, Richard Baxter (1615-1691), is most frequently cited as the intellectual engine behind the Protestant ethic. See *Protestant Ethic,* p. 155 for Weber's reasons for reliance on Baxter.
[122]*Economy and Society,* 3:1198.
[123]"To the Catholic the absolution of his Church was a compensation for his own imperfection. The priest was a magician who performed the miracle of transubstantiation, and who held the key to eternal life in his hand" (*Protestant Ethic,* p. 117).
[124]*Protestant Ethic,* p. 104.
[125]*Economy and Society,* 2:573.
[126]*Economy and Society,* 3:1199.
[127]*Protestant Ethic,* p. 162.

[128]*Protestant Ethic,* p. 157.

[129]*Protestant Ethic,* p. 172.

[130]*Protestant Ethic,* p. 54.

[131]*Protestant Ethic,* p. 72.

[132]*Economy and Society,* 3:973.

[133]*Economy and Society,* 3:975.

[134]*Economy and Society,* 3:957.

[135]*Economy and Society,* 3:987.

[136]*Economy and Society,* 3:992.

[137]*Economy and Society,* 3:975.

[138]This seems to put Weber square in the camp of his fellow social theorist, Marx. However, Weber believed that Marx's blindspot was a lack of recognition that socialism would require as much, if not more, reliance on bureaucracy if it hoped to compete economically. As a result, the alienation and depersonalizing qualities characteristic of capitalism would not be eliminated by simply exchanging it for a new economic infrastructure.

[139]*Economy and Society,* 1:5-6.

[140]Freud's works are available in collected form in The Standard Edition of the Complete Psychological Works of Sigmund Freud, ed. and trans. James Stachey, 24 vols. (London: Hogarth, 1953-1974). Major individual works by Sigmund Freud are *Totem and Taboo,* trans. James Strachey (London: Routledge & Kegan Paul, 1960); *Civilization and Its Discontents,* trans. James Strachey (New York: W. W. Norton, 1961); *The Complete Introductory Lectures on Psychoanalysis,* ed. and trans. James Strachey (New York: Norton, 1966); *The Interpretation of Dreams,* trans. A. A. Brill, 3rd ed., (London: Allen & Unwin, 1913); *Future of an Illusion,* trans. W. D. Robson-Scott (Garden City, N.Y.: Doubleday, 1957). An anthology of Freud's works is *The Basic Writings of Sigmund Freud,* ed. and trans. A. A. Brill (New York: Modern Library, 1938). The standard biography of Freud is Ernest Jones, *The Life and Works of Sigmund Freud,* 3 vols. (New York: Basic Books, 1953-1957). This biography is available in abridged, one volume format in Ernest Jones, *The Life and Works of Sigmund Freud,* ed. Lionel Trilling and Steven Marcus (New York: Basic Books, 1961). The number of secondary works on Freud is staggering. Good sources to begin with are Maryse Choisy, *Sigmund Freud: A New Appraisal* (New York: Philosophical Library, 1963); Erich Fromm, *Sigmund Freud's Mission: An Analysis of His Personality and Influence* (New York: Grove, 1959); Erich Fromm, *Psychoanalysis and Religion* (New Haven, Conn.: Yale University Press, 1950); Jerome Neu, ed., *The Cambridge Companion to Freud* (Cambridge: Cambridge University Press, 1991); Hans Küng, *Freud and the Problem of God,* trans. Edward Quinn, rev. ed., (New Haven, Conn.: Yale University Press, 1990); Richard Wollheim, *Freud,* 2nd ed. (London: Fontana, 1991); Richard Wollheim and James Hopkins, eds., *Philosophical Essays on Freud,* (Cambridge: Cambridge University Press, 1982); Herbert Marcuse, *Eros and Civilization: A Philosophical Inquiry into Freud* (Boston: Beacon, 1966); Philip Rieff, *Freud: The Mind of the Moralist* (New York: Viking, 1959). For the development of Freud's theories by his intellectual descendants, see J. A. C. Brown, *Freud and the Post-Freudians* (Baltimore: Penguin, 1961).

[141]Ernest Jones, *The Life and Works of Sigmund Freud,* ed. Lionel Trilling and Steven Marcus (New York: Basic Books, 1961), p. 17.

[142]*An Autobiographical Study,* in The Standard Edition of the Complete Psychological Works of Sigmund Freud (hereafter SE) 20, ed. and trans. James Stachey (London: Hogarth, 1953-1974), p. 8.

[143]*Autobiographical Study,* p. 9.

[144]Postcript of *Autobiographical Study,* p. 72.

[145]*Future of an Illusion,* in SE 21, p. 48.

[146]*Civilization and Its Discontents,* p. 24.

[147]"New Introductory Lectures on Psychoanalysis," in *The Complete Introductory Lectures on Psychoanalysis,* ed. and trans. James Strachey (New York: Norton, 1966), p. 623.

[148]"New Introductory Lectures," p. 643. In case one suspects that Freud had temporarily overlooked sociology in his brief list of the sciences, the prior sentence asserts, "For sociology too, dealing as it does with the behaviour of people in society, cannot be anything but applied psychology." Freud argues that actions are not primarily a matter of cultural conditioning or biological determinism but grow out of our unique experiences. This individualistic perspective dictates that the key to human behavior is found in psychology, not sociology.

[149]"Introductory Lectures on Psychoanalysis," in *The Complete Introductory Lectures on Psychoanalysis,* ed. and trans. James Strachey (New York: Norton, 1966), p. 21.

[150]"Introductory Lectures," p. 22.

[151]See *Christianity & Western Thought,* 1:30 for the three functions Plato attributes to the soul.

[152]"Introductory Lectures," p. 413.

[153]*The Ego and the Id,* in SE 19, p. 59.

[154]*Ego and the Id,* p. 35.

[155]*Future of an Illusion,* 21, p. 11.

[156]*Ego and the Id,* p. 48. While the superego can absorb the ideals of sources other than the parents long after the internalization process begins, its decisive character is established by the child's relationship with the parents, particularly the father. "By giving permanent expression to the influence of the parents it [the superego] perpetuates the existence of the factors to which it owes its origin" (*Ego and the Id,* p. 35).

[157]*Ego and the Id,* p. 17.

[158]*Ego and the Id,* p. 40.

[159]"Introductory Lectures," p. 357.

[160]*Ego and the Id,* p.25. For Plato's parable of the charioteer and the two horses, see *Phaedrus* 253d-254e.

[161]Freud's thought closely parallels that of Nietzsche's on this point. Freud states that, in the capacity of conscience, "aggressiveness is introjected, internalized; it is, in point of fact, sent back to where it came from—that is, it is directed towards his own ego. There it is taken over by a portion of the ego, which sets itself over against the rest of the ego as super-ego, and which now, in the form of 'conscience', is ready to put into action against the ego the same harsh aggressiveness that the ego would have liked to satisfy upon other, extraneous individuals" (*Civilization and Its Discontents,* p. 70). Unlike Nietzsche, however, Freud does not view conscience itself as a sign of weakness but as an aspect of human psychology that cannot be eliminated. Instead the goal is maintaining the proper balance between the external and internal outlets of the id's energies.

[162]"Three Contributions to the Theory of Sex," in *The Basic Writings of Sigmund Freud* (hereafter *BW*), trans. A. A. Brill, 2nd ed. (New York: Modern Library, 1938), p. 622).

[163]"Introductory Lectures," p. 314.

[164]"Three Contributions to the Theory of Sex," p. 584.

[165]"Three Contributions to the Theory of Sex," p. 622.

[166]"Introductory Lectures," p. 335. Freud sees this as the foundation of taboos against incest.

[167]"Introductory Lectures," p. 332. While Freud is known for all but ignoring females in his discussion of sexuality—except as the object of male desire—he states, "Things happen in just the same way with little girls, with the necessary changes: an affectionate attachment to her father, a need to get rid of her mother as superfluous and to take her place a coquetry which already employs the methods of later womanhood" ("Introductory Lectures," p. 333).

[168]"The Interpretation of Dreams," in *BW*, p. 308.

[169]"Introductory Lectures," p. 337. Failure to accomplish this results in neurosis, in which "the son remains all his life bowed beneath his father's authority and he is unable to transfer his libido to an outside sexual object" ("Introductory Lectures," p. 337).

[170] "Introductory Lectures," p. 287. Another reason the patient resists cure is that the symptoms of mental illness, although harmful to the patient, play an important role for that person. "The construction of a symptom is a substitute for something else that did not happen. Some particular mental processes should normally have developed to a point at which consciousness received information of them. This, however, did not take place and instead—out of the interrupted processes, which had been somehow disturbed and were obliged to remain unconscious—the symptom emerged" ("Introductory Lectures," p. 280). Since the symptom fulfills a need in the patient's life, they believe that relieving it puts them in danger.

[171] "Interpretation of Dreams," pp. 192-93.

[172] "Interpretation of Dreams," pp. 223-24.

[173] "Interpretation of Dreams," p. 235. Discerning the wish expressed by a dream is further complicated by the fact that events from our immediate daytime experiences are also drawn into the dream. The ideas of repression, resistance and the unconscious help explain the methods of psychoanalytic therapy. Dreams are interpreted by the therapist in an attempt to discover wishes and meanings disguised within the often bizarre features of our dreams. Slips of the tongue, body language, initial association of one word with another and other unguarded behaviors may also allow past experiences within the preconscious to slip past the censors and are thus important data for the psychoanalyst. Because of the encoded nature of the root problem that gives rise to symptoms that appear unrelated to the cause, the psychotherapeutic process is an extended one in which, as Freud puts it, many tons of ore must be mined in order to locate the material of value.

[174]*Civilization and Its Discontents*, p. 36. See *Future of an Illusion*, 21.6 for a similar definition.

[175]*Future of an Illusion*, p.15.

[176]*Future of an Illusion*, p. 7.

[177]"Introductory Lectures," p. 312.

[178]*Civilization and Its Discontents*, p. 44.

[179]"Introductory Lectures," p. 311.

[180]*Civilization and Its Discontents*, p. 71.

[181]*Civilization and Its Discontents*, p. 80.

[182]*Civilization and Its Discontents*, p. 81.

[183]*Civilization and Its Discontents*, p. 62.

[184]*Civilization and Its Discontents*, p. 90. Freud views love as a commodity. Any love expended in one direction is unavailable for use for another potential object of love, oneself included. Therefore, he concludes that loving our neighbor as ourselves is logically impossible. "But if I am to love him [the stranger] simply because he, too, is an inhabitant of this earth, like an insect or an earth-worm, or a grass-snake, then I fear that only a small modicum of love will fall to his share—not by any possibility as much as, by the judgment of my reason, I am entitled to retain for myself. What is the point of a precept enunciated with so much solemnity if its fulfilment cannot be recommended as reasonable?" (*Civilization and Its Discontents*, p. 57).

[185]*Civilization and Its Discontents*, p. 90.

[186]"New Introductory Lectures," pp. 625-26. Roughly corresponding to these needs, Freud states, "The gods retain their threefold task: they must exorcize the terrors of nature, they must reconcile men to the cruelty of Fate, particularly as it is shown in death, and they

must compensate them for the sufferings and privations which a civilized life in common has imposed on them" (*Future of an Illusion*, p. 18).

[187]*Civilization and Its Discontents*, p. 19.

[188]"New Introductory Lectures," p. 628.

[189]*Future of an Illusion*, p. 19.

[190]*Totem and Taboo*, p. 148.

[191]*Totem and Taboo*, p. 129.

[192]*Totem and Taboo*, p. 141.

[193]*Totem and Taboo*, pp. 154-55.

[194]*Future of an Illusion*, p. 43.

[195]*Future of an Illusion*, p. 30. Prefers to call religion an illusion rather than an error or mistake. The latter have means by which they can be tested and corrected. Since, by contrast, religion springs from our wishes and needs, "the reality value of most of them [religious teachings] we cannot judge; just as they cannot be proved, so they cannot be refuted" (*Future of an Illusion*, p. 31.

[196]*Future of an Illusion*, p. 33. While Freud seldom directly confronts traditional philosophy, he does not see it as a useful foundation for one's worldview. "Philosophers stretch the meaning of words until they retain scarcely anything of their original sense. They give the name of 'God' to some vague abstraction which they have created for themselves; having done so they can pose before all the world as deists, as believers in God, and they can even boast that they have recognized a higher, purer concept of God, notwithstanding that their God is now nothing more than an insubstantial shadow and no longer the mighty personality of religious doctrines" (*Future of an Illusion*, p. 32).

[197]"New Introductory Lectures," p. 624.

[198]*Future of an Illusion*, p. 35.

[199]"New Introductory Lectures," p. 635.

[200]*Totem and Taboo*, p. 88. Freud offers a chronology of science's demolition of human narcissism. "In the course of centuries the *naïve* self-love of men has had to submit to two major blows at the hands of science. The first was when they learnt that our earth was not the centre of the universe but only a tiny fragment of a cosmic system of scarcely imaginable vastness. . . . The second blow fell when biological research destroyed man's supposedly privileged place in creation and proved his descent from the animal kingdom and his ineradicable animal nature. . . . But human megalomania will have suffered its third and most wounding blow from the psychological research of the present time which seeks to prove to the ego that it is not even master in its own house, but must content itself with scanty information of what is going on unconsciously in its mind" ("Introductory Lectures," pp. 284-85). A form of this dictum with more bite states that Copernicus discovered that the human is not the center of the universe, Darwin discovered that the human is actually an animal, and Freud discovered that the animal is sick.

[201]*Civilization and Its Discontent*, p. 23.

[202]*Future of an Illusion*, p. 54.

[203]"Introductory Lectures," p. 312.

[204]*Future of an Illusion*, p. 36.

[205]*Future of an Illusion*, p. 33.

[206]Hans Küng, *Freud and the Problem of God*, trans. Edward Quinn, rev. ed. (New Haven, Conn.: Yale University Press, 1990), p. 77.

Index